THE SOCIOLOGY OF REVOLUTION

THE SOCIOLOGY OF REVOLUTION

BY
PITIRIM A. SOROKIN

New York · HOWARD FERTIG · 1967

FOREWORD TO THE 1967 EDITION

More than forty years have passed since the first publication of this book. During this time I have continued my study of revolutions, particularly as regards their movement and fluctuation in the history of the Greco-Roman and the Western peoples from 600 B.C. to the present, their causes and sociocultural effects, and the uniformities present in most full-scale revolutions that run their complete life course. These studies are published in my *Social and Cultural Dynamics* (Vol. III, Chaps. 12, 13, 14), *Society, Culture and Personality* (Chaps. 31, 32, 33), and *Man and Society in Calamity* (Chaps. 9, 10, 11, 12).

In the light of these studies one emendation needs to be made in my theory of revolution as outlined in this book. It stresses the "behavioristic" and biopsychological too much and does not sufficiently take into account the sociological. It overestimates the role of hereditary factors and unconditioned reflexes and underestimates somewhat the role of the acquired, sociocultural forces in the engenderment, development, suppression, and life course of revolutions; but the relationship between the unconditioned and acquired actions-reactions of individuals and groups in revolutions remains essentially the same as outlined in this study.

This volume does not analyse the course of revolutions beyond their second restraining phase. If it had, it would have shown that while some societies could not stand the fiery ordeal of a great revolution and have temporarily or forever lost their identity, unity, and independence, other societies have successfully overcome this danger and have established a new, post-revolutionary sociocultural order, system of values, and a nobler, better, more creative way of life. The Russian Revolution exemplifies this last course. The Soviet peoples have passed beyond the second phase of their revolution and are now building their post-revolutionary society, culture, and way of life.

PITIRIM A. SOROKIN
Winchester
March, 1967

PREFACE

THIS book was written in the Czecho-Slovakian Republic where I found the most hospitable refuge and friendship after my banishment from Russia in October, 1922, by the Soviet Government. Only thanks to the hospitality of the Czecho-Slovakian people and government was I able to accomplish this work. Therefore it is for me not only the greatest pleasure but my social duty to express my deepest gratitude to the most esteemed President of the Czecho-Slovakian Republic, Dr. Th. G. Masaryk; Dr. A. Masaryk; the Czecho-Slovakian Prime Minister, Dr. A. Shwegla; the Ministers of the Foreign Office, Dr. E. Benesh, Dr. J. Girsa; Dr. K. Kramarj, Senator Klofach and to many other representatives of the Czecho-Slovakian Nation.

For the publication of this book I am particularly obliged to Professor E. C. Hayes, who not only gave me this possibility but kindly took upon himself the irksome work of the correction and improvement of my English. I must thank him also for his valuable scientific advice and sympathetic interest in my fate by which he has encouraged and aided me very much. This acknowledgment is only a very imperfect expression of my sincerest thankfulness to him.

In characterizing the effects of the Russian Revolution, I give almost exclusively the Bolshevist figures. I

PREFACE

do so not because the Communist statistics are reliable, but because I want to be objective. Being inaccurate and often quite contradictory, these statistics have one valuable quality: they do not depict the situation worse and do it rather better than it is in reality. In this way they prevent the exaggeration of the negative results of the Revolution by its investigators. For the sake of the same objectivity, I add to the book some notes and recent data which were not available while writing and composing the book.

PITIRIM SOROKIN.

December 5, 1924.

CONTENTS

PART I

PART II

PART III

PART IV

CONTENTS

PART IV.—*Continued*

PART V

PART I

THE PERVERSION OF HUMAN BEHAVIOR
IN REVOLUTION

THE SOCIOLOGY OF REVOLUTION

CHAPTER I

THE PERVERSION OF HUMAN BEHAVIOR IN REVOLUTION

AFTER many years of peaceful " organic " evolution the History of Mankind has entered again into a " critical " period. Revolution hated by some people and welcomed by others has come at last. Some societies are burning in its fire already, toward others this danger is approaching. Who can predict how wide this conflagration of revolution will spread? Who can be quite sure that this hurricane will not sooner or later destroy his own house? No one. But if we cannot predict that, we can at least know what revolution is. We live amidst it. Like a naturalist we can observe, analyze and study it.

For five years the author of this book has lived in the circle of the Russian Revolution. Day after day during this time he has watched it. This book is a result of this observation. It represents not an ideographic description of the Russian Revolution, but an essay in sociological analysis of the phenomena typical of all serious and great revolutions. The task of a historian is to portray a strict description of a concrete historical event in all its individuality and unrepeated singularity. The task of a sociologist is considerably different: in all social phenomena only those traits are interesting for him which are general for all facts of the same type whenever and wherever they may have happened. Sombart says quite rightly: " the battle *at Tannenberg* is the object of historical investigation;

3

4 THE SOCIOLOGY OF REVOLUTION

the battle at Tannenberg is the object of sociology. The University *of Berlin* belongs to the sphere of History; *the University* of Berlin to the department of sociology." [1] Similarly the *Russian* Revolution with all its details is the object of a historian. The Russian *Revolution,* as a type of revolution, is the object of the sociologist.

It is true that we are very often told: " The History of Mankind does not repeat itself." But is the history of the earth repeated and that of the solar system and of the accessible part of the world? With all identity organisms, cells and their elements are not repeated either. Does this fact prevent the repetition, in this unrepeated process, of many phenomena which are described in the laws of physics, chemistry and biology? Is it not true that on the earth H_2 and O have given water innumerable times in spite of the unrepeated history of the earth? Have not the phenomena and causal relations described in the laws of Newton, Mendel, Avogadro and Gerard been repeated countless times? By this I want to say that the historical process though unrepeated as a whole is woven out of repeated elements. This is as true of the History of Mankind as it is of the history of organic and inorganic nature. Here also " similar causes under similar conditions produce similar results." War and Peace, Famine and Prosperity, Conquest and Liberation, Growth and Decay of Religion, Government of Minority and Government of Majority, etc.—all these phenomena taken as causes have repeated frequently in different relations of space and time. In spite of all the different conditions in which these processes have taken place, the fundamental similarity of the phenomena of the same type, for example, of war wherever and whenever it has taken place, could not be annihilated absolutely by these different accom-

[1] Sombart: *Soziologie,* 1923, S. 7.

panying conditions. Therefore the results of these similar causes had to be repeated in a more or less complete degree. The theory of the Book of Ecclesiastes was not far from the truth. The fundamental fault of the many theorists of the philosophy of History has consisted only in that they have looked for " repetition " not where repetitions ought to be sought. The latter are seen not in the complicated and great events of History, but in the elementary, usual and daily facts, from which the former are composed and into which they can be analyzed.[2]

From this point of view it seems that the uninterrupted creation of History is not so endlessly new and inexhaustible as they imagine. History is like an author who without interruption is writing ever new dramas, tragedies and comedies with new characters and heroes, with new scenery and environment, but . . . with the old subjects which many times in the previous works of this indefatigable author have been repeated before. Like the writer who has written himself out, History, in spite of all its creative forces, has to be repeated.

All of the above may be said of the great tragedy called " revolution." It has been given on the historical scene rather often. Every staging of it is new. The conditions of time and space, scenery and actors, their costumes, monologues, dialogues and the chorus of the crowd, the quantity of the acts and of " striking scenes " —all these are variated. But, nevertheless, in all this dissimilarity a great many similarities are repeated. All these different actors amidst the different scenery act the same play called " revolution."

---

[2] See about this principle of repetition in my *A System of Sociology.* See also Tarde: *Social Laws,* ch. I. A. Bauer: *Essai sur la Revolution,* 1-8; corresponding pages in *Introduction to the Study of Sociology,* by E. Hayes; and *Foundations of Sociology,* by E. Ross.

Let us now ask ourselves: " *What is Revolution?* "

We have a great many definitions of the latter. The most numerous amongst them represent very incorrect conceptions. To these belong " the sweet " definitions, on the one hand; and the " bitter," on the other. I mean by this the definitions which deal with imaginative but not with real revolutions as they have been given in History.

E. Bernstein says,[3] " At the present time it is possible to name as revolutions only those periods in which the amount of liberty is increased." Another writer asserts, " The October *coup d'état* is usually described as revolution; but torture and revolution are incompatible. As in Soviet Russia, where tortures are usual phenomena, there is only reaction but not revolution." [4]

These conceptions of revolution may be taken as examples of the fictitious—" sweet "—definitions for, as the reader will see further, almost all revolutions during revolutionary and post-revolutionary periods have not only augmented the sum of the freedom of the population but have regularly reduced it. May it be inferred from this that many ancient and mediæval revolutions, as well as the great French Revolution, are not revolutions? Revolution and torture not only do not represent incompatible phenomena but, on the contrary, in fact every revolutionary time has always been stamped with a great increase of murders, sadism, cruelty, bestiality and tortures. Does it follow from their cruelties that the Russian or French, English or Hussite Revolutions are not revolutions ?

These examples show the incorrectness and subjec-

---

[3] *Dni*, Nr. 17.
[4] *Dni*, Nr. 117.

tivity of such conceptions of revolution. Their authors are Don Quixotes of revolution who do not want to see the real prosaic girl of Toboso or the barber's basin, and see in them the beautiful Dulzinea or wonderful knight's helmet. Some of these " illusionists " try to get out of these contradictions by pointing out that all these negative traits of revolution do not belong to its essence and represent only " occasional elements " in it or are the expression of " reaction " but not of " revolution." In this argument is hidden the same illusionism. If almost all revolutions are regularly accompanied with such negative traits (torture, diminution of liberty, pauperization, growth of bestiality and so on), then what objective reason have we to call these traits " occasional accompaniments? " To consider them as " occasional accompaniments " of revolution is no more possible than to consider the abatement of mercury in the thermometer as an " occasional accompaniment " of abatement of temperature. The " illusionists " like to appeal to " the reaction," as a source of all negative phenomena connected with revolution. Alas! They scarcely give themselves an adequate account of the great significance of this reference.

It is possible that they may be surprised at the statement that every revolutionary period as a whole inevitably consists of two stages indissolubly connected with one another. " Reaction " is not a phenomenon beyond the limits of revolution but is an unavoidable part of the revolutionary process itself, its second half. The dictatorship of Robespierre or Lenin, Cromwell or Zizka, signified not the end but the flare of revolution. The former was only the mark of its transition into the second stage—the stage of "reaction" or "restraint" but not its end. Only when "reaction" is finished, when society enters the period of its normal evolution—only then revolution may be considered as finished. These "illusionists" condemning "reaction" do not understand that by this they blame nothing but revolution itself in its second stage.

This idea is illustrated in the following scheme:

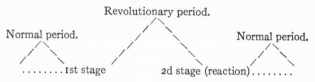

Revolutionary period.

Normal period.   Normal period.

. . . . 1st stage   2d stage (reaction). . . . .

What is said above of the "sweet" illusionists may be likewise applied to the "bitter" ones.

Regarding revolution as a "creation of Satan" they are as far from understanding real revolution as the former. By praising "reaction" they are not aware that in spite of their hating revolution they laud it, only not in its first but in its second stage.

Some other definitions of revolution are more scientific. "Revolution is the change of the constitution of society realized by violence." [5] "*Das wesen der Revolution besteht in einem plötzlichen unstetigen Ubergang von einem politischen Gesamtzustand zu einem anderen, inbesondere von einer Rechtsordnung des öffentlichen Lebens zu einem andern . . . in einer plötzlichen Ver schiebung der Machtverteilung.*" [6]

There is nothing to be said against this sort of definitions save that they are too formal and do not give quite a complete representation of revolution. It is not my

---

[5] A. Bauer: *Essai sur Revolution,* Paris, 1908, 11, 16 p.
[6] A. Vierkandt: *Zur Theorie der Revolution.* Schmoller: *Jahrbuch fur Gesetzgebung. 46 Jahrgang. zweites Heft.,* 1922, 19-20.

intention to add to all these definitions one more. Social sciences abuse definitions too much, often giving nothing in essence but only a formal conception. I will act in another way, as naturalists usually do. I will make a study of a series of revolutions of different times and peoples: The Russian Revolutions of 1905, 1917–24, and that of the seventeenth century; the French Revolutions of 1789, 1848, 1870–71; the German Revolution of 1848; the English Revolution of the seventeenth century; some mediæval and antique revolutionary periods; the Egyptian, Persian and other great revolutions. This study should give the fundamental traits of what is styled as revolution.

Only such revolutions as the Czecho-Slovak of 1918 and the American of the eighteenth century which do not represent the struggle of one part of the same society with another but rather the struggle of a society with another quite different from the former, I exclude from my study. Revolutions of this sort are rather the processes of war and differ considerably from revolutions proceeding within the confines of the same society.

Of the latter revolutions my attention is fixed principally on the great and deep ones because they show us the typical characteristics of them most clearly. Among them I analyze with the greatest attention the Russian Revolution proceeding before our eyes. It is worthy of this attention: it is one of the greatest revolutions—I have had the opportunity to study it directly, and, finally, it pours light upon many sides of other revolutions.

The two latter conditions, from my point of view, are particularly important. In spite of the popular opinion about " the judgment of history " expressed in the statements that " it is better seen from the distance; " that "after many generations a better valuation of historical events is possible;" that "not through the present must the past be explained, but on the contrary"—in spite of this, I think the opposite opinion is more true.

Not the descendants, but the contemporaries, are the better observers and judges of historical events. The experience of the former founded only on certain documents is very unsatisfactory, while the experience of the latter is direct; the acquaintance of contemporaries with events is adequate, they perceive them daily and personally, while the knowledge of the descendants is indirect, occasional, fragmentary and disfigured. This statement is at any rate true in the case of those contemporaries who enlarge the circle of their personal experience by the experience of other people, by statistical observations and other scientific methods of supplementing and correcting the individual experience. Utilizing these aids the contemporary generation is better guaranteed against mistakes than a historian who studies these events some generations after and against the errors of a foreigner observing from a distance the rare and occasional facts that reach his notice.

In natural sciences the direct experience has long been preferred to the indirect. Here usually the past is explained by the present observations or experiment. In social sciences the full value is not yet sufficiently understood of explaining the past by the present, of trying to understand many outlived historical events by the direct observation and investigation of the processes proceeding around us.

The above explains why I give the greatest attention to the Russian Revolution. Its direct observation helps to understand other revolutions and makes their many sides comprehensible. A series of revolutions studied in this manner provide us indeed with many similarities and regularities of which in their total is composed the typical phenomenon styled as revolution. What these traits are the reader will see later. Here I will say only that the definitions criticised above not only fail to point out all the characteristics of revolution but scarcely indicate the characteristics that are most fundamental.

First of all, revolution is a change in the behavior of the people on the one hand and their psychology, ideology, beliefs and valuations on the other. To this problem is devoted the first part of this book.

Secondly, revolution signifies a change in the biologic composition of population, and of the reproductive and selective processes in its midst. This problem is studied in the second part of the book.

Thirdly, revolution represents the deformation of the social structure of society. I deal with this matter in the third part.

Finally, revolution means the change of fundamental social processes. These facts are investigated in the fourth part.

The fifth is dedicated to the study of the causes of revolution.

Such are the contents of this book.

The valuation of revolution is very subjective—therefore its scientific investigation must be particularly objective.

The phenomena of revolution are very exotic and romantic—therefore the investigator must be especially prosaic; he has to study with the methods and purposes of a naturalist. The purpose of this book is neither to blame, praise, apotheosize nor to condemn revolution. It is only to study revolution in all its reality.

For this purpose I try to confirm every statement by the facts. Of course, for the sake of brevity, I may give only the minimum of the proofs. But in the works quoted the reader will find ample confirmation.

Only in exceptional cases do I break this rule and rarely allow myself to give moral valuations. However, the latter are so definitely separated from the scientific (descriptive) statements that nobody will mix them.

Such are the methodological principles followed by me in this book.

The real nature of revolution is very different from these romantic representations of it which are usual among its apologists. Many of its traits pointed out in this book may appear to them as offensive, as disfiguring "the beautiful face of revolution." Therefore they may find "a reactionary mind" in my book.

What, then? I willingly agree to this accusation and am ready to accept the name of "reactionary" but a reactionary . . . of a very unusual type.

The reader will gather from the book that revolution is a bad method for the improvement of the material and spiritual conditions of the masses. Verbally promising the realization of many of the greatest values, in fact it leads as often and as much to opposite results. Revolution does not tend to socialize so much as it tends to biologize the people; does not only increase but also reduces the sum of liberties; does not improve alone but also impairs the economic and spiritual state of the working classes. Whatever gains it yields are purchased at a prodigious and disproportionate cost. It punishes not only and not so much those aristocratic classes which, thanks to their para-

sitism, licentiousness, incapacity and oblivion of social
duties deserve, if not punishment, then at least degradation
from great position, as it punishes millions of the poor
and working classes who in the paroxysm of despair think
to find the end of their misery in revolution. If such are
the objective results of revolution then in the name of man,
his prosperity, his rights, his freedom and for the sake
of the material and spiritual progress of the working classes
it is not only my right but it is my duty, to abstain from
the idolatry of revolution. Amongst many " idols " of
Bacon there is also " the Idol of Revolution." Amongst
numerous idolators and dogmatists who sacrifice man to
different idols there are many idolators of revolution. In
spite of many millions of men sacrificed to this " god "
its worshippers continue to demand new and ever new
hecatombs. Is it not time to abstain from this demand
and finish this sacrificing? Like every dangerous illness
revolution represents the results of many causes. But
the inevitability of disease does not oblige me to welcome
and laud it. If this ideology is " reaction " I willingly
accept the epithet of " reactionary."

The history of social progress teaches us that all fundamental and really progressive acquisitions have been the
results of knowledge, peace, solidarity, coöperation and
love; but not the results of hate, bestiality and mad struggle which are inevitably connected with every great revolution. This explains why in answer to the calls of
revolution I should like to say: " My Father, let this cup
pass from them." It is true that all these apprehensions
are considerably diminished in connection with " little "
revolutions not followed by great civil war. At first it
seems very commendable to overthrow without blood-
struggle incapable government and degenerated aristoc-

racy which hinder social progress. If the real situation were such I should not have objected at all to revolution. I am not a defender of any parasitic, talentless and corrupt aristocracy. But, alas, revolutions, spoken of in the terms of medicine, represent *maladie a-typique,* the development of which it is impossible to foresee. Sometimes, beginning with a slightly dangerous symptom, it suddenly becomes worse and ends with death. The same may be said of revolution. Who can be quite sure that by setting fire to a little pile of revolution he does not start the beginning of a great conflagration which will burn not only the tyrants but . . . the incendiaries themselves with many thousands of innocent people as well. Therefore in this problem it is absolutely necessary to " consider seven times before cutting once."

This is necessary to bear in mind especially now when the air is full of combustible material, when order—a necessary condition of every progress—is troubled and the storm of the horrible revolution threatens to spread over many societies.

At the present time mankind more than at any time needs order. Even imperfect order is now better than disorder, as " a bad peace is better than a good quarrel."

Instead of revolutionary experiments there are other methods of improvement and reconstruction of social organization. The principal canons of the latter are the following:

1. A reform must not violate human nature and contradict its fundamental instincts. The Russian revolutionary experiment, as well as many other revolutions, give us examples of the opposite.

2. An attentive scientific study of concrete social conditions has to precede every practical realization of reform

in them. A great part of revolutionary reconstruction breaks this rule.

3. Every reconstructive experiment at first must be tested on a small scale. Only when it gives a positive result is it possible to realize it on a greater scale. Revolutions neglect this canon.

4. Reforms have to be realized only by legal and constitutional means. Revolutions disdain these restrictions.[7]

A violation of these canons renders every endeavor at social reconstruction unsuccessful. Similar canons are understood and applied for example at the construction of a bridge or at the improving of a breed of cows. But, alas, these canons very often are considered unnecessary in the reconstruction of human society. An ignorant man here often becomes a leader of revolutionary reforms; a consideration of real conditions is not seldom condemned as " bourgeois prejudice; " demand for prudence as cowardice or civil dishonesty. The demands of peaceful and legal methods—as " reaction," " the spirit of destruction," here *eo ipso* is recognized as the " spirit of creation." These " revolutionary methods " make the failure of revolutionary reconstructions and their sacrifices quite comprehensible. An inhabitant of some other planet watching these facts might conclude that on the earth cows and bridges are more valued than human creatures: the former are often treated with more consideration than the latter, they are not sacrificed so willingly and in so numerous quantity as men are sacrificed *ad majorem gloriam* of revolution.

---

[7] See about this E. Hayes: *Introduction to the Study of Sociology,* ch. of Social Control, and his *Sociology and Ethics.* See also E. Ross: *The Principles of Sociology,* ch. XLV.

It is difficult to decide whether every one observing these facts ought to weep or smile.

At any rate it will not be unjust to equalize the rights of man in this respect to the privileges of a bridge or of cows. This demand is rather modest and easier of realization than the demands of many " Declarations of the Rights of Man and Citizen."

CHAPTER II

THE NATURE AND MECHANISM OF HUMAN BEHAVIOR

THE more we study man, his conduct and psychology, the stronger grows the conviction that he in nowise resembles the " good little boy " that the eighteenth century and the modern rationalists love to depict.

" Man is a being guided by intellect, naturally virtuous; peaceable, devoid of animosity; full of altruism, always thinking and acting according to logic and intellect;" such is the conception of the rationalists. " If," they add, " he has certain failings, it is only because they are called forth by imperfect conditions of social order, by lack of culture. Suffice it to abolish ignorance and prejudice, to eliminate the imperfections of social organization, and man will again be transformed into the perfect being nature had fashioned." " Evil is not in, but outside man—such is another formula of the same idea. Substitute another social environment and poverty, crime, warfare, guilt, injustice and ignorance will all disappear. " Our epoch has struck a mighty, we might say deadly, blow to such a conception. The world's butchery, revolution, and the still existing seditions and antagonisms have shown a man totally different from the rationalistic " good little boy."

Before us we have not only a sensible being, but the elemental man, who is not only peace-loving, altruistic, compassionate, but also full of rancor, cruelty, bestiality; not only consciously clear-sighted, but often blind; not only gentle and creative, but wild and destructive. Of course certain features claimed for man by the rationalists have not been wanting, but they have been overshadowed by quite opposite qualities.

The clearer insight which events have given us makes it utterly impossible to adopt the optimistic, rationalistic viewpoint. Even before the war and revolution, beginning from the end of the nineteenth century, scientific thought has gone through a series of modifications in its method of investigating the revelation of nature, and in its appreciation of man's conduct. This change has grown still more deliberate during the war and the years following it. First of all, according to Galton, Pearson and others, biology has proved, and is still proving, the tremendous importance of heredity, not only for the physical, but also for the psychical qualities of man. The value of heredity, as compared to that of environment and education, is now being given a more prominent place than it used to have.[1] This was the first blow struck at the rationalistic view of man.

Secondly, the development of the theory of tropisms and taxis (Loeb and others) has shown that they play an important part in the conduct of man.[2]

Thirdly, the theory of inner secretion which is only now being developed has proved, especially if taken in connection with the experiments of Steinach, Voronoff and others, the immense dependence of all our actions and psychological life on the character and activity of the organs of inner secretion, the formation of which depends but little on our consciousness.[3]

---

[1] A compilation of theses, theories and facts can be found in the book of D. Starch: *Educational Psychology*, as well as in the latest works of Gertwig, Shallmayer, Johannsen, Ch. Richet and others.

[2] Loeb: *La Nature Chimique de la vie. Revue Philosophique,* December, 1921.

[3] Among other numerous works on this subject see: I. Vassilieff: *Studies of the Physiology of Spirit*, St. Petersb., 1923 (Russ.), wherein he attempts to establish a connection between inner secretion and the character of spiritual activity and psychical life; and L. Berman: *The Glands Regulating Personality*, 1921.

The investigations of psychologists of the most varied tendencies have proved no less destructive to rationalism. Already Lange, Petrajitzky, Ribot and others have laid sufficient stress on the part played by feelings and emotions in the psychology and conduct of man.[4] Freud, his school and a whole series of psychologists have given predominance to the immense importance of subconscious and unconscious impulses.[5] On the other hand Thorndike, McDougall and others have demonstrated the presence, variety and great determining power of man's inborn reflexes or instincts.[6] Among these instincts are not only social, but combative instincts; not only the parental, but that of the hunter; not only that of subordination, but that of dominion and self-assertion. To sum up: Man is the bearer not only of peaceful, gentle, virtuous and social impulses, but also of their opposites. On the other hand the Russian school of the objective method of analyzing

---

[4] Lange concludes "that not only are emotions one of the chief factors in the life of individuals, but that they are in general one of the mightiest inborn powers known to us. Every page of individual or national life demonstrates their unconquerable power. The storms of passion have ruined more human lives, have devastated more countries than any whirlwind has ever done; more towns have been destroyed by the torrent of passion than by inundations." Lange: *The Movements of the Soul* (Russ. transl., 1896), 14. "A blind belief in the strength of ideas," confirms Ribot, "is apt to be an endless source of illusions and mistakes. An idea as long as it remains purely an idea is powerless: it grows to be active only when it passes into the realm of feeling. We can study Kant's: *Critic of Practical Reason,* both thoroughly and deeply; write volumes of brilliant commentaries and yet add absolutely nothing to our own practical morality, which has a totally different source." Ribot: *Psychology of Feeling* (Russ. transl., 1898), 25. See also Petrajitzky: *Preface to the Study of Law and Morality,* 1907.

[5] See Freud: *Psychical Analysis,* as well as many other works of his and those of his followers.

[6] See Thorndike: *The Original Nature of Man.* McDougall: *Introduction to Social Psychology.* G. Patrick: *The Psychology of Social Reconstruction.*

the behavior of man and animals and the behaviorists [7] have given still greater predominance to inborn or unconditioned reflexes, showing how completely conditioned or acquired forms of behavior depend on them. Sociologists have also studied this question.

L. F. Ward and C. Patten have given predominance to the position that suffering and pleasure occupy in the conduct of man and in social life. *The Trattato di Sociologia Generale,* by V. Pareto, shows the fundamental influence exercised by subconscious feelings (residui) on human conduct and the subordinate place occupied by reason and consciousness (derivazione). He draws our attention to the discrepancy existing between " the logic of feeling " and the " logic of reason," the latter, in his view, giving only concrete form to the dictates of the former; he shows us the numerous " illogical acts " in human conduct.[8] This work of V. Pareto has laid special stress on man as an " illogical, irrational being," swayed by impulses, not only peaceable and social, but also evil, violent, cruel and wild. On the other hand sociology has shown us in the words of men like Tarde, Rossi, Le Bon, Michailowsky, Sigelet, F. Giddings, E. Hayes, E. Ross, A. Small, Martin, Ellwood and others the immense part played by suggestion and imitation in the blind impulsive conduct of the crowds and masses.[9] At the same time in all lectures on sociology a more prominent place is being

---

[7] See I. P. Pavlov: *Twenty Years of Experimental Objective Study of the Higher Nervous Activity of Animals,* Moscow-Petrograd, 1923 (Russ.). V. Bechtereff: *General Foundations of the Science of Reflexes,* St. Petersb., 1918 (Russ.). Also his: *Collective Reflexology,* 1922. See the works of Watson, Paton, Meyer and other " behaviorists " quoted below.

[8] See V. Pareto: *Trattato di Sociologia Generale,* Vols. I, II, 1916.

[9] See E. H. Hayes: *Introduction to the Study of Sociology.* E. A. Ross: *The Principles of Sociology and Foundations of Sociology.* Tarde: *Laws of Imitation.* Michailovsky: *The Heroes and the Crowd, etc.* (Russ.). Martin: *The Behavior of Crowds.*

given to instincts and blind impulses as " factors of conduct " and " Social Forces."

Towards the end of the nineteenth century the same
tendency can be seen in philosophy. For instance: in
Hartmann's *The Unconscious* and Nietzsche's *The Will
for Power;* in Bergsonn's *Intuition,* and in the prominent
part it takes among the Anglo-American Neo-Realists
and Pluralists. All these are symptoms of the same order.
If the peaceful pre-war conditions have somewhat tended
to minimize the total change of viewpoint on human nature
and conduct, the events of the last ten years, the present
atmosphere so rife with bloodshed, gunpowder and elemental forces let loose, with sedition and madness of millions of men, have forced this new conception into much
greater evidence. The fallacy of the rationalistic conception of human nature now grows clearer.

" The real man is restless, aggressive and aspiring." [10]
He is the bearer of various inborn reflexes.[11] His instincts
force him to desire not only peace, but warfare; not only
self-sacrifice, but murder; not only justice, but the satisfaction of his necessities, though at the cost of his fellow-
men; not only work, but idleness. They spur him to
independence, at the same time, make him seek subjection
to, or, upon occasion, domination over others; they teach
him not only to love, but to hate others; the list of instincts
includes such tendencies as pugnacity, gregariousness,
ownership, rivalry, self-assertion, love of adventure, of
leadership, of migration, of domination, of self-expression, etc. I do not even allude to such wants as man's
desire for food, clothes, sexual satisfaction, etc. To sum

---

[10] Patrick: *Op cit.,* III p.
[11] The terms: inborn or hereditary reflex, instinct, impulse, are
used by me as synonymous, for there is no real difference between them;
the same may be said of the terms: conditioned or acquired reflex or
reaction, habit.

up: the quantity and quality of man's impulses and reflexes render him, singularly, like a bomb full of different kinds of forces and tendencies capable of bursting and
presenting us with a picture of wild disorder. To use
Pascal's words: " Man is like an angel with a devil hidden beneath."

If this " wild devil " is not always visible it is only
because, first of all, the long process of historical development and cruel historical schooling has, up to a certain
point, curbed and mutually balanced the conflicting
instincts, bringing them into coördination with their
environment including their fellow-men; secondly, because
through education it has created certain " brakes," or
restraining bonds, called juridical, moral, religious, conventional, etc.—the forms of social control; and thirdly,
because it has created certain socially harmless channels
through which they can find an outlet and be satisfied
without giving vent to wild, mad, bestial forms of rioting,
a so-called " canalization of instincts " into socially harmless forms of sport, competition and so on.

Thanks to all these conditions human conduct presents a certain degree of " balance." Man resembles a wild
colt tamed and harnessed. He is bound on all sides by hundreds and thousands of hereditary and acquired links
between the stimuli and organism preventing this rioting
and setting limits to his behavior. From this evolves the
usually normal and comparatively peaceable conduct of
man, the balance between man's actions and his psychology,
the relative coördination and mutual adaptability of the
actions of different individuals. By means of repetition
and the strengthening influence of habit, this process of
" socialization " creates a more stable kind of balance; as
if the inner fire of a volcano were being covered by an
always thickening coating of " culture lava."

However it suffices that social conditions should change in such a way that one, two or more of the fundamental instincts should not find sufficient satisfaction, that they should be hard pressed . . . for all this " balance " of human conduct to collapse. The reflexes which are hard pressed, press, in their turn, on their neighbors; these latter on the next ones—and we stand before an eruption of the volcano. The outward coating of social forms cracks and bursts on all sides, and the fire of biological impulses bursts loose, and instead of a cultured " socius," we see a wild animal, devil-possessed, totally dissimilar to the cultured being you knew. Peaceable man changes into a murderer, the pacifist into a militarist, the honest man into a thief, the chaste into a profligate. We constantly see such transformations happening to individuals. They call forth in all kinds of societies the organization of protective police institutions and of justice courts with the gallows and prisons they entail; institutions whose business it is to extinguish the fires and explosions of human conduct.

However, if the conditions of the environment are modified in such a way that they violate the fundamental instincts of the masses, then we have to face a complete disorganization of conduct; we stand before an outburst of the masses, a social earthquake, called riot, rebellion, revolution. Such, in general terms, is the origin of revolutions and such are their fundamental causes.

Let us dwell a little longer on this point, so as to get a clearer insight into the thesis which till now we have described rather in artistic, than in scientific terms. At this point I am forced to make a slight digression, which will enable me to state the whole matter more exactly. I must remind my reader of certain fundamental statements established by modern science as regards the conduct of animals and men; otherwise all that follows will be unintelligible.

Referring my reader for all details and proofs to the authors named further on I shall formulate them as concisely as possible.

1. Long ago Spencer stated that life was an unceasing adaptation of the inner relations of the organism to outward environment. Cut off from this unceasing adaptation the organism cannot continue to exist as a unit, that is, cannot continue to live.

2. This adaptation to environment or balance is achieved by acts of the organism, which thereby respond to each of the stimuli of its environment, or to the complex situation created by them.

3. Such acts of man can be subdivided into two categories, according to their relation with man's environment and its stimuli: 1. Inborn or unconditioned acts—reflexes, instincts, reactions. Here the connection between a given stimulus or environment and reaction of organism is hereditary. 2. Acquired or conditioned acts—reactions, reflexes, habits, wherein the connection between the stimulus and the reaction is instilled, inculcated in the individual during the course of his life. They differ in many ways: a. The nervous mechanism of the action is different. b. The inborn acts are more stereotyped and less variable than acquired ones. c. The first usually cannot be destroyed; you can but modify, reinforce or weaken, retard or accelerate their outward manifestation; the second can be ingrafted or cast away like clothes which can be put on or taken off and exchanged.

4. Unconditioned reflexes accomplish the fundamental functions of adaptation to environment and preservation of life; such are the reflexes of nutrition, self-preservation, multiplication and others. The conditioned ones are

only an additional corrective to the first, giving pliability to the behavior of man, allowing him to respond to the stimulation of his environment in a more skilful, in a finer manner. In a constant environment they would be superfluous. In the varying and complex environment in which man is destined to live the unconditioned reflexes are insufficient; they are too coarse. To supplement this defect the higher animals and man have acquired a great number of habits whose mission it is to facilitate the adaptation to complex and varying conditions.

5. Habits in general are ingrafted only on the basis of hereditary reflexes, when the action of the hereditary and the non-hereditary tendency happen to coincide. Hereditary reflexes lie at the basis and are their point of issue. Without the former the latter could not exist; moreover, if the action of a non-hereditary tendency is a few times running not corroborated by that of the unconditioned one (for instance, if the lighting of the electric lamp which had become the stimulus of an acquired tendency to the secretion of saliva by a dog is not followed by feeding), the habit will also grow fainter and disappear. (The secretion of saliva following the sudden light will not be forthcoming.)

6. All of the above statements prove that the power of hereditary tendencies and reflexes in determining human conduct is much greater than that of conditioned habits and reactions. The first can be compared to steam urging the man-machine onward, and the second to nice adjustment in its mechanism. The hereditary impulses of nutrition, of sex life give the organism the order to accomplish certain acts to satisfy its hunger, or the functions of sex life. The habits only define the details best fitted to the accomplishment of the given order, according to existing circumstances.

7. Consequently, the whole conduct of man consists of a series of inborn reflexes on and around which many acquired reflexes have grouped themselves. The first resemble the trunk of a tree and the large branches; the second the small boughs and the leaves covering them and hiding the naked form.

8. The hereditary reflexes of human conduct are numerous. An accepted classification of them does not yet exist. Of existing classifications some differentiate only between fundamental groups of inborn reflexes such as nutritive, self-protecting (individuals and groups) and sexual, and regard all other groups as complications and variations of these fundamental ones.[12]   Others give a much more detailed classification of inborn reflexes or instincts.[13]   Not attempting to present here the classification we consider to be the most correct, we only want to state that they are numerous which, however, does not prevent their being grouped into a few fundamental groups, that they are dissimilar, often opposed to each other, and that they include not only reflexes of social character, but also those which are rather anti-social—

---

[12] See W. Wagner: *Biological Foundations of Comparative Psychology*, Vol. II (Russ.).
[13] See the classification of Thorndike, McDougall, Ellwood and specially Patrick who makes the following subdivision of instincts: The instincts of constructive workmanship, curiosity and manipulation; of ownership, individual possession, acquisition and collecting; of pugnacity, gregariousness, of emulation and rivalry, of loyalty and devotion, of parental bent and motherly behavior; the instinct of thought, invention and organization; of housing and settling, of homing and migratory; of hunting, of love of adventure and change; of leadership and mastery; of love of dominion, of subordination and submission, of display, vanity and ostentation.   Patrick: *Op. cit.*, 67. The following scientists are also adherents of detailed and numerous classification: I. Pavlov, L. Petrajitzky and V. Pareto.   See Pavlov: *Twenty Years of Experimental Objective Study of the Higher Nervous Activity of Animals*, 1923, Passim and 209-10, 193 and foll. (Russ.). See for other classifications Parmeles: *The Science of Human Behavior*, ch. XIII. Sorokin: *System of Sociology*, Vol. I, 87 and foll. (Russ.).

impulses of pugnacity, of acquisition, of power, of self-expression and so on. In this sense man presents a kind of *coincidentia oppositorum*.

9. As regards acquired reactions we can say that in their concrete form they are incalculably numerous in man. A great majority of concrete habits generally called religious, moral, æsthetic, conventional actions, even such habits as writing and speaking a particular language, are but habitual reactions or conditioned reflexes. The act of making the sign of the cross, or of Holy Communion, acts of politeness, of decency, of compliance to fashion, even the cultivated appreciation of what is beautiful or hideous, of what is moral and immoral, etc., all these are but conditioned reactions that have grown out of a series of unconditioned reflexes. From the first day of the man's existence promptings to develop such habits envelop the man on all sides, and in the long run a definite relation is established with certain conditioning stimuli furnished by the environment; for instance, with the actions of persons: father, acquaintance, chief; with certain places or buildings: church, cemetery, bar, school; with certain periods of time: Easter, Sunday, Namesday; with certain events: chimes, cries, and such situations as law court, church service, battlefield, shopping, which evoke a definite way of reacting, *i.e.*, the acts of praying in church, saluting a general, dancing at a ball, etc. The conditioned reflexes or habits can be classified according to the degree of their complexity. There exist conditioned reflexes of the first category, which are grafted on unconditioned ones; there are reflexes of a second category springing from the reflexes of the first category; and there are reflexes of the third category founded on those of the second; also those of the fourth, fifth, etc. The higher the category of the conditioned reflex or habit, the less stable.

the more brittle is it, and the easier is it to extinguish
and destroy it. A change in the functioning of an
unconditioned reflex, out of which the whole pyramid of
habits has grown, calls forth a general upheaval similar to
the trembling of the upper stories during an earthquake.
The destruction of a reflex of the lower category leads
to the destruction of all the reflexes of the higher order
founded on it.[14]

10. The subjective ingredient among these objective
phenomena consists in man's possession of corresponding
convictions and rules of conduct named: religious, moral,
etc. " Thou shalt not lie," " Pay your debts," " Don
your dress coat for dinner," " Give up your seat to a lady,"
" Pray to God," etc.—these are subjective phenomena
involved in the corresponding conditioned habits. Their
modification or disappearance manifests itself in the modification or disappearance of these convictions. In other
words: a modification of habits is accompanied by
unavoidable modification of convictions in the subjective
world of man.

11. The interrelationship between different unconditioned reflexes, between the different conditioned reflexes
and lastly that existing between conditioned and unconditioned reflexes can be classified under three distinct heads.

a. When a whole series of different stimuli reacting
upon a man urge him to accomplish the same kind of
action, we have a case of solidary, or, according to
Sherrington,[15] allied interrelationship. For instance, the
stimuli of hunger + cold + a " socius " offering bread and
meat, all urge the hungry man in the same direction and

[14] See A. Lenz: *Method of Conditioned Reflexes in Investigation
of the Higher Nervous Activity.* Ivanov-Smolensky: *Conditioned
Reflexes in Psychiatry and Neurology,* Vol. I, 1922 (Russ.).
[15] See Sherrington: Association of Spinal and Brain Reflexes,
Journal Progress of Biology (Russ. transl., 1912, 26-7).

give us an example of solidarity of interrelationship. If no other stimulus exists, and man is only under the influence of the above-named ones, he will, without any doubt, energetically set about satisfying his hunger. His convictions and opinions as to what his conduct should be will be perfectly clear.

b. If the stimuli reacting on man at a given moment demand reflexes which are opposed to each other, which mutually exclude each other, then we face a case of antagonistic or mutually inhibiting interrelationship of different reflexes. As example: the sexual determining force (in the shape of a whole series of stimuli awakening the feeling of profligacy) spurs a man to what is "evil;" but a whole series of other stimuli (demands of morality, religion, etc.) keep him back, restrain him from the "evil act." The determining force of self-preservation urges the soldier to forsake the battlefield; a whole series of other impulses prevent his doing so. If we look upon the convictions of man as the subjective component of his reflexes, we can clearly see that a discrepancy among the latter must, in such a case, lead to contradiction in the realm of his convictions. They, too, are in a state of conflict. You "want to have your cake and eat it, too"—"you desire and do not dare."

c. In cases when various stimuli urge man onward to perform various, though not conflicting, actions we feel a state of neutral interrelationship with corresponding mutual reactions. This case, however, is comparatively rarely to be found in an unalloyed state.

12. The actual environment in which man lives and acts consists of such a number of various stimuli that some of them are always sure to be antagonistic to the others. Consequently the case when the stimuli-reflexes are antagonistic to each other is the most usual one in

human conduct. Our organism, capable of accomplishing the most various kinds of acts (sexual, nutritive, self-preserving, etc.), is like a tense battlefield of various stimuli, each of which strives to force it to be its obedient servant fulfilling its dictates; striving to twist and turn it so that instead of a " check payable to bearer " it should be changed into a " check to a certain person." During each moment of his life the conduct of man is but a result of countless " duels " fought by various stimuli-reflexes.

13. In such duels the victory always falls to the lot of the strongest stimuli-reflexes; the weak ones go to the wall. When the strength of the duellists is equal the victory falls either to the " tertius gaudens," or man begins to act inconsistently, contradicts himself, grows timorous, a very Hamlet, and often . . . perishes. Here we see a corresponding inconsistency, a want of logic, and a contradiction in the realm of his ideology and convictions. One day, inspired by the victory of such and such a stimulus, man proves that $A = B$ (e.g., capital punishment is not to be tolerated, war is a crime). The next day under the influence of a new victorious stimulus he declares that A is not equal to B (that capital punishment is allowable for bourgeois and counter-revolutionists, that war in the name of God, Justice, the Internationale, etc., is praiseworthy). Such facts in man's conduct are not exceptions, but the rule; and the common conception of man's nature being logical, is a great exaggeration.[16]

14. As unconditioned reflexes in their unalloyed state are stronger than conditioned ones we can easily say that, as a general rule, the first will usually be victorious in a duel between the two. Conditioned reflexes (if not

[16] See V. Pareto: *Trattato di Sociologia Generale*, Vols. I, II, and Passim.

strengthened by other also unconditioned ones) are snuffed out, extinguished, no more obeyed.

15. The extinction of the habits restraining unconditioned reflexes sets the latter free from bounds which had handicapped their activity and liberty.   It means the liberation of man from winding sheets which had hampered the free play of instincts.   In such cases human behavior is actuated only by hereditary reflexes and their stimuli.

Summing the above up we come to the conclusion that human conduct is an extraordinarily complex phenomenon that, in an immense majority of cases, it is determined by the inborn reflexes and their stimuli, that the balance of conduct is achieved by way of self-restriction and a complex mutual struggle of various stimuli and reactions.[17]

---

[17] The development of all these statements can be found in the works of Pavlov (cited above) ; of Bechtereff : *General Foundations of the Science of Reflexes*. See further the dissertation of the school of Pavlov and Bechtereff; the works of Deriabin, Lenz, Orbelly, Tzitovitsch, Babkin, Zeleny, Protopopoff, Frolof and others. See also J. Watson : *Psychology from the Standpoint of a Behaviorist*. S. Paton : *Human Behavior*. See detailed literature in my *System of Sociology*, Vol. I, and *Famine as a Factor*.

CHAPTER III

GENERAL CHARACTERISTICS OF THE CHANGE OF BEHAVIOR DURING REVOLUTION

THE behavior of people changes even in ordinary times. What, then, are the particular characteristics of the changes which occur in times of revolutions?

1. The change of the unconditioned and conditioned reactions in ordinary times are of an individual character. As regards extent, the change does not affect numerous persons at the same time. During revolutionary periods the extent and spread of the change affects at once a considerable proportion of the total population.

2. Suddenness of change is the second manifestation. The disappearance of old habits and the development of the new ones, a process which previously occupied several decades, now occurs during a few weeks or months. Slaves, who only yesterday were obedient to their masters, lose all sense of obedience, arrest and kill them. Citizens, who some days before never thought of resisting the authorities, now attack them. A peaceful and good-hearted individual becomes a cruel and bloodthirsty murderer. In the course of some days or weeks a monarchist becomes a republican; an individualist—a socialist; a pious person—an atheist. It seems as if some electric current flows through the veins of the citizens and leads them at once to rejection of numerous traditions respected for centuries, and, on the other hand, to speedy adoption of many new forms of thought and

32

behavior: religious, moral, æsthetic, political, professional, etc.

3. Let us turn to the third characteristic. As mentioned above the fundamental springs of human behavior consist first of all of inherited or unconditioned impulses; habits are woof and pattern woven on the warp of the latter. We have observed above that their mutual relations are either solidary or antagonistic. When the fundamental inherited impulses (impulses of individual self-preservation, alimentary, sexual, group-defense, self-expression, etc.)[1] are satisfied under the given conditions and habits the latter can very well coexist together with the unconditioned. But when one of the fundamental inherited impulses is, using Freud's terminology, "pinched" or pressed and cannot be put in action nor the corresponding biologic necessity satisfied without breaking the habit preventing this satisfaction (e.g., the religious habit forbidding eating certain foods hinder the appeasement of hunger, or moral habits hinder the satisfaction of sexual impulses) then between the former and the restraining habit a sharp conflict commences. The "cramped" hereditary impulse begins to put a pressure on the "brake"— that is on the habit. In this "duel" one of the rivals must be beaten. If the "duel" is fought between the inherited reaction and pure habit, it nearly always ends in the victory of the first.[2] The conditioned reactions

[1] See for their notion and characteristic in my *Elements of Sociology* and in *Famine as a Factor*.

[2] In my *Famine as a Factor* I give the following approximative index of the relative force of different unconditioned and conditioned impulses and respective reactions. Taking the force of absolute starvation of a normal organism during 48-70 hours for 100, the relative force of the other impulses—reactions—will fluctuate in the following limits: 1. The inherited reactions of individual self-preservation provoked by the stimuli menacing with the inevitable death—100-150; by other stimuli—according to the degree and character of danger—20-80. 2. The inherited reactions of group-defense and

in their pure form are weaker than the inherited impulses and their reactions. Therefore as a general rule, they disappear. When the facts seem to be against this view, when the unconditioned reactions seem to be subjugated by the habits; for example, in " hunger-strikes " in prisons, self-sacrifice because of duty—a more attentive analysis shows that in such cases we usually have before us not a conflict between some unconditioned reaction and a purely conditioned one but a conflict between the first and the latter with the help of some other inherited impulse; the conditioned reaction hides it but the decisive force lies in the latter. If it were not for their unconditioned " ally "—this battle would not be won by acquired or conditioned reaction tendencies. Let us bear this in mind.

Now for the moment we will accept as an axiom (further on proofs will be given) that the fundamental causes of revolutions always were circumstances that caused the strongest cramp of one or several of the inherited impulses in very many individuals. From this is comprehensible the character of the perversion of human behavior in the first period of revolution.

It consists first of all in the extinction, suppression and weakening of numerous conditioned reactions which under the given circumstances hinder the satisfaction of the pinched hereditary impulses of the population. This fact is the result of the pressure put by the cramped instincts on all opposing habits. Together with them

---

live interests of the most near persons (relatives, close friends, etc.)— 90-140; of remoter group (state, church, party, etc.)—10-70. 3. Sexual reactions—40-90. 4. Totality of different conditioned reactions in their pure form (legal, religious, moral, æsthetic and other habits)— 5-20. The force of different reflexes fluctuates from man to man. These figures give their approximative average force in human behavior. The foundation and the method applied in finding these indexes is to be found in *Famine as a Factor*.

GENERAL CHARACTERISTICS 35

numerous other habits, directly or indirectly connected
with them, are also extinguished. We have observed that
only the conditioned reactions of the first order (a) are
directly grafted on the inherited. An immense number
of the conditioned reactions of the second order (b) are
implanted on the first (on a). The habits of the third
order (c) fed on (b), reactions of the fourth order (d)
fed on (c) and so on. As soon as a great number of
habits of the first order (a) disappear in the "duel,"
their extinction leads to the extinction of all the other
habits (b, c, d, e, f) of higher orders based on and
brought up on reactions of the first order. Their extinction resembles the extraction of the bottom cards from a
complicated card-house. Extract these cards and the
whole edifice collapses. This is the reason why it is a
mistake to think that such an extinction concerns only a
few habits. An immense part of the "social dress" of
habits of the higher orders, deprived of the support of
reactions of the first order, falls to pieces, exposing the
naked tissue of the hereditary reflexes to our sight.

Secondly, the revolutionary perversion consists in the
biologization of the behavior of the multitude, as a
result of this extinction. The more restraining habits are
extinguished the stronger this biologization, this transformation of man-socius into man-animal takes place. With
the release of these "brakes" in the form of religious,
moral, legal and other habits declared to be "prejudices"
by revolution the hereditary reflexes attain full freedom.
The primary impulses are hindered now only by other
primary impulses. They can develop to their full natural
expansion. Under such circumstances human behavior
becomes almost exclusively a function of the primary
tendencies. But this is not all. This biologization reaches
its climax here; the biologic tendencies must here mani-

fest themselves in their most extreme and "sadistic" form, not only because they are released from pressure of the brakes of restraining habits, but also because of the revolutionary environment in the form of a fight, as the fundamental activity, in revolutionary periods, most intensely excites and stimulates them. The longer this fight lasts and the crueller it is—the more intense is this effect.[3] Hence—a feverish, agitated and furious character of behavior of multitudes in such periods. It is all impetuosity, agitation, emotional rage imbued with immense energy. Like unpiloted and rudderless ships on a stormy sea, human individuals are tossed by the immense force of the liberated primary impulses. This explains the greatest destructive activity of people in revolution.

Thirdly, side by side with this extinction of the restraining habits in the same first period of revolution we see the appearance and strengthening of new conditioned reactions acting not as "brakes," but, on the contrary, aiding the satisfaction of the pinched hereditary tendencies. We have indicated above that the biologic impulses are seldom expressed in their naked form in a human being. The human being is a creature who cloaks even the worst of his actions with good words. The great majority of our actions we "powder" and disguise in a pretty frock of numerous conditioned reactions, especially speech-reactions. Unlike an animal a human being will rarely commit murder without some pretentious excuse—" in God's name," "in the name of Progress," "Justice," "Democracy," "Revolution," "King," "Republic," "Socialism," "Liberty," "Equality," "National Welfare," etc. He will rarely rob his

---

[3] This phenomenon quite accurately has been stated by Ch. A. Ellwood, in his *Introduction to Social Psychology*, ch. VIII and in his *Sociology in its Psychol. Aspects*, 1912, 163 and 86 pp.

fellow-men without the same " cosmetics; " rarely indulge
in sexual intercourse without " romance; " rarely will one
nation fight the other without an accompaniment of
numerous " noble " reactions. The existence of consciousness and thinking makes it inevitable for him to " veil "
his primary tendencies with numerous pretty habits.
Right or wrong—this is a fact.[4]

The pressure of pinched primary impulses not only
extinguishes the retarding habits, but also brings into being new ones that countenance and aid the madness of the
former. These are the " wings " on which the hereditary
tendencies fly in the heights. Their exterior changes from
a naked animal impulse to noble deeds of the highest
order, thus helping both—actors and audience—to see in
them not animal prose, which they really are, but the
loftiest poetry of " God," " Truth," " Justice " and
" Beauty." Thanks to them acts of murder and robbery,
provoked by biologic impulses, are transformed into acts
of a " Struggle for Liberty, Fraternity and Equality; "
the desire to seize the goods of others is transformed
into the " Holy Social Requisition; " incendiarism and
vandalism into the " Creation of an Ideal Society," etc.
Such is the part they play. The conditioned reactions of
this type now are multiplied and strengthened.

Such are in short the fundamental characteristics of
the perversion of human behavior during the first period
of revolution.

4. Let us now trace the outlines of the perversion of
the behavior during the second period of revolution, in
the phase of its decline. As a result of the wild play of
excited primary impulses anarchy comes in. The revolu-

---

[4] See for details V. Pareto: *Trattato di Sociologia Generale*, Vols.
I and II. G. Le Bon: *Psychology of Socialism* (Russ. ed.), 4-5, 16-17
and Passim.

tionists begin to fight among themselves, crushing each other, individual against individual, and group against group. Every adaptation to life and life itself becomes difficult, if not impossible. In these conditions the primary instincts begin to be pressed even more strongly than before. Trying to find an outlet from this unendurable situation they begin to exert a pressure upon and to restrain each other. In this way the first "brakes" come into action. Exhaustion of energy called forth by especially wild activity and by poverty, starvation and want of necessities of life—usual satellites of revolution—leads to the same results. In a few months or at most in two or three years people are exhausted and become feeble, as also does the energy of inherited impulses. As a result these become easier to restrain. As in the preceding period the primary impulses attained their "boiling point" and human beings were brutalized to the utmost; it now becomes necessary to introduce the rudest and strongest brakes to limit their wild play. Such measures are usually administered in the form of "white" or "red" terror. By "iron" and "fire," by the most brutal and purely mechanical measures—i.e., strong unconditioned stimuli. Thus the mad society begins to be restrained. The direct result of such brake-work is a state of lethargy and apathy—an overture to the second revolutionary period. A great mass of people, who only yesterday were madly agitated, are now bound hand and foot. On their liberties of press and speech a muzzle is placed; on their actions, a veto; on society—a straitjacket. The onrush of inherited impulses is wrong but within its banks. Society is put in iron, bound and gagged. Agitation is replaced by a stunned silence. Society is inert and apathetic. Sometimes these brakes are put in action by "red" dictators (Cromwell, Robespierre,

Lenin), sometimes by " white " (Cavaignac, Wrangel in 1848, Thiers), but the objective part of their activity is the same in either case: they all do the same work of " reaction " or restraint.

After this period of quelling mad society comes a period of certain awakening out of apathy, followed by the implanting of brake-habits. The latter, like live tissue, gradually—under the " bandages " of terror-stimuli— grow over the hereditary reflexes; the more the stronger, and thus they gradually begin to replace the mechanical and strong brakes of terror and compulsion. The swifter and more energetic this growth of conditioned brakes, the sooner are the brutal restraints removed. Often a lull occurs: sometimes the " straitjacket " is taken off from society before the brake-habits are inculcated. Then revolutionary activity released from the " bandages of terror " flares up again. This flareup leads to a new reversion to terror and other measures of suppression. The latter leads again to apathy and to a further inculcation of brake-habits until at last they are sufficiently redeveloped. Then only is society fully released from the brakes of terror. And only then can revolution be considered as finished. Without repression and oppression revolution may become a permanent social state sooner or later leading society to perdition.

From the above it follows, that in the second as opposed to the first period of revolution we see: 1. The biologic essence of behavior is beginning to be draped in conditioned brake-habits, extinguished during the preceding stage. A " restoration " or " regeneration " of an immense majority of them takes place, partly in their old, partly in a new changed form. 2. Therefore the restraining processes begin to dominate over agitation, " socialization " over " biologization," " inhibition " over

" impetuous   action."   3. The   " beautifying "   habits
created in the preceding period disappear: as no expansion but a restraint of primary impulses occurs here they
become useless and baseless, and fade under the pressure
of brake-stimuli.   The above gives us, it is true, only the
basic scheme, obviously not excluding deviations and
variations of characteristics of a secondary order.   But
it gives the outlines of the fundamental essence of revolutionary perversion of human behavior.   Let us now turn
to the confirmation of the above by concrete examples.
We shall investigate in greater detail the character of
perversion of certain groups of reactions.

CHAPTER IV

THE TRANSFORMATION OF
" SPEECH-REACTIONS "

THE (oral and written) speech of man is a special
form of habits. These " speech-reactions " are interesting
in many respects. They are extremely variable and flex-
ible in their contents. They indicate the aspirations of the
individual and show the stimuli under which he acts.
Every important change of circumstances and stimuli
and every variation of reactions, their complicated performance and replacement is directly manifested in the
speech-reactions. In this respect they are a thermometer
of the state of the organism and its environment though a
very peculiar "thermometer." It shows the actions of
impulses, especially of the inherited, in a "beautified"
form. The speech-reactions give these impulses "wings"
with which to soar, beauty to dazzle and a noble character
to provoke necessary enthusiasm and at times fanaticism.

From the above we clearly see that they are naturally
the first to be transformed during revolution. Even
before revolution our thermometer shows us in the form
of growth of speech-reactions of discontent the growth
of "pinching" circumstances, on the one hand; and serves
as a precursor of the explosion of other reactions, on the
other. At the same time, it acts as a brake-remover.
Discontented speeches, undermining propaganda and
criticism of the foundations of the retarding régime—
in newspapers, pamphlets, books and meetings—the
expansion and success of liberal ideologies—the Encyclo-

pedists, Rousseau, Voltaire in France, Huss in Bohemia, Wycliffe, the Lollards and Independents in England, Marxism, Socialism and Radicalism in Europe—all appear before the revolution. Its beginning is characterized by an exceedingly strong " liberation " of the speech-reactions from brakes. " Man's tongue is loosened." He ceases to hold his tongue. An endless flood of speeches begins. Meetings and assemblies, sittings and demonstrations are convoked. A stream of newspapers, pamphlets, proclamations and placards flood the country. Unlimited " liberty of press and speech " begins to reign. The tongue which was silent before, and did not allude to numerous " sanctities," now begins to scourge, damn and accuse them, and stimulate the destruction of all the circumstances that oppressed the now liberated impulses—religion, church, property, morality, authorities—as the restraining and pressing conditions. " Down with them! " is the monotonous chorus of all these numberless cries. A plea for moderation and self-control meets with no response. Ideologies, acting as brakes on this unlimited freedom of pressed appetites, are not well received. Ideologies, however, that call for more freedom, demand the removal of all social brakes and instigate robberies, murder, revenge, etc., ennobling these actions as the demands of " Equality," " Deity," " Justice," or " Socialism "—such ideologies spread with the swiftness of an epidemic and infect thousands of converts.

Such is the transformation of speech-reactions during the first period of revolution. The second phase is a period of restraint. Here also speech-reactions go ahead of the other reflexes. Their restraint is a precursor of the inhibition of the other primary impulses and a symptom of the transition of revolution into its second period. Independently of the question whether the brakes are put in action by "white" or "red" government, a gag is placed on the tongue of man. Numerous newspapers vanish. Liberty of press is limited, liberty of speech is annulled, meetings prohibited, propaganda punished. For violation, there are punishments beginning with prison and ending with the guillotine or shooting. Under the pressure of such brakes " people begin to hold their tongues." The flood of speeches dries up. In the place of unlimited verbosity a period of hushed voices and silence begins. The success of " liberating ideologies " of the first period is over. They are replaced by ideologies whose watchword is " order " and " restraint! " With the return to normal life the regulation of speech is gradually resumed.

Such is the essence of the transformation of speech-reactions during revolutionary periods. Together with this fundamental process other processes take place. 1. Numerous new expressions appear for the purpose of expressing new experiences. 2. Each period has its favorite and its proscribed words. Usually the favorite expression of the first period is the object of hatred in the second. 3. The same can be said of ideologies. 4. During each period a Bacchanalia affects the " conquerors " and a restraining silence, the " vanquished foes." Each party restrains the other.

The Egyptian Revolution (1600–2000 B.C.). Abstinence from verbosity was here in normal times a pious virtue. In the *Book of the Dead,* as we should expect, it is said of an act agreeable to Osiris: " I uttered no useless word." This virtue, according to the following words of a contemporary of the revolution—Ipouver—vanished during the revolution. The tongue was " loosened." " There is enough noise in noisy years . . . The noise is endless . . . Oh, if the noise on the earth would cease . . ." He remarks in his elegaic chronicle of the Egyptian Revolution: " The female slaves are not moderate in their speech, and they do not like when their mistresses talk." [1]

The same " loosening " of the tongue is to be observed in Rome during the numerous revolutions of the final period of the republic, beginning with the time of the Gracchi. From this time on congregating became a permanent feature. The " corn-plebs " grow and attend such meetings. There appear professionals of speech-reactions, the popular orators. Politics are made on the forum; ideologies of equality, liberty, radicalism and socialism emerge. During the " quelling " periods, which occurred several times, strong " restraints " were brought into action. But after each period of restraint once more it is recorded: " The motley street crowd never has such a good time and never attended such merry meetings. The name of all these little, great men is legion. Demagogism has become a profession." The mob is permanently in the forum. The propaganda is immense. " The significant words, that only a poor man can represent the poor and that a dictatorship of the poor must be proclaimed, are already pronounced." [2]

Characteristic shibboleths and watchwords arose. " Down with restraint! " Senate, patricians, aristocracy, the rich, property, family, ancient gods, etc., on one hand and *aequatio bonorum, aequatio pecuniae,* the annulling of debts and the distribution of land, etc., on the other, flooded the country like a wide stream. " There was no lack of elements, full of enthusiasm for the most extreme

---

[1] V. Vikentieff: *Revolution in Ancient Egypt. New East* (Russ.), Vol. I, 1922, 290. Turaeff: *Ancient Egypt,* 1922, 120-1.
[2] Mommsen: *Roman History* (Russ. ed.), Moscow, 1887, Vol. III, 260, 81 pp.

socialistic and destructive ideas." [3]   In the periods of
"suppression," for example, in Sulla's time and later,
"the speechless horror oppresses the whole country and
no freely-expressed opinion was to be heard." [4]

In Greece we observe the same during the revolutions
of the sixth and seventh centuries B.C.—in Athens,
Mileth, Mithylene, Mehar, Syracuse; in 427 in Corcyra,
in 412 in Samos, in 370 in Argos, as well as in the revolutions led by Agis IV, Cleomenes II, Nabis, etc. One has
only to read the description of the Corcyraean Revolution
by Thucydides for confirmation of this. " The use of fair
phrases to arrive at guilty ends was in high reputation." [5]
Endless and wild riots were preceded and followed by
similar " riots " of speech, which were restrained during
the periods of revolutionary ebb.

The same is seen, for example, during the Peasants'
Rebellion in England in 1381. It was followed by the
teaching of Wycliffe and his disciples, the " Vision of Piers
Ploughman," the propaganda of John Ball and the Lollards. " The seed sown by Lollards grew like young
trees and spread all over the country." The speech-reactions undermined property, church dogmas, the privileges
of classes (" when Adam delved and Eve span, who was
then the gentleman? ") and the foundations of government. " They taught that property is a gift of God and
that the sinful lose the bliss that property gives " and so

---

[3] Pöhlmann: *History of Ancient Communism and Socialism*, St.
Petersburg, 1910, 503, 514-21, 533, 582 p. Pöhlmann: *The Early
Christian Communism*, Kazan, 1921; look for details by Ferrero:
The Greatness and Fall of Rome. Duruy: *Histoire des Romains*,
1885, Vol. V. Rostovtzev: *The Birth of the Roman Empire*, St.
Petersburg, 1918.
[4] Mommsen: *Op. cit.*, Vol. II, 347.
[5] Thucydides: *Peloponnesian War*, book III, ch. X, 225 p.
(Dutton) look for details by Pöhlmann, *op. cit.*, Passim, F. de
Coulanges: *La cité Antique*, the books of Buzolt, Niese, Böckh men-
tioned further.

on.[6] After the suppression of the rebellion the usual pressure begins.

The same occurred during the Bohemian Revolution in the fifteenth century. It was also preceded by a "loosening" propaganda of the Hussitism that undermined the foundations of the Catholic Church and rebelled against obedience to the Pope, and all ecclesiastical institutions, whose authority is not acknowledged by the Holy Scripture. This propaganda was gradually followed by criticism and repudiation of numerous other social "restraining beliefs" which led during the periods of the Hussite Wars to the condemnation of property, government, and even of family by Taborites, Millenarians, and among other sects by the naked Adamites and Piccards, who even preached the community of wives. In the second period after the wars of Zizka and Prokop, we observe the quantitative and qualitative "restraining of speech-reactions." [7]

Similar events are also seen in the Dutch Revolution in the sixteenth century, whereby in periods of restraints "the tongue of each prisoner was screwed in an iron ring and seared with hot irons." [8] As soon as the restraints were loosened rebellion raised its head.

The same state of affairs existed during the English Revolution of the seventeenth century. "Before the rev-

[6] Weber: *General History* (Russ. ed.), Vol. VIII, 1894, 43-8; look for details by Ch. Oman: *The Great Peasants' Rebellion in England*. Kovalevsky: *The Economic Growth of Europe* (Russ.), Vol. II. Petrushevsky: *The Rebellion of Wat Tyler* (Russ.). Green: *A Short History of the English People* (Russ.), 1897, Vol. I, 277, 285 ff.

[7] Weber: *Ibid.*, 205-7; look for details in Denis: *Huss et la Guerre des Hussites*, 1878, 219, 265-7. F. Palacky: *Geschichte v. Böhmen.* Kautsky: *Von Plato bis zu den Anabaptisten. Vorläufer des modernen Socialismus* (Russ. ed.), 1907, Vol. I.

[8] D. Motley: *History of the Dutch Revolution* (Russ. ed.), St. Petersburg, 1866, Vol. II, 67, 218 p.

olution the discontent with the policy of Charles I was demonstrated by the upper classes in the form of abstinence from court and liberty of thinking (*i.e.*, speech-reactions) never heard of before. Even more strongly was this evident in the lower classes." The loosening of the tongue began and grew crescendo. An immense harvest of "loosening" pamphlets was reaped in 1636. In Parliament and in the street tongues were loosened as well. Criticism grew bolder; " liberty of speech," " free-thinking " and extreme teachings increased. " The speeches of extreme independents denying aristocracy and the authority of the Monarch, hotly in the Church, but also in the chairs of State and demanding equality of rights and the distribution of riches, found a strong echo. The free-thinkers liked such speeches, they wanted to lead the revolution to its extreme limits." [9] Even more. " In the lower classes a stormy agitation commenced. Demands for unheard-of reforms were made in every quarter." " Their self-confidence and imperious language was as great as their ignorance and insignificance. Summoned before the judges, they declared their disbelief in the authority of the judges themselves. In the churches they stormed the pulpits, and drove away the (moderate) preachers." The ideologies of radicalism, equality, communism, republicanism, whirled round in a storm. " Meetings " began, a flood of " loosening " pamphlets streamed forth. The following was written in them: " Law is the sign of cunning suppression," " Prisons are sanctities of the rich and places of torture for the poor." The religious non-restraint is illustrated by the following words of a

[9] Guizot: *History of the English Revolution* (Russ. ed.), St. Petersburg, 1868, Vol. I, 62-3, 70; Vol. II, 23. S. Gardiner: *History of the Great Civil War*, 1886-91. *History of the Commonwealth and the Protectorate*, Vols. I, IV, 1903 and *O. Cromwell* (1899).

soldier: "If I choose to worship that pint pot, what is that to you?" "Good Lord!" writes a contemporary of the preachings of the Anabaptists, "how many horrible disgusting calls for destruction, murder and fire. Listening to them, I thought of the Savior's answer to His disciples: 'You know not, what spirit fills your hearts.'" [10] The theatres produced plays that mocked catholicism. After this they began to mock the reformers themselves, so that "the reformist clergy was forced to take measures against this, fearing to be themselves overthrown by the revolutionary movement." [11] "Overthrow, overthrow, overthrow, this was all that was in the minds and hearts of people." Thus Cromwell himself characterized the situation in his speech before Parliament in 1654.[12] From the second period beginning with Cromwell's dictatorship the restraints were again put into action in the form of arrests of Lilborn and other pamphleteers of disobedience, including members of Parliament; in the form of suppression of the liberty of speech and press. The right to print books was given only to four towns. A severe censorship was introduced. "No magazine, no periodical could be issued without the permission of the government, the printers had to give securities. Not only were the authors persecuted and punished, but every purchaser of the rebellious work was fined." Meetings were prohibited, theatres closed, street-singers and vendors persecuted. The head of the family was obliged to keep his children and servants indoors except for a few hours a day, etc. In short, there was the strongest restraint. The result was as follows: "Everyone yielded, everyone was silent." Inertia reigned. Later on a revival

[10] Guizot: Vol. II, p. 1, 96-7; Vol. III, 7, 63-4.
[11] Cabanes and L. Nass: *Revolutionary Neurosis* (Russ. ed.), St. Petersburg, 1906, 294.
[12] Guizot: Vol. III, 109.

took place in the form of pamphlets and attacks against Cromwell, but the latter successfully restrained till his death the new "loosening of tongues." [13]   During the French Revolution the loosening of speech-reactions in the upper classes began. Also long before the revolution, the Encyclopedists, Rousseau, Voltaire and others successfully spread their preaching of rationalism, cosmopolitanism, geometrism, republicanism, atheism, rights of man and their criticism of restraining "superstitions." With the commencement of the revolution, "the flood of speech-reactions" expands and acquires a furious character. Endless meetings began. Clubs, pamphlets, newspapers, etc., appear. The number of Jacobin clubs at the beginning of 1791 amounts to 227. After three months their number is 345 and at the end of the National Assembly 406. The loosening is clearly demonstrated in instructions, in the "declaration of the rights of man," in newspapers, in speeches and in theatrical performances. All the old restraints—Government, the King, the Tyrants, the Aristocracy, the Church, Religion, Family— were ridiculed and criticised. The number of "revolutionary plays" and poems grew incessantly. They contained an "apotheosis of liberty, republic and equality" on the one hand, and supported various biologic impulses on the other. They released the individual from the "superstitions" of authority, church, family, property, etc. All these plays: "Modern Equality," "The Tenth of August," "Buizot," "The King of Calvados," "The Republican Widow," "The Guillotine of Love," "The Last Judgment of Kings," "Charles XI," "The Husband Confessor," "Another Parson," "The Marriage of J. J. Rousseau," "The Storming of the Bastille,"

---

[13] Guizot: Vol. I, ch. XXIV; Vol. II, 51-2, 123, 176. Gardiner: *History of the Commonwealth,* Vol. IV, ch. XLII.

" Friendship and Fraternity," etc., monotonously sang these motifs. They all were full of watchwords: " Off with the Chains," " Down with the Tyrants, Kings, Clergymen, Aristocrats." " Let us Break the Hated Chains," etc. The same is contained in the numberless poems, beginning with the " Marseillaise " and ending with the poems of Lagarpe, Marcus Chenier and others.

The newspapers were full of the same ideas, especially the most popular of them, as for example: Marat's *L'Ami du Peuple* and *Père Duchesne*. Their language was strong, half-pornographical and half-feverish. From Marat's pen the same words incessantly poured forth: " Scoundrels," " Villains," " Devils." Cries of " Down with "—" Away with "—were inevitable. The demand for execution was general. Michelet reckoned that Marat alone demanded no less than 270,000 heads. *Père Duchesne* continually demanded the general removal of restraint.[14] The riot of tongues was unlimited in all respects. Together with this, the language changed in its essence. Numerous new expressions were introduced or the sense of the old underwent a change (budget, club, motion, constitution, aristocrat, revolutionary, lanterner, septembriser, guillotine, regicide and sans-culotte). New jokes appear ("to poke one's head out of the window," "to sneeze in a sack "—to be guillotined). A number of words were prohibited (the use of the plural of respect, " you," and of Monsieur). Certain other words became obligatory ("thou," "citoyen," etc.). In short, we have before us a general revolution of language.[15]

---

[14] The import-tax on wine was for example abolished. He wrote: " At last our boys who love a drink won't be ruined any more. Instead of a 'small scoundrel,' we can now grab a big one. What happiness!" This is as usual followed by an unprintable expression.

[15] Cabanes and L. Nass: *Op. cit.*, 250-310. Aulard: *Les Orateurs de la Constituante*, 1905. Madelin: *The French Revolution*, 1921, Vol. I, 25-6, 143 (Russ. ed.). Taine: *Les Origines de la France Contemporaine*, Vols. I-III. *Histories of the French Revolution*, by Michelet, Jaurés, and others.

From the beginning of the Jacobin dictatorship a one-sided restraint commences. The anti-Jacobin speech-reactions are persecuted. " Pamela," " The Friend of Law," " Figaro's Marriage " and even Molière are not permitted to be played without alterations. A censorship of speeches, theatres and newspapers is introduced. A strong restraint is laid· on anti-Jacobin language. After the Termidor the latter is less strict,[16] but instead the Jacobin speech-reactions are restrained. Under the Directoire the "restraint" is intensified and extended, especially after such rebellions as the one in Fructidore. The clubs and newspapers were closed. A permit-system together with securities, fines and arrests was introduced. The theatre was placed under control, etc.[17] Under Napoleon this process grew even stronger and nearly led to the utter abolition of freedom of oral and written speech.[18]

In the Revolution of 1848 in France again we see the same picture. At the beginning of the revolution endless meetings and the growth of clubs, whose number amounts to 700. " Hundreds of clubs existed, where every person said what he thought at the moment. Everyone proclaimed his wishes and put forward plans." The walls were covered with immense posters. Every day new papers appeared, which tried, as it seems, to create fear by their loud and fearsome names: *Le Père Duchesne, La Commune de Paris, Le Tribun du Peuple, La Voix des Clubs, La Voix de Femme, La Peuple, L'Ami du Peuple,* etc.[19]

---

[16] " The press suppressed under the tyrant (Robespierre) revenged itself. It increased . . . Newspapers together with a great number of pamphlets, that attacked the disciples of Robespierre, appeared." Madelin: Vol. II, 156-7.

[17] Madelin: Vol. II, 294. Look for corresponding parts in the works of Taine, Jaurés and *The Political History of the French Revolution,* by Aulard, St. Petersburg, 1920.

[18] E. Tarlé: *The French Press Under Napoleon I,* Petrograd, 1922.

[19] Gregoire: *History of France in the Nineteenth Century* (Russ. ed.), 1896, Vol. III, 21-52, 140-41, 446-50 ff.

As usual, endless festivities, illuminations and demonstrations. In the clubs the " proletarians " were overwhelmed with flatteries and called " the People, the infallible People." The newspapers vied with each other in the forcible tone of their articles. " It seemed as if some madness had affected the whole population." Every day more and more threatening demonstrations took place. The papers devoted themselves to the most furious utterances and all instigated to " rebellion and civil war." The inevitable " Down " addressed to all restraints and " Vive " !!!—to " liberty " (from restraint).

After the rebellion of the twenty-second to twenty-fifth of June, a strong restraint begins, inaugurated by Cavaignac. Numerous newspapers close down. A security (a bond) of 24,000 francs is introduced. (This provokes Lamenes' answer: " We are not rich enough, the poor be silent " !!!) Oppressions grow stronger, clubs and meetings close. The general cry is for " Order! " Later on we again observe a certain slackening, but after the thirteenth of June, 1849, Napoleon orders the suppression of propaganda " to reassure the good and to make the bad tremble." By the laws of the fifteenth of May, 1850, a strong restraint is laid on the " speech-reactions " in the form of control of the press, the school, the church, the closing of newspapers, clubs, etc.

Similarly history monotonously repeats itself during the German Revolution of 1848. " In the spring and summer of 1848 every day in Berlin brought new meetings and placards. Clubs and newspapers grew like mushrooms. The liberty of opinion and coalition was realized. Government tried to limit this freedom, but it had to tolerate it for some time. There was as yet no possibility of satiating their fanatic thirst for order." In Austria " there was no opposition press before March."

With the beginning of the revolution "a new press grew up at once. The majority of papers had a revolutionary character. Innocent magazines were transformed into radical political papers. The number of political papers in Vienna amounted to 220. Many of them used a rough and vulgar language." At the end of 1848 a new restraint was put into action in Berlin. On the twelfth of November "all clubs and unions in Berlin were dissolved, the democratic newspapers closed. The soldiers tore down all placards. A military dictatorship began." [20] Later on searches, arrests and the usual group of restraining activities took place.

The same occurred during the French Revolution of 1871. As early as 1868 " the opposition in Parliament increased, and the press grew bolder." The restraint placed on the press grows weaker. Rochefort's *La Lanterne* had an unusual success. The speeches of 1869 were so bold that even *Delecluse* condemned them. After Sedan the liberation from restraints had at once an immense success. There arose a general call for " Dethronement!" " The Liberty of the Press, meetings and proclamations were unlimited." Endless demonstrations took place. The growth of extremism in all respects led to the Commune. But the Commune also commenced to restrain. The anti-communistic press was prohibited. Lissagarés declared that: " we demand the prohibition *sans phrase* of all newspapers that are hostile to the Commune." With the latter's fall—the restraint was laid on anti-Thiers papers; after the massacre—all papers were controlled.[21] Thus the regular succession of events ran its course.

---

[20] Bloss: *The German Revolution* (Russ. ed.), Moscow, 220, 269, 392-3.
[21] Gregoire: Vol. IV, 185, 260, 372, 425. Lissagarés: *The History of the Parisian Commune*, St. Petersburg, 1906, 320, 417-31.

Exactly the same course of events is repeated in the Russian Revolution of 1905–6, and again during the Revolution of 1917–24. As early as the end of 1916 the "loosening" of tongues began in the Duma (speeches of Miliukoff, Kerensky, Tshkeidse, Shulgin and others) and in private meetings as well as in the street and in the press. With the approach of the end of February, 1917, the "loosening" increased. On February 27th the unrest made an immense jump.[22] Incessant meetings are held at all times and places, in the Duma, in private houses, barracks, governmental offices, etc. The tone of the newspapers, even of the *Novoje Vremja* changes at once. During a week or two numerous newspapers appear: one more radical than the other. The walls of the town were covered with numberless placards. The expenditure on paper, on manifestoes and placards was immediately multiplied several times. In one day the "monarchic" speech-reactions were replaced by "republican."

Already in the first declaration of the Provisional Government all liberties were proclaimed. After this came at once the liberation of the soldiers from military discipline together with suggestions that were equivalent to instigations to kill their officers: do not obey orders, finish the war. The citizens hunted, caught and killed the police. Things daily grew worse. A flood of speeches about the six–eight-hour day and about the futility of hard work, streamed out. The peasants received manifestoes inciting them to take possession of the landlords' estates and to rob the mansions. Odes to freedom—to unlimited and boundless freedom—were addressed to everyone. Sometimes the following watchwords were distributed to the mob: "The workmen to their benches, the soldiers to

[22] See already published memoires: *Dni*, by Shulgin: *History of the Second Russian Revolution*, by Miliukoff. *Notes on the Revolution*, by Sukhanoff and especially the newspapers of that time.

arms, peasants wait;" but all this was only a drop in the ocean. The " loosening " progresses. Soon calls for the destruction of capitalism and the bourgeois class were to be heard. The socialization of everything, the liberation from all " bourgeois and family prejudices " was demanded. Religion was declared to be " opium for the people," the members of the Provisional Government to be " traitors," the Soviets to be compromise-makers helplessly trying to restrain the " intensification of the revolution." As a result all speech-restraints were broken. Tongues were absolutely free and uttered what the biologic impulses ordered. Songs, poems, plays, stories, etc., acquired a similar character. Their fundamental motive consisted in " Down " and " Three Cheers for Freedom." The Bolsheviks came. During the first weeks after the October revolution they could not yet control. But in 1918 the restraint began. All non-communistic papers were closed. Non-communistic meetings and societies were dissolved. Arrests, searches, and the first executions took place. The restraint acquired one-sided, but nevertheless unlimited, character. For any word of protest—imprisonment and thrashings. For the anti-Soviet proclamations, execution; for a non-permitted meeting, " to the wall."

At the end of 1918 all was silent. The voice of the people, with the exception of the communists, was silenced. Nineteen hundred and nineteen to nineteen hundred and twenty-one, the whole country except the communists was deprived of its tongue. No non-communistic newspaper, no free speech, no book, edited without the permission of the censorship; no visiting card, printed without the permission of a commissary—were issued. Only in a whisper, suspiciously looking around, two or three near " friends "

dared to tell each other " whispergrams." Even this did
not always occur. Terminology also strongly changed.
Numerous new words and expressions appeared: " Sow-
dep," " Narkom," " Tsheka," " Narobras," " Sownar-
hos," " Samkompomorde," " Tovarish," " Kombed."
Certain former expressions were prohibited : " Gentlemen,"
" Sir," etc. Some words acquired a specific significance :
" To the wall," "to spend," " to liquidate " (to shoot),
" bourshuika " (an iron small stove), " scoundrel-mobil "
(motor-car), etc.[23] In short everything was repeated
here in the same way as in other revolutions.

With the beginning of the " New Economic Policy "
(N. E. P.) in the second half of 1921 and early in 1922
the restraints grew slightly weaker. People again gradually acquired the gift of " articulate speech." They
tried to say something oppositional. Two or three magazines appeared, several books with a shadow of oppositional tendency were published. They were successfully
sold. The word " tovarish " (comerade) began to meet
with disapproval. The public began to grow a little bit
bolder. But . . . in the middle of 1922 these magazines were suppressed, the grumblers arrested, several of
them were banished, the others shot. Russia became silent
again, taking refuge in the " whispergrams " of yesterday and Russia remains silent now, as I write these words.
The " restraint " of speech of 99.5 per cent. of the population continues. The wise rulers teach it saying : " Words
are silver, silence is gold." But themselves they speak all
the more.

The result of our investigation is : that history repeats
itself. The fundamental difference between various revolutions in this respect consists only in the fact that different groups of speech-reactions are released from restraint

---

[23] Cornfeld: *New Words and Expressions,* 1922 (Russ.).

—the tongue "accuses" different restraining institutions —and that the loosening process reaches various degrees. In some revolutions it stops at a certain limit, in others it goes further, till it burns down and covers with mud all restraining "sanctities." The deeper the revolution goes, the greater is this loosening; the greater the latter, the harsher and crueller the subsequent restraint is. Action is equal to counteraction. The disciples of unlimited freedom of speech must bear this in mind. Again the stronger the mechanical "bridles" of liberty of speech were before the revolution, the further the loosening goes and the wilder forms takes the speech-bacchanalia. This has to be remembered by all suppressors of liberty of speech—and press.

CHAPTER V

PERVERSION OF THE REACTIONS OF OWNERSHIP

AMONG the unconditioned reactions there exists a whole group of reactions manifesting themselves by the acts of possession, acquisition, utilization and appropriation of certain objects necessary to the maintenance of life and in acts of self-protection against the encroachment of others. This group of hereditary reflexes can be classified under the title of reflexes of "ownership." We can find their rudiments in animal and even vegetable life.[1] In man these hereditary reflexes have been overgrown by numerous conditioned ones. An essential function of the latter consists partly in shaping and directing the actions of the unconditioned ones; in deciding when, where, how and in what conditions they can be exercised; in fixing the border

[1] "Ownership is a natural fact existing prior to any kind of organization. From the latter it only receives the sanction which justifies and codifies a fact existing already. Among all the different existing theories as to the origin of the right of ownership, the one that affirms that legislation creates the right of ownership appears to me the most fallible. The right of ownership, as Petrucci so rightly states, is the result of a tendency, all the more instinctive, because it originates in the very organism of man, in the forms of his activity, in his social feelings." Petrucci goes on to clearly prove that the fact of appropriation and ownership of outward material objects necessary to the life of the organism forms the foundation of ownership in the animal and vegetable kingdoms. As long as an organism exists it has to take and appropriate some objects of the outward world (as *e.g.,* food, land, air, light, warmth, lodging, etc.). Without it life were not possible.

Petrucci: *Les Origines Naturelles de la Propriété,* 1905, ch. I, II. See on the existence of unconditioned reflexes of acquisition Thorndike: *The Original Nature of Man.* McDougall: *Introduction to Social Psychology.* G. Patrick: *The Psychology of Social Reconstruction.* G. Wallas: *Human Nature in Politics,* 1919, 36 p.

line existing between " mine " and " thine ; " and, partly, in restraining and limiting the insatiable appetites of the unconditioned reflexes of ownership. Conditioned, restraining reflexes prevent the encroachment on others' property and hold back from acts of spoliation and appropriation.

These two combined groups of reflexes of ownership determine our conduct in regard to property. I can take from the table and put into my pocket " my " watch and do not touch yours. I peacefully pull out the vegetables from my own vegetable bed and do not molest the neighboring ones belonging to " others." I pay money for a book in a shop and " appropriate " it, though I would not have considered it " mine " without having handed over the money for it. All these acts are the results of the combination of my unconditioned reflexes of ownership with ingrafted, conditioned habits by which they are fashioned, directed and restrained.

The economic and legislative organizations of society, with their corresponding legal principles, are, in their very essence, the result of its member's conduct, and an attempt to give it shape and to define it.

In normal times the reflexes of ownership are stable among a great majority of society. In epochs of revolution they are considerably perverted. During certain revolutions this perversion is very acute, during others less so. The first are so-called " social " revolutions, the second may be political, religious, or other, only not social in that narrow sense. Wherein does the perversion of the reflexes of ownership consist?

From the objective viewpoint the perversion of reflexes of ownership during times of revolutions consists in the following: During the first stage we see: a. Among the poor, and those whose reflexes of ownership have remained pinched and unsatisfied, a falling off of those habits which restrain the appropriation of other people's property. b. As a result of this we witness a strong manifestation of hereditary reflexes of ownership in the form of appropriation of others' property no more restrained by habits, now grown obsolete. c. Among the rich a weakening of property-protecting reflexes.

As the result of such a perversion we witness a tremendous process of appropriation of the property of the wealthy (estates, capital, etc.) by the poor; of the belongings of one group by other groups—in form of robbery, requisitions, " nationalizations," " levelling." The border line between " mine " and " thine " is obliterated. People whose restraints upon the reflexes of ownership have faded are spurred onward by their cramped unconditioned impulses of appropriation, and set about to satisfy appetites with mad primitive wildness. In the cases where formerly they were held back from appropriating other people's belongings, they now feel no restraining element. The catchwords are: " Steal what has been stolen," " Long Live the Expropriation of the Exploiters." Those whose belongings are taken away generally have weakened property-protecting reflexes. This process is accompanied with an outburst of oratorical and subvocal reflexes (ideas, ideology, convictions), all propagating ideas of equality, communism, economic levelling, protesting against the right of ownership, against the greed of the rich, and sanctioning appropriation, communisation, etc. This ideology of the levelling-communistic type develops swiftly, is easily caught up by the masses who have cramped reflexes of ownership and spurs them onward to acts of appropriation, " equalizing," and repartition.

Later on such a period is followed by a second one of a totally different character. This takes various forms according to whether the revolution has run its full course, or has taken an abortive form. But in both cases the essence is identical. It consists in a new and intense awakening of the weakened restraints upon reflexes of ownership, a new development of restraints upon spoliation. The causes which call forth this second stage of the process are: on the one hand a general impoverishment, famine, pauperism, which are the consequences of the destruction, spoliation, nationalization and requisitions of the first period; and, on the other, the satisfaction of the cramped instincts of ownership of the more energetic "communists" and "levellers." The latter are now interested in protecting their own property; the people in protecting themselves from the misfortunes brought on by the wild orgies of unrestrained reflexes of ownership. If the former rich get the upper hand and stem the revolutionary process this reëstablishment of habits of restraint is due to them and their strength. If on the other hand revolution runs its full course, if riches exist no more, if there is nothing left but nationalized belongings, if private wealth is destroyed and divided among all kinds of communisers; then any new repartition threatens only them, and those who have now grown to be representatives of the new bourgeoisie, new fresh energetic owners, hasten to reëstablish restraining habits. They are upheld by all the groups that have acquired material wealth from the revolution and have, up to a certain degree, satisfied the previously pinched reflexes of ownership.

In both cases it is now forbidden to "rob," to touch the property of others. Each act of spoliation is severely punished. The strongest restraining sanctions are established; fines, prisons, capital punishments. Society is governed "by a rod of iron." The wildly impetuous impulses of ownership are bridled. As a result, little by little, with many backslidings, the elemental forces are driven back

into their natural channels, and the restraining reflexes get
the upper hand. "Ownership" is looked upon as sacred.
The old order of things lifts up its head: *Beati possidentes.* The difference lies only in the fact that the new
owners are much more staunch adherents of this principle;
are much more energetic in defending their belongings
than the enfeebled owners of the old régime were with
their half-atrophied reflexes of property protection. These
new owners will be perplexed neither by threats, nor
reproofs, nor "good words." They know too well the
worth of them; they have used all these arguments during
the first period of the revolution and, consequently, are
not impressed by them. Their answer is quiet and positive: "We know, we've heard it often enough," "our
own words" . . . And they will continue to stand
up for their own "sacred" property. *In the realm of
ideology and speech-reactions this period is characterized
by the falling off of the levelling-communistic ideologies* of
the first period of revolution. They lose credit and popularity. An ideology directly opposed to it lifts up its head
and strengthens all such as sanction the "sacred right
of property."

This is the essence of the transformation in this realm
of reflexes. The forms in which they manifest themselves
are not equally evident in every revolution, but every
revolution has the same tendency and manifests it, though
sometimes only in a slight degree. Let us now take up
the facts.

THE RUSSIAN REVOLUTION, 1917–24

For some time before the revolution the waning of the
restraints upon acquisitive instinct could be observed;
first of all in the sacking of stores, market places, etc.;
secondly, in the popularity socialistic ideology was gain-

ing; thirdly, in a whole series of nationalizations and restrictions of ownership by the government (actuated by the demands of war and " military socialism "). But from the first days of the revolution this decay of the socially inculcated reflexes was suddenly accelerated. Workmen appropriated enterprises, peasants sacked the estates of the landowners, carried away the live-stock and furniture, took possession of the land. The per cent. of crimes committed against the rights of ownership rose inordinately. In two to three months, this process took on catastrophic proportions. Since the October revolution this has been legalized. In 1918 a law was issued confiscating all private landed property, all the factories were requisitioned, capital and houses likewise. The border line between " mine " and " thine " was swept away. First property was taken away from the wealthy: the workmen took away from the capitalists, the peasants from the landowners, the house porters from the wealthy lodgers, the soldiers from the officers, the communists and sailors from everybody. When all the riches were broken up and divided, requisitions were started: corn, live-stock, butter, milk, clothes, were taken from the peasants. Men, having lost the restraints upon the reflexes of ownership (chiefly communists and sailors), requisitioned everything they could—foodstuffs, jewels, pictures, books, lodgings—all, carrying away the last shirt, the last silver spoon. To sum up: the great majority has lost all restraining reflexes. Others, the rich, had lost property-preserving reflexes, and showed themselves to be pitifully weak. They allowed nearly everything to be taken away, without resisting.

This same process can be observed in the statistics of crimes perpetrated against the right of ownership. In 1918 in Petrograd, there were 387,000 thieves (twenty-two per cent. of the population). They stole by presenting unlawful food-cards to get more rations than they had a right to. In Moscow their number attained the figure of 1,000,000 (seventy per cent. of the population).[2]

If we take 100 to be the figure designating the criminality in Moscow for the year 1914 we have for the year 1918 the following figures, which do not include the " crimes " of the Soviet's agents:

Thefts	315
Armed robbery	28,500
Simple robbery	800
Trickery	370
Appropriation	170[3]

On the railway lines thefts of luggage were one hundred and fifty times more frequent in 1920 than they had been in peace times.[4] In 1922 we also see no amelioration. According to the data of the *Soviet Workmen and Peasant Inspection* the following items were stolen on the railway lines during 1922:

> 2,640,000 pouds[5] of foodstuffs.
> 65,000 pouds of stuffs, boots, leather and furs.
> 196,000 pouds of different kinds of valuables.
> 4,826,000 pouds of fuel.
> 680,000 pouds of raw material.

In all 11,400,000 pouds having a value of 50,000,000 gold rubles, that is twenty-two per cent. of the whole budget of the Commissariat of Ways and Means. However, the official figures are but a faint shadow of what has really taken place. Yet even these figures show clearly enough how weakened the restraining reflexes of ownership have grown to be and what an actual form communism had acquired.

All this was accompanied by a loud clamoring of

---

[2] *Statistical Material for St. Petersburg,* Vol. III, 4-5. *Red Moscow,* 1917-20, 53.
[3] *Red Moscow,* Chapter " Criminality."
[4] *Isvestia,* October 2, 1921.
[5] A poud—about 36 English pounds.

speech-reflexes, by slogans of " material equality," " communism," " abolition of capital's exploitation," " justice," " general welfare," and many similar. But did this correspond to what really existed? In reality the communists define the situation very exactly. Commissary Ossinsky says : " When factories are appropriated by the workmen, they do not look after the interests of the majority, they do not nationalize them, but develop a meanly bourgeois feeling of ownership towards the enterprise. Every group that appropriated a factory looked upon itself as its rightful owner, pilfered and parcelled it amongst its members." [6] The same picture can be seen among the peasants. Already in 1918 the communist Mesheriakov said : " The peasants, as a mass, do not admit of socialism, and do not want to have anything but a free grant of land. Their meanly bourgeois prejudices rise to the surface and grow evident." [7] " When," disconsolately adds Ossinsky, " the villagers succeeded in getting the landlords' property into their own hands, they turned an absolutely deaf ear to questions of socialism and resolutely refused to listen to any idea of a commune." The same is corroborated with even more authority by Lenin.[8]

Instead of general welfare and plenty, we see general pauperism. Instead of material equality, already in 1918 dozens of different kinds of rations, " paiki," were established, beginning with the plentiful " sovnarkom paiek " (Soviet of Peoples' Commissaries) which includes caviar, fruit, wine, etc., and ending with starvation rations. At the same time thirty-four categories of salaries were established. In 1919, during the communistic congress, a reso-

---

[6] Ossinsky : *The Building Up of Socialism,* 1918. *The Review of Labor,* 1921, No. 3, 91 (Russ.).

[7] Mesheriakov : *Agricultural Communes,* 1918, 11-12, 17-25 (Russ.).

[8] See his speech in *The Eighth All-Russian Congress of Soviets,* 1921, 29-31 (Russ.).

lution was carried, which not only approved of material privileges of communists, as compared with non-communists, but also decreed a higher remuneration for " responsible communists," as compared with the small fry. While the majority was starving, the minority was pilfering all that came to hand. They travelled in " wagons de luxe," they had automobiles, mistresses, tropical fruits, furs, the best perfumes, diamonds, etc. Wedding rings, clothes, boots—were taken away from the executed in the name of communism and were worn or sold by the spoiler.

Instead of the destroyed restraints upon reflexes of ownership, the communists were possessed by a hateful, unbridled greed, spoiling both the living and the dead. Such was the first stage of the revolution. In 1920 all had already been divided; former wealth had disappeared. Nothing was left that could be divided. The bourgeois existed no more. General poverty and famine reigned everywhere. Then those in power decided to " requisition " the peasants. Bread, live-stock, all was taken away from them. Now it was their reflexes of ownership which were being pressed. As a result we witness the riots of peasants endeavoring to protect their property. This movement grew and widened. It spread over the towns and inflamed the soldiers and sailors who had no more occasion to " communise " the bourgeois, as the latter were non-existing. At the same time some of the communists who had succeeded in making their own pile were eager to protect their belongings, holding on to " communism " did not suit them any longer. As result we see the anti-communistic movement which reached its zenith in March, 1921, during the Cronstadt Rebellion. The Cronstadt sailors, who one or two years ago were extreme communists, now proclaimed the program of " soviets without communism." What a remarkable transformation! Here we witness " a new economic policy," a " decommunisation," a resuscitation of capitalism, in a word—private ownership. The restraining reflexes of ownership which had been decaying are again brought into full play by the new owners. During the two years of 1921-23 the process has manifested itself clearly both in practice and in the decrees issued by the Soviet Government. The chief of these are: The decree concerning the right of concessions, the denationalization of plants and factories and houses, the actual admission of the right of ownership, the right of possessing an unlimited amount of money, the reëstablishment of the right of inheritance, the right of private individual leasing and cultivating landed property for an indefinite period of years, etc. In other words, at the present moment, from an economic standpoint, very little has remained of communism except the Asiatic lawlessness of the Soviet authorities.

Practically during these two years we see the reëstablishment of social brakes to the reflexes of ownership, as well as all the negative sides of capitalism, which have taken tremendous proportions. Its positive sides are still in abeyance. The feverish stock jobbing, profiteering, underhand dealings, the mad growth of luxury, the fathomless contrast between the luxurious life of the communist and the so-called " nepman " (new economic policy men) on the one hand, and the millions of starving on the other. The merciless execution of any thieves and robbers who had an eye to the " property of others," and the comparatively colossal capitals accumulated by the " communistic leaders " and the active part they take as directors or shareholders in all the chief trusts and joint stock companies,[9] appropriating to themselves all the revenues, letting the government pay the expenses; the merciless exploitation, the sweating of the workmen, the spoliation of the state's reserve gold fund, etc.—all this has again come to the front, but, alas! in a degree unheard of before.

At the same time the feeling of individual ownership has taken hold of the masses, and particularly the peasants, to an unheard-of degree. It manifests itself first of all in the immense quantity of peasants deserting the "obschina"—"village commune" and settling down on individual tiny farms or "otrouba" (cut-off). This movement took such proportions that the government was obliged to legalize it, issuing a decree October 30, 1922. The Russian peasant, member of the village community, is now transformed into a small bourgeois individual owner. In a word, the communistic revolution has resolved itself into a growth and development of reflexes authorizing but regulating individual ownership, in a degree so extensive and deep-rooted, as was till then unknown in Russia. At the present moment we can look upon the resuscitation of the reflexes defining private ownership as upon an established fact. The chief Beatitude is again *Beati possidentes*. However these new *possidentes,* sprung from the ranks of the "destroyers of property," have infinitely stronger acquired reflexes of ownership than the former wealthy. Unlike the latter, they will protect their rights of ownership with all their

[9] The investigations of the left communists have shown that the richest men, those that receive the greatest revenues, are Trotzki, Zinovieff, Radek, Kameneff, Krassin, Dzerdzinsky, etc. See also the *Red Gazette,* 1922, the article "The Bush of Trotzki," which described most naively that the Joint Stock Company of which Trotzki is the director and a shareholder has had a revenue of a few million gold rubles. The investigation of the controlling commissions of the Third Internationale has shown that Zinovieff and Radek cannot render account of three million gold rubles.

strength and will not allow it to be "nationalized." Parallel to this process of reëstablishing the weakened habits defending private ownership we witness a change in the general ideology. An example of this is clearly to be seen among the communists themselves. Suffice it to compare their speeches, articles, papers and books of 1917–19 and these of 1921–24. They are diametrically opposed to each other, and what is approved of during the first period (nationalization, ration system, material equality, collective management, the necessity of absolutely abolishing private property, the spoliation of the bourgeoisie, the flattery of the workmen, etc.) is now looked upon negatively. Not much has remained of the former communistic phraseology. Towards 1921 all the communistic catch-words, so popular a short time ago, have lost credit among the population. Socialism and communism have lost their charm. Quite other theories, a new ideology, anti-socialistic and anti-communistic, is growing popular. It idealizes and approves of capital, private property, individuality, personal initiative, personal interests. We have accomplished a full circle and are now again facing an ideology not urging on to the appropriation of property, "to communism and nationalization," but, directly and indirectly, upholding private property; bowing down before commandments such as: "Thou shalt not steal," "Leave other people's goods alone," "Touch not the sacred rights and property of others." Such are the fundamental outlines of the process of perversion and transformation of the reflexes of ownership, which took place during the Russian Communistic Revolution. It has resulted neither in communism, nor in material equality, nor in general welfare, nor in the abolishment of private property and capitalism, but only in the ruin of the country; a change of place among the different members of the economic pyramid has taken place as well as a strengthening of the reflexes of ownership, according to the scheme shown in the above pages.[10]

We find a similar process in other revolutions. The difference lies only in the degree.

THE EGYPTIAN REVOLUTION

We read in Ipouver: " They hide by the roadside and kill the traveller. They take away his clothes. The gate-keepers say, ' Let us go and rob.' The poor have grown rich, and those that possessed riches have grown destitute; he whose cup is brimful now used to be glad of a crust, . . . He who possessed has now ' no shade ' (*i.e.,* no house), ' nowhere to lay his head.' The princes of the earth are starving, noble ladies go hungry and say: ' Oh, if we had some food.' Their clothes are ragged. ' But the necks of the female slaves are encircled by gold and lapis lazule, by silver and malachite, by cornelian stone and bronze.' The King's shops became a general possession." [11]

These lines denote a wholesale destruction of the restraining reflexes of ownership; an appropriation of others' heritage, a nationalization which, however, in no wise did away with inequality; in other words, the

---

[10] A daily detailed report of this whole process can be found in the Soviet papers, *Isvestia, Pravda* and *Economical Life.* See also speech of Lenin about the tax in kind, the book of Dalin: *After the War and the Revolution.* Maslov: *Russia After Four Years of Revolution.* Sorokin: *The Present Conditions of Russia.* Miliukoff: *The History of the Second Russian Revolution,* Vols. I-II. Soukhanof: *Reminiscences of the Revolution,* Vols. I-VII. *The Economical Life of the People,* 1921-22 (official edition). In the *Economical Review,* the article of Prokopovitch; " About Land," Vols. I-II (official public.), *Economist,* Nos. 1-5, 1922. *Peasants' Russia,* Vols. I-VII. Prokopovitch: *The Studies of The Economics of The Soviet Russia,* 1923. All these books and publications are in Russian.

[11] Vikentieff: cited above.

same characteristics as those we witness in the Russian Revolution.

In the Greek Revolutions of the third, fourth, fifth and sixth centuries B.C., here also the position is similar: " all who were prominent and rich were killed and their goods confiscated; the churches were sacked; houses, fields, wives and children were given over to the proletariat, to the helots and the rabble." Confiscations, requisitions, wholesale pillage, nationalization, etc., are the general accompaniments of these revolutions.[12]

The same can be said of the Roman Revolution towards the close of the Republic. The Gracchi, Marius and Sulla, Crassus, Pompeius, Augustus and Antonius, they and their followers all turn the right of ownership into fiction. Pillage, appropriation, confiscation, requisition, etc., were on a colossal scale. For instance, Sulla alone confiscated and divided among his followers over 120,000 portions of landed property. Pillage, robbery and theft reached an unheard-of dimension and led to the foundation of powerful pirate states. Robberies were perpetrated daily, both in the capital and in the more thinly populated districts of Italy. Unheard-of greed and pursuit of riches, bribery, corruption, were to be seen everywhere. " Poverty was looked upon as the only and worst disgrace and crime. For money a statesman was willing to sell his country, a citizen his liberty; a noble lady sold herself for money; perjury and counterfeit of documents were so usual that an oath was called " a ground for debts." At the same time, in spite of all requisitions and nationaliza-

---

[12] See Pöhlmann: *Op. cit.*, Passim. Niese: *Geschichte d. Griechischen und Makedon. Staaten, Gotha*, 2 Teil, 296 and following pages; Teil 3, 42 and follow. Buzold: *Griechische Geschichte*, Band III, Teil 2, 1402-3, 1456, 1614, 1628 pp., Teil I, 560-82 pp. Thucydides, book III, 223-27 pp.

tions, "a terrible inequality reigned everywhere." Rome was a "republic of millionaires and beggars." [13] We quote from the words of Pöhlmann, who makes the following résumé of all the ancient revolutions: "In Greece (and Rome) in the course of a few centuries a struggle was waged, the motto of which was: equality, justice and fraternity. The attempt to establish in practice an economic and social equality was accompanied with unbridled outbursts of hatred and rancor, pillage, robbery, wild licentiousness. Also with righteous indignation, called forth by extreme poverty and exploitation, we constantly witness greed towards the wealth of their neighbors, whom they cast out only to set themselves, and only themselves, in their places. Consequently it is not by chance during the last centuries of the Greek culture, that in nearly all cases when equality was the slogan, every individual strived to set himself above all others, and practiced the coarsest of tyrannies. The latter was a characteristic embodiment of the greed of the masses. Those who profited by the revolution were not apt to show that spirit of solidarity and justice to which social democracy aspired. No traces of equality or fraternity were to be found anywhere. As soon as the primary aim of the social revolution was achieved, that is, as soon as a more or less considerable number of its agents had acquired money and landed property it would regularly become evident that not self-denying loyalty to a common idea, but personal interests had supplied the actuating motive. And these interests required that each individual should retain what he had acquired during the general pillage. Now these people had reason to fear the saturnalia of revolutionary

---

[13] Mommsen: Vol. III, 68, 453, 461 and others. Friedlaender: *Pictures of Everyday Roman History* (Russ.), 20-21.

speeches, for a new revolution could only make them lose, not gain, and so they had no reason to go about masquerading as proletarian-revolutionists. Usually they suddenly acquired the most reactionary ideas, both in the realm of economics and politics. *Beati possidentes*. The new owners were little worried by the new growth of inequality and poverty. They would not listen to the idea of a new division of property now that they themselves were the owners. Consequently, fraternity lasted only till the opposing side was conquered and the process of spoliation had been accomplished." [14]

Need we still look up references and quotations testifying that the same process had taken place during other revolutions, in other countries at different epochs?

Let us take the Persian Revolution, during the time of Kobad or the rebellions during the reign of Hurmuz III. We see the appropriation, division, pillage and nationalization of the property of the rich, not only of the material goods, but even of women (during the Mazdak Revolution). [15]

Try to get a clearer insight into the numerous revolutions of Islam—that of the Haradgits, Alides, Karmats, Ismaelites, Kopts, Communists, Babekists, Vakhabits, etc.—everywhere we see the same pictures, the same processes. [16]

Passing over to Japan, we also find in the revolution of the fifteenth century the same " Jacqueries, the same

---

[14] Pöhlmann: *History of Ancient Communism and Socialism*, 469-70, 494-8, 503-82. See details in the above-named works of Ferrero, Rostovtzev, Duruy, O. Seeck. Der Untergang der Antiken Welt.

[15] See Malcolm: *The History of Persia*, Vol. I, 100, 106, 120; Vol. II, 344, 353.

[16] See Müller: *History of Islam* (Russ. transl.), Vol. II, 29, 33, 161, 178, 182, 187-92, 195-6, 297-9, 278-81 and foll.

Pragueries." [17] And in the revolutions of the Middle Ages
we witness similar events, even communism itself. Did
not the Hussite Revolution in Bohemia begin by the
spoliation of the riches of the church, the clergy, the Germans and the nobles and later on of the property of other
nations? Here also the events were accompanied by a
communistic ideology, by the foundation of a communistic state of the Taborites and numerous other communistic
sects: the Nicolaites, Beggards, Adamites, etc. "To take
the property of others is not sin, but an action with which
God will be pleased "—such is the teaching of the preachers, such is the ideology of the beginning of the revolution. In accordance with it the property of the rich, the
churches, the Germans, etc., was taken and nationalized.
Communistic sects and communities were organized
wherein even women were considered to be public property.
"Greed is the root of all evil." Such is the comment
of the contemporary of all this high-flown communism.[18] However, all this was not of long duration.
Parallel with the growth of riches, accumulated through
pillage and appropriation, we see the decay of the communistic ideology and the regeneration of the reflexes of
ownership. "The Taborites put down the Adamites and
admitted the right of private ownership among themselves. This, and its inherent feelings of envy and
greed, excelled communism and all feelings of fraternity.
Equality of property began to disappear. Among the
Taborites you could find the poor and the rich, the latter
becoming more and more unwilling to share their wealth
with the poor." [19]

[17] See De la Mazelliere: *Le Japon*, Paris, 1907, Vol. II, 389 and
others.
[18] Denis: *Op. cit.*, 287.
[19] Kautsky: *From Plato to the Anabaptists, The Forerunners of
Modern Socialism*, Vol. I, 198 (Russ. transl.).

" The revolutionists forgot their promises and showed themselves more greedy than the old rulers. Those that were loudest in clamoring that all property should be in common, excluded their own comrades from a participation in it. Riches, which were considered criminal as long as they belonged to Catholics, were ruthlessly appropriated by themselves. They had promised absolute freedom of the use of forests, waters and meadows and they were the first to prohibit it and to reduce the people to a state of serfdom." [20]

The same process, in the sense of ever-increasing pillages and robberies, appropriation of others' property, and freedom from all obligations included in the right of property is repeated in the French and English Jacqueries, in the revolutions of the Middle Ages, up to the communistic revolutions in Münzer and Mülhausen.[21] The colossal pillages among the Irish, where a wholesale appropriation of all their landed property (2,500,000 acres) and riches took place, the growing number of thefts and pillages, the numerous appropriations and confiscations of the property of the royalists; the many requisitions among the peaceable population, and many other transgressions against the right of property during the first period of the English Revolution of the seventeenth century on the one hand, and the hindering of all such actions during the second period on the other hand, are sufficiently known

---

[20] Denis: *Ibid.*, 348-9.

[21] For instance in the New Jerusalem of John of Leyden the leaders of the communistic party, having got all the riches into their hands, appropriated the lion's share for themselves, and even during the period of famine showed not the least desire to share it with the starving masses. Kautsky: *Ibid.*, 364. Details of the behavior of the masses during the Jacqueries in the works of Oman, Petrushevski, M. Kovalevsky: *The Economic Growth of Europe*, Vol. II. Levasseur: *Histoire des Classes Ouvrieres*, Vol. II.

and need not be dwelt upon.[22] The greed and cupidity of revolutionary conquerors who attained such a doubtful renown as members of the Parliament were only one more corroboration.[23] Here also we see the communistic ideology, for instance, among the diggers and men of the fifth monarchy.[24] The tendency to reëstablish the restraining reflexes is also very evident during the second period.[25] It is unnecessary to dwell on the absence of material equality, as a result of revolution. Material inequality grows more, not less marked.[26] During the Russian Revolution of 1603–1612, the rebellions of Razin,

---

[22] Gardiner: *History of the Commonwealth and the Protectorate,* 1903, Vol. I, 39; Vol. II, 22, 200; Vol. IV, 82-4 and others. Gardiner: *History of the Great Civil* War. Guizot: the work above quoted, Vol. I, XI, XII, XXII, XXIII, 192-4 pp.; Vol. III, 113.

[23] Guizot: Vol. II, part I, 78-9.

[24] Here is an example of a contemporary proclamation. We read in the manifesto of Everard: " All landlords were thieves and murderers. It was now time for the English to free themselves from the landlords. Break in pieces quickly, the bond of private property . . . and give thy full consent to make the earth a common treasury, etc." Gardiner: Vol. VI, 43.

[25] It is clearly expounded in the speech of Cromwell, 1654. " The nobles, the gentlemen, the farmer, the landlord—these are the real kernels of the nation. The equalizers wanted to level all ranks, all property, all ownership; they wanted to make the master and the tenant equally rich. But even if they had been successful, such an order of things could not have been durable: if those people should have achieved it, they would have been the first to glorify and protect the right of ownership and property, and, at the same time, would have caused a great deal of harm by their principles, because these words have a great attraction for the poor and the ne'er-do-wells." January 22, 1655, he goes on to say: " If it is ordained that the Republic is to suffer—it were better it should suffer from the rich, than from the poor, for Solomon likens the oppression by the poor to a devastating storm, that destroys all on its way." Consequently, during this period we witness the energetic suppression of different kinds of communistic movements, of pillages, robberies, etc. Guizot: Vol. III, 108, 127-8. Gardiner: *History of the Commonwealth,* Vol. IV, 28 and foll.

[26] See Bernstein: *The Communistic and Democratic Socialism Tendencies in the English Revolution of the Seventeenth Century. Forerunners of the New Socialism,* Vol. II, 64, 263.

Pougatsheff and others,[27] the same process, that is, the same loosening of the ownership reflexes, the same growth of pillage took place. During the great French Revolution this process took much greater dimensions. The decay of the socially inculcated restraining reflex of ownership began some time before the revolution itself (the rebellions of 1785–89, the pillage of shops, storehouses, barns, the growth of thefts, robberies, etc.).[28] At the beginning of a revolution all such restraining brakes fall off. We see wholesale appropriations of priceless riches, legalized and illegal pillage. The process goes on crescendo. First only the aristocrats and the rich are robbed; then, especially since the epoch of the Jacobin dictatorship, the pillage of the poor commences and manifests itself in ceaseless confiscations, requisitions, appropriations, profiteering, all done in the name of equality, fraternity, liberty. The inviolability of property grows to be in reality a fiction. Parallel to this movement, all kinds of equalizing and communistic theories crop up.[29] Everybody snatches what he can. Though nearly everyone is relatively poor there exists no material equality. The warmest partisans of the revolution are only too glad to pillage and to appropriate huge properties. " The huge properties of the terrorists were accumulated in this way; this is the origin of their immense riches. After Termidor all the wretches who had been Robespierres on a smaller scale

---

[27] See Karamzine: *History of the Russian State*, Vols. XI-XII. Platonoff: *Lectures in Russian History*, 1917, 249 and foll. Firsoff: *The Peasant Riots till the Nineteenth Century, in The Great Reform*, Vol. II (Russ.).
[28] See Taine: *Les Origines de la France*, 1889; *L'Ancien Régime*, 200-13, 280-93. Kropotkin: *The Great French Revolution*, 1919, 23, 39-41 (Russ.). Afanasieff: *Historical and Economical Articles*, Vol. I, 398, 402, 434-5 (Russ.).
[29] See Taine: *Ibid.*, Vol. II, 1-199; Vol. III, 1885, 69-159. Kareeff: *History of the Western Europe* (Russ.), 1913, Vol. III, 146-288. Tocqueville: *L'Ancien Régime et la Revolution*, 1877, 234-43.

are allowed to spend their accumulated fortunes in peace. Now these patriots built castles near Orleans, in Valenciennes; having destroyed the existing private and public property, they establish their own rights to the houses and the estates of the emigrants." [30] After the repartition is accomplished the second period sets in—the stabilization of the plunder and the redevelopment of the deteriorated reflexes of ownership. A decree is issued, proclaiming the sacred right of ownership. Every attempt to violate it is rigidly put down. All socialistic, communistic movements are repressed (Babeuf and others). Society throws itself avariciously into stock-jobbing and spoliation. Greed of wealth, of material values, possesses it; we see a new class of " nepmans " (new economic policy men), a new profiteering zoological bourgeoisie. For money women sell themselves, consciences are bought. All can be bought, all can be sold.[31] This process resulted in the Code of Napoleon with its strict principle of the sacredness, inviolability and protection of private property on the one hand, and in a cruel wholesale repression of pillage and robbery, and the introduction of the court-martial on the other hand.

---

[30] Taine: *Les Origines de la France,* Vol. III; *Revolution,* 289-379, 360-64. See also Michelet: *Directoire,* Vol. I, 79-80 (Russ.). Also the works of Kareeff, Madelin, Jaurés and Kropotkin.

[31] Among the revolutionaries: Barras was the owner of Grobois, Barrère of the castle of Clichet, Taillien—the palace of Chaliot, Merlin—Montvalerien: " In the Committee of only the third year thirteen future counts can be found (so much for equality), five future barons, seven future senators of the Empire, six future statesmen. The Convention boasts fifty levellers from the future Duke of Otranto to the future Prince of Merlin. Before fifteen years will pass they will all own titles, coats-of-arms, liveries, carriages, majorats, castles and palaces. When Fouchet dies his wealth is estimated at fifteen millions." Madelin: Vol. II, 168 and foll. See description Madelin II, 163-5, 245, 314 and others. Michelet: *Ibid.,* 71-4, 80, 110-12, 158-254, etc. The above-named works of Taine, Kropotkin, Jaurés and Vandal, The Rise of Napoleon.

On a smaller scale the same tendencies manifested themselves during the revolutions of 1830–48 in France and 1848 in Germany. It is true that in, this case, especially in Germany, the loosening of reflexes did not go very deep (even during the rebellions the slogan proclaimed was: " Property is sacred "). Nevertheless, cases of appropriation of castles, lands, throwing off financial obligations, different encroachments on the right of ownership, especially on those of the rich, took place. If it did not go very deep it is only because the revolutions were stemmed and restrained at their very beginning. It need not be proved that a loosening of reflexes of respect for ownership took place during the Paris Communist Revolution of 1871 and the Russian Revolution of 1905 (the peasant movement); also during the Hungarian Revolution of 1918–19, and even during the German Revolution of 1918 (slightly).

All the above-made statements bring us to the conclusion that: 1. Our principle of the perversion of the reflexes of respect for ownership is fully corroborated. 2. Material equality, proclaimed by so many revolutions has been achieved by none. 3. Still less have they succeeded in destroying or even weakening the reflexes of individual greed. 4. All revolutions during their second period not only do not weaken, but even excite these reflexes to hideous degrees, cause hypertrophy of selfish greed, profiteering—and in a word, instead of socializing man, they make out of him an egotistical, zoological proprietor, and the stronger, the more communistic the revolution is, the more striking is the reaction. 5. The beautiful slogans and phrases in the name and under the cover of which the revolutionary processes in the realm of private ownership were performed are merely a pretty screen for the commonest form of appropriation of other people's belongings, a passing symptom of the freeing of reflexes from all restraining stimuli and an excuse for their animal greed. The objective behavior of men in no wise corresponds to them. 6. This means that violent revolutions and the real socialization of men; that violent revolutions and the better control of the selfish reflexes of ownership—are absolutely incompatible.

To think of this would do no harm to those who see in revolution the means of socializing men and their reflexes of ownership.

CHAPTER VI

THE PERVERSION OF SEXUAL REACTIONS

THE group of sexual reactions is one of the most important in the conduct of human beings. These reactions are hereditary. In man this unconditioned kernel is enveloped in numerous habits. During normal periods of social life the unlimited manifestation of sexual reactions, or unbridled satisfaction of sexual appetites, is restrained by numerous conditioned and unconditioned stimuli, including severe chastisements following forbidden sexual relations.[1] Besides there are other forms of punishment: the censure of public opinion, disgrace, dishonor, religious penance, as well as religious, moral and other habits which are inculcated through education and form inward restraining forces.

The total sum of these stimuli present a kind of "brake" which restrains the satisfaction of sexual impulses and forces them into certain fixed channels, determined by contemporary legislation and the moral conditions of a given society.

Revolution calls such restraining "brakes"—"superstition," "bourgeois prejudice," thereby often destroying them. The same result is also achieved in a more direct way by the modification of family and marriage legislation. Wild revolutionary struggles which stimulate sexual nervous centres also tend that way; here, too, must be

---

[1] See the corresponding passages in the Bible, Laws of Manu, in the Laws of Hammurabi and other ancient law codes. See Sorokin: *Crime and Punishment,* 365 and foll. (Russ.). Westermarck: *The Origin and Development of the Moral Ideas,* ch. Adultery. Westermarck: *The History of Human Marriage.*

added indulgence in strong liquors. The weakening of these restraining reflexes betokens the destruction of all such " bridles " as held back the impetuosity of sexual impulses. That is why sexual licentiousness follows in the wake of many deep-rooted revolutions. But revolutions which are not deep-rooted may avoid these results.

However, the mischief does not stop here. The bloody struggle which is an inherent part of the first period of revolutions calls forth not only growth of sexual license, but very often adds a taint of sadism which finds a sexual satisfaction in seeing the suffering and torture of its victims.

As sexual reflexes are among the least variable their social transformation commences at a later period of revolution than that of many others. But on the other hand, it also takes more time and is more difficult to subject them anew. Very often it happens that other instincts have already been forced back into their normal channel, while sexual instincts still continue their ungovernable " excesses." They are behind time, both in the process of disorganization and in the process of restraint. Such is the result to which our study of revolution has brought us. Let us now speak about concrete facts.

THE RUSSIAN REVOLUTION, 1917–24

The first symptoms of sexual license grew apparent in the corresponding discoursive reactions (speeches, articles, propaganda, books) of the Bolsheviks. In the speeches of Mme. Kolontay, Liline-Zinovieff and Poletaeff —vice commissary of education—and many other Bolshevist leaders, even Lenin and Lunacharsky, not to speak of the average Bolsheviks, a marriage and family life are qualified as a " bourgeois superstition; " sexual moderation, purity, conjugal faithfulness—as " bourgeois prejudice," as a manifestation of the ownership instincts of capitalism. " If a young man and a young girl love each other let them manifest this love freely. The sexual relation is not a forbidden fruit for us. Marriage in our eyes is only a legally recognized corrupt perversion, a moral swamp of the hypocritical dwellers of the bourgeois society "—such is an example of these speeches.[2] The pregnancy of two fifteen-year-old high school pupils was characterized by the Commissary of Education, Mrs. Liline-Zinovieff, as a perfectly legal satisfaction of sexual appetite and the fulfillment of the obligations of motherhood. This point of view has been spread and is still spread among the students in the " Communistic Association of Young Men and Women," in whose midst sexual license is not restrained, but rather encouraged. This propaganda of " sexual liberty " has in some places (Saratoff) demanded a " communisation of women."

The second more important symptom is the modification admitted in the marriage and divorce legislation. A decree of December 20, 1917, has thrown open the door to divorces so widely, that a marriage can now be dissolved, if one of the parties simply states his, or her, desire to do so. This decree gives full liberty to marry today, and to divorce and marry again tomorrow; in other words it legalizes all chance sexual relationship. Legislation concerning abortion speaks of the same ten-

---

[2] *Youths' Pravda*, November 13, 1923. See also Gerile: *Social Education of the Youth* (Russ.). Kolontay: *The New Morality*, Petrograd, 1919; and the answer of Lenin to my article (*Economist*, No. 1, 1922) which points to the growth of sexual license, as one of the features of the revolution. After showering a whole bucketful of abuse against me, Lenin qualifies this growth as a priceless acquisition of the revolution, which, it appears, has liberated 50 per cent. of the population from hypocrisy, imposture and all bourgeois trammels. See Lenin's introductory article for the magazine " Under the Banner of Marxism," Nos. 2-3, 1922 (Russ.). Kolontay: *The Love of Labor-Bees*, 1924 (Russ.), quite frankly propagating the permanent change of mates in sexual life.

dency. Abortion which used to be an act reprehended by law is no more looked upon as demanding chastisement. Above that, abortion is now permitted in so many cases that it is very easy for anyone to obtain permission to have it done. During years of revolution statistics first of all show an unheard-of increase of divorce cases; secondly, an unusually short duration of wedded life; thirdly, by its very nature a Soviet marriage is but a legalized form of chance sex relation.

All this, taken as a whole, testifies to the fact that all "brakes" and "bridles" restraining sexual license have been thrown off.

Witness the growth of divorce cases immediately after the decree of December 20, 1917, had been proclaimed. During the first months after its proclamation the number of divorce cases attained colossal proportions. After that, when the greater mass had satisfied their craving for it, we see a certain slackening in their number; but in 1920, the figure, apparently, rises again and stabilizes itself at an unusually high level. Here are the figures for 1918 in Moscow:

January	98	July	611
February	384	August	507
March	384	September	343
April	1053	October	436
May	980	November	384 [3]
June	804		

In Petrograd, in 1920, there was one divorce case out of every sixteen marriages occurred in the same year; in 1921—one divorce case out of eight marriages; in 1922 —one divorce case out of 6.6 marriages (Goyhbarg: *Isvestia*, September 24, 1923). These figures are

[3] Goyhbarg: Some More Words About Wedlock and Divorce, in the magazine: *Proletarian Revolution and Right*, Nos. 2-4, 1919; Nos. 5-6, 1918 (Russ.). I do not remember the exact figures for 1919-22 for Moscow, that is why I do not give them.

something absolutely unheard of before for Petrograd.
Out of each 100 per cent. of these divorce cases in:

51.1 per cent. the marriage had lasted less than 1 year.
17.8 per cent. the marriage had lasted from 1-2 years.
8.2 per cent. the marriage had lasted from 3-4 years.
22.9 per cent. the marriage had lasted over 4 years.

Out of the first 51.1 per cent.

11 per cent. had lasted for less than 1 month.
22 per cent. had lasted for less than 2 months.
41 per cent. had lasted for less than 6 months.
26 per cent. had lasted for from 6 to 12 months.[4]

In 1921 and 1922, the situation became still worse. In
1921 there was one divorce for every eight marriages
solemnized; in 1922, one divorce for every 6.6 marriages.[5]

The figures in the provinces are yet worse. In 1922
we see:

for every 4.9 marriages in Poltava 1 divorce case.
for every 3.9 marriages in Nikolaeff 1 divorce case.

In the towns of the Zaporojsky, Ekaterinoslavsky,
Krementchougsky, Podolsky provinces for every 3.8 marriages one divorce case.[6]

For all Russia in 1922 we had 1,027,910 marriages
and 85,938 divorces; that is one divorce out of 11.2 marriages.[7] If we take into consideration that formerly in
Russia we had a divorce case for every 470 marriages, we
can easily fathom the catastrophic transformation, in
this direction, that we are facing during the revolutionary years.

Further indisputable symptoms of the " license " of
sexual reflexes can be traced in numerous facts which
everyone can observe. The *Pravda* writes (June 21,

---

[4] Materials for the Statistics of Petrograd, No. 5, 1922, 27.
[5] Goyhbarg : The Marriage Law, *Isvestia,* Sept. 12, 1923.
[6] Bulletins of the Central Statistic Administration of the Ukraina,
1922, No. 7, p. 29; No. 11, p. 50.
[7] Goyhbarg: *Ibid., Isvestia,* Sept. 13, 1923.
See " Notes and Addenda," p. 415.

1923) that at the police stations: " In the part of the building set apart for the incarcerated there is for men and women a common W. C. As soon as the thieves see that a woman goes to the W. C. they rush there also and violate her."

Nearly from the first days of the revolution the people started dancing, dancing in a literal sense. Innumerable " hops " were started. " Hops " with concerts, with meetings; " hops " after debates; " hops " in the midst of starvation, typhus, executions. They have not ceased dancing even now. And during all this dancing, primitive, coarse flirtations are being carried on which generally end in amorous embraces.[8]

Sexual licentiousness amidst the younger generation has attained unheard-of proportions, especially among the communistic youth. Every semblance of restraint is done away with. In the towns boys and girls of twelve to thirteen years old have sexual relations. Soviet marriages are a usual everyday occurrence among them, especially in towns.

The figures quoted below will help us to get a faint idea of the existing state of things. The following number of girls had been deflowered. They were medically examined in 1919 at the Central Distributing Station in Petrograd, from which station they were distributed among different children's colonies, asylums and children's houses. Out of all girls under sixteen years old 96.7 per cent. were deflowered. Even among the girls under ten years old ten per cent. were deflowered.[9] A communist

---

[8] " They dance till they are ready to drop, till they forget themselves; they dance in a kind of frenzy. The young men and women scrape together their small little savings, hire a hall, and dance on and on. Not unusual is it to see a young girl and her cavalier going through their steps on the snow." *Dni*, No. 89.

[9] I take these figures direct from the unpublished material of the Distributive Station.

woman writes: "The immorality among children, the corruption of children, the immense per cent. of venereal diseases, broken lives, distorted humanity—that is the result of the straits we have come to." [10]   It is, therefore, not astonishing that the children of the colonies, asylums, etc., not only lived and still live a sexual life, but that a great part of them are infected with venereal disease.   In a thousand small incidents that pass before his eyes, an attentive observer can notice the development of sexual license.

The same *mutatis mutandis* can be said of the adult population.   The woman communist quoted above writes: "What is happening to the family? Freedom of feeling, falsely understood, often takes the shape of licentious instincts. It has grown to be quite common for a laborer to live with two or three workwomen, and for a workwoman to have several husbands. Attachments are thrown off, like an old glove." [11]   It is interesting to observe from day to day the loosening of sexual reflexes, from the very commencement of the revolution.   During the very first months of the revolution the behavior of the prostitutes in the streets of Petrograd grew more and more shameless. The revolutionary slogan: "Proletarians of all the countries unite," grew to be their slogan in a professional sense, too.   With time this process spread wider and deeper.   From the time of "military communism" prostitution vanished from the streets; there was no more need for it; prostitution had entered into the house and the family.   Girls and women lived openly with those who maintained them—communistic sailors, commissaries, etc. New words were even coined: *Sodcom* (mistress of the commissary) ; *soderjanka* (mistress) ; *Sovbar* (Soviet

---

[10] I cite *Dni*, No. 202.
[11] I cite *Dni*, No. 202.

miss); *barishnia* (miss); designating the numerous new types of mistresses.[12]

Family ties were dissolved. Morality grew loose. The propaganda of " sexual freedom " replaced it.[13]

With the advent of " a new economic policy " prostitution reappeared and immediately gained more ground. At the present moment the streets of Moscow and Petrograd are thronged with prostitutes. Still stronger is it in its " secret forms " among the employees, typists, etc., who try to add some luxuries to their meagre daily bread by prostituting themselves. There is a much greater number of women willing to sell themselves now than there was formerly. To sum up: The development of sexual license [14] has grown to be immense.[15]

During the last year and a half we begin to see the first symptoms of a restraint of this licentiousness. For instance, in the villages women demand to be married not only civilly, but in church as well. The unlimited facility of divorce is being somewhat restricted both in practice and by new clauses being added to the divorce decree. Public opinion grows more and more hostile towards libertinage; the feeling of shame seems to be reawakening. But all this is not yet clearly manifested. Probably some

[12] Often those in power after saving a victim from execution or imprisonment demanded from the woman who had solicited their help a corresponding "reward;" this gave rise to much blackmail.

[13] See the sketches of modern life so vividly depicted by the pro-communistic authors; B. Pilniak: See his *Naked Year, The Past,* also the stories of Iakovleff, Kozireff, Nikitin, Veressaeff and other authors living in Soviet Russia and whose works are published in communistic magazines such as *The Red Virgin Soil* (*Crasnaja —Nov.*), etc.

[14] See the circular of the Commissary Semashko who officially admits the unheard-of development of prostitution. *Dni,* No. 186, 194, 193. *Rul,* No. 777.

[15] Proportionately great has also been the number of miscarriages. *Isvestia* writes: "the number of miscarriages grows from year to year."

years will elapse before the " brakes " restraining sexual license will be fully repaired.

Parallel to the development of sexual license, we observe a very decided manifestation of *sadism and sexual perversion*. Beginning with the Bolsheviks' brutal violation of the women's battalion during the days of the October revolution, cases of violation were pretty frequent; at any rate much more frequent than formerly. Violation was often accompanied by sadism, with gibes and horrible tortures of the victim (cutting off the female breasts, jamming of the masculine genital organs, cutting them off, stuffing grass, straw and sticks into the vagina, pricking it with knives, etc.).

At the same time we have reason to believe that all kinds of sexual perversions have increased greatly. The Russian Revolution fully corroborates the thesis which we have proclaimed.

THE RUSSIAN REVOLUTION, 1905–06

Though on a smaller scale, we see also here the increase of sexual license. It manifested itself in dozens of symptoms similar to the following one: " During the October riots (1905) in Odessa the hooligans violated girls openly in the streets, violated them time after time till death ensued. They slashed open the abdomens of pregnant women, etc. On the ninth of December in Moscow the crowd literally stripped naked two girl students." [16] Such facts were rather often published in the papers of that time.

But apart from such individual cases, the licentiousness of sexual reflexes among the younger generation manifested itself in a whole series of actions of a more general

---

[16] *Novoe Vremia* (New Times), II, December, 1905. Notes of the translator of the book, Cabanes and L. Nasse: *The Revolutionary Neurosis*, St. Petersb., 1906, 19.

character. First of all in the founding of societies and clubs called " Ogarki " (candle-ends). Secondly, in the organization and development among the " *Intellegentzia* " of "Athenian Nights." Thirdly, in the importance attached to sex questions in the theatre and in the literature. During 1906–07 sex questions and sex indulgence grew to be the central point of discussion in all speeches, papers, books and conversations. This state of affairs has been reflected in contemporary artistic productions, which have had such a sensational influence on our times. Artzibasheff; *Ogarki* (candle-ends), Skitaletz; *The New Magic,* Sollohub; *The Last Border Line,* Artzibasheff; *The Hole,* Cuprin; *Spring Corn,* Gorodetzki; *Stories of Erotism,* Kouzmin; Kamensky, Hippius, Nagrodsky, *Sanin,* etc.; the erotic poetry of Balmont and Brussoff; these were particularly popular at the time and were the most realistic. Erotism, propaganda of free love, discussions upon sex questions; these were the topics spoken of at five o'clock teas in drawing-rooms; at meetings of religious and philosophical societies; on the pages of newspapers, magazines, articles, etc. In a word there cannot be two opinions as to the development of sexual license, fully corroborated by eye-witnesses and contemporary documents.

THE FRENCH REVOLUTION, 1870–71

A whole series of facts gives us reason to believe that here also a certain degree of license of the sexual reflexes was to be found (strengthened by war, but somewhat mitigated by hunger).

The number of prostitutes in Paris was:

In 1868	5938
In 1869	5768
In 1870	6372 [17]
In 1871	....
In 1872	6007

[17] Oettingen, Moralstatistik, 1882, 203.

We see that their number had risen in 1870. It is true that the Commune promulgated a law for the *suppression du traffic odieux des marchands d'hommes* (suppression of the horrible man-traffic). But this law, according to Lecour, remained only *une declaration emphatique* (an emphatic statement), for the police stations—*bureaux des moeurs*—were all closed, as it was considered that they infringed on the liberty of women, and as a result the evil grew more rife than ever.[18]

The statistics for France of children born out of wedlock corroborates the same. We see a systematic rise from 1871–73.

For every 100 births we see:

	1871	1872	1873	1874	1875	1876
In France	7.15	7.21	7.46	7.26	7.03	6.69[19]
In Prussia	7.77	7.05	7.65	7.15	7.38	7.36

The years 1870–73 were years in which the sexual reflexes were set loose, consequently from 1871–73 there had to be an increment of illegal births. From 1873 restraining influences are again put into motion, and the number of children born out of wedlock diminishes likewise. In Prussia, where there had been no revolution, we see nothing like it, notwithstanding that Prussia had also taken part in the war.

Let us now look at the requests for separation (*separation de corps*—separation of board and bed) and for divorce. In studying the diagram of Levasseur we see that there is an abrupt fall in the number of such requests (*demandes d'assistance judiciare*—demands of legal aid) caused by the war. From 1869–70 they decrease from

---

[18] Lecour: *La Prostitution à Paris et à Londres,* 1872, 326 and others.

[19] Oettingen: *Anhang,* tab. 36 (Supplement, tab. 36); Levasseur: *La Popul. Française,* Vol. II, 32.

6000 to 3699. From 1870–72, on the contrary, we see a continual rise. In 1870 about 4400; in 1871 about 6100. In 1873 the number remains stationary, and in 1874 it falls again to 5700.[20]

These figures, as well as the descriptions of historians and contemporaries, depicting very vividly the growth of sexual license during the revolution and Commune, give us sufficient reason to believe that our statement is correct in this case as well.[21]

THE REVOLUTION OF 1848

" In France there used to be, as an average, 200 cases yearly of *attentats aux moeurs* (crimes against morality). In 1848–49 their number reaches 280–505. In Saxony the number of children born out of wedlock, in comparison to the average number of the forty preceding years, augments 14–15 per cent. and more.[22]

Taking 1000 as being the figure for children born out of wedlock in 1847, we have in 1849–50 an increase of that number in all those countries through which the revolutionary wave had swept. From 1850–51 there is an ebb in the revolutionary movement. The following figures are sufficiently eloquent:

Year	France	Bavaria	Saxony	Hanover	Prussia	Würtemberg
1847	1000	1000	1000	1000	1000	1000
1848	1042	895	932	996	919	1018
1849	1092	1126	1135	1230	1239	1283
1850	1088	1140	1129	1220	1312	1284
1851	1104	1131	1107	1092	1304	1195 [23]

[20] Levasseur: *La Population Française*, Vol. II, 90.

[21] See for instance L. Gregoire: Vol. IV, 410. *Lissagarés,* 328. *The Diary of the Brothers Goncourt,* and others.

[22] Oettingen: 240.

[23] *Ibid.,* 76, 311, 1847 was a critical year—one of famine; this is a reason for the falling off in 1848 of the birthrate. The result of the conceptions of 1848-49 could be seen only in 1849-50. The years 1848-51 in France are years of perpetual sedition, ending in the *coup d'état* of Napoleon. We see the same results in the figures indicating the percentage of children born out of wedlock to children born in the latter. See tables of Oettingen, p. 312.

In a whole series of countries this liberty shows itself in the scale of divorces and separations " from board and bed." In Saxony for each one hundred marriages we find in the year:

1845	2.16
1846	2.43
1847	2.04
1848	2.50
1849	2.27 [24]

The same can be seen in France where the diagrams show a decrease in 1847–48 and an increase in 1848–50.[25]

The number of foundlings is also much higher during the years of revolution and those directly following them. We see this in France in 1849–50, in Austria in 1848–50 (see figures given by Oettingen, pp. 331-5). All these data clearly state that the revolution of 1848–49 was accompanied in all countries by a growth of sexual license.

THE GREAT FRENCH REVOLUTION

Here the licentiousness attains enormous proportions. Beginning from 1790–91 it advances crescendo, and only during the first Empire is it stemmed.

This is, first of all, manifested in the " Divorce Decree " of September 20, 1792, which gives the full liberty of divorce (like the Russian decree of December 20, 1917) and lowers the age limit for marriage, fixing it at thirteen for women and fifteen for men.[26]

Secondly, in the tremendous growth of divorce cases. During the first twenty months after the promulgation of

---

[24] Oettingen: 154.
[25] Levasseur: *La Population Française,* Vol. II, diagram, p. 90.
In the year 1837-40 for every 1000 marriages we have 2.1 divorces.
In the year 1841-45 for every 1000 marriages we have 2.7 divorces.
In the year 1846-50 for every 1000 marriages we have 2.8 divorces.
Ibid., 89.
[26] See Levasseur: *La Population Française,* II, 67.

the decree 5994 divorces took place, and in 1796–97 their number surpassed that of marriages.

Thirdly, in the tremendous number of foundlings. The number of abandoned children born out of wedlock had not been above 23,000 in 1790. In 1798–99 it was over 63,000.[27]

Fourthly, in the tremendous growth of prostitution during the years of revolution; up till the revolution of 1789 the number of prostitutes in Paris was not above 20,000. During the years of revolution it surpassed 30,000. " During this revolution the disorder and shameless behavior of the Paris prostitutes surpassed in heinousness all that can be conceived." [28]

Fifthly, the observations of contemporaries: " Children of thirteen to fourteen behaved both in word and deed in a way that would have been scandalous for a man of twenty. The restraints of sexual instincts were weakened. In summer among the crowds standing in line before the shops, abominable scenes of human bestiality and Paris impudence could be seen. Prostitutes did not hide their profession. Their loud sensual laughter could be heard from far. The shaded nooks of the boulevard suited them to perfection. Many of them brought their bedding and openly gave themselves up to all kinds of abominations. Men threw themselves upon women, embracing one after another." [29] " The scenes amid the crowd are more than indecent."

Needless to describe the orgies and saturnalia during the festival of " Liberty," " The Goddess of Reason " and other popular assemblies (for instance the fifth of October), etc. After Termidor " the young men and

<hr>

[27] Taine: *Les Origines*, 1885, Vol. III, 108.
[28] Levasseur: *Ibid.*, II, 431-32. Parent-Duchatele: *De la Prostitution dans la ville de Paris*, Vol. I, 521.
[29] Taine: *Ibid.*, III, 108, 499.

women grew licentious and ribaldry becomes fashionable."
" All else is forgotten in the lust of pleasure." " Fashions
become eccentric." " Antiquity grows to be the fashion."
Next to the *sans culottes* we see the " shirtless girls."
" Not much need be taken off from a woman for her to
appear in the garb of Venus of Medici." Foreigners and
newspapers confirm existing immorality. " The family
pot is overturned." " Women pass from hand to hand."
Some marry one sister after the other, even their own
mothers-in-law. The dregs of society resemble " Sodom
and Gomorrha." The newspapers say that " Immodest
books are the popular reading of our girls." " Everybody comes to the conclusion that no moral principles exist
any more." [30]

As in Russia the population dances, dances madly,
ceaselessly. They dance everywhere. In Carmah where the
blood of the one hundred and sixteen executed clergymen
is still fresh on the walls; in the cemetery of St. Sulpice;
in the houses; on the squares, etc.[31]

Even the prisons are under the dominion of Eros.
Prisons get nicknamed " trysting houses." " By common
consent it is agreed to waive the accepted rules of social
decency. No feeling of shame restrains. The most ardent
impulses are acted upon publicly. An earthly Eden is
sought after and often the last night before execution is
transformed into a night of free love's transports." As a
result many women were pregnant [32] when they forsook
the prisons. In a word, we observe a complete license of
sexual reflexes.

---

[30] Madelin: Vol. II, 105-6, 156, 280-85, 289-90.

[31] *Ibid.*, II, 166-7.

[32] Cabanes and Nass: *The Revolutionary Neurosis,* 130-32.
Michelet: *History of the Nineteenth Century.* The Directory, Vol. I
(Russ.), St. Petersb., 1882, 49, 110-13, 254 and others. See also
Madelin: Vol. II. Taine: Vols. III-V, describing the Jacobins and the
Directoire. Vandal: *The Rise of Napoleon.*

Here also we see a tremendous growth of sexual sadism. As an example of it we cite the following facts: The crowd crammed straw into the vagina of a flower girl in the *Palais Royal,* then stripped her naked and bound her to a post, nailing her feet to it, and ended by cutting off her breasts and setting fire to the straw." [33]

In Marseilles " seven or eight women were stripped naked and then with fiendish cruelty the lower part of their stomachs was scorched." [34]

In the Salpetriere thirty women were killed, " both the living and dead were simultaneously violated." In an orphanage " heaps of little children were violated." " It is not possible to describe the outrageous lewdness of the scenes which accompanied the murder of Princess Lambale. Her breasts were cut off, then her stomach cut open and all the intestines pulled out. One of her murderers cut out her sexual organs and fashioned artificial whiskers out of them."

A kind of epidemic of pulling off the clothes of women, of thrashing them with rods, " of seizing them by the most tender parts of their bodies," breaks out. " The filthiest, most bestial, sensual instincts are satisfied." [35]

After Termidor sadism grows more refined. Balls and hops are organized during which the favorite pleasure is to represent the guillotine and the executions. Blood-bespattered places of execution are specially chosen for dancing, etc. (Madelin, II, 166-7).

It were useless to add still further details to these facts. Suffice it to say that they were numerous enough. All that was most heinous and disgusting, all that bestial-

---

[33] Cabanes: 30.
[34] Michelet: 259.
[35] Cabanes: 30-68. Many similar facts can be seen there. See also Sigelet: *The Criminal Crowd.* Lasseur: *La Perversion Sadique,* 1898 and the above-named authors on the French Revolution.

ity of man could invent, took, during the revolution, proportions immeasurably surpassing all that was known in
times of peace.

THE RUSSIAN REVOLUTION OF THE SEVENTEENTH CENTURY

The contemporary, Abraham Palitzyn, writes: " The
heart throbs at the remembrance of all the villainies perpetrated in places where the spilt blood of the victims had
not yet cooled, where the murdered corpses were still
lying—there heinous lasciviousness sought to satisfy its
lust. Holy nuns were stripped naked and violated. Some
women found delight in depravity and were attracted by
foreigners." Wives forsook their husbands; young girls
had lovers. " Beautiful women and young girls were
given to fornication and so died defiled and depraved,"
etc. " They were addicted to overeating, drunkenness
and fornication." [36]

The same was repeated during the Netherlands Revolution in 1663 and the following years. Here we also find
a general loosening of reflexes. Here, too, we see wholesale massacres. Among them " certain individuals were
spared for the express purpose of making them assist at
the violation of their daughters and wives. Miracles of
bestiality were performed. Neither the home nor the
church was held sacred." [37]

On a small scale we observe an appreciable growth
of sexual license during the English Revolution of the seventeenth century; this is corroborated both by direct witnesses and by the excessively severe measures which,

[36] Karamzine: *History of the Russian State* (Russ.), Vol. XI,
190-91; Vol. XII, 79-80, 311, St. Petersb., 1897.
[37] Motley: *History of the Netherlands Revolution*, Vol. II, St.
Petersb., 1866, 493.

towards the end of Cromwell's Protectorate, were taken to restrain license and to elevate the level of morality.[38]

It is superfluous even to mention that such loosening of reflexes accompanied by sadism took place during the Jacqueries, especially during the French, German and Bohemian ones; and in general during the whole of the "Troubled" period of the fourteenth and beginning of the fifteenth centuries in France, the end of the fifteenth and beginning of the sixteenth in Germany and the period of the Bohemian Revolution. During the latter matters had grown so bad that certain sects—the Adamites, Nicolaites, etc., publicly announced the "use of wives in common"—walked about without clothes.[39]

A similar state of affairs existed during the communistic "New Jerusalem" of John Leyden. The state of revolutionary France towards the end of the fourteenth and beginning of the fifteenth century is described in a few words by contemporaries: *Unde cedes rapine et incendia, et hucusque spolacionis ecclesiarum, violationes virginum, et quicuid rabies Sarracenica excogitare potuisset fuerant subsequenta, etc.*[40]

---

[38] See Guizot: Vol. I, pp. 7, 8, 22. Gardiner: *History of the Commonwealth,* Vol. IV, ch. XLII. On the whole the loosening of a whole group of reflexes is much less marked during the English Revolution of the seventeenth century than during other revolutions. This can probably be explained by the fact that the restraining reflexes themselves were infinitely more stable among the Anglo-Saxons. It is to be believed that this stability is not only conditioned, but unconditioned. The degree of stability of certain reflexes is not equal. not only individually, but among whole groups. The same can be observed among animals, as the experiments of Pavlov have shown.

[39] Weber: *General History,* Vol. VIII (Russ. transl.), 190-91, 243. Kautsky: above named work, p. 190 and foll. "All ties of friendship and home were dissolved. Neither property, nor family existed. Property and wives were owned in common. It is not possible to put down in print the details given on this matter by Aeneas Sylvius and Bress." Denis: *Huss et la Guerre des Hussites,* 1878, 267-88.

[40] See Levasseur: *Histoire des Classes Ouvrieres,* 1900, Vol. I, 522-7.

During the revolutionary period of the thirteenth and fourteenth centuries in Italy: " Pilgrims were robbed and murdered; nuns violated; there was no one from whom to seek protection." According to the words of a contemporary, " In Florence moral depravity knew no bounds. The sacredness of wedlock was no more respected. The rich thought nothing of buying the wives of the poor. It was so common an occurrence that it was looked upon as quite a legal commercial transaction." [41]

THE ROMAN REVOLUTIONS

Beginning from the time of the Gracchi, " divorce, which had previously been unheard of, grew to be an everyday occurrence." Even such a model family man as Metelus of Macedonia says that " marriage is a social burden which it is, of course, heavy to bear, but which a feeling of duty must prevent the patron from neglecting. If it were possible to do so, of course, every one of us would free himself from this burden; but nature has fashioned us so that it is equally awkward to live with wives and to manage without them." [42]

" Women felt that they had freed themselves from the tutelage of their fathers and husbands. Love intrigues of the most various kinds occupied them all. Ballet-girls (*mimae*) could have competed with modern ones for the manifoldness and skill with which they gave themselves up to their profession. However, they found no less skilful competitors among the ladies of the aristocracy. Love intrigues grew so common among the most renowned families that only some unusual scandal could make them the object of gossip." [43] " Transparent tissues, whose aim it was to denude, not to cover, the shape of the body, and

[41] Weber: Vol. VIII, 378.
[42] Mommsen: Vol. II, 412.
[43] Mommsen: Vol. III, 462-3.

silk garments took the place of the ancient woollen dress, not only among women, but men also." [44]   Varro writes with sadness: "Formerly the housewife would ply her spindle with one hand, and at the same time have an eye on the boiling pot; but now the daughter begs her father for a pound of precious stones and the wife a bushel of pearls. Formerly a woman was silent and shy during the wedding night, but now a woman gives herself to the first handsome coachman she sees. When a lady travels to her elegant villa a crowd of Greek rascally servants follows her. Virtue has disappeared; ungodliness, treachery and sensualism are rife everywhere." [45]

It were needless to cite further evidences of historians. The growth of sexual licentiousness, orgies, "masculinization" and emancipation of women and the effeminization of men, the modification of marriage legislation in the sense of "giving women freedom from the serfdom of wedlock;" sensual perversions, the declining of the sacredness of marriage and stability of the family ties, etc., all this is more than sufficiently proved. And all this happened during the revolutionary period which began approximately at the time of the Gracchi and ended with the reign of Augustus. In a word, here also we see proofs of the infallibility of our theorem.

The same happened during the Greek Revolution and manifested itself most clearly during the third and second centuries, when these revolutions grew to be frequent.

Even in the papyrus of Ipouver we see certain indications of such a growth of sexual license: "Scented and overdressed young cavaliers and ladies used to meet to adore the goddess 'Merth;' in other words, to sing and enjoy themselves." [46]

[44] Mommsen: Vol. II, 411.
[45] Mommsen: III, 537-8.
[46] Vikentieff: 293 (Russ.).

Let us cast a glance at the great Persian Revolution of the Mazdakists (in the time of Kobad). It is known that it proclaimed: "the ownership of women in common" and carried out this principle in practice.[47]

Our cursory review is, I presume, sufficient to prove the truth of our statements. In such revolutions as have had a deep-rooted and important influence on the mass of the people, causing them all to take part in the struggle, this licentiousness of sexual reflexes takes a sharp and wholesale character. In revolutions of less importance it limits itself only to those individuals and groups who take an active part in the struggle. Apart from the importance and deep-rootedness of a revolution the degree of licentiousness greatly depends on the inherited and acquired stability of the restraining habits of the population. A people like the English who possess such a restraining strength will not permit it even during a lengthy revolution to take great proportions. A people of a weaker restraining force: for instance, the Russian and French, allow it to take catastrophic proportions. But that is a difference only of degree, not of essence. The latter consists in both cases of a tendency to weaken, or to do away with all bounds, restraining sexual license. Revolution attempts to break restraints encompassing man, and therefore strives to give him " freedom " also in this matter. I leave it to the apologists of revolution to sing dithyrambs in honor of this kind of human " freedom." Personally I prefer not joining in their songs.

[47] See Malcolm: The above-cited work, Vol. I, 100, 106, 120; Vol. II, 334, 354.

CHAPTER VII

PERVERSION OF THE LABOR REACTIONS

Among human reactions there exists a special group: the reactions of labor. They consist in the accomplishment of certain acts necessary to gain a livelihood. The performance of such actions when they are harmless; when they are neither monotonous nor fatiguing and so long as they represent what the Americans call "creative workmanship," awakens no negative reactions. Man does not then try to avoid labor. At a work that he loves he is willing to remain not eight, but ten to sixteen hours. Quite other are the reactions of a toil which is fatiguing, monotonous, uninteresting and biologically harmful. However, the number of such undesired toil-reactions is very great in human conduct. The necessity of procuring a livelihood forces man to perform them. But only this necessity can spur him on. If by chance the stimulus of necessity (hunger, cold, compulsion, ethics, right, etc.) is absent or grows feeble man strives to liberate himself from such "toil."

In normal life different measures are taken to educate men to perform such work: punishment, example, rewards; moral, legal, religious and other stimuli are all put into action; man is inoculated with a whole series of conditioned reactions which give him the habit—"in the sweat of his face to eat bread," and which restrain the reactions of laziness.

In this respect the advent of revolution is marked by a sharp change in the behavior of man.

During the first period it is marked by the destruction

of the conditioned factors " restraining " laziness. This is due to different causes : the diversion of man's strength in a common struggle which occupies all his energy and, like war, makes him lose the habit of peaceful labor; the loss of prevision and thought for the morrow in the belief that the revolution will find sufficient food for everybody; the hope of profiting by the goods of others, their laid-up.stores of provisions, which is held out by the revolutionary propaganda.   A falling off of an immense majority of conditioned reflexes restraining laziness (which the revolution so often nicknamed: " bourgeois prejudice ") is the usual phenomenon in revolution. Liberated from these shackles man's natural tendency to avoid acts involving toil manifests itself without any restraining " brakes " or trammels.   These are the causes for the growth of laziness, for the growth of the desire to live on the labor of others, *i.e.,* the development of parasitism as a usual manifestation of the first stages of a revolution. The social results of such a deformation are : a decrease of labor capacity among a revolutionary society; the eating up of the provisions formerly laid up; the destruction of economic life; pauperism and famine.

When these inevitable results of the development of idleness grow evident, the second stage of the revolution is arrived at; the stage of a new inoculation of the extinct toil-reactions, the stage of bringing into activity stimuli restraining laziness.

Hunger, cold, want, called forth by revolution now get the upper hand.   It was they that had already once taught and forced primitive man to labor.[1]   When the

---

[1] The savage is lazy or industrious according to the ease or difficulty he finds in obtaining means of living. See Westermarck: *The Origin and Development of the Moral Ideas,* Vol. I, 268-9. Bücher: *Industrial Evolution* (Russ. transl.), Vol. I, 16, 18, 24 and others. A detailed investigation of this problem was given by me in my book: *Hunger as a Factor,* a book which has been destroyed by the Bolsheviki.

conditional habits restraining laziness are extinct and inactive—new cruel stimuli to toil proclaim an ultimatum to revolutionary society: " Work or perish from hunger, cold and want."

Society either perishes or accepts the ultimatum. These teachers force man to reacquire the habit of work; they do so both indirectly and directly through the power of society. It is of little account if the latter be white or red. With the merciless cruelty of a slave-owner it forces: " the free people which had overthrown slavery " to toil like galley-slaves. And man begins to toil not eight but sixteen hours a day; not according to his strength, but far beyond his strength. For merciless is the whip of death and famine: however, revolutionary society is bound to submit to its lash.

As a result every profound revolution, which begins by proclaiming the slogan of an " eight- or six-hour labor day " in reality achieves just the contrary: not a reduction, but an increase of labor hours; while the work itself is rendered harder and more irksome. Such is the usual " irony of history."

Let us turn to history to illustrate our proposition.

In the Russian Revolution of 1917–24, from the very beginning of the revolution the extinction of all the reflexes of labor grew evident. The demand for an eight-hour working day, even in enterprises working for the war, was the first corroboration of what is said above. But in reality even the eight-hour day was not complied with: instead of working, the laborers went to meetings and spent endless hours in discussions. Strikes grew more frequent. The general opinion was that: " Now we have liberty; and since we've achieved liberty, let the bourgeois work." Labor discipline, diligence, attentiveness—had all disappeared; no one was willing to obey. Each attempt made by the technical directors of an enterprise to bring some kind of order into the work, such, for instance, as reprimanding a defaulter, or discharging a good-for-nothing workman, etc., was regarded as a " counter-revolutionary " act. The call of : " All laborers to their looms and presses," remained " a voice crying in the wilderness." All persuasions that because of the war and revolution it was just the time to redouble productiveness were received with unanimous opposition by the masses and the socialists.

Such was the beginning of the extinction of the reflexes of labor reaction and the destruction of national well-being in Russia. This process spread wide and reached other classes of the population; later on the infection reached the peasants. The landowners and proprietors were forced to forsake their land and estates, because the peasants expropriated them; the manufacturers, directors and engineers forsook their enterprises, because of the threats of the workmen and their protest against every rational demand for systematic work; the peasants did not till the fields because their right to the expropriated land remained doubtful, and later on because it was useless to labor when the products of their labor were taken away by the communists. The October revolution brought this process to a climax. We now witness a demagogy sanctioning the idleness of the proletariat, introducing into many enterprises a six-hour working day. It is true, that at the same time, it introduced compulsory physical labor for the bourgeois (labor camps, labor tasks, etc.) ; but no serious results could be expected from these measures, except a higher death rate of the bourgeois. Already in 1917 the industry of the country began to degenerate. Through 1918 and 1919 this process continued. The reflexes of labor were weakened not only quantitatively but also qualitatively as well: the work grew to be careless, slip-shod and unproductive. Work which formerly would have been produced by one laborer during one day required now two to three days. The calls to work for the " Revolution," for " the general welfare," for " their own workmen and peasants, government," etc., were ineffective. The masses continued to be demoralizingly lazy.

The following tables are eloquent:

Out of all the working days the days missed in nationalized industries formed:

In 1920 first	third of year			40.8	per cent.
In 1920 second	"	"	"	33.2	per cent.
In 1920 third	"	"	"	23.5	per cent.
In 1922 first	"	"	"	25.3	per cent.
In 1922 second	"	"	"	45.9	per cent.

In the match industry one workman produced yearly:

In 1913	187	boxes of matches	100	per cent.
In 1914	207	boxes of matches	111	per cent.
In 1915	153	boxes of matches	82	per cent.
In 1917	152	boxes of matches	81	per cent.
In 1918	113	boxes of matches	60	per cent.
In 1919	85	boxes of matches	45	per cent.
In 1920	65	boxes of matches	35	per cent.
In 1921	75	boxes of matches	40	per cent.

One workman produced yearly:

	Peat	Coal
In 1916	100 per cent.	100 per cent.
In 1917	72.9 per cent.	65.7 per cent.
In 1918	55.6 per cent.	45.7 per cent.
In 1919	52.3 per cent.	34.3 per cent.

According to the data furnished by the communist Strumilin the gross productiveness of a factory laborer can be calculated as follows:

In 1913	100	per cent. of productiveness
In 1914	101.5	per cent. of productiveness
In 1915	125.8	per cent. of productiveness
In 1916	127.5	per cent. of productiveness
In 1917	85.5	per cent. of productiveness
In 1918	44.0	per cent. of productiveness

In 1919 .... 20.2 per cent. of productiveness
In 1920 .... 24.3 per cent. of productiveness
In 1921 .... 29.6 per cent. of productiveness [2]

The communist Kaktyn gives the following summary of the growth and decrease of the productiveness of one man's labor:

Industry	The yearly productiveness of one man calculated in pouds			
	1913	1920	1921	1922
Coal Industry	9165	2348	2893	4212
Naphtha	15460	——	14510	13150
Metallurgy (in gold rubles).	1988	342	415	636
Cotton	43	5	—	23.6
Linen	48	16	30	32 [3]

In short, the productiveness of work fell for 1918–21 to thirty per cent. of its pre-revolutionary state.[4]

During the first Soviet's Economical Congress the communists characterized this degeneration of labor reflexes very exactly.

" It sounds comical to me," says one of them, " when I hear people speak of a bourgeois sabbotage. We are witnessing a national proletarian sabbotage."

Somebody else calls it: " an epidemic of unconscious sabbotage." [5] Many workmen only registered their names at the factories, sometimes they also went there, but rarely did a stroke of work.[6]

As a result: all the old provisions were eaten up; want, famine and cold reigned supreme. The Russian population had to choose between starvation and work. These stimuli imperatively demanded the reëstablishment of labor reflexes.

Beginning from 1920 this takes place; at first scarcely perceptible. Hundreds of different kinds of labor taxes

[2] Prokopovitch: *Op. cit.*, 1923, 23-7 (Russ.).
[3] *The Economical Building Up*, No. 2, 1923, 35 (Russ.).
[4] Prokopovitch: 27.
[5] *Professional Journal*, 1918, Nos. 7-8, p. 7.
[6] Prokopovitch: The above-cited works.

are introduced; transport taxes, river taxes, timber taxes, fuel taxes, ice-clearing taxes, street-cleaning taxes, etc. Tens and hundreds of thousands are mobilized to form this labor army.[7]

In the guise of so-called " Saturdays," or Saturday work, and other forms of work, the six- to eight-hour working day is in reality transformed into one of ten to fourteen hours. The governing powers, which had so recently encouraged "the right of idleness," now find themselves obliged to force the population to work. They do so in a mercilessly and idiotically irrational manner. The severest punishments are fixed for the avoidance of labor taxes. The coarsest, but most efficient brutal stimuli are brought into play.[8]

At the same time nature itself brings forward stimuli such as famine, cold, etc., which force the population to work with all its strength and beyond its strength. People are forced to work sixteen to eighteen hours a day to gain the barest livelihood. The recent *dolce fare niente* is forgotten. Formerly they protested against nine hours' work, now they are forced to submit to double that period of work. This bitter experience reminds an oblivious society

---

[7] See Prokopovitch: The above-cited work, 48 (Russ.).

[8] During the Third Congress of Professional Associations the wordy ideology of compulsory inoculation was set forth as follows by Trotzki: "We are advancing towards compulsory labor for every workman. This is the basis of socialism. Compulsory labor, *i.e.*, a labor wherein each laborer occupies the place fixed for him by those in authority . . . This is the meaning of labor taxes. Hereby we admit that the state has the right to delegate each workman or woman to whatever place it deems they may be needed, in order to fulfil certain economically necessary tasks. Hereby we also admit the right of the state to punish the workmen and laborers (for non-accomplishment of tasks). Militarization of labor is unavoidable." See *The Third All-Russian Congress of Professional Associations*, April 6-13, 1920. Such is the ideology of so-called "socialistic" labor which is in reality that of a galley-slave.

of the eternal commandment: " In the sweat of thy face shalt thou eat bread."

Thanks to the regeneration of the reflexes of labor the destruction of the economical life in Russia is somewhat less rapid since 1921; and in certain cases shows signs of amelioration.

Of course this regeneration is produced with tremendous effort. The tendency to parasitism developed during the preceding period shows itself in hundreds of symptoms; instead of productive labor people are even in 1921–24 scrambling to procure a livelihood by means of cheating, speculation and rapacity. Consequently we see an unheard-of development of these phenomena in Russia. Nearly the total population of cities has been turned wholesale into profiteerers. Yet notwithstanding all this the regeneration of labor reflexes has really begun. If it were not for the deadly system of communism, the general state of ruin, and the idiotic measures of regulating labor on the part of the Soviet authorities, this process would make much more rapid progress. The revolution has nearly made a full circuit and is approaching its starting point. During the first period it began by the extinction of the reflexes of labor; since 1921 it commences to regenerate them again, reminding the Russian population of the eternal law. " He that will not work neither shall he eat."

Similar is the process during other revolutions. " The Nile overflows, but no one tills the ground." We read of the Egyptian Revolution in the chronicles of Ipouver, " No ship goes off to the North to Biblo (βύβλος) to bring back cedar-trees and precious ointments. They are no more brought here. The Nedgeces (the city proletariat) who formerly had never seen the light of day and the pitiful journeymen who used to water the earth from sunrise till sunset now ' walk about without restraint ' and ' welcome the day without fear.' All work is at a standstill. As a result, we witness famine. ' Because of hunger and terror moaning intermingled with weeping is heard all over the country.' ' Men are without clothing, grain or oil. How much grain used to be sown formerly and how little now ! ' Yet even this ' small quantity ' perishes in the field for lack of laborers .   .   .   Men feed upon lupinus, durro and herbs, snatching them out of the jaws of swine. ' Spices and oil are unheard of.' ' The fields remain untilled; buildings are not erected. Nothing new is created; only that which existed already is distributed anew.' "

The observing Ipouver notes a tendency towards parasitism spring up among the lower classes. Compulsory labor is introduced for the former wealthy and the aristocrats are turned into slaves.[9]

The same picture often repeats itself during the Greek revolutions from the seventh to the second century B.C.[10]

This repeats itself still more clearly during the lengthy revolutionary period of Rome; beginning with the epoch of the Gracchi and ending with the fall of the Republic. It is just from this period that the lazy, idle and parasitical Roman plebs, demanding only the free gift of bread and amusements (*panem et circenses*), enter upon the scene.

Towards the epoch of Cæsar the number of individuals who profited by a free gift of rations, given out by the state, had reached the figure of 600,000 (counting the members of the family). From the time of the Gracchi begins the growth of expropriations, plunder, repartitions, and other easy means of gaining a livelihood; from this moment we witness the intensive development of slavery; crowds of plunderers roam about; greed, profiteering,

---

[9] Vikentieff: The above-cited work, 284-300 (Russ.). Turaeff: The above-cited work, 70-72.

[10] See actual details in the above-cited works of Pöhlmann, Niese, Buzold and Beloch, especially in the comedies of Aristophanus.

avidity, idleness—all these symptoms of the extinction of the reflexes of labor begin to abound. From this moment begins the impoverishment and destruction of national economic life. The revolution "brought forth a terrible financial crisis . . . a universal impoverishment and depopulation. In the interim between the Battle of Pydna and the advent of the Gracchi many buildings had been erected, but after 122 B.C. hardly any." [11]

Not until after the time of Cæsar, and particularly after those of Augustus, does the strengthening and regeneration of the reflexes of labor begin.[12]

Similar is the process during the important revolutions of modern times; during the Jacqueries of France, England and Germany; during the Hussite Revolution [13] and the Russian troubled times of the seventeenth century. The deformation which we have been depicting repeats itself in all its details in the most stereotyped manner.

The same repeats itself during the English Revolution of the seventeenth century. The development of civil war brought on the ruin of the material interests of the country. Continual, disorderly war brought ruin to towns and villages, destroying the means which were indispensable for the existence of the people; it also demolished national industry. The financial measures taken by parliament and all kinds of abuses called forth disorders; every vestige of safety which alone could encourage the popula-

---

[11] Mommsen: Vol. II, 40-44, 46, 134, 399-400; Vol. III, 446-7 and others.
[12] See details in the above-cited works of Ferrero, Duruy, Rostovtzev, Friedlaender, Salvioli: *Capitalism in the Ancient World.* Waltzing: *Etude Historique sur les Corporations Professionnelles chez les Romains,* in the *Memoires Couronnées of the Belgian Royal Academy,* Vols. I and II. Vipper: *Studies of the Roman Empire,* 1908 (Russ.).
[13] "The Revolution of Huss soon developed an indifferentism towards labor and a laziness which brought poverty and want in their wake." Denis: The above-cited work, 289.

tion to put up provision and to give thought to the future had disappeared. At the same time the number of pillages, thefts and other means of easy gain had greatly increased. A decrease of the reflexes of labor sets in and the country grows "to be a prey to depression." [14] The signs of poverty could be seen everywhere. Only towards the end of Cromwell's Protectorate and towards the beginning of the Restoration does a compulsory regeneration of labor reflexes commence. (The Act of 1662.)[15]

It is not necessary to dwell upon the fact that the same process took place in a most extreme form during the great French Revolution. Levasseur concisely sums up the state of affairs in the following words: "Revolutions are always critical periods for labor: they destroy capital, bring disorder into consumption and paralyze productiveness. In 1789 this manifested itself particularly clearly."

With the commencement of revolution the amount of work produced in a country diminishes; the development of revolution brings it near to extinction. Expropriation and plunder grow more frequent. These phenomena are increased by struggles, by economic crises and the great number of those out of work. Among the masses, particularly in cities, we witness the growth of parasitism. "The laborers," says Levasseur, "produced no more useful work. The productiveness of their labor in works undertaken by the state was minimum. Mendacity developed in the country in the most terrific manner." In consequence we see . . . famine, illness, want and a tremendous growth of pauperism. This all acts as a stimulus forcing the population back to work. Conse-

---

[14] Guizot: Vol. I, XIII and following pp.
[15] Kovalevsky: *From Direct Government by the People to a Representative Government*, Vol. II, 178 (Russ.). Rogers: *Six Centuries of Work and Wages*, N. Y., 1884, 432-33 pp.

quently there are first of all measures taken by the
government, the laws of Chapelier forbidding strikes, reg-
lementations of labor, abolition of freedom of labor, introduction of a compulsory labor tax and a law which
punished with arrest and even capital punishment workmen
who refused to work for their masters, and commanded
that they should be sent to work by compulsion, and permitted their being turned into journeymen, etc. The government showed great brutality in forcing the dissolute
population to work. Secondly, we witness the renewal of
exhausting labor; for men were spurred thereto by the
threat of famine. These phenomena already began in 1791
and continued during the epoch of the Directoire and that
of Napoleon until the reflexes of labor were reawakened.[16]

The same result brought on by voluntary and involuntary causes repeats itself in the revolution of 1830 and in
the rebellions of 1831–34. " The revolution increased the
industrial crisis. All work was at a standstill. The workmen lost their jobs. In the works organized by the state
the productiveness of labor stood on a very low level."
Further on symptoms of the same kind can be seen in the
demand for shorter working hours and for the increase of
the wage tariff. Famine and the use of firearms crush
rebellions and put an end to the extinction of the reflexes
of labor.[17]

During the French Revolution of 1848 this process
was much more clearly defined. From the very beginning
of the revolution the reflexes of labor among the workmen
quickly began to grow extinct. The workmen " did not
want to work for more than eight or nine hours." The

[16] See Levasseur: *Hist. des Classes Ouvrieres,* 1789-1870, Vol. I,
57, 61-62 and Passim, book I. E. Tarlé (Russ.): *The Peasants and
the Workmen During the Epoch of the French Revolution,* St.
Petersburg, 1922, ch. 4.
[17] Levasseur: Vol. II, 1-6.

introduction of a ten-hour workday instead of the existing twelve-hour workday, satisfied them no more. After the opening of national workshops, those of private owners were forsaken, for in the former they received 1 fr. 50 cent. a day and had the possibility of . . . not working. "The workmen led an idle life and yet received their pay; they only made a semblance of working; many mocked at the government which gave them payment for dawdling about the whole day." Thanks to this possibility of spending the whole time in idleness, "the crowd of workmen in the national workshops always grew larger; towards the end of May there were no less than 115,000, not counting the 5000 aspirants." The same happened in other towns. V. Hugo clearly sums up the position; he says: "There was a time when our eyes were irritated by the sight of the idlers of luxury; nowadays we see the idlers of want. During monarchy men existed who did absolutely nothing,[18] but is it possible that the Republic will also give us such sluggards?"

After that follows the usual history: the aggravation of the crisis; the growth of expenditure for these workshops, financial straits, famine, the closing of the national workshops, rebellions and . . . the regeneration of the labor reflexes under the influence of starvation, punishment, and the repressive measures of Cavaignac and Napoleon (the introduction of a twelve-hour working day, etc.).[19]

The German and Austrian Revolutions of 1848 give us a similar picture. We hear the same demand for shortened work hours; the same attempts to live at the cost of the government; the same growth of laziness, loss of time

---

[18] Gregoire: Vol. III, 16-17, 30-32, 109-10.
[19] Gregoire: Vol. III, 25-28, 35. Levasseur: *Op. cit.*, Vol. II, 383 and foll., book V, Passim.

during meetings; endless chattering, drunkenness, etc., and finally the same fate of the national workshops as in France. In Vienna "many grew lazy and would not labor" on the works organized by the state. We witness a great inflow of those desirous to work (they came from private workshops). Their number reached 50,000. Each attempt to force anybody to work seriously evoked a protest. All the appeals to high-flown sentiments such as: "Liberty," "Revolution," "Common Welfare," in the name of which the laborers were urged to work, fell flat. And as result, we again see pauperism, which makes it necessary to use "strong medicine" to revive the extinct reflexes of labor.[20]

The blockade, and later on the civil war and revolution, called forth a similar process during the Paris Revolution of 1871; a process which, however, was interrupted.

From the moment of the triumph of the Commune a rapid extinction of the labor reflexes was noticeable, though it really had commenced some time before. A whole series of measures and decrees issued by the Commune at the beginning of its activity reduced the discipline of labor (prohibition of night labor, pecuniary help rendered to those out of work without any obligation to refund the sum, abolition of fines and deductions, abolition of rent, postponement of the discharge of debts, nationalization of enterprises). Civil war rendered this discipline completely impossible. As a result: "All enterprises were stopped; pauperism grew to be universal. All traces of industrial or other activity had disappeared from the town. A great number of shops and stores were closed; the rest remained without customers." Thereafter came

---

[20] Bloss: 201-2, 221 and foll.; 310 and foll. Hartmann: *Volkserhebung der Jahre, 1848-49 in Deutschland*, 1900.

famine, sickness and the usual consequences of such a state.[21]

From the moment of the Commune's downfall there commences a rapid regeneration of the labor reflexes of the Paris population.

All we have said proves that every revolution calls forth a perversion of labor reflexes such as has been described above. The degree of this perversion depends on the depth and length of the revolution.

Revolution sings the praises of productive labor, but it takes away from the laborers the habit of work. It blames idleness—and augments the number of the idle. It rails against profiteering and parasitism—and turns men into parasites.

It is true that revolution also annihilates that class of society which had been idle until then, and by direct or indirect measures forces it to work. But alas! that is but a drop in the ocean which does not compensate for the opposite results. Instead of one idler it produces hundreds of them. Instead of one parasite, profiteerer, machinator, it creates dozens.

And so the same " lesson " is again and again repeated to humanity. To some, the formerly idle, it says: " Your parasitism has awakened the righteous indignation and storm of the revolution, which will annihilate and burn up you and your offspring." To the others, those who have been weighed down by toil, it says, " Bloodthirsty revolutionary measures are least of all capable of lightening your yoke of labor. This method is worth nothing. The attempts to adopt it have brought, bring, and will always bring down a merciless retribution on the heads of those who employ it."

---

[21] Gregoire: Vol. IV, 307-8, 352-7, 409-10. Lissagarés: 259-61.

CHAPTER VIII

PERVERSION OF THE REACTIONS OF AUTHORITY AND SUBORDINATION

AMONG the numerous activities of man there exists a special group of reactions which can be subdivided into reactions of *subordination and authority*.

The first are the answer to certain stimuli—complex or simple—which call forth in the individual such reactions as the execution of given orders (such a stimulus could be for instance an order issued authoritatively by a policeman, governor, minister, etc.). On the other hand an individual endowed with authority, when he finds himself in a suitable environment (for instance when in possession of an official post with the requisite outward circumstances and paraphernalia of authority), answers the given stimulus by so-called reactions of authority, for instance by issuing orders requiring obedience.

The tendencies to reactions of both these categories exist in nearly every man. They do not limit themselves to the relations existing in state government and to the obedience of a subject. The mutual relationship of those in authority and those yielding obedience exists also among other numerous and different groups, among members of a family, of the church, of political parties, professional associations, trade companies, and the members of any given society. Among every kind of population existing under normal conditions we find such a complex network of interrelationship. When the members of such an aggregate answer the demands of such reaction constantly and persistently the result is " a state of order."

The advent of a revolution changes the whole picture. Every political revolution is in its first stage characterized by the extinction of a vast majority of reactions of subordination among a great many citizens. The conditioned connection existing between the stimulus to obedience personified by those set in authority (from a policeman to a king), by their acts and the symbols accompanying their office, and the corresponding reactions of subordination called forth among the citizens is broken. The reaction of obedience does not follow the accustomed stimulus to subordination.

On the other hand many of the reactions of authority among the governing classes also grow extinct. The outward stimuli which would formerly have called for the exercise of immediate and indisputable authority either remain unanswered, or are reacted to in an undecided, half-hearted, vacillating manner. Here also the connection between stimulus and reaction is broken.

As a result the whole complex chain of interrelations existing between these groups of reactions is destroyed and the order of government disappears. When this extinction of the reflexes of subordination and authority concerns only relations existing between citizens and agents of state authority, and does not spread its influence over other social groups (children and parents—in the family; the community and the clergy—in the church; the workmen and the owner—in economic life; the pupil and teacher —in school; the members and leaders of professional associations; the negro and the slave-owner; the subjected and the governing nationalities: for instance, the Hindoo and the English, etc.), we are facing a superficial, purely political revolution (such, for instance, as the revolution of 1848). When, on the other hand, this extinction of reflexes spreads over the above-mentioned groups—then the revolution takes a more profound character; the more groups it embraces, the greater the number of reactions that grow extinct—the deeper does it go.

Let us throw a cursory glance at the character and development of such a process: the extinction of this kind of reaction.

1. As a rule the extinction of the reflexes of subordination begins prior to revolution. This manifests itself in sporadic disturbances, riots, and a refusal to submit to certain representatives of authority, when the latter prevent the fulfilment of the demands of certain reflexes—which have been oppressed. These are the precursors of a coming storm.

2. If large masses are suffering under oppressed reflexes; if those in authority do not know how to turn the current of these oppressed reflexes and are not capable of strengthening the reflexes of subordination by stimuli which can act as a " brake," then the process of destruction develops quickly and spreads wide and deep.

Such a " loosening of all screws " spreads over vast masses. First obedience is refused to the policeman; later on to the governor, the minister, the king. The downfall of the latter calls forth a complete breakdown of the reflexes of subordination towards all agents of former state authority.

3. But not only towards them. For most of the other reactions of subordination were acquired in connection with obedience to state authority; were a result of these very reflexes, and so their extinction leads to a more or less complete extinction of the reactions of subordination towards all authorities connected with it. The closer the connection, the greater the brightness shed from the imperial light over church dignitaries, privileged classes, the wealthy, etc., the more complete will their extinction

be. This is the reason why, in countries which possess only one fundamental " centre of authority," the fall of the latter implies the downfall of all other authorities. In countries where " self-government " is the order of the day, where many independent centres of authority exist, the breakdown of the reflexes of subordination towards state authority need not seriously influence the reactions of subordination to other centres of authority. In such cases the downfall of the King's authority need not be accompanied by the denial of the authority of church, family, class, and other dignitaries, for the reactions of obedience to each of them had been acquired independently.

4. If this process of extinction finds no serious barriers, it progresses, being repeatedly stimulated by acts of strife, and, reaching its climax, leads to anarchism. A period of license, a limitless display of freedom of the reflexes sets in. The downfall of existing authority is soon followed by that of the very opposition which had overthrown it, as soon as the opposition attempts to stem wilfulness without having the means to accomplish it.

The same fate awaits the next authorities if they decide to follow the same tactics. Each one of them is strong only in so far as it encourages : " the loosening " of all restraining factors. As a result : life grows insufferably difficult, nearly unbearable; unless new reflexes of obedience be inculcated society begins to perish.

5. This can only be achieved if the strongest of unconditioned restraining factors are put into play : merciless terror, court-martial and such like stimuli, to which less extreme measures can also be added, such as propaganda, electioneering campaigns, suggestions, imitation, etc. The completer " the loosening of restraining factors," the more merciless will the measures taken against it have to be. They are carried through by " white " or " red "

dictators. Under the severe binding compulsion of such measures the half-destroyed reflexes of subordination are speedily reawakened. This stage of process admits of certain relapses. As a result of this process the reflexes attain their normal state and the revolution comes to an end.

Such is only the general scheme. Certain conditions may produce some variety, but we need not enter into details here.

All that has been said above shows clearly that terror and dictatorship are the inevitable results of revolution. He who wants the last must want the first as well. He who spreads revolution prepares the soil for the play of unbridled terror and dictatorship.

Let us illustrate this with one or two examples. We shall begin with the Russian Revolution. In 1916 the first symptoms of a dwindling of the subordination reflexes manifested themselves. Subjectively this showed itself in the loss of authority by the governing class. Objectively—in a whole series of "soldiers'," and so-called "bread" riots. In January and February of 1917, this process developed itself. We are in the presence of workmen's street demonstrations, of the first struggles, the first manifestations of the insubordination of the masses. The police are no more obeyed. Soldiers and cossacks refuse subordination to officers. The governmental machine remains inactive. Certain sections of it work on, but in a half-hearted manner. On February 26th–27th revolution breaks out. During two or three days the destruction of the reflexes of obedience to imperial authority spreads from the capital far and wide over all the other large cities of Russia ; its influence reaches also deep down —from the authority of the Czar to that of the policeman. The Czar is overthrown.

In Russia all other authorities enjoyed but a reflected

light; the masses acquired reflexes of subordination to them only as a result of subordination to the Czar. These belonged to a first-rate category of reflexes; the others only to second- and third-rate categories engrafted on the reflexes of subordination to imperial authority. The annihilation of these was the destruction of the foundation of the complex structure of the reflexes of subordination. Naturally all other authorities would be engulfed in its downfall, and such was the case. After the reflexes of subordination to the Czar were extinguished those of his agents followed suit: the reflexes of subordination of soldiers to officers and generals; workmen to directors of factories and other enterprises; of peasants to landowners to nobles to representatives of city and " Zemsky " self-government; of all subordinates to everybody in authority. As long as the state Duma was busy " loosening " the reflexes of subordination to imperial authority it enjoyed popularity with the masses. But when, after the downfall of monarchy, it tried to put bounds to limitless self-will it lost all authority after two or three weeks. A " Provisional Government " and the First Soviet took its place. But they also were short-lived. During the first weeks they made no attempt to restrain anything, letting the reins drop out of their hands. As soon, however, as they tried to resume them even though only in words, it grew evident that they possessed no authority. After many crises they were overthrown.

Their place had to be taken by the Bolsheviks. These gave full free play to the self-will of the masses; they restrained nothing; they sanctioned license of every kind; at the same time enveloping it in idealistic noble words. To the workmen they said: " Take the factories, destroy the bourgeois; " to the soldiers: " Give up fighting, kill your officers; " to the peasants: " Sack the estates, take away the land; " to all: " Do not submit, expropriate, sack, kill the bourgeois, the capitalists, the nobles—all whose death you desire in order to ' Deepen the revolution.' "

Their success was inevitable. Their opponents, beginning with those of the Soviets of the First Assembly and ending with the " Provisional Government " possessed no strong will; they neither knew how to, nor had the power to, stem the mad "loosening" of subordination reflexes. Capital punishment was abolished. Any serious repression was tabooed, being considered a manifestation of reaction. Even incarceration was looked upon as a " counter-revolutionary" action. The sole restraints admitted by the Soviets and the Provisional Government consisted in: " persuasion," proclamations and addresses directed to " conscience," to " revolutionary judgment," in appeals " to protect the revolution and Fatherland." But even these appeals were equivocal and more liable to weaken all restraining factors than to strengthen them. On one hand the soldiers were told: " Protect your country, obey your officers; " at the same time they were encouraged to conclude peace; war was depicted as the intrigues of imperialists and all the time they were taught that the staff was reactionary. The same took place during all the debates of the First Soviet and the Provisional Government.

As a result " elemental forces burst forth breaking through all bonds and restraints." [1]

The same *mutatis mutandis* was the fate of the other authorities. Everywhere we find the same process of letting biological features get the upper hand and " loosening of restraining factors." The only authority which gained power during the process was that of those who egged

[1] Denikin: *Sketches of the Russian "Troubled Times,"* Vol. I, part I, 44, 63-64; part II, 91-93, 104, 145-6.

the masses on, who justified and sanctioned wilfulness, *i.e.,* that of the Bolsheviks. They let themselves float down the stream. Never restraining the self-will of their subordinates, but directing it against the "bourgeois," they attached the masses to themselves and formed a "coalition of bloodshed and crime" by instigating the population to destroy and kill, and by now and then throwing out to them some gifts.

And they conquered. During the first stages of their victory they still refrained from restraining the wildly surging elements. Later on they were forced to do so, but here also they followed the same method: they restrained one group by giving full liberty to the oppressed impulses of other groups. To this they added the influence of propaganda and the privileges showered on the more active members of the "pretorian guard" of Bolshevism, such as the right to rob, to violate, and the grant of good rations during the famine period. By these means Bolshevism created a so-called "Fist" which was indissolubly bound up for life and death with its own fate.

The "Cheka"[2] was inaugurated. By means of this institution it grew possible to restrain others, among them the soldiers. A revolver placed at the temple of a citizen, a machine gun situated in the rear of the soldiers, merciless executions, convictions, confiscations, such were the methods with which the reëstablishment of the extinct reactions of subordination was begun.

As soon as the Bolsheviks entered the stage of restraint, we observe the fading away of the reactions of subordination towards them: peasants' and workmen's riots are heard of (in Tamboff, Jaroslav, on the Don, the Volga, etc.). But the Bolsheviks were already prepared;

---

[2] Cheka: Extraordinary Commission for the Suppression of Counter Revolution by Terror.

they had an " apparatus of restraint " ready to hand, and they put down the riots. The first dam was raised; after that other rebellions took place, but were again put down. As a result towards 1919–20 society is "benumbed." The insubordination is broken down with the help of merciless restraints.

The army which had been so adverse to fighting obediently went into battle when subjected to such determining agents; citizens who had protested against the faintest infringement of their " freedom " were obliged to endure the full loss of it. The reflexes of subordination to the Soviet authority began to take root; fear, not duty, being the compelling motive. Decrees were obeyed, taxes and duties paid. To sum up—the reëstablishment of the extinct reflexes of subordination of subjects towards state authorities was achieved.

However, this reëstablishment is not very stable so far as the Bolsheviks are concerned. The " strait-jacket " into which they have forced society is so narrow that a whole series of biological reflexes suffers from it; it not only restrains their uncontrolled manifestation, but suffocates the life of society. Consequently a new outburst of insubordination can be expected, if the " strait-jacket " is not rendered wider and are going in fact.

The Russian Revolution as we have seen is characterized by a "loosening" of the reflexes of subordination not only in regard to state authority, but also towards many other derivative forms of authority. In 1918–20 we witnessed the setting loose of the reflexes of subordination among many members of the church community in regard to church dignitaries; of members of a family—children in regard to their parents; of workmen—towards the owners and directors of enterprises; of servants—towards their masters; of pupils—towards teachers; of

the masses—towards the cultured classes, the "intellegentzia " and " bourgeois " in general.

It could not have been otherwise in Russia where
all authorities derived their weight from imperial power,
where the reaction of obedience to other authorities was
acquired from the feeling of obedience given to the former.
How many authorities and groups there were which were
busily occupied undermining imperial power, not knowing
that in undermining it they were also undermining their
own power; and that the precipice towards which they
were pushing it would engulf them, too. Yet such has
been the case.

But here also since 1921 we see a change; a whole
series of authorities has begun to be reëstablished. Beginning from this period we witness the regeneration of
reflexes of subordination of workmen towards engineers
and owners; of the faithful towards the authority of the
church; of pupils towards teachers; of children towards
parents, etc. At the present moment this process is clearly
defined. But not everywhere, and not yet in full measure.

During seven years the Russian Revolution has almost
accomplished a full circuit. The degree and intensity of
the "loosening of all restraining factors " which it has
attained rendered it one of the profoundest revolutions
history has ever known. We must therefore not be astonished if the process of regeneration is also slow, painful
and cruel. Here also: " the action equals the resistance; "
the more complete the extinction, the more painful the
regeneration of the extinct reflexes of subordination.

A similar process took place in every other revolution.
We read of the Egyptian Revolution: " Not a state dig-
nity can be found at the post that ought to be his. The
population resembles a frightened herd without a shep-
herd. The statesmen are killed, the judges have fled or

been exiled from the country. The serpent (emblem of Pharaoh's power) has been taken out of its nest. The secrets of Upper and Lower Egypt have been divulged. The laws of the court of justice are thrown under the feet of the mob, and they are broken by the needy."

In Egypt the power of all authorities proceeded from one source: that of Pharaoh's power; their light was but the reflection of his light. Consequently it is easy to understand that the destruction of Pharaoh's power necessarily led to the annihilation of all other authorities. Such evidently was the case: "The former slaves have grown to be masters of slaves. The children of princes are thrown into the street, or dashed against walls. The father kills the son; the son the father. Brother rises against brother. The priests have lost all authority. Egypt has no more pillars, Egypt exists no more. 'All is lost!'" exclaims Ipouver in despair.[3]

He also describes the stage of numbness which set in: "People wander on earth like half-dead fish. The country is abandoned to its own lassitude; like a field of mown flax." We do not know whether this state of anarchy was of long duration, but we do know that in the long run here also the stage of "restraining factors" set in and the regeneration of the subordination reflexes took place.

In the great Greek and Roman revolutions we see the same conditions. Here, especially in Rome towards the end of the Republic, this replacement of processes, *i.e.*, the extinction and the regeneration of the reactions of subordination repeats itself several times. Let us take, for instance, the revolution in Corcyra described by Thucydides. Here we see clearly how deep and diverse the "loosening of restraining factors" was for all the reflexes of subordination. "Death thus raged in every

---

[3] Vikentieff: 279-300. Turaeff: *Ancient Egypt*, 70-71 (Russ.).

shape; there was no length to which violence did not go; sons were killed by their fathers; . . . even blood became a weaker tie than party. Society became divided into camps in which no man trusted his fellow. There was neither promise to be depended upon, nor oath that could command respect. In the confusion into which life was now thrown, human nature, always rebelling against the law and now its master, gladly showed itself ungoverned in passion above respect for justice, and the enemy of all superiority" and so on. To sum up, we witness the complete wreck of all authority and of those reflexes of subordination which it demanded; we witness anarchy, a return to animal instincts and . . . after it the reacquisition of the extinct reactions of subordination by similar cruel measures.[4] The same took place in other Greek revolutions.[5]

The advent of the Gracchi denotes the beginning of the extinction of the reflexes of subordination towards the authority of the senate and other legal institutions of Rome. " The proletarians demanded that the consul should respect the authority of the people in the person of every ragamuffin." The reactions of subordination were being weakened in the people; those of authority, among the corrupted dignities.[6]

The actions of the Gracchi gave great force to their " loosening " of restraining factors. As a result we see: the growth of insubordination and of demagogy, and then a transition to violence and bloodshed with finally use of bloodthirsty measures of restraint. " Gracchus was devoured by the demon of revolution he himself had set free." " The governmental system began to grow vindictive; acts

---

[4] Thucydides : Book III, 223-27 pp.
[5] See description in the works of Beloch, Niese, Buzold, Pöhlmann and others.
[6] Mommsen : II, 71-73.

of terrorism were constantly perpetrated; violence and cruelty were the qualities that commanded respect and so grew to be the rule." We witness tremendous slave insurrections. Pillage grew to be a normal practice and demagogy to be the chief essence of politics. Authority of religion degenerated, so also the authority of the husband and *pater familias*. Varro writes: " Formerly the father pardoned his son; now the right of pardoning has gone over to his son. Nowadays no one subjects himself to law "—such is his concise summary of the situation. The introduction of restraining factors here also assumed a particularly cruel character. In the Roman Revolution subordinates refused obedience to those in authority; children to parents, slaves to masters, allies to Romans, wives to husbands, the poor to the rich, the low-born to the nobles. They slaughtered, pillaged, rebelled, did violence—at their own free will. Doubtful questions would be decided not by law, but by war; the sword grew to be the arbitrator. Such stages of extinction of reflexes of subordination to authority would be followed by stages of " restraint," during which such cruel measures would be put into practice that " the whole country would be crushed with dumb horror and not a single free expression of opinion could be heard." [7] We know that these two different kinds of periods repeated themselves several times from the time of the Gracchi to those of Augustus.[8]

During the Russian Revolution of the seventeenth century there was witnessed an "extraordinary degree of self-will among the population—mental turbulence . . . The heads of everybody seemed turned. Each wanted to occupy a superior position. The slaves wanted to be mas-

---

[7] Mommsen: Vol. II, 374; Vol. III, 35.
[8] See the actual development of these processes in the above-cited works of Mommsen, Pöhlmann, Ferrero, Rostovtzev, Duruy and others.

ters; the low-born, nobles; the nobles, princes." The authority of the Czar, the church, the nobles, of all that was sacred had disappeared. As a result there followed the cruelty and bloodthirstiness that is characteristic of the ' restraining ' period." [9]

The same happened during all the medieval revolutions beginning with the Jacquerie and ending with the rebellions of the cities.

A contemporary of the Czech Revolution writes: "The population, like ancient Lucifer, refused to submit itself to anybody: neither to pope, nor king." Later on submission was achieved by Zizka, but at the cost of mercilessly cruel measures. After his death we again see " no semblance of authority." A whole series of years passed by . . . the energy of the Bohemians was exhausted before the reflexes of subordination were reëstablished—by the sword and bloodshed—after the battle of Lipany.[10]

Similar was the situation during the English Revolution of the seventeenth century. Here, however, thanks to the habit of self-government of the English people, and to the fact of the existence of many comparatively independent centres of authority, the extinction of the subordination was not so widespread and did not manifest itself seriously as regards non-governmental authorities and dignitaries. But in the realm of subordination to state authority the extinction went much further (as it always does) than the first instigators of the revolution and rebellion against the king had planned.

Here also we first see the extinction of the reactions of subordination towards individual agents of state and church authority (Strafford and other nobles), then— towards the king himself. Then towards parliament

---

[9] Karamzine: Vol. XII, 79-80 (Russ.).
[10] Denis: *Huss et la Guerre des Hussites*, 1878, 286, 286, 346, 478.

when the latter tried to introduce restraint; then towards the army and Cromwell. The process runs its full course and attains its logical end: *i.e.,* it swallows up all the authorities of the revolution and leads to a restoration.

Little by little: " all passions, hopes, longings floated to the surface and began to develop themselves. A seething mental unrest took possession of the people and the army. Everywhere unheard-of reforms were demanded. Reformers sprang up from all sides. Neither law nor facts seemed to baffle them." " Overthrow, overthrow, overthrow," such is the characteristic appreciation of this period by the Lord Protector himself.[11]

From the time of Cromwell the Dictator the reinculcation of the extinct reactions of subordination commences again. Remaining alone he tightly screwed up all the springs of power and with the aid of the army forced the population into obedience; one part of the army crushed the rebellion of the rest; with the aid of the institution of general-majors and at the cost of executions, convictions, fines, confiscations and similar measures he reinstalled the habit of obedience, crushed plots and rebellions, and towards the close of his own life forced society into submission, thereby paving the way to the restoration of the authority of the Stuarts.[12]

During the French Revolution of 1789 we first see the fading of the reflexes of subordination towards individual representatives of imperial authority (development of robbery, pillage, etc.). The restraining factors grow weak. Those in power show a weakening of the reflexes of authority. Louis XVI " did not know how to will,"

---

[11] Guizot: Vol. II, ch. I, 96-97, 109.

[12] The actual development of the process and some exceedingly interesting details, into which I cannot enter here, can be found in the works of Guizot and Gardiner: *History of the Great Civil War* and *History of the Commonwealth and Protectorate.*

and " did not know what it was that he wanted." The aristocracy was infected with the spirit of free-thought and,
in the words of Malet du Pain, " was debilitated by worldliness, epicureanism and effeminacy." The old order
demonstrated " an absence of energy." [13]

From the time of the convocation of the États Généraux, the process of extinction of submission advanced
crescendo; the same happened with the " reactions of
authority." The governing members proved themselves
impotent to cope with the soldiers, both on the sixth of
May in the Salle du Jeu de Paume, and in the Church of
St. Louis on the twenty-fourth and twenty-eighth of June
and on the twelfth of July. Their unsuccessful attempts
at restraint irritated the reflexes of insubordination still
more. After the taking of the Bastille Louis had " neither
law, nor power on his side; " the provinces came to the
conclusion that what was permitted in Paris could be
allowed outside of it, too; that the state officials were to
be set aside; that the castles—these 40,000 small Bas-
tilles—should be taken by assault; thus the extinction of
the reflexes of subordination grew to be universal. As a
result, " we witness," in the words of Bailly, " that everybody knows how to command—no one how to obey.
. . .   each district deems itself endowed with sovereign power." [14]

The reflexes of obedience towards the king with his
slogan of " carefully, carefully; " to the feudals, the aristocracy and clergy speedily grew extinct. The National
Assembly during its first period encouraged this loosening of all restraining factors and was very popular, but
very soon—from the moment it attempted to restrain elemental forces (like other centres of restraint, for instance

---

[13] Madelin: *The French Revolution* (Russ. transl.), Vol. I, 45-49.
[14] Madelin: Vol. I, 86-95, 108-113.

the Communes of 1789)—it lost authority and was easily submerged by the waves of rebellion. Already in October, 1789, " the revolution set apart the active men of 1789; later on it completely devoured them." [15]

The Jacobins take their place; they do everything to encourage the self-will of the masses; restrain nothing, sanction slaughter, pillage, butchery. They, like the Bolsheviks, skilfully direct the mob's passions against their own foes and against the wealth of the latter. Like the Bolsheviks, they form a " coalition of bloodshed." With their advent, however, begins the stage of reinculcation of the reactions of subordination. With the aid of the mob they first train the " aristocracy " to submission, then with the aid of their " fist " they subjugate the rest of their opponents, and lastly the people itself. Their methods are the usual " revolutionary bonds : " terror, dictatorship, revolutionary tribunals, executions, convictions, confiscations and hostages.

The stage of numbness sets in. " The years 1793–94 (till Termidor) are terrible just because of their silence. You might hear the flight of an insect." [16] After Termidor we again witness some animation and at the same time the final fading away of the reflexes of subordination.

A new stage of restraints begins after the days of Terminal, Prerial, Vendemiere and Fructidor. " Deputies are condemned, the aristocrats deprived of their rights, the press subjugated, the clergy exiled, the emigrants executed, a hypocritical terror reigns everywhere." [17]

" Thereafter the nation appears exhausted, like a mad-

---

[15] *Ibid.*, 137. Not in vain did Mirabeau when dying say : " I am indignant at the thought that I have taken part only in a work of tremendous destruction." Barnave, Vergniaud, Brissot, Danton and Demoulins—were all popular as long as they " unscrewed " restraining reflexes, Vol. I, 216.
[16] Madelin : Vol. II, 156-7.
[17] *Ibid.*, 296.

man brought low by bleeding, hot baths and hunger. A collapse followed the period of the high fever." [18]

Paroxysms of rebellion repeated themselves several times, but were easily quenched. Napoleon finally accomplished the task of reëstablishing the extinct reactions of subordination, bringing them into their normal state. At the same time the reëstablishment of other reactions of subordination; subordination to authorities other than that of the state, such as the church, family, the new bourgeois, the new aristocracy, etc., was also taking place.

The same process repeats itself in the history of the German Revolution of 1848. In this case the first demands were very modest. The reactions of subordination towards the king were not yet extinct. Later on the demands go much farther than those granted on the eighteenth of March. The annihilation of taxes, cloisters, privileges and poverty was demanded. This process was not allowed to develop itself. The government had strength enough to put a stop to it. The twelfth of November a military dictatorship was introduced and the "strength of the revolution was broken. The peasant felt satisfied, the workmen grew indifferent." [19]

During the French Revolution of 1848 the throne is overthrown, the temporary government speedily loses all the sympathy of the people. The process approaches its culminating point. The Red Republic looms a danger to the tricolored one. The reflexes of subordination towards the Temporary Government and the Constituent Assembly, begin to grow extinct (the movement of March 17th, April 16th and May 15th). Anarchy, *i.e.,* complete absence of authority sets in.

---

[18] Michelet: 48-58, 158, 254 and others. See also the works of Taine and Jaurès.

[19] Bloss: *The German Revolution,* Moscow, 1921, 94, 160, 392-4, 408 and others.

"The army was in a state of anarchy." "The soldiers threw away their ammunition and departed for their homes." "The towns were full of consternation and unrest." The workmen left off working. Nobody was willing to obey. The process advanced crescendo till the rebellion of June 22d to 25th. After it was crushed an energetic reinculcation of the reflexes of subordination was undertaken by Cavaignac, who used the severest of repressions and punishments. "After the absence of all restraints a superabundance of restraints was the order of the day." [20] Napoleon the Third completed this "education" during the first years of the Empire.

The same repeated itself in 1871. Here also during the beginning the police were absent. "All confidence in hierarchy was at an end. Law courts were organized by the government of National Protection for judging actions of rebellion; but all criminals were acquitted because the judges did not believe in lawfulness" (extinction of the reactions of authority). The reflexes of subordination towards the government of National Protection speedily fade away. At the time of this universal absence of authority the Commune takes power into its own hands. But even it is but little obeyed. "The youngest subaltern refuses to accept orders, but wants to issue them." A complete absence of discipline and great license reigns among the soldiers. [21]

The Commune started the process of reëstablishing restraints, killing and depriving of all liberty. But this task was accomplished by the Versailles government, which used the habitual methods of terror and subjection.

We have passed in review a whole series of revolutions

[20] Gregoire: *History of France—Nineteenth Century,* Vol. III.
[21] Gregoire: *Ibid.,* Vol. IV, 226, 361 and others. Lissagarés: *History of the Paris Commune,* Passim.

and have seen that in the particulars specified they all repeat themselves. Two stages are prominent and indispensable in each of them. The extinction and the reinculcation of the reactions of subordination. The methods of the latter are always similar: " bloodshed and iron." It is a detail of little importance if the strait-jacket be put on by a Cavaignac or a Robespierre; by a Lenin or a " white general." One as well as the others do the same work, pressed thereto by necessity. Only the degree of their skilfulness may be different. From this technical point of view the white " bridlers " generally are more skilful and perform the restraining operation with the less bloodshed, cruelty and destruction. The deduction is clear: he who does not want such a strait-jacket must be very careful when he tries to " undermine authority." Before doing so he must think seriously: how deep the process of " extinction " will go? Whether it will not lead to anarchy and through the latter to the deadly " strait-jacket? "

CHAPTER IX

PERVERSION OF RELIGIOUS, MORAL, ESTHETIC AND OTHER ACQUIRED FORMS OF CONDUCT

THE greater part of these forms of conduct represent a complex of habits of a higher order. Some of them are grafted on unconditioned reactions, others on habits of a lower order, which are, in their turn, added to the first. Each group of hereditary reflexes, in each individual case, is overlaid by a growth of restrictive habits. For example the sexual reflexes are wrapped in a series of habits defining the conditions and forms in which they may be gratified. The complex of these habits is prescribed by those religious, moral, legal and esthetic rules, which regulate sexual conduct, marriage and family life in society. The same *mutatis mutandis* can be said of other primary impulses and of the habits wrapping them.

The whole complex of religious, moral and legal habits may thus be regarded as a development or expansion of the primary unconditioned reflexes, upon which they are founded.

They may also be regarded as the garb in which these latter are clothed. Clothing, however, may in many ways regulate or hinder the movements of the wearer; a machine determines the action of the steam; in the same way conditioned reflexes, having once become existent, necessarily exert more or less of an influence upon the unconditioned reflexes, in the sense of regulating and correcting them. In this sense they may be regarded as the regulators of these latter, or as factors correcting their manifestations.

This end is attained in two ways. In certain cases these regulating factors stimulate the individual to certain actions: "help thy neighbor," "love God," "pray," "honor thy parents," "be polite," "obey the authorities," "offer your seats to ladies," "dress for dinner," and so on. In other cases these same factors act as a check and hinder the completion of certain actions: "thou shalt not kill," "thou shalt not commit adultery," "thou shalt not steal," "thou shalt not lie," "thou shalt not be rude," etc.

The chief action of these factors consists in bringing such harmony into human conduct as will best enable each individual or group of individuals to subsist and attain the highest development under given conditions.

These general considerations make it clear in what sense these factors undergo a deformation in times of revolution, namely: those habits which formerly acted as a restraint and check upon the unconditioned ones, are liable in the first place to become extinct, whereas the unconditioned reflexes become inordinately stimulated by the struggle and violent impulses pertaining to revolutionary conditions.[1]

This means that revolution in its first stage inevitably leads to demoralization. The second stage of revolution in a community which has escaped final disintegration is distinguished by a revival of religion, morality, lawfulness and other discarded reflexes, which serve to regulate and rectify human action.

We have seen this to be the case while studying the different groups of reflexes pertaining to sexual relations, speech, property, labor, etc. In addition to what has already been said, we will now briefly expose the enormous range of action of this process.

[1] See Ellwood: *Op. cit.*, ch. VIII.

THE FIRST STAGE OF REVOLUTION

In the first place, there appears an obliteration of all the religious, moral and legal habits which acted as a barrier against acts of murder or of aggression against personal inviolability.

In legal terms we observe an enormous growth of criminality, and the law " thou shalt not kill " ceases to be observed. The path of revolution is sodden with blood and spread with the bodies of the dead; it is peopled with wrecked human lives. Human life has become a thing of no account; all of which is performed *ad majorem gloriam* of the revolutionary idea and clothed in the high-sounding terms of " Progress," " Humanity," " Fraternity," " Equality," " Freedom," " Communism," " Internationality," and similar expressions intended to palliate these wholesale crimes of revolution. There are, indeed, a certain number of persons who consider individual murder to be wrong, whereas they justify wholesale slaughter; the taking of life, unaccompanied by high-flown words, is to them a crime; but when cloaked in " lofty phraseology " it becomes a deed of heroism. These persons are apt to consider the wholesale hecatombs of revolution as something highly to be commended. We will not deprive them of this consolation because it is not our aim to preach morality. Suffice it to say that even they cannot turn the act of killing into anything else than murder. That is all we need to state here.[2]

---

[2] To the same class of " illusionists " may be added those criminal statisticians who, in recording the murders perpetrated during a certain revolutionary epoch, take into account only those occasional individual cases which happened to be officially registered. They pass in silence the slaughter of thousands and tens of thousands, performed by order or without the order of " red " and " white " authorities, under street barricades, on battlefields, in cases of wholesale massacre of prisoners of war or of those confined in prison cells. Surely this is a peculiar system of statistical reckoning.

From this realistic standpoint, which is at the same time one of true morality, free from any taint of hypocrisy—revolutionary epochs are most abundantly fertile in acts of murder and unspeakable cruelty, attended by the infliction of bodily and mental tortures. This is a fact so well established that no confirming figures or facts are needed.[3]

Two million Russians were killed during the years 1917–20 by their own countrymen. Such a " harvest of murders " has never happened before in the history of Russia. The same is to be said of other revolutionary epochs. The aggregate numbers of people killed, during revolutions in any country, show an extraordinarily sharply ascending curve of murder, much exceeding that of the most criminal non-revolutionary years. As regards the cruelty, brutality and sadistic lust attending these murders, revolutionary years have also richly earned the right to " first prize."

Extraordinary cruelty is manifested in the act of killing. Men are drunk with blood, and with the brutal lust of inflicting pain. The bodies of the killed are torn asunder, their limbs and heads are carried through the town on pikes and thrust before the eyes of those nearest to them (as illustrated in the execution of Montrose and the murder of De Launay and Foulon).

Such methods of murder as the crushing of the sexual organs in a vise; of slowly tearing the victim asunder by tying him to two trees bent together and allowed to spring back into their natural position; of burying alive; of skinning alive; of consecutively cutting off the limbs; of putting out the eyes, etc., had for a long time been unknown in the annals of Russian criminology. But they were com-

---

[3] See certain figures in the following sketch upon the influence of revolution upon the biological composition of the population.

monly practiced in the Russian Revolution by the " whites,"
principally by the " reds." [4] The barbarity and sadistic
cruelty of long-past ages came back to life with its
refined atrocities of torture. It would be necessary to
present a long and detailed description of these atrocities
in order to give any idea of them to anyone who had not
personally witnessed them from day to day.[5]

They killed for no reason whatever. Before the revolution it was utterly unheard of that any one should be
put to death because he had spoken against the Czar, or
confessed his religion, or written a proclamation, or
reported some irregularity to the authorities, or for having said a word of opposition to some minor official, or
for not having paid his taxes, or simply for nothing
at all, because somebody had reported against him. Any-

[4] A series of facts in M. Gorky's pamphlet: *On the Russian
Peasantry;* in Melgounoff's book: *The Red Terror,* 1923 (Russ.).

[5] The following may serve as an illustration: " I have summed up
the quantity of human flesh," says the Russian writer Schmeleff,
" of people murdered without trial, in the course of three months in
the Crimea alone, and estimate that it would have filled with fresh
human flesh, with young, strong flesh three hundred trains, or eight
thousand cars. One hundred and twenty thousand heads! I have
calculated the quantity of blood which had been spilled and it would
have been sufficient to start an albumin factory—for export into
Europe, if commerce with the communists is taken up. What an
invaluable asset to the history of ' socialism!' What a strange thing
it is that the communists, with all their ranting talk, have not succeeded
in making one little nail for common use, have never dried one
human tear, although their mouth is full of talk about humanity and
happiness. What an insatiable lust of blood! They live upon it like
lice. In truth, what a stupendous renovation! And the other nations
wait and watch curiously to see what will be the end of such portentous
events; they are very careful not to interrupt the course of this interesting experiment: the inoculating of 150,000,000 with the virus of
socialism. Two million human ' frogs ' have been subjected to vivi-
section, have had their breasts cut out, their heads beaten in and the
walls of the cellars where they were tortured smeared with their
brains. Is this not a most interesting experiment? Meanwhile the
onlookers in foreign countries are waiting for results and now and
again making little experiments of commerce—as required in the name
of ' humanity ' " (Schmeleff: *Solntze Mertvich, Okno,* Russ.).

thing remotely approaching this state of things was utterly impossible and unthinkable. Murder, or attempt at murder, of members of the Imperial family, or of high functionaries, was sometimes, but not always, punished by death for the principal culprits. All other crimes were punished with imprisonment or at the worst with hard labor. Minors were not subjected to capital punishment.[6]

During the last revolutionary years, these executions for no reason whatever have become a daily occurrence. Children and adults have been shot down wholesale, by tens and thousands.[7]

Average yearly number of executions was during the years:

1881-85	15.4
1886-90	18.0
1891-95	9.6
1896-1900	15.6
1901-05	18.6

In connection with the revolution of 1905–06 the number of executions reached a much higher figure, rapidly decreasing again as soon as order was again established.
Number of executions:

1906	547
1907	1139
1908	1340
1909	717
1910	129
1911	73
1912	126 [8]

During the years 1917–21 no less than one million persons were executed on both sides, without counting

---

[6] See *The Russian Criminal Code.*

[7] After the Cronstadt revolt of 1921 had been put down, 5000 sailors who had taken part in it were put to death. After the Bolshevists had taken Crimea, they put to death no less than 50,000 persons (according to other records—120,000) in the course of three months, under the leadership of the Hungarian commissary Bela-Khun.

[8] Cf. Gernett: *Capital Punishment,* 57-76 pp. (Russ.).

those who fell in battle in the course of civil war. The number of the victims of the "red terror" could be established only approximately. Professor Sarolea gives the following figures: 28 bishops, 1219 priests, 6000 professors and teachers, 9000 physicians, 54,000 officers, 260,000 soldiers, 70,000 policemen, 12,950 landowners, 355,000 intellegentzia, 193,290 workmen, 815,000 peasants. See *The Scotsman,* November, 1923, No. 7. Mr. Komnin (*Rul,* August 3, 1923) takes as an average for a year 1,500,000. These figures I find too exaggerated. But on the other hand, the number for 1917 to 1922 was no less than 600,000 human beings killed by Tcheka without any trial.

These figures need no commentary.

It was unheard of that hundreds of innocent people should be put to death for one guilty person, with whom they had nothing whatever to do. But this has now become a current practice. As punishment for attempting Lenin's life more than three thousand persons were shot in the prisons where they were confined all over Russia. " Collective retribution " and the taking of " hostages " has become part of the system. " We exterminate not the individuals but the bourgeoisie as a class. Don't look in our records for the evidences of the criminal actions or of the words of the accused persons. The fate of them is decided by the fact to what class they belong, what education they have got. This is the essence of the red terror." These words of Latzis, one of the heads of the red terror, clearly show the character of the " revolutionary justice." [9] The same mode of action, though in a lesser degree, was practiced by the " whites " in the territories occupied by them.

[9] See official Bolshevist paper *The Red Terror,* Nov. 1, 1918. See also *Weekly Journal of The Tcheka,* Kasan, No. 1.

We should never finish if we tried to enumerate even the principal victims of the storm of murder which is still raging over the limitless plains of Russia.[10] In the course of six years revolution has erected to itself a monument of human flesh—of two and a half million human beings, done to death; the victims of famine, epidemics, etc., not being taken into account. Is not this monument too grand? Is not the number of victims crushed by the triumphant chariot of "the Great Revolution" too large? Let the "troubadours" of revolution answer these questions.

The same facts are repeated in every revolution. It is only a question of greater or lesser numbers. "*La sainte guillotine,*" the rivers of France and her prison cells witnessed the death of thousands who were killed with less compunction than one would kill a kitten. The September massacres, 3000 guillotined in Paris and 17,000 in the French provinces in the course of two years, 2000 slaughtered at Lyons, 382 at Toulon, 120 at Marseilles, 332 in Orange, 1800 shot by Carrier in the stone-quarries, 300,000 dead in the Vendee, thousands and tens of thousands butchered by their countrymen all over France, the atrocities committed by the Chouans, by the Royalists and by the companions of Jehu—all these facts are well known, as well as the sadistic cruelty manifested in these butcheries.[11]

All revolutions take the same course : " Kill, in order to escape being killed." These words of Barras describe the peculiar characteristic of revolutionary epochs.

Countless murders and slaughters without end—such

---

[10] The following example speaks for itself. During the five years of 1901-05, ninety-five persons were subjected to capital punishment. Whereas in one month only (May, 1923) when the wholesale reign of terror was practically at an end, 2370 persons were put to death.

[11] Cf. Mortimer-Terneaux : *Histoire de la Terreur,* 1820. G. Le Bon : *La Revolution Française et la Psychologie des Revolutions,* Paris, 1912, 62-65, 208-11 pp.

is the summary of revolutionary events in Greece and Rome; in Egypt, China, Persia and Turkey; in the Middle Ages and in later times, up to the Russian and German Revolutions of 1917–24.

"Death thus raged in every shape; there was no length to which violence did not go; sons were killed by their fathers; and suppliants dragged from the altar or slain upon it; while some were even walled up in the Temple of Dionysus and died there. While some hanged themselves upon the trees and others destroyed themselves as they were severally able." [12] " Men are killed at their brother's side. How is this thing possible that man should kill his brother. Brother rises against brother, and fathers are at strife with their children as with their bitterest enemy." . . . " Men are being slaughtered everywhere. Death is rampant in the country. The crocodiles are glutted with food." [13] These descriptions of the Corcyraean Revolution by Thucydides and of the Egyptian Revolution by Ipouver present a true picture of all revolutions in this respect. During the Hussite Rebellion men were hunted down like game. Thousands were thrown into mine-pits. The soldiery of Sigismund and of Zizka, surnamed the " Angel of Death," swept like a hurricane over the country and exterminated all who did not join them.[14] Taine is perfectly right when he compares revolution to a crocodile, which devours first the rich and the fat, then the thin and the poor, and finally its own leaders—the arch murderers themselves.[15]

These facts show clearly how completely the restraining moral, legal and religious habits are wiped out of

---

[12] Thucydides: III, 81-85.
[13] Vikentieff: 285.
[14] Denis: *Op. cit.*, 233, 247-48, 259, 268-69.
[15] Taine: *Les Origines de la France contemp.*, Vol. III, Revolution, Preface.

human consciousness in times of revolution, and this applies not only to the makers of revolution, but to the entire community. *" Revolutions ne voulaient plus admettre dans la nation que deux classes: les bourreaux et les victimes,"* truly said anonymous author of the *Théorie des Revolutions.*[16] Revolution is not only a factor breeding crime, but it is in itself the very essence and element of bloody and brutal crime.

After what has been said it is superfluous to turn to criminal statistics, which only deal with a fortuitous portion of murders. Whether statistics show a growth or decline of their numbers does not alter the picture in the least.

At certain epochs, as during the civil wars in the United States and in France in 1830, 1848 and 1870, the frequency of crime diminished; but this apparent abatement is only due to the fact that the murderous impulses found ample satisfaction in the form of wholesale legally organized slaughter, as is very rightly pointed out by A. Corne.[17] He would be very foolish who, in times of war or revolution, wished to satisfy his lust for blood in an " illegal " manner. There were so many cleverer ways of doing so by " legal " means: he has only to become a commissary, or a " tchekist," or a soldier and he could " lawfully " and " by order " kill, rob and outrage his opponent. This was always practiced, and most abundantly so during the Russian Revolution.

The great majority of criminals entered the ranks of the tchekists and could thenceforth act under cover of the law. The assumption that individual tendency to crime is absorbed in legally sanctioned wholesale ones is proved to

---

[16] See *Théorie des Revolutions* par l'Auteur de l'Esprit de l'Histoire, Paris, 1817, Vol. IV, 45-6 pp.

[17] Cf. A. Corne: *Essai sur la Criminalite. Journal des Economistes,* 1868, Janvier.

be correct by the fact that after the close of a revolution, the business of "legal" slaughter having become an impossibility, the increased murderous tendencies immediately manifest themselves by a sharp rise in the number of "criminal" murders. This was the case in France in 1849–52, and later in 1871–73,[18] as well as in the United States.

We have made it clear that the above-named instances do not in the least refute our assumption. But these instances are very rare in history. In the great majority of revolutions and social crises, criminal statistics show a strongly increased number of murders, notwithstanding they left the wholesale slaughter of hundreds and tens of thousands out of their reckoning. For instance, in Moscow in 1918, there were committed eleven times more murders, and sixteen times more attempts at murder than in 1914—without counting political murders.[19] Add to these the innumerable gangs that murdered and plundered right and left, slaughtering whole villages and towns,[20] and you will gain some faint notion of the tremendous growth of crime, even within the limits of the cases recorded by criminal statistics.

Events took the same course, on a smaller scale, in the Hungarian Revolution of 1918–20 and even at the beginning of the German Revolution; but here they were promptly checked.

We observe the same in all revolutionary epochs: in Rome, in Egypt, in Italy in the thirteenth and fourteenth centuries, in France at the time of the Jacquerie and in the revolts of the fourteenth and fifteenth centuries; during the

[18] See Levasseur: *La Population Française*, Vol. II, 442-45. Corne: *Loc. cit.*
[19] Krasnaia Moskwa: Article upon criminality (Russ.).
[20] See a whole series of facts in the article of Kolosoff: in *The Past*, No. 21 (Russ.).

religious wars in Germany in the fifteenth and sixteenth centuries, during the anarchy of the seventeenth century in Russia, in the Hussite wars, in the English and Dutch Revolutions, in Italy in the nineteenth century, in France in 1788–1801, in India in the eighteenth century, etc. For details we refer to the sources mentioned below.[21]

Richard is right in saying: " Organized resistance against criminal propensities is exacted, either spontaneously or with conscious intent, by every normally existing community, that is, one whose condition is that of gradual and harmonious development. As soon, however, as a community comes to an acutely critical stage, it inevitably engenders criminality."

" Every crisis, by which the religious and political discipline of a people is shaken to its depths, gives rise to an identical criminal process in the social plane; that is to say, a process of general and murderous criminality, which gradually abates in proportion as the social crisis relaxes." [22]

There may probably be people who will vindicate these facts by the argument that only " aristocrats," " rich people " and " bourgeois " are killed, but not the common working people. This, however, is an utterly erroneous supposition. Two-thirds of the "clients" of Fouquier and Samson were artisans, small shopkeepers and employees.[23]

---

[21] Cf. Mommsen: Vol. II, 138-9, 150, 160, 229, 334-6; Vol. III, 68, etc. The tremendous growth of piracy, banditism, murders and robbery. Vikentieff: *Loc. cit.* Weber: *Loc. cit.,* Vol. VIII, 25-27, 29, 242, 271, 302, 317, etc. Levasseur: *Histoire des Classes Ouvr.,* Vol. I, 503, 522-7; Vol. II, 55, etc. Motley: *Loc. cit.,* 67, 164-5. Karamzine: Vols. XI, XII. Guizot: Vol. I, XXII, 190. Denis: *Op. cit.,* 189, 233, 247, 259, 268. Richard: *Les Crises Sociales et les Conditions de la Criminalite. L'annee Sociologique,* 1899. Sorokin: *Crime and Punishment, Heroism and Reward* (Russ.), ch. X, 1914.
[22] Richard: *Op. cit.,* 17, 30.
[23] Madelin: Vol. II, 155. Taine's investigations prove that 7545 out of 12,000 persons executed were workmen, artisans and common citizens. L. Blanc writes that only 650 out of 2755 persons who died by the guillotine belonged to the better classes.

Who but peasants perished in the Vendee? Of the two millions slaughtered in the course of the Russian Revolution, only a very small number belonged to the "aristocracy " and the "bourgeoisie." The great majority were peasants, manual and intellectual workmen.[24] How large was the number of "aristocrats " who were killed in 1830, 1848 and 1871? The above argument is utterly devoid of foundation. It is true that, in its first stage, revolution devours the "fat," but very soon it turns upon the "thin" and destroys them in innumerable quantities.

The gradual extinction of the moral, legal and religious reflexes which repress the instincts of murder is followed by the extinction of the corresponding "subvocal" reflexes: meaning the religious and moral consciousness of the sinfulness, iniquity and inadmissibility of murder.

With the fading of the sense of wrongdoing, the corresponding rules and standards are distorted or disappear, and are replaced by their opposites. It is a state of consciousness in which murder becomes a meritorious action, instead of an iniquity and a crime. The following statements of the Bolshevist newspaper showed this frame of mind "We ought to kill by hundreds. Let us murder by thousands. Let our enemies choke themselves with their own blood. Kill as many as can." [25] " Let us show a bloody lesson to bourgeoisie. For one of our heads they have to pay by thousands of their heads." [26]

This perversion of the moral consciousness is glorified in all revolutionary songs like the "Carmagnole," "Ça ira," the "Marseillaise," both French and Russian, the "Internationale," and many others. They are nothing but one continuous call to slaughter:

---

[24] See Melgounoff: *The Red Terror* (1923).
[25] Krasnaia Gazeta: Aug. 31, 1918.
[26] Ib. Septem: 1, 1918.

" Kill the priests, kill those dogs, kill the wealthy,
Kill that wretched vampire—the Czar;
Kill, destroy them, the scoundrels confounded,
And watch for the new life's dawn."

This is a sample of the revolutionary " morality of slaughter." Every antagonist becomes *le sang impur.* The spilling of his blood, far from being a crime, is an action of the most excellent merit.

New creeds arise, such as that of " the Angel of Destruction," of " The sacred executions of the Tche-ka," the cult of " *La sainte guillotine.*" Instead of inspiring aversion, murder affords delight. Here are a few samples :

" Christ, destroy these heretics, these subverters of morality ; do not suffer these wolves, these mad dogs to devour Thy lambs "—such is one of the prayers of the Hussite wars (Denis, 201).

After the butchery of August 10, 1789, one of the participants, an " honest artisan," exclaimed : " Providence has been kind to me today : it helped me to kill three Swiss." After the murder of De Launay and of the invalids " women and children danced round the corpses and gave vent to clamors of regret that the heads did not number a thousand " (Madelin : Vol. I, 109-10, 316, etc.).

The words written by the Jacobin Hochard to his friend after the slaughter of 209 victims, are typical in this respect : " What delight you would have felt, if you had witnessed the death of the 209 scoundrels sentenced by national justice. What a sight worthy of " Freedom ! *Ça ira.*" " Let us go to the foot of the great altar " (the guillotine), cries Amar at the Convention, " and let us watch the celebration of the Red Mass." " The essence of republicanism," says St. Just, " consists in the destruction of everything which is antagonistic to the Republic.

Those who rely upon the aristocracy are guilty; those who do not love virtue are guilty; those opposed to terror are also guilty." Marat clamored daily for " murder, murder, murder, in the name of morality." Couthon, while urging the convention to greater severity, brings forward the following argument: " Every hesitation is a crime, every formality is a public danger; the time necessary to destroy an enemy should be no longer than the time needed to detect him." There are to be no witnesses and no defense; nothing but death—sentences admitting of no exception.

Later, after Termidor, the Royalists demanded the same course of action. Entraygnes aspires to become a " Marat of royalism " and claims the heads of 400,000 patriots.

Such is the state of moral consciousness at times of revolution. Such are specimens of the morality dictated by anthropoids in human shape who have lost all the restraining ethical reflexes.

We heard the same during six years from the Bolshevists. The disgusting murders in the " Tche-ka " are praised by them as a great virtue; the most efficient murderers are rewarded with decorations and riches. Dzerdzinsky has been called a saint! [27]

It could not be otherwise with people whose moral, legal and religious habits have become extinct. When they regain possession of them they will be like the French terrorists who " a year after the end of the terror could

---

[27] See the foundations of that morality of absolute cynicism in Trotzki's book, *Terrorism and Communism;* in the work of one of the principal Tche-ka'ists, Latzis: *Two Years on the Inner Front;* and especially in Trotzki's speech of June 18, 1923, addressed to the young revolutionaries, when he said: " A revolutionary should find no moral obstacles in applying unrestricted and pitiless violence. Therefore atheism, materialism and amoralism should constitute the fundamental principles of his conception " (cf. *Pravda:* June 24, 1923).

not understand how they could have done it." [28] " People have gone mad," briefly says Barrère.

At times of revolution everything is dear except human life. Its price goes down to zero and it is destroyed without trial, without evidence, without defense. There is no bread, but there is plenty of human flesh to which a " free and happy " people is sometimes treated by the " Sacred Revolution."

The moral, legal and religious habits that restrain from murder are not the only ones that get stilled during revolutionary epochs. Sometimes even stronger reflexes, those restraining from cannibalism, are extinguished at such times. Since the fifteenth century Russia experienced many most serious famines; but it is only during one or two of them that anthropophagy became widespread: these were the famines of 1601–03 and of 1921–22, and these were both revolutionary periods. Ever since the fifteenth century [29] hunger alone has never been a factor strong enough to stifle the reflexes preventing *homo sapiens* from devouring his fellow-citizen. But at times when demoralization and bestiality engendered by revolution were coming to reinforce the motive of hunger, the restraining habits found themselves weakened and men began to devour each other.

" Fathers and mothers (during the anarchy of the seventeenth century) devoured their children, children ate their parents, hosts their guests; human flesh was sold on the markets, travellers were afraid to stop at inns "—such is a picture of the time in the description of a contemporary, A. Palitzyn.[30]

---

[28] Madelin: Vol. II, 92.

[29] Earlier than the fourteenth and fifteenth centuries anthropophagy was a rather common occurrence in Russia as well as in Western Europe; since that time the reflexes restraining from anthropophagy became sufficiently strong to make it a rare phenomenon during famine periods.

[30] Karamzine: *Op. cit.,* Vol. XII.

The same thing happened in 1921–22, perhaps on a greater scale. Anthropophagy took enormous proportions. Not individuals, nor scores, but hundreds and even thousands of people were eaten. Human flesh was also sold and murders for cannibalistic purposes were frequent.[31] Let us repeat it, Russia starved many times, and very badly, since the fifteenth century, but then there was no anthropophagy, or it was very rare. According to the " differentiative " method the increase of cannibalism during these revolutions has to be credited, apart from hunger, to the " Emancipating Revolution." This is confirmed by facts of sadistic devouring of the flesh and blood of people killed during a revolution that have been recorded in Europe. Such facts, according to several sources, took place during the French Revolution; e.g., compulsory drinking " the health of the nation " in blood of the killed; the challenge to taste some of Madame de Lamballe's heart in order " to prove true patriotism with one's own teeth; " Lequigny's desire to taste blood, etc.[32] During the Dutch Revolution, a surgeon in Veer cut out the heart of a prisoner, nailed it to the prow of a ship and invited the citizens to bite into it, which " many did with savage delight." [33] It is probably such facts as these that Plato had in view when he said that during revolutions the antagonists not only want to seize another's property, but want to bite and to eat each other . . . Such facts, however exceptional and rare, point to the tendency towards *moral insanity* that is engendered by revolution. Luckily at the present time these reflexes are steady and

---

[31] See, for instance, the statement of Bolshevist newspapers: *Krasnaia Gazeta*, Dec. 31, 1921; *Pravda*, January 5, February 10, March 26, May 22, 1922; *Isvestia*, January 29, 1922, etc. Photographs of cannibals were reproduced in many publications, *e.g.*, in the book *On Famine*, published by K. N. Georgievsky, Kharkov, 1922.

[32] Cabanes: *Loc. cit.*, 31, 46, 47.   Madelin: II, 82-92.

[33] Motley: II, 343-.44.

disappear only during rare revolutions accompanied by great starvation and among a minority of the population.

Anyway, such rare facts prove the following: if a revolution, however seldom, succeeds in extinguishing even the anti-cannibalistical reactions, that are the most inveterate ones, what is there to be said of other restraining habits, of a religious or moral character, that prevent from inflicting injury to another man's health; from physical violence, beating, wounding and flogging; from causing physical pain, from rape and other crimes against human personality. The tremendous increase of such acts of violence against human personality, as we have enumerated, is easily understood.

Such acts as beating people with rifle-butts or sticks, flogging, and all sorts of bodily punishment are extensively used among a revolutionary population; they become a custom, even a rule. Physical violence becomes the best "educational" method.

Along with such physical punishments as these, there are other ones in use, more elaborate ones. Torture by starvation that leads to equally destructive results is a good instance. Also the introduction of the "class-ration" of the Russian Revolution when people belonging to the "third category" were doomed to death by starvation, and when, to quote Zinovieff's words, a diminutive ration of bread ($^1/_8$, $^1/_{16}$, $^1/_{32}$ of a pound) was issued to them only in order "not to let them forget the smell of bread;" intentional torture by hunger in prisons, concentration camps, etc.; all these methods were extensively used during the last years. The same may be said of the use of *cold, filth, scant clothing, dampness, darkness, exhausting labor, privation of fresh air and so on, that were intentionally inflicted by one side upon the other.* A man after staying in such a camp for a few months either

died or came out a " shadow," an invalid for life. To this
may be added real mediæval tortures : the " cork room "
of the " Tche-ka " where prisoners were slowly suffocated
to death; the insertion of pins under finger-nails, cutting
up with a knife, roasting on fire, beating up through a
wet sheet, so as to leave no marks on the body; menace of
being shot, compulsory presence at executions, the rape
of women, etc.[34] This chapter could not be brought to
an end if I had attempted to describe even the principal facts pertaining to the extension of crimes against
personal inviolability of man during the Russian and
other revolutions. I may simply say that their crop
was enormous.

The same relates to crimes against *personal freedom*.
The religious, moral reflexes restraining attempts at the
freedom of the neighbor are still more easily extinguished.
This is best to be seen from plain figures showing the
number of people arrested and deprived of liberty during
the revolution. The prisons are not merely overcrowded,
but are of insufficient capacity. Convents, palaces,
schools, churches are turned into prisons; special concentration camps are arranged.[35] During these years the
percentage of people in Russia who were not arrested at
least once is not great. At any rate it is several scores of
times *less* than it was before. We see the same in other

---

[34] Cf. Melgounoff : *The Red Terror. The Tche-ka,* published by the
" Social Revolutionary Party." *The Kremlin Behind a Grating.* Also
photographs and special disclosures on the *Tche-ka* published by the
" whites " after recapture of Kharkoff, Kiev and other cities. Also
publications by the " reds " upon the work of intelligence departments
of the " whites " after the seizure of " white cities."
[35] *E.g.,* in February, 1923, the number of political prisoners in
the Moscow prisons alone was 15,290. Of these 60 per cent. were
workmen and peasants; 40 per cent. " intellegentzia." In the preceding
years the number of prisoners was still greater (*Dni,* No. 194).
In France, before the ninth of Termidor, there were 400,000 prisoners
in confinement (Taine : Vol. III, 283).

revolutions. All *habeas corpus* guarantees of personal freedom and inviolability are forgotten. People are arrested not only on the faintest suspicion, but without any reason at all. No formalities are necessary for the authorities to prove the culpability of the prisoner; it remains for the latter to prove his own innocence, which, as it is well known, is a very hard thing to do.

People are arrested in their houses, enormous beats are organized in the streets, markets, moving pictures, theatres, churches and schools, where hundreds and thousands of " free citizens " are taken in. The normal procedure of the authorities consists in wholesale arrests, and their principle seems to be that it is better to keep a thousand innocent people in prison for a month than to let one single offender escape. The reader should not think that I am exaggerating, this statement strictly corresponds to the facts. Apart from the first moments after a revolution, all the revolutionary society can consider itself as being under arrest, for it suddenly gets under the action of " extraordinary," " martial " and " siege " laws. " Revolutionary tribunals " take the place of the usual courts; they are free from any legal formalities and act quite arbitrarily, according to a " revolutionary conscience," that is to say, an absolute absence of conscience.

While proclaiming freedom, revolution is actually busy at destroying it.

The same applies to the right of the individual to enjoy freedom of speech, of thought, of religious belief, of press, of meetings. People, brutalized by revolution, do not hesitate to get beyond all boundaries and lose all respect for such rights. During the first phase of revolution it is the revolutionaries who silence their opponents; during the second stage, the victorious elements do the same. Society, as a whole, becomes degraded in that respect. The nine-tenths of the public are compelled to silence. Any open criticism, even a suspicion of disagreement, is relentlessly punished. " Suspicion towards any opinion—overheard conversation—noticed tears—recorded sighs—spied silence—police at the family's hearth—spies and sneaking everywhere," [36] such is the picture of a revolution.

"Freedom must be established by violence, and despotism of freedom must be established in order to destroy the despotism of kings," once said Marat. Alas, freedom and despotism of freedom are irreconcilable; therefore revolutions never established freedom, but only arbitrary despotism.

Mutatis mutandis, everything stated above may be repeated in respect to *man's property rights.* The habits restraining from attempts against other people's property also get smothered. We have already seen this when describing the deformation of property reactions. In other words, *revolution leads to a tremendous growth of burglary, robbery, theft, swindle, graft, forgery, deceit* and other crimes against property.[37]

During the French Jacquerie (also in England, Bohemia and Germany), a tremendous banditry prevailed.

---

[36] Le Bon: *Psychologie du Socialisme,* 539 (Russ. ed.).

[37] Here are some illustrations. During the Egyptian Revolution: highway robbery, house burglary, thefts on roofs of houses, etc. (cf. Vikentieff: *Loc. cit.*). During the Corcyraean Revolution—debtors murdered their creditors. " The majority of people prefer being called clever swindlers than honest simpletons; the latter name inspires shame, the former gives pleasure. Thus, owing to anarchy, there appears a complete distortion of morals " (Thucydides: III, 81-85). In Rome, " wealthy people and paupers joined in an equal dishonesty, demoralization, and in equal propensity to ignore property rights." Prevailing piracy, extensive robbery, unheard-of speculation, forgery and swindling, general graft assumed immense proportion. (Cf. Mommsen: I, 37-38, 158, 211, 253, 316, 317, 343, 349; II, 99; III, 15, 29, 68, 79, 461, 464, 563, sequ.).

" Gangs of robbers gathered into enormous detachments. They robbed, destroyed, burned down the villages and cities that did not buy them off by paying a contribution." " *Oh, le miserable temps pour n'oser sortir des villes!* " exclaims a contemporary. " *Cedes, rapine et incendia,*" says another.[38]

During the English Revolution in the seventeenth century, " while the revolution proceeded the respect for rights declined. Mendacity, violence and cupidity rapidly increased among the people. On the highways round the cities there appeared a growing number of thieves and robbers; they walked in bands and admixed political designs to their own iniquities." The cavaliers robbed; so did their political opponents, the members of parliament, who also robbed, took bribes and displayed rapacity (Guizot, Vol. I, 12, 13, 17; Vol. III, 22-23, etc.).

The tremendous growth of robbery and other crimes against property during the French Revolution is well known. Some figures relating to their increase during the revolution in Russia have been quoted above. Suffice it to say that Russia has hardly ever experienced such a growth of theft, swindling, forgery, bribery and other such crimes. " We find bribery at every step," says Lenin authoritatively. This evil attained such proportions that a special commission under Dzerdzinsky was appointed in 1921-23 to fight it; many people were shot, but to no

---

[38] (Cf. Weber: Vol. VIII, 27-29. Levasseur: *Histoire,* Vol. I, 522, sequ., II, 55.) During the Peasant Revolt in England, serfs and peasants . . . " destroyed and robbed houses, plundered the estates of the gentry, demolished fences, burned property titles " . . . In London, " houses and palaces of lords were plundered and destroyed," etc. (cf. Weber: Vol. VIII, 44-45). In Bohemia, "the Hussite wars were a long series of sieges, murders and robbery " (Denis: 287, 340). At the time of the Italian Revolution in the thirteenth century " morals declined, robberies and tumult were an everyday occurrence, gangs of bandits travelled over the Roman province, wandered in the streets of Rome and rioted without restraint " (Weber: 317, sequ.).

avail. The corruption became general. Whether we call such actions criminal or not, does not matter; what matters is their enormous growth in number.[39]

Revolution usually leads to the development of great cupidity and rapacity. Bribery and corruption blossom as never before. There is a deluge of the basest, most selfish actions. All this we see in the Russian Revolution. " The number of crimes, theft and robbery increased, they are growing to tremendous proportions," says a communistic newspaper.[40] Infantile criminality, as compared to pre-revolutionary days, augmented in Petrograd 7.4 times.[41] Similar pictures we see in the whole of Russia.

Truly enough some naive people, carried away by the flow of fine revolutionary parlance, mistake words for reality. But it has been said long ago, it is not words that matter, but acts. The deeds of the actors and understudies of the revolutionary dramatic stage are in direct opposition to their words.

We have already seen how the same process of smothering of religious and rightful habits develops in the domain of sexual behavior (cf. chapter on sexual reflexes). Here also the crimes against public propriety, to use the legal term, grow enormously.

The same takes place in the realm of social service and in the performance of social duties. Beginning from the peasants who stop paying taxes, to the workmen who stop working honestly, and finishing by the judges, the

[39] Cf. Pravda: Oct. 22, 1921. *Krasnaia Gazeta*: April 15 and 16, 1921.
[40] Cf. Makhovic: July 27, 1921; *Isvestia*, February 12, 1922.
[41] Cf. Aronovitsch: Infantile Criminality, in *Psychiatry and Neurology*, No. 1, 1922 (Russ.).

officials and the policemen—everyone begins to neglect his social duties.[42]

Official efficiency is displayed only where obedience to bestial reflexes is concerned—in acts of slaughter or of battle. But this is easy to understand: good robbers always proved to be courageous fighters, plucky burglars and desperately defended their lives.

"Interests of the society," "common welfare," such

[42] Here are some instances: In Rome, "the majority of the citizens were good for nothing"—"Discipline among the soldiers was slack,"—"no justice could be obtained against influential persons" —"many senators were worthless"—"officials betrayed the state for bribes, . . . citizens betrayed liberty"—"forgery of documents and perjury were widely spread. Honor was forgotten: a man who refused a bribe was not considered as an honest man but as a personal enemy . . . Jurors neglected their duties and got intoxicated." "Officers' commissions and jurors' balls were bought for money." "Authorities were rotten to the marrow, speculated excessively" . . . etc. In one word "every honest Roman should have blushed when looking at the terribly fast decay of his nation" (cf. Mommsen: Vol. II, 72-73, 195, 211; Vol. III, 76, 79, 461).

In England, "abuses and illegal deals were growing in number and parliament, the absolute ruler of the state's wealth and destiny, soon became known as the abode of unrighteousness and corruption." Cromwell when talking to Whitelocke characterized parliament in still stronger words (cf. Guizot: Vol. III, 31, 22-23).

The corruption of such officials as Mirabeau, Danton, Tallien, as well as of minor revolutionary officials, especially during the Convention and the Directory, are well known. "There is no administrative office where immorality and corruption have not found their way," says the official report of an investigating commission (cf. Madelin: Vol. II, 314).

As to the officials of the Soviet government, the less said the better. There is no government with such an enormous quantity of corruption, of thieves, unprincipled scoundrels who spill blood in order to obtain wealth and who disguise their crimes by proclaiming high ideals; such is the Soviet government beginning with the "leaders of the world-revolution," such as Zinovieff, Radek, Krassin and Trotzki, and up to the last agent of the "Tche-ka." For instance: the bribery of officials was so extensive, that beginning November 1, 1922 and until May 1, 1923, the Central Commission for the prevention of bribery conducted 4800 cases of prosecution that finished by giving sixty-one death sentences, six hundred and twenty-nine sentences of imprisonment for from five to ten years, while the remainder were condemned to prison for periods ranging from six months to three years (cf. Dni, No. 175).

words are on all lips during a revolution. And at such times people are less than ever inclined to do their duty for that common welfare. We have seen that already when studying the work (labor) reflexes. We see it confirmed by the bribery, cupidity, laziness and dishonesty of officials during revolutionary periods.

Just the same should be said concerning the remaining moral and religious habits. Even such of them as seem very deeply-rooted, as family affection, aversion to harming one's own husband, father or children—even such habits disappear. A revolution cuts short even such ties of family-altruism and solidarity.[43]

Actually, to whatever sphere of morally-rightful conduct we may turn, we arrive at the same conclusion:

---

[43] Here are a few instances: "Brother rises against brother, a father looks upon his own child as an enemy," says Ipouver, speaking of the Egyptian Revolution.

"Faith was not sealed by Divine law, but by a common crime "— " Father killed son, blood relationship became a weaker tie than party-comradeship," says Thucydides, describing the Revolution of Kerkir. The same relates to the Roman Revolutions. Scipio, when informed of the death of his relative Gracchus, said: " let everyone who commits such deeds perish in the same way." His mother held the same view. Scipio, in turn, was murdered by followers of Gracchus. The same applies to the murder of Cicero by Augustus and so on.

During the revolution in Holland "people were often seen who calmly assisted in the hanging of their own brothers."

In Russia in the seventeenth century "people became worse than beasts: they abandoned their wives and families in order not to divide a piece of bread with them. Mothers strangled their children."

In the French Revolution we find a good instance in the relations between the Bourbons and Philippe-Egalité. A general picture is given in a play, very popular at the time, "A Republican Husband," where the husband denounces his wife to the revolutionary court and succeeds in getting her executed. Everywhere here, just as during the Russian Revolution, different members of one family frequently found themselves fighting behind opposed barricades and killed each other (cf. Vikentieff: 285. Thucydides: III, 81-85. Mommsen: Vol. II, 97, sequ. Motley: Vol. II, 343-44. Karamzine: Vol. XI, 67. Cabanes: 290-91).

demoralization and smothering of all moral and rightful restraining habits.[44]

Naturally, such demoralization of conduct is accompanied by that deterioration of moral and legal consciousness among the masses which we have termed as a "modification of subvocal reflexes."

As we have seen, the old moral consciousness gets dulled and readily disappears. A "revaluation of moral standards" takes place and results in pure nihilism, leads to the assumption that "everything is permitted" or to a further development into totally reversed moral standards as represented by a "glorification" of animal instincts. The situation is clearly and vividly described by Thucydides: "Words had to change their meanings and to take that which was now given them. Reckless audacity came to be considered courage; prudent hesitation, specious cowardice, moderation was held to be a cloak for unmanliness. Frantic violence became the attribute of manliness; cautious plotting, a justifiable means of self-defense. The advocate of extreme measures was always trustworthy; his opponent a man to be suspected. To succeed in a plot was to have a shrewd head, to divine a plot a still shrewder. In fine, to forestall an intending criminal, or to suggest the idea of a crime, was equally commended. Revenge was held of more account than self-preservation—men are readier to call rogues clever than simpletons honest, and are as ashamed

<hr>

[44] Guizot's words concerning the moral influence of the English Revolution may be applied to any other one: "In this general and universal disorder, amid abuse of force and amid extremes, every bad feeling had chances of success. Strong people developed hatred and vindictiveness; weak people indulged in cowardice and poltroonery . . . Mendacity, violence, cupidity, meanness of every kind rapidly grew among the people who took a part in the struggle." The rest of the masses "lost any idea of right, of duty, justice and morality, or kept it in a very confused form" (Guizot: Vols. I, XII, XIII).

of being the second as they are proud of being the first. Thus every form of iniquity took root. The ancient simplicity into which honour so largely entered was laughed down and disappeared; and society became divided into camps in which no man trusted his fellow."[45]

This picture is true and clearly represents the character of the deformation undergone by moral and righteous consciousness during a revolution. Whether it works for the better or for the worse is a question of personal taste. The task of the investigator is only to establish its indubitable and unquestionable presence.

Exactly the same is to be found in the domain of strictly religious reflexes. Being similar to the moral ones, inasmuch as they restrain from socially wrong actions and stimulate the good ones,[46] such habits are also extinguished, and for the same reasons, during the first period of a revolution. Their extinguishing begins even earlier and serves as a symptom of coming upheavals.

It is to be noticed in the decline of the authority of religion, in persecution of the latter, in the growth of atheism and of religious indifference. The number of church-going people, believing in dogmas and following the rites declines; the number of people freed from the " religious opium " increases.

Parallel to this process another one develops: new habits are substituted for the extinguished ones and these new ones do not restrain from, but sanction the acts of murder, plunder, brutality, etc., towards which

---

[45] Thucydides : III, 81-85.

[46] For that influence of religion see Durkheim : *Les Formes élémentaires de la vie Religieuse*. Ellwood : *The Reconstruction of Religion*. F. de Coulanges : *La Cité Antique*. Also the chapters on religion in : E. Hayes : *Introduction to the Study of Sociology*. E. Ross : *Social Control*. Sorokin : *Sociological Conception of Religion*. Zaveti : 1915.

the rioting biological impulses are pushing the crowd. Such is the essence of the deformation of religious reflexes during the first stage of a revolution.

The contemporaries of the Egyptian Revolution state this clearly: " The designs of the Gods are trampled upon." . . . " people boast openly of their unbelief." " They stopped burning incense and offering sacrifices of fattened oxen; sanctuaries are plundered, corpses are thrown out of their graves, in a word it is a complete crisis of religion." [47]   In the Corcyraean Revolution " religion was in honour with neither party " (Thucydides, b. III, 225 p.).

We find the same in Rome. " The political and social revolutions were bound to destroy the existing religious order. The ancient Italian popular beliefs are disappearing. Over, the ruins of the ancient faith there appear disbelief, state religion, Hellenism, superstition, schisms and the oriental creed with its mysticism." [48]

The peasant revolt in England was preceded and accompanied by a religious revolution started by Wycliffe, the Lollards and John Ball. The same occurred before and during the English Revolution in the seventeenth century.

The Hussite Revolution had the same character. It was preceded and accompanied by a decline in the authority of the Catholic Church, by the growth of Hussism and its fall into extremes and its separation in Utraquists, Taborists and other radical sects. [49]

We also find analogical facts before and during the German Jacquerie (Reformation period) and during the

[47] Cf. Vikentieff: 298-99. Turaeff: 70-71.
[48] Mommsen: Vol. I, 860-65; Vol. II, 419; Vol. III, chapter upon religion. Rostovtzev: *The Birth of the Roman Empire*, 111-13.
[49] Cf. Ch. Lea: *History of Inquisition*, Vols. I and II. Also Palacky and Denis: *Op. cit.*

series of civil disturbances and wars in France in the fifteenth and sixteenth centuries (the period of religious wars). The disappearance of religious habits that preceded and accompanied the French Revolution is well known; suffice it to mention the persecution of the clergy, the attempts to establish the " Cult of Reason," etc.[50]

The same happened in France in 1848 and 1870–71. Also during the Russian Revolutions of 1905 and 1917–24.[51]

In Russia before the revolution the Greek-Orthodox Church was already discredited in the eyes of many people. Nine-tenths of the intellectuals were open or secret atheists; to be religious was considered the same as being superstitious and backward.

This setting loose of religious restraining habits developed rapidly after the revolution; from that time it gained the peasant and working classes and atheism was making enormous progress. After the Bolshevist Revolution of 1917 began an open persecution of religion and its servants, an intensive propaganda of atheism and of a " communistic religion." During 1917 and 1918 this movement was very successful and contaminated many people. Religious habits and faith were rapidly disintegrating, while the persecution of the church by the government went on and increased. This persecution acquired a most cruel form in 1922 and 1923. But as early as 1920 a reaction set forth in the popular masses, this being a symptom of a beginning of a revival of religious habits. We will come back to that question further on.

We thus see that the religious reactions are subject to

---

[50] For details cf. Cabanes: Ch. " God and Revolution."

[51] We might also point out analogical facts in the Persian Revolution in the reign of Kobad, during the series of Turkish revolutions, and the many Islamic revolutions beginning by the one of Mohammed.

distortion in the same way as the moral and righteous ones. Since we know that the fundamental rôle of both consists in constructing, widening and reinforcing of solidarity ties between the members of society, we should not wonder when we see them disintegrate during revolutionary periods, these actually representing a rupture of social-solidarity ties and relations. It would be a miracle if such a disintegration did not take place.

We have now examined various groups of legal, moral and religious habits and we saw that they all are subject to deformation in one and the same direction—that is, in the direction of weakening and extinguishing of those of their number that tend to restrain biological impulses. Their extinction means a return to savagery, "biologization" and "primitivization" of man. To be sure there are new habits being grafted to the place of the old ones; but these are not the restraining ones and but sanction and encourage biological impulses. Therefore they do not prevent the "biologization" but rather intensify it. They are but "fine gloves" that do not prevent a hand from accomplishing murder; on the contrary, they incite to murder by disguising blood and filth under sacred words and slogans.

THE SECOND PERIOD OF A REVOLUTION

If society, after having become the playground of biological impulses, happens not to be utterly destroyed by anarchy, there generally comes, sooner or later, the second period of revolution that marks the dawn of renaissance of the extinguished legal, moral and religious reactions together with a corresponding moral, religious and righteous consciousness. Sometimes these return in a concrete form, and closely resemble the old ones; some-

times in outwardly different forms. But in both cases
they are similar to the old ones in their principal and fundamental part, that is, in their restraining action and their
general functions.

When comparing the older concrete form of the
restraining habit, " Do not kill, for God commanded not
to," and its present form " Do not kill, for such is the
demand of progress and humanity," we see that for all
the difference in the latter part of both commandments,
their fundamental part is one and the same. *Mutatis
mutandis,* this is applicable to all other cases.

There begins a trying period of speedy reëducation of
the dulled legal, moral and religious reflexes. In order to
do it quickly, the strongest stimulants must be devised
and applied. We actually see them at work. The brutalized revolutionary society is compelled to go in two, five
or ten years' time through a course of moral, religious and
legal education for the initial acquirement of which
humanity had to spend scores and hundreds of years . .

Murder is being punished by merciless murder. Theft,
robbery and burglary bring about the same punishment
. . . Sexual reflexes are gradually brought back to
normal. A modest, but still a greater freedom of speech,
of press, etc., is granted . . . Some few guarantees
from arbitrary despotism of the authorities are also introduced. At the same time a teaching and propaganda of
morality and righteousness is commenced. There begins
a rapid revival of religion, a return to the old forms of
decency, conventional manners and morals. In one word,
society begins to dress rapidly in the garment of the extinguished moral, legal and religious habits. The biological
nakedness diminishes. Life is gradually normalized,
which in its turn aids in the rebirth and strengthening of
moral, legal and religious reactions. Their gradual

strengthening makes the application of cruel stimulants and repressions less necessary.[52]   Naturally this process does not go on without interruptions, very complicated ways and a great number of victims, but its essence is such as it was painted above.

Whether that reëducation is commenced by the revolutionary or counter-revolutionary authorities is only a detail, a fortuitous occurrence of no importance to the generalization.   It would be a lengthy task to describe all the details of that process.   The reader is referred for them to the literature concerning the final periods of different revolutions and those closely following them.   Such periods are to be found at the time of Cæsar, of Augustus and of his successors in Rome; at the epoch of liquidation of the Jacqueries in France, Germany and England; the period of the " Compacts of Prague " and the years following the Hussite Revolution, Cromwell's Protectorate and the Restoration of the Stuarts in England; the times of Mikhail Fedorovitch and Alexei Mikhailovitch in Russia; the Directoire and Napoleonic era in France; the period of Cavaignac and the first years of the presidency and reign of Napoleon III; Thiers' time and the first

---

[52] An incomplete, but vivid, picture of this process may be seen in the number of executions that grows during the first years after a revolution, or the first years of reëducation of dulled restraining reflexes, and gradually falls while they are grafted on, and while social life is getting more normal.   In France this has been noticed by Prof. Garçon.   Thus, Napoleon's Consulate began with 605 executions (1803, the beginning of a serious "application of brakes "); about 1813 their number falls to 325.   The Restoration—another serious step towards " braking "—starts with 514 death sentences in 1816; later, their number decreases to 91.   In 1831 their number again reaches 108 and falls back to 65 in 1847.   After the suppression of the rising of 1848 hundreds of people were shot; in 1870 this number decreased to 11 death sentences.   The figures of death sentences in Russia before and after the revolution of 1905-6 which were given above are also illustrative (Cf. Gernet: *Op. cit.,* 75-76, Sorokin: *Crime and Punishment,* 428-29).

years after 1871; also the period of Witte and Stolypin after the revolution of 1905 and the revolutionary period of 1921–24 in Russia.[53]

While studying these historic materials the reader will find a full confirmation of all the features that have been described here, and that was indicated in the form of a generalization in the introductory chapters as to the characteristics of that second period. Notwithstanding all the practical differences of actors and scenes of such a period, the play performed is the same one. It could be entitled "The Revival and Reëducation of the Extinguished Habits of Righteousness and Religion" by "blood and iron."

Such is the ever-revolving circle of history.

---

[53] There are many symptoms in the Russia of 1922, tending to show that the population has reached the phase in question.

CHAPTER X

THE PSYCHOLOGY OF REVOLUTIONARY SOCIETY

In the foregoing chapters we have seen that the perversion of conduct provoked by the first stage of revolution renders society more primitive and brings men nearer to the conduct of animals. For one acquainted with psychology and the science of behavior these suffice to explain the direction in which the psychology of revolutionary society alters itself. Each extinction of a conditioned or acquired reflex corresponds physiologically to the partial effacement or at least to the temporary inhibition of the functioning of a connecting path between receptive and effective parts of the nerve arch of a conditioned reflex in the gray matter of the hemisphere of the cerebrum which path had been formed during the acquisition of this reflex. This means that the acquisition of each conditioned reflex denotes the establishment of an additional communication between the outward world and the organism; a keener knowledge of the former, a more perfect adaptability towards it on one hand, and a more thorough activity of the nervous system, on the other. Every extinction of conditioned reflexes means both the rupture, the annihilation of the former communication between the world and the organism; and a simplification, a returning to primitive motives; a decentralization of activity of the cerebral matter and the whole nervous system.[1]

---

[1] See details in the above-cited works of Pavlov, Bechtereff, Lazareff, Paton, Watson and F. H. Allport: *Social Psychology,* ch. II.

If such an extinction spreads over many conditioned reflexes, it means that the channels of communication in the hemispheres will be more or less completely obliterated and the communication annihilated; that the organism will be transformed into an apparatus guided exclusively by unconditioned stimuli and reflexes; it means a rupture between nervous centres and a lessening of the integrative action of the nervous system; [2] a transformation of the whole organism into *membra disjecta,* disjointed members having lost a supreme governing centre. This makes it clear that when the extinction of acquired reflexes renders the mechanism of the nervous system primitive it must also lead to "primitiveness" of the psychical life and activity.

We come to the same result from another standpoint. The development of conditioned reflexes marks the establishment of more and more numerous communications between the organism and its environment; this means that new "connections" are being created in the gray matter of the brain; this produces their mutual cohesion, their mutual dependence, and their mutual restriction. The gray cortex matter grows similar to a complex telegraph and telephone station into which all the telegrams and phonograms transmitted by the receptors from the outer world pour in. All these various, often contradictory, messages are "sorted here;" part of them mutually "restrict" each other, and the organism reacts only in answer to their conjoint message. This process of "sorting and appraisement" demands time and energy. It is usually called "reflection" or "the activity of consciousness and mind." The greater the number of acquired conditioned reflexes, and the more numerous the telegrams pouring in, the stronger does their mutual inhibitions grow; the more complex and difficult does the work of "sorting" become; the more time and energy does it

[2] See Sherrington: *The Integrative Action of the Nervous System.*

require from the organism, and the longer is the act (*i.e.,* the answer of the organism) postponed. Speaking subjectively this means: the more intense and serious the process of reflection and thought, the more time will it require to come to a conscious definite decision. In cases where this does not exist, for instance in unconditioned reflexes and in habitual automatic actions, the answer of the organism to stimulus follows immediately and automatically, without any reflection. In the cases where reflection sets in (how to act? what to decide upon?) the restraining element always exists as well; the organism does not immediately answer the stimulus; *i.e.,* a difficult process of "sorting" all the "pros" and "cons" is going on in the cortex matter. Sometimes this "sorting" lasts for months or years (scientific problems). Subjectively we mentalize this process as "reflection." The more serious and complex the environment we are conscious of, the profounder is our reflection. The profounder our reflection, *i.e.,* the more we appraise all the circumstances, all the numerous "pros" and "cons," the more time do we require, the more energy does this inner effort take up; and the more the influence of inhibiting factors bears upon our actions, postponing decisions; making us careful, vacillating, sometimes resembling Hamlet in our indecisiveness and outward inactivity. A whole series of unquestionable experiments corroborates all this. These experiments prove that the more complex the mental tests presented by the experimenter to the one experimented upon (1) the longer time elapsing before an outward answer is forthcoming, *i.e.,* the more time is taken up by sorting the "pros" and "cons" in the cortex matter of the cerebral hemispheres; (2) the less muscular motor strength will be expended in the answer, or in other words, the greater the energy taken up by the process of "inner inhibition " (reflection), the less will there remain for outward manifestation.[3]

This causes an antinomy existing between " reflection " and " action." The culminating point of the first is achieved in Rodin's " Thought," or in ancient Russian religious images. They represent complete repose; complete " inhibition." We see the culminating point of extreme decisiveness of action, in " automatic reflexes " in " direct action," untrammelled by doubts or vacillation; or in the actions of animals, which are in greater part pure reflexes or automatic actions.

It is now clear why the extinction of conditioned reflexes, taken not in the figurative, but in the literal sense of the word, renders physiologically and psychologically the whole spiritual activity of man primitive, and makes the work of his nervous system, and all his psychical life akin to the type of the savage and to animals, *i.e.,* to the type of automatic and narrowly instinctive acts. This " primitiveness," this " simplification " and degradation of spiritual activity is the fundamental feature of the psychical perversion of revolutionary society and render it akin to the psychology of the savage and the animal.

When a great quantity of reflexes, and that of a very one-sided character, grows extinct in man, his nervous apparatus begins to resemble a complicated machine in which the screws have grown slack. Because of this, the machine begins to work all wrong. The telegrams passed on by the analyzers to the higher nerve centres no longer correspond to existing facts, as the work of the nerve centres appointed to analyze and interpret them becomes imperfectly done. Consequently, we witness a

---

[3] Korniloff: *The Science of Human Reflexes,* Moscow, 1922 (Russ.). Meymann: *Intellectuality and Will Power,* 1919 (Russ. translation).

" separation from reality." The reactions lose their faculty of adapting themselves to circumstances. This is an aspect of the disorganization of regular functions of the nervous system, accompanied by disorganization of psychical—that is to say of conscious—life which forms the second feature of the psychical perversion of revolutionary society. Famine, cold, want, all the horrors of revolution are illustrations of this inability to adapt conduct to reality.

Let us describe the consequences of this breakdown in the mechanism of consciousness. 1. In the realm of " perceptive experience " such as feeling, perception, attention, conception, association, and combination of ideas, the " primitiveness " and " disorganization " of spiritual life manifests itself in the following phenomena. Revolutionary society begins to see the world and its environment in a one-sided and false aspect. This fact manifests itself in a thousand phenomena. Society sees hundreds of plots where they do not exist at all. It accuses innocent individuals of the most heinous crimes. It is ready to see enemies in perfectly harmless and friendly groups, and looks for friends among those who actually work at the destruction of society. It expects to gain from events that are in reality harmful and *vice versa*.[4]

This tendency is also shown by the fact that revolu-

***

[4] We could cite hundreds of examples proving this. " During every revolution the atmosphere is heavy with imagined plots." Let us remember the *Pacte de Famine* during the French Revolution; the murder of Flesselles, de Launay, the destruction of the houses of Henriot and Revellion; the accusation against the Girondins of their being in league with the emigrants; of the accusation against the followers of Hebert and even Danton of their giving assistance to Pitt and Coburg—an accusation of which they were perfectly innocent (see Madelin: Vol. II, 57-8). The Russian Revolution has given examples such as the murder of Kokoshkin and Shingareff: the accusation thrown out against the Czar of his having wanted to open the front to the Germans; the accusation against numerous individuals—socialists,

tionary society manifests no desire whatsoever to investigate the true state of affairs. For example, let us take a revolutionary court of justice: even when life and death depend upon the decision of a case, it does not consider it necessary to provide either witnesses, or advocates, or a competitive process, or other conditions, guaranteeing a thorough investigation of the accused's case and the justice of the judgment. All these are set aside and an arbitrary: "condemn to capital punishment and let God Himself decide who is innocent and who is guilty" is introduced in their stead.

Further on, a whole series of other facts will be cited. The same feature manifests itself in the fact that events which previously would not have attracted its attention are now felt most acutely by revolutionary society; whereas it grows absolutely "unresponsive" towards other events which in normal times would have concentrated the attention of everybody and been acutely felt by the whole of society.

The economic life of the nation is destroyed; the death rate, famine, cold, sickness, epidemics grow. Yet during the first period of the revolution, society thoughtlessly ignores these facts and uses all its energy in combatting against . . . the officer's shoulder-straps, tearing off armorial bearings; spying upon each other to ascertain that the proper salutation should be used (comrade, not sir; thou, not you), and similar childish games.

A great dearth of textile material is felt, but this does not prevent thousands of yards of material being used for sewing flags. Formerly a case of capital punishment used to be an "event." Now society remains nearly completely

---

for keeping up friendly relations with the followers of Korniloff, Kaledin, etc.; which accusations were absolutely unfounded; the accusation against the merchants and shopkeepers, for a supposed organization of famine, etc.

unresponsive to a ceaseless stream of executions. Formerly the sight of death, sorrow and suffering attracted
attention. Now, even death leaves everyone, in the best
of cases, utterly indifferent.[5]

Formerly if a house caught fire, if a bridge, or water
conduit, or building was threatened with destruction, it
provoked a general panic. Nowadays towns and villages
are destroyed, factories and plants perish in flames and
awaken no particular alarm. Society's faculty of respond-
ing has dwindled tremendously. It is sensitively alive to
all small and narrow and objectively unimportant events,
and absolutely unresponsive to everything else. It sees no
further than the narrow round of small events, it neither
feels nor is in touch with anything else. All the rest does
not enter the field of its vision, it is incapable of appre-
ciating its significance.

2. Perceptions are but the material for thought;
therefore the false perception of events leads revolutionary society to false association and interconnection of ideas
and conceptions formed from these perceptions. Levy-
Brühl has proved that the fundamental law, governing
thought amongst primitive men is " the law of participation " [6] but not the law of mental logic, the law of identity, the law of contradiction, etc. The law of participation consists in assuming the existence of a " causal "
connection where there is only some outward connection
or proximity of events. The savage does not admit of the
law of identity or contradiction, or of any other fundamental laws of logic. We see the same happening in
revolutionary society. Its reflection is governed by the
same " law of participation." For example, during the

---

[5] Madelin: Vol. II, 287. " In France where the cult of the dead
was always particularly respected, death no more calls forth either
respect or attention."

[6] See Levy-Brühl: *Les Fonctins Mentales Dans les Societés
Inférieures*, 1912.

Russian Revolution, all those who were comparatively decently dressed and wore spectacles were considered to be "bourgeois" and the "enemies of the people." It sufficed for the Bolsheviks to nickname all the non-Bolshevik socialists "Monarchists," "Koltchakovists," or "Kornilovists" for the mob to identify all these various groups; though the groups properly bearing these names had all fought against each other in a death-like struggle. It was enough to be a member of a collective body, two or three members of which had been arrested (for instance, that of professors); or to live in the same house or flat with a suspicious individual, or to appear in a theatre when a "search" for counter-revolutionists was being made; or to have the same family name as the one inscribed on the pocketbook of some arrested individual; or to be a member of the same commission; or to be caught in the market where you had perhaps gone to sell your last pair of trousers—for you to be arrested and even executed without further discussion. A casual outward connection —either one of time, place, or profession was sufficient to identify you with counter-revolution or profiteering, to create the presumption of a plot and execute you, though any normal reflection would have shown such an identification to be inadmissible. I shall not cite a thousand other facts of a similar order. Both the Russian and every other revolution is saturated with them and clearly proves that the reflection of revolutionary society is governed by the primitive law of participation.[7]

---

[7] An individual case and demonstration of the law of participation is to be seen in the fact of "Collective Responsibility" introduced during revolutionary times. If one of the members of the family is an "enemy of the people" the law of participation identifies all members of the family with him. All the nobles are reckoned as "enemies of the people," even though many of them have been imprisoned for years for having abetted revolution. On the other hand, if a criminal and cut-throat is willing, in common with revolutionists, to murder the "bourgeois" he is, according to this simple symptom, identified with the "Heroic Champions of Liberty."

The logic of revolutionary reflection is a continuous transgression against the law of contradiction. It appears somewhat strange for a morally logical mind to sing the praise of liberty—and in the name of liberty to execute all those who are of a different opinion; somewhat strange to preach the brotherhood of man and to demonstrate that brotherhood by means of the guillotine and execution! Does it not strike you as inconsistent, from a logical point of view, to preach full liberty of expressing the Will of the People and, at the same time, to take away every possibility of freely expressing that will and mercilessly crushing every freely-expressed dissension? Does it not seem somewhat inconsistent to promulgate the abolition of capital punishment; to accuse your opponents for having recourse to it, for crushing liberty, for using violence; and, at the same time, to try to prove the necessity of applying capital punishment, violence, etc., in an unheard-of degree? Yet such are the actions and logic of the revolutionists during epochs of revolution.

Read the speeches of the Jacobin orators, take any number of a Bolshevist newspaper and you will find a limitless amount of infringements of the basic laws of logic. This inconsistency manifests itself more clearly as time goes on. Up till the moment of the convocation of the Constitutional Assembly the Bolsheviks actively intrigued for its convocation, demanding that it should be endowed with supreme power. On the day it was opened they dissolved it and began to prove that the Constitutional Assembly, as well as the whole system of parliamentarism, was bourgeois and useless. Till January, 1918, the justice of "universal, equal, secret, and direct voting" was insisted upon. After January this formula was proved to be counter-revolutionary. The same process was practiced as regards freedom of speech, press and assembly. This was still more sharply defined in the case of advocacy of collective government, of necessity of nationalization, of abolition of inheritance, of destruction of capitalistic enterprises, of annihilation of money system, etc. From 1921 they began to prove quite the opposite. The reflective logic of revolutionary epochs is a logic of inconsistency.

The mechanism of associating and of combining perceptions and ideas in revolutionary society shows a resemblance to that of primitive society. It is primitively chaotic, inconsistent and unstable. Today a certain action will be qualified as "a crime;" tomorrow as a "virtue;" today the "enemies of the people" are those who associate with monarchists; tomorrow those who associate with liberals, the day after with communists, and after a few days more—with anarchists. Today the "State Douma," or the Girondins, are termed "Saviors;" tomorrow—"Executioners of the People." Today certain groups fight against each other; tomorrow they embrace. Society's "field of perception" resembles a disturbed ant hillock, where numerous perceptions and ideas are full of activity without plan or consistency, without system or order—giving the most foolish and absurd combinations, if judged from the standpoint of generally accepted logic.

3. The process of reproducing and memorizing also grows deformed. Revolutionary society, up to a certain point, loses its memory, the power to "memorize and reproduce." Suddenly it forgets traditions, beliefs, ideas, and is cut away from the past. All historical memories, all the mental luggage of the past, are cut off, as if touched by a magical wand. Society forgets its own likeness, its own name (*e.g.,* in the present name of Russia; The Union of the Soviet Republics, the name of Russia is absent), its national traditions, its heritage, its historical

features. The internationalism of revolutionary society is but another name of the same process. The face of society is deformed and denationalized. This fact of forgetfulness can be followed in small details. How quickly are the former merits or crimes of certain individuals or groups forgotten. From the twenty-seventh of February to the first of March the mob thanks the Douma for the great part it had played in the struggle for liberty. Towards the end of March the Douma is cursed. The same occurred with the " Temporary Government " and the socialistic parties. From the fifth to the tenth of July, 1917, the Bolsheviks were cursed for their insurrection of the third to the fifth of July. In a month this crime was forgotten. In the relations existing between certain individuals, this feature is still more prominent. Relations of many years' standing are broken, the remembrance of past service and long struggles is forgotten and effaced. Yesterday's friends are today's foes.

4. The same process of disorganization can be traced in the realm of sensory-emotional experience in revolutionary society.

" The sensory-emotional tone " of public activity grows to be particularly impulsive, unstable and disorderly. Despair and joy, outbursts of hatred or admiration, dejection or unbridled merriment, intense admiration or contempt, vengeance or magnanimity, feverishly follow each other. Today the mob acclaims you, tomorrow it tears you to pieces. Today Lafayette, Robespierre, Kerensky, Miliukoff, Tchernoff, are the idols of the people; tomorrow they are traitors.

" It is as if a fever had taken possession of the people," writes a contemporary of the Czech Revolution. " The contemporary men of science did not know how to explain this phenomenon and ascribed it to the influence of the

stars." [8]   " The people have grown mad," writes a contemporary of the French Revolution. The same can be
remarked of other revolutions. A whole series of investigations puts into relief the impulsiveness of the sensory-
emotional life of savages. We see the same feature in
revolutionary society. It is impossible to trust the frame
of mind of the mob. It often changes completely in the
course of a few days, hours, or minutes. If it makes
merry, it does so as if it were intoxicated; if it admires,
it does so with rapture; if it hates—it grows bestial. It
admits of no uniform sensory-emotional tone. We see
ceaseless manifestations, festivals—of Reason, of Liberty,
etc.—dancing, on one hand; on the other hand, outbursts
of fiery hatred, anger, vindictiveness and fear. All this fills
out the first phase of the revolution and shows its special
instability and impulsiveness. Feelings and passions seeth
and boil. The smallest pretext: a sentence in an article, an
act of the government—provokes the outburst of the mob;
a trifling incident awakens its admiration. We can say
that every mob is unstable—but a revolutionary mob is so
in a superlative degree.

During the second half of the revolution, fatigue,
exhaustion, famine and misfortune turn this state into one
of passivity, depression and indifference. Society grows
to be not a " wild madman " but a " silent madman,"
apathetic and sullen. It were a serious mistake to look
upon this wild bull-like energy as upon a demonstration
of will power.

During the second period of the revolution this grows
evident when the stage of " restraining factors " and the
exhaustion of energy sets in. Society loses all will-power
and grows characterless. It grows incapable of active
effort. You can do what you please with it. This com-

[8] Denis: Above-cited work, 219.

plete numbness of will-power presents a fertile soil for the growth of the flowers of red or white dictatorship and tyranny. Dictators strike at society in a most merciless fashion, insult it, torture it, lash it and society humbly bears the stripes. It does not even find energy enough to protest loudly. It is like "new-mown flax." [9] Here we see still more clearly the above-mentioned features of primitiveness and disorganization which are the result of the sudden extinction of many conditioned reflexes.

5. A whole series of investigators have noted the tremendous development of reflexes of imitation during revolutionary epochs.[10] Imitation must, from the behavioristic standpoint, be looked upon as a simple reflex. The fewer the acquired reflexes or the greater the number of extinct ones, the more easily will the reflexes of imitation be performed. This explains why children and savages are more imitative than adult and cultured individuals; why persons suffering from progressive paralysis, in whom cerebral dissociation is in an advanced stage,[11] are exceedingly liable to be imitative, and why the mob, when situated in conditions producing the "somnolence of the higher centres of consciousness," is also imitative.[12] When we recollect that a great number of reflexes grow extinct during periods of revolution, it is easy to understand that the part played by imitative reflexes grows to be much more dominant in the psychology and activity of a revolutionary mob.

---

[9] See a whole series of correct remarks by Galeot: *La Psychologie Revolutionaire* (1923) and Vierkandt: *Zur Theorie der Revolution.*
[10] See Sigelet: *The Crimes of the Mob.* Martin: *The Behavior of Crowds.* Cabanes: The above-cited work, ch. I. Tarde: *Psychology of the Mob.* Bechtereff: *Collective Reflexology,* 1922 (Russ.).
[11] See: The Doctor Dissertation of A. Lenz (Russ.).
[12] See corresponding chapters by Hayes: *Introduction to the Study of Sociology.* Giddings: *The Principles of Sociology.* Ross: *Foundations of Sociology.* Allport: *Op. cit.,* 239-52 pp.

Such is the case.   After all that has been said by Tarde, Le Bon, Michailovsky, Sidis, Sigelet, Bechtereff, Giddings, Baldwin, Rossi, Hayes, Ross, Ellwood, Martin and a whole series of social psychologists, it is useless to cite new facts.   It is known that in all the examinations of the psychology of the mob and of its imitative tendency the chief facts and examples are taken from epochs of revolution.

The same has been witnessed in Russia.   The part played by reflexes of imitation has acquired a tremendous predominance in the behavior of the masses. They have grown to be " somnambulists."   The stimulus of activity given in the form of a vocal reflex—the speech of an orator—is repeated by the mob; or if published in a newspaper, it is iterated all over the country; if promulgated by a communistic leader, it is caught up by his herd-like adherents.   It is very characteristic that thousands of orators repeat in the most stereotyped manner the terms and expressions of their leaders, often not understanding the sense of the foreign words they use, distorting foreign words and pronouncing speeches which are but a string of phrases without sense or reason, but which are compiled out of the stereotyped expressions used by their " models."

The active stimulus, inciting to murder, to the pillage of stores, given by one individual has spurred on hundreds and thousands to devastation.   Panic, fear, flight, or on the contrary, courage and decisiveness displayed by one individual has carried away the rest of the soldiers and citizens.   The population has presented a mass over which waves of imitation were ceaselessly rolling.   Children and the young generation need not even be mentioned: they grew to be nothing but imitators.   However heinous an act it would be sure to find an immense number of imitators, if only it had been expressed or performed with clearness and decision. Society was transformed into a tremendous hypnotized being which could be pushed on to perform the most unexpected actions, could become obsessed by the most foolish dreams.[13]

The same happened during other revolutions. This development of imitative reflexes clearly shows the return to primitiveness of the psychical life of revolutionary society. Beginning with the second revolutionary stage, that of the reinculcation of extinct conditioned reflexes, the steam of imitation grows less profound.

6. What has been pointed out with reference to the perversion of perception and of reasoning prepares us to understand the *lack of practical judgment* which is another characteristic of the revolutionary psychology.

For the savage, the child, the physically abnormal, the border line between what is real and phantastic, attainable and utopian, is vague and not clearly defined. It is difficult to establish where the former ends, where the latter commences. Beyond the limits of their narrow everyday environment there opens the world wherein the " actual " and " improbable," " fancy " and " reality " get mixed up. Even the division of things into " natural " and " supernatural " is one that does not appeal to them.[14]

The same can be seen in a revolutionary population. Its ideas of the world, of the environment and character of the processes it witnesses, its comprehension and appraisement of given events, are a complete distortion of reality. What is impossible appears to it to be possible and *vice versa*. It looks for safety there where it can only find perdition. Illusions seem to be realities. It begins to live not in a world of realities but in a phantastic world. It begins to grow delirious and to see hallucinations.

---

[13] See facts in Bechtereff's book: *Collective Reflexology*, chs. V-XII.

[14] See Durkheim: *Les Formes Élémentaires de la Vie Religieuse.*

The first general symptom of these features is the so-called law of revolutionary illusionism and childish superstition. A society which is on the way to revolution believes in the possibility of attaining the most improbable fancies, the most utopian aims. It proclaims grand slogans and believes in their realization. " Perfect Justice," " an Eden on Earth," " Universal Plenty and Happiness," " The Advent of Christ on Earth," " The Coming of the Kingdom of a Thousand Years," " Egalité, Fraternité, " Liberté," " The Declaration of the Rights of Man," " The Advent of the Fifth Monarchy of Christ," " Universal Peace," " The Internationale," " The World's Revolution," " Communism," " Psychical and Physical Beatitude," etc., these are but some of the numerous catchwords proclaimed by revolutions. A watchword, a dream seems to be its own guarantee of being attainable. The masses—during the first revolutionary stage—believe that they can be realized. Not the shadow of a doubt enters their heads. The question: " Is it possible? " does not crop up. They are bewitched by these great illusions.[15] They are hypnotized and do not see what actually takes place around them. All around, ferocity and slaughter reign supreme, but they do not desist repeating that the

---

[15] " Man's mind had so far drifted from the anchorage of use and wont that to some of them every counsel of perfection seemed capable of immediate realization!" This characteristic of revolutionary psychology in England can be considered correct for all revolutions. Gardiner: *History of the Commonwealth*, Vol. I, 29, London, 1903. " A new era commences; now no more scandals will take place, no more crimes, nor laziness, nor treachery; prerogatives and distinctions will exist no more; property will be annulled; humanity will be liberated from toil, pauperism and hunger. . There will be neither learned nor ignorant, the light of eternal truth will shine before everyone. The wicked will forget their evil actions," such is one of the illusions which during the Czech Revolution was looked upon as immediately attainable. Denis: *Op. cit.*, 266. The same under a different shape is to be seen during other revolutions.

brotherhood of man is being realized. Famine and pauperism increase—they do not perceive it and believe that on the morrow the revolution will bring not only plenty, but the beatitude of paradise to all. The economical life of the people is crumbling away, the fields lie fallow, the factories do not work, the cost of living grows constantly higher. All these do not disturb their quietude; all this is but casual, tomorrow revolutionary genius will accomplish wonders. War and civil war are surging all around—they appear to the masses to be precursors of eternal and universal peace. The growth of an unheard-of inequality is actually taking place; the majority is deprived of all rights; the minority is transformed into a class of dictators, and limitless despotism reigns; the masses continue to look upon it as a realization of equality. All around morality crumbles away, license, sadism and cruelty are everywhere—the masses call it a moral regeneration.

From 1920 European society entered the phase of " reaction " (it is in reality convalescence). In Russia they daily continued to expect the outbursts of a world's revolution; just as during the English Revolution the men of the " Fifth Monarchy " continued to expect its advent, and the Medieval Revolution expected the " Kingdom of a Thousand Years." That is, we witness a society which has lost all feeling of actuality, and which lives in a realm of illusion and fancy. These examples repeat themselves during all revolutions. Only the concrete details vary.

But after the terrible blows dealt by real life, the people wake up, during the second period of the revolution. They " come round " and, like a madman recovering his senses, begin to perceive all the horror of their actual environment; only then do they lose their illusions and begin to grow conscious of the actual state of things.

This "illusionism" and separation from realities of life manifests itself in the acceptance of all extreme theories. The development of revolution and the extinction of conditioned reflexes is accompanied by the prevalence of an extreme ideology. The more extreme an ideology the greater its chances of acceptance. In revolutions which do not take an abortive turn this ideology soon conquers all the more moderate ones, that of the: Faillants, Girondins, Cadets, Moderate Socialists, etc. The more utopian the program, the more unattainable and the greater the beatitude it promises to the masses, the more chance has it to succeed; the sooner is it admitted and becomes popular. Such ideologies spring up like mushrooms, each more extreme left, more utopian, than the others. It is a wild competition of who will achieve the most extreme point "to the left of common sense." The masses follow those who promise the most unattainable, "the land of honey and rivers overflowing with milk." Their psychology is such that not for a moment do they doubt that on the morrow such rivers will really overflow the land. Ideas which during normal periods would be looked upon—like the utopia of a not quite normal person, or the fancy of a poet, or the ravings of a madman, are now accepted as entirely practical. Society, with the obstinacy of a maniac, starts building a bridge towards the moon. Obstacles? They do not exist for it, as they do not exist for a madman. If it is necessary to overthrow the world, it will cost nothing to do so; if the course of the planets has to be changed, it suffices for society to issue a decree. It believes in its own omnipotence, believes in the possibility of actually fulfilling its program; like a child that believes in its own invention. In this fact, which is inherent to all revolutions, the above-mentioned features of primitiveness and disorganization are particularly evident. Only the exceptionally severe blows which real life inflicts, when revolutions long continue, little by little, force society to regain its senses. The second period of revolution is one of " coming to one's senses." Extreme illusions begin to fade. A state of scepsis, followed by disenchantment, and lastly by complete loss of credit of all the extreme theories takes the place. Their charm disappears, bandages fall from the eyes of society, and it clearly sees the actual " breaking through," the crumbling ruins it faces. The stage of denying and hating all extreme theories, so popular but a short while ago, sets in. It is true this does not take place without vacillation and backslidings. But on the whole, the ideology of society makes a sharp deviation towards the opposite side.

7. A general manifestation of the facts above expounded is the direct method of reflection and action employed during revolutionary epochs. The developed system of conditioned reflexes results in complexity of sinuous ways of achieving a given aim. This thought has been very clearly stated by L. Ward [16] who showed that the development of thought sometimes demands that direct means (often inadequate for attaining a given end) should be replaced by indirect circuitous, more complex ones. The development of thought and civilization all tends in this direction. What we have called " primitiveness " is a return in the opposite direction.

This being so, it is easy to understand why the extinction of numerous conditioned reflexes during revolutions must call forth an increase of " direct actions " and " direct reflections " instead of indirect, circuitous ones; and why this fact indicates a return to " primitiveness " and a psychical regress. We witness this during all revo-

---

[16] See L. Ward: *The Psychic Factors of Civilization.*

lutions. It can even be traced in the name by which revolutionary methods are called: *l'action directe*. The name
is strictly correct, though I scarcely think that its adherents have seriously taken into account its significance.
Professor Ellwood is perfectly right in saying: The methods of achieving the aims of revolution are methods that
characterize the lowest stages of civilization; they are non-
reflective, exceedingly direct and cruel.[17]

It is the method of a wild bull dashing himself against
a wall. The method of applying churlish strength; the
belief in the universal usefulness of physical violence.
The maxims of revolutionary wisdom, reflection and
action are simple and not complex.

" Smite and hew down the cursed villains,
    And   .   .   .   the dawn of a new life will arise."
                    (*The Russian Marseillaise.*)

The greater the number of heads struck off, the
sooner will the promised land be attained. The greater
the reign of violence and terror, the surer the approach
of the Kingdom of Brotherhood, Equality and Liberty,
Communism and Socialism. The greater the destruction
—the better; for the " spirit of destruction is a creative
spirit "   .   .   .   The conduct of man grows to be identical with that of the bear, who attempted to bend a bow
by force, described in Kryloff's Fable. The results were,
as we know, rather pitiful.

Therein " is the law and the prophets " of the revolution. We see this in the wild and senseless elements of
violence and destruction that accompany revolution.
Everything and everybody is destroyed: man and relics
of culture, fields and factories, villages and cities, museums
and libraries, a kind of bacchanals of destruction spreads
over all; in most cases the masses destroy the very objects

---

[17] Ellwood: *Introduction to Social Psychology*, ch. VIII.

they need themselves. Fundamental human impulses freed from all restraining factors develop a mad impetus and wild energy. All persuasion, calls, arguments not to demolish remain fruitless. Man, having broken his chains, is like a whirlwind spreading senseless ruin, death and destruction.[18]

Everywhere revolution exhibits not only "direct action," but also thought assumes a character similarly simple and primitive. Some dozens of "direct slogans" grow to be the key to all the treasures of wisdom. Two or three rather narrow and somewhat pitiful ideas (for instance that of "Class Struggle," "Nationalization," "The Dictatorship of the Proletariat" and the extremely primitive materialism of the Russian Revolution), grow to be the beginning and the end of all wisdom and knowledge. All else, all that is of another opinion, is denied. Every more complex construction is nicknamed: "Counter-revolution." The rod, prison, conviction, exile, execution—all come to take the place of reasoned argument. Every doubt as to the soundness of revolutionary dogma is characterized as a crime. In place of serious mental labor, we find a revolutionary sectarian dogmatism, more intolerant than that of the inquisition, for here also we see "primitiveness" in its most extreme form.

8. A further manifestation of the primitive psychology of revolution is a kind of "*megalomania*," or *mania of grandeure*, which takes possession of the revolutionary masses and their leaders. If we pass in review all revolutionary speeches, pamphlets and articles, we see that each most important step of a revolutionist is described as

---

[18] This passion of destruction grew particularly evident in Russia during the years 1918-21, even in the daily conduct of children. The pedagogues stated that "an epidemic of destruction" had taken possession of them: for no particular reason whatsoever the children broke school benches, cupboards, windows, locks, doors, made incisions on the walls, etc.

"The Discovery of a New Era," as a "New page in history," as something absolutely new and exceptionally important in human history. That is why many revolutions—the English, French and Russian—inaugurate a new chronology and count the year of the revolution as the year one; they introduce a new almanac; they change the holidays and saints' days, introducing new revolutionary saints in place of the old ones. That is why they change the names of streets, towns, counties, naming them after themselves during their lifetime. They consider themselves to be—to use the terms of the Russian Revolution—the vanguard of humanity, supermen, titans, infallible saints, in comparison with whom others are but "sinners" and paltry beings. The revolution is termed: "A Discovery of a New Era." The triumph over a handful of counter-revolutionists is again termed "A Discovery of a New Era." The confiscation and division of the wealth of a few rich—again "The Discovery of a New Era;" the decrease of the work day for one hour—again a "New Era." The simplest events are described in high-flown words. What appears comical to a healthy-minded man appears to them heroically titanic. In the eyes of the masses they themselves, and especially their leaders, appear to be giants. A newspaper reporter is transformed into a "Great Tribune." A most second-rate bookkeeper, into a "Great Organizer;" a second-rate publicist, into a "Great Thinker." This megalomania gives birth to a "Revolutionary pose," to classical movements, to speeches appealing to "God" or to the heroes of Rome and of previous revolutions. It encourages luxurious festivals, demonstrations, manifestations and "mysteries." You are in the presence not of normal individuals, but of actors playing a pseudo-classical tragedy.

9. The same feature of primitiveness and disorganiza-

tion of the psychical life displays itself in the fact that personal responsibility disappears and is replaced by a collective responsibility, which we know to be a common feature among primitive groups. For the crime of one, hundreds and thousands of individuals, having nothing in common with him, are punished ("hostages," "mutual responsibility," "general terror," the punishment of entire cities and villages, of entire social groups and categories).

10. And lastly, the disorganization of psychical life evoked by the revolution displays itself in a considerable increase of actual insanity of psychical illnesses and psychical disorders (see the following chapters).

All the above-said is sufficient to illustrate and substantiate the correctness of our statements concerning the primitiveness and disorganization of psychical life among revolutionary society which inevitably follows the extinction of conditioned reflexes. This is the origin of the peculiarities of revolutionary psychology which have been described, as well as of other features of it which I shall not describe here.[19]

With this we close the study of the perversion of conduct and psychology during revolutionary epochs. Its fundamental features are here evident and do not require repetition. They make up a picture essentially different from the "romantically fantastic" conception of the beneficent influence exercised by revolution. They lead us to the conclusion that those who desire that biological features should be the predominant ones in man, who desire his conduct to resemble that of animals, have only to pave the way for the approach of revolution, and deepen its influence: it surely leads to these results.

[19] See descriptions of some of these in the books of: Galeot, Vierkandt, Cabanès and Taine—the chapter of the Psychology of Jacobinism.

PART II

THE INFLUENCE OF REVOLUTION ON
THE COMPOSITION OF THE POPULA-
TION AND ITS DEATH, BIRTH AND
MÁRRIAGE RATE.

CHAPTER XI

THE INFLUENCE OF REVOLUTION ON THE COMPOSITION OF THE POPULATION AND ITS DEATH, BIRTH AND MARRIAGE RATE

THE revolution not only changes human behavior, but also modifies the biological structure of the revolutionary population by its effect on the process of births, deaths and marriages. These modifications can be summed up as follows:

1. Revolutions tend to diminish the number of population through direct destruction of life.

2. Revolutions as a rule further diminish the population and retard its growth by heightening the death and diminishing the birth rate while in most cases, though not always, they augment the number of marriages. If there is but a slight falling off in the birth rate, we usually see a very great rise in the death rate, so that, in the long run, the natural growth of the population is still retarded.

3. Revolution is an example of a " selection of the unfittest." It exterminates the " best " elements of the population (as to hereditary qualities) and protects the vitality of the " worst."

By thus exterminating the " best " revolutions destroy the bearers of desirable hereditary qualities, the progenitors of a corresponding posterity and, consequently, impoverish the " biological hereditary fund of positive national qualities."

4. At the same time they cause deterioration of the physical health and vitality of the survivors.

All these effects of the revolution (admitting all other conditions to be equal) manifest themselves more or less strongly in proportion to the bloodthirstiness, length and severity of the revolution. In revolutions that do not go deep they are scarcely appreciable. We shall give some concise explanations to corroborate these statements.

1. **Revolution Diminishes the Population Numerically.**—This does not require detailed proofs. Revolutions are generally accompanied by civil war. The latter, like every other kind of war, devours mankind. The same results are also achieved by revolutions in other ways : such as a low birth rate, a high death rate, epidemics, pauperism, famine and other factors which are its constant satellites, parents and children, of the revolution.

The population of the Soviet Republic has during the five years of revolution, 1917–22, diminished by fifteen to seventeen millions. That is, the revolution has not only destroyed all natural addition to the population but between fifteen and seventeen millions more.[1]   During the French Revolution of 1870-71 the total sum of the fallen is calculated at " 25,000 French killed by their own compatriots," not counting those that could also be considered indirect victims of the revolution.[2]   In Paris (in the revolution of 1848), during the rebellion of June 22nd to 25th no less than 1000 men were killed. However, if we should also add the indirect losses in different parts of

[1] Official statistics tell us that the population living on the territory of the contemporary Soviet Republic has diminished from eighteen to nineteen millions for the years 1914-20. The years 1921-22 carried away still two or two and a half millions. If we deduct from this number of 21 to 22 millions the three millions devoured in the World War and one million of emigrants, we arrive at the above-named figure. See: *The Works of the Central Statistical Administration*, book III, p. 4, Moscow, 1922 (Russ.). *Economist*, Nos. 4-5, p. 44, Petrograd, 1922.
[2] Gregoire: Vol. IV, 427-8.
See " Notes and Addenda," p. 415.

France, this number would be infinitely greater.[3] It is a generally accepted fact that during the French Revolution of 1789 there was a sharp decrease of the population. Tours lost a third of its citizens, Bordeaux one-tenth, Rennes one-eighth, Lyons over 80,000, etc. The war of the Vendée carried away 300,000 to 400,000 men. The reports of the prefects state that in thirty-seven departments the population had diminished, in nine it remained stationary and only in twelve had any increment been noticed. Most of the historians are agreed that the revolution and the wars of Napoleon—offspring of the former—carried away about two millions of the population. According to Juglar and Raudot about 1,400,000 men perished during the years 1789–1801.[4]

On a smaller scale we can see the same in the English Revolution of the seventeenth century. A whole series of years of civil war brought forth similar results here. On the other hand, certain episodes of the revolution, such as the wholesale extermination of the population in Drogheda, Wexford; the massacre of 200,000 (according to May), or 100,000 (according to Gardiner) Irish in 1651, evidently, greatly added to the number of victims of the revolution.[5] It is needless to speak of the tremendous devastations of the population calculated in tens of thousands during the Hussite Revolution and the ensuing wars (Zizka and Procopius) which in the long run com-

---

[3] *Ibid.*, Vol. III, 132, 119, 129.

[4] Michelet: *History of the Nineteenth Century,* Directoire, Vol. I, 133, St. Petersburg, 1882 (Russ. transl.). Levasseur: *La Population Française,* Vol. III, 506 and foll. Levasseur: *Histoire des Classes Ouvrieres, de 1789 à 1870,* Vol. I, 276-7. Taine: *Des Origines de la France Contemporaine,* Vol. VIII. Though Levasseur is inclined to consider that the decrease in the city population is compensated by the increase of the rural one, it must be remembered that his viewpoint is not accepted by most specialists (F. de Flax, C. Juglar, Raudot, Taine and others).

[5] See Guizot: Vol. I, 34. Gardiner: Vol. IV, 82-4.

pletely ruined the population of Bohemia, both quantitatively and qualitatively.[6]

Let us now cast a glance at the French Jacqueries of the
fourteenth century and the numerous rebellions accompanying them: *les Maillotins, les Cabochiens,* etc., which,
with only short intervals of peace, worried France for
many decades, during the second half of the fourteenth
century and the beginning of the fifteenth century. They,
and the plague, called forth by them, cut down one-third
of the population.[7] The like *mutatis mutandis* can be
said of the peasant insurrection of Watt Tylor in England
and the peasant insurrections in Germany towards the
end of the fifteenth and sixteenth centuries. All of them
directly or indirectly were accompanied by famine, plague
and other epidemics that carried away many tens of thousands of men. To all of them the words of the historian
may be applied: " The peasants raged and ravaged, murdered, and tortured the knights, their wives and children.
The nobles pursued them, killed them in thousands,
burnt down their villages, and covered the fields with
their corpses." [8]

The same can again be repeated of the Netherlands
Revolution of the sixteenth century during which about
one-third of the population perished; also of the years
of sedition in Russia in the seventeenth century. The
revolutions of ancient Rome and Greece again give us the
same picture. The revolutionary period of Rome, begin-

---

[6] See the above-cited works of Denis and Palacky.

[7] See Levasseur: *Histoire des Classes Ouvrieres,* Paris, 1900, Vol.
I, 521-33. *La Jacquerie* he writes *n'eut d'autre effet que de depeupler
plusieures campagnes,* Paris, whose population numbered at the beginning of the thirteenth century more than 200,000 inhabitants, had now
the appearance of a city abandoned by its population. More than
24,000 houses stood tenantless. In Provence out of 3200 artisans there
remained only 30; in Salses out of 500 houses only 35; in Roussillon
out of 80 only 30, etc.

[8] Weber: Vol. VIII, 25-6.

ning at the time of the Gracchi, passing on through the civil wars of Sulla and Marius and those of the First and Second Triumvirates, which were all accompanied by colossal massacres of the opponents on both sides, ended in what approached extermination of the Italics, Samnites and Etruscans, and in a great degree of the original population of Rome and Italy. The total number of victims far surpassed 300,000.[9] "The Latin race was speedily dying out in Italy"—we witness a dreadful depopulation. "Instead of the former inhabitants, Italy was inhabited by a proletariate of slaves and freemen from Asia, Syria and Egypt. In many districts of Italy even this replacing of nobler elements by the baser ones was not forthcoming, and the population obviously decreased."[10] The same happened during the third and fourth centuries A.D. under a system of constant anarchy, seditions and insurrections. Analogous was the fate of the Greek aggregates during periods of revolution. Here also ceaseless murder speedily and appreciably decreased the population. When during the third century B.C. revolution and insurrection grew to be the permanent state (Agis IV, Cleomenes III, Nabis, etc.), we witness, as direct and indirect result of it, the terrible depopulation described by Polybius.[11]

Let us now turn to the revolutions of such enormous aggregates as, for instance, China. Here the population is numerically so immense that the figures of its decrease also take impressive proportions, running into tens of millions. Let us take, as example, the civil war of 755–81. It is said to have diminished the population of

[9] See Rostovtzev: *The Birth of the Roman Empire,* St. Petersburg, 1918, pp. 29, 42–4, 100–101. Mommsen: Vol. II, 404.
[10] Mommsen: Vol. III, 463-4.
[11] See Fahlbeck: *La Decadence et la Chute des Peuples, Bulletins de l'Institut Intern. de Statistique,* XV, part II.

China from fifty-three to twenty millions. The insurrection of the Thai-Pings is estimated to have diminished it from three hundred and thirty-four to two hundred and sixty millions, etc.[12] Ipouver also testifies to the tremendous death rate during the Egyptian Revolution. " Death is rife in the country. Wherever you turn you see man putting his brother into the earth and the covering of the mummy calls out to men before the latter approach it." " So many die that no one is left to bury them." " Many of the dead are buried (thrown into) in the river." " Famine, murder, civil butcheries and war on different fronts— all contribute to heighten the death rate, but above all the plague which ravages the whole country." [13]

It is unnecessary to cite further facts, nor is it a great exaggeration to add that, though the number of direct and indirect victims of revolutions, insurrections and riots is smaller than that of the victims of international wars and conflicts, still it mounts to a formidable total. In both cases of Humanity's struggle for " right and justice," death gleans a rich harvest. Part of this harvest it gathers not so much directly through murder, as indirectly through a lowered birth rate and heightened death rate of the revolutionary population. Let us look at this side of the question.

2. The Death, Birth and Marriage Rate During Revolutions.—The heightened death rate and lowered birth and marriage rate among the civil population during years of war is a fact of usual occurrence. The death rate generally grows higher soon after the commencement of the war and falls after its termination. The marriage rate

---

[12] Concerning the decrease of the population during the insurrection of Thai-Pings, Dounkans, etc., see the statistical data given by Parker: *China Past and Present,* London, 1903, p. 26. Steinmetz: *Philosophie des Krieges,* 1907, p. 60.

[13] See Vikentieff: p. 245.

falls during the commencement of a war and shows a sharp increase—generally above the normal average—after its termination, when the weddings, held back by war conditions, generally take place. A year or two later their number approaches the average level. The birth rate begins to decrease only nine to ten months after the declaration of war, and nine to ten months after its termination it also shows a sudden increase, reaching its pre-war level a year or two later.[14]

It is clear that as civil war is only another type of war, its influence on the birth and death rate must be analogous. Famine, epidemics, want, diminished vitality of the population are unavoidably the result of all deep-rooted revolutions.

Figures show that during the revolutionary years the death rate is generally high and the birth rate is low. If this latter is not much below the average, then the decrease of the growth of the population is achieved by a corresponding increase of the death rate.

The marriages, however, show a certain deviation from the above-named scheme. If civil war does not separate the soldier from his family, if revolution has played havoc with the sexual reflexes and has increased sexual license; if it creates conditions which render life and the struggle for life easier for the married than the unmarried (as *e.g.*, in Russia during these last years. Thanks to the division of labor between the wife and the husband, married couples found life easier than the sin-

---

[14] We have watched these facts of the population's increase and decrease during the Prussian-Danish War, 1864; the Prussian-Austrian War, 1866; the Napoleonic Wars; the Crimean War; the Franco-Prussian War, 1870-71; the Russian-Turkish War, 1877-78; the Serbian-Bulgarian War, 1885; the Balkan War, 1912-13; the Russian-Japanese War, 1904-05; the Civil War of the United States; the World War of 1914-18. See the statistical data in my article: " The Influence of the War on the Composition of Population," *Economist*, No. 1, 1922, St. Petersburg. The sources are indicated here (Russ.).

gle) ; if, on the other hand, the revolution, needing human " food for the cannons," encourages wedlock and even grants certain privileges to those who enter into that state (several meters of material for the bride's dowry, better monthly food rations, etc.), then, in such cases, we witness a high level of the marriage rate even during the years of revolution. This can be observed in Russia. When these conditions do not exist, then the marriage rate decreases in times of revolution and increases after the termination of the civil war. But even in the first case the marriages remain childless, unstable, casual, short-lived, easily dissolved. They are, in reality, but a legal transformation of chance sexual connections, they bear less numerous offspring, and are as easily dissolved as they are formed. The statistics of divorces and the short-lived " revolutionary marriages " cited above witness to the fact. Such is the influence of revolution on the " natural " movements of the population. Let us give some figures beginning with the Russian Revolution.

A clear picture of the vital movements of the population can be seen from the following statistics given by the R.S.F.S.R. Unfortunately we have no figures for the whole of Russia.

Increase of the death rate.

Out of every 1000 inhabitants there died :

Provinces	in 1914	in 1920
Kostroma	27.6	49.6
Moscow	26.8	40.8
Nisgni Novgorod	29.1	33.8
Orel	26.8	36.4
Penza	30.0	40.8
Riazan	22.3	27.2
Tver	25.7	27.0
Smolensk	25.3	33.4 [16]

[16] *Statistical Yearbook of Russia for 1918-20*, Moscow, 1921, 9-3. " The Works of the Central Statistical Administration," Vol. I, book III, p. 4, Moscow, 1922 (Russ.).

Here we have taken, as examples, provinces that have not been battlefields of civil war.   But even here there is a considerable increase of the death rate.   In provinces which have been the seat of warfare the increase of the death rate is even more frightful.

The like can be said of the fall in birth rate.   During the years of revolution, up to the end of the civil war in 1920, it had greatly decreased.   After 1920 it ought to have risen, but famine, poverty, epidemics, terror and similar conditions existing nearly all over Russia, with the exception of the capitals, continue to lower the birth and raise the death rate.

The following figures are very eloquent.

Decrease of the birth rate.

For every 1000 inhabitants there were born:

Provinces	in 1911	in 1920
Novgorod	41.04	24.0
Smolensk	46.2	29.7
Tver	43.3	26.1
Moscow	41.5	24.5
Kostroma	46.4	33.2
Nigni Novgorod	47.9	24.9
Viatka	52.7	16.2
Perm	55.1	19.0
Penza	54.8	28.0
Riazan	43.4	25.4
Orel	47.3	24.2 [16]

The coefficient of births all over Russia for the whole of the nineteenth and the beginning of the twentieth century vacillates between forty and fifty-two for every thousand inhabitants.[17]   During the revolution it was never above thirty for every thousand.

It is easy, therefore, to understand that during the rev-

[16] *Statistical Yearbook of Russia for 1913*, p. 1-2. " The works of the Central Statistical Administration," book III, p. 4 (Russ.).
[17] *Encyclopedia of Brockhaus and Effron*, Vol. XL, 628-9 (Russ.).

olutionary years Russia, which has always been looked
upon as having a particularly high birth rate and a rapid
increase of population (the normal increase during the
nineteenth and the beginning of the twentieth century
being from 12.0 to 18.1 to the 1000), could not even compensate her death rate. The following figures prove it.

For every thousand inhabitants during the year 1920
there were:

Provinces	Births	Deaths	Excess of the latter
Tcherepovetz	24.0	29.6	5.6
Novgorod	24.0	25.3	1.3
Smolensk	29.7	33.4	3.7
Tver	26.1	27.0	0.9
Moscow	24.5	40.8	13.3
Ivanovo Vosnesensk	32.8	46.3	13.5
Kostroma	33.2	49.6	11.4
Nigni	24.9	33.8	8.9
Viatka	16.2	24.1	7.9
Perm	19.0	26.0	7.0
Penza	28.0	40.8	12.8
Riazan	25.4	27.2	1.8
Orel	24.2	36.4	12.2 [18]

In the Nikolai Province the difference between the
death and birth rate had changed from the rate of 1914
in the following way:

Years	Surplus of birth + Surplus of death −
1914	+5981
1915	+2762
1916	+1828
1917	+1822
1918	+1399
1919	−4698
1920	−1977 [19]

[18] "The Works of the Central Statistical Administration," book
III, p. 4 (Russ.).
[19] "Bulletins of the Central Statistical Administration of the
Ukrainia," No. 9, 1922, p. 29 (Russ.).

In different towns of the Ukrainia the decrease in 1921 manifested itself in the following figures:

Towns	Surplus of birth + Surplus of death −
Cherson, Aleshky	− 1987
Poltava	− 1646
Loubny	− 1192
Gadiatch	+ 27
Zenkof	− 82
Kobeliaki	+ 81
Constantinograd	− 44
Lochwitza	+ 95
Mirgorod	− 151
Romny	− 103
Sebastopol (March–July, 1922)	− 1064

Towns of the Zaporoshsky Government	− 34
Towns of the Governments of Ekaterinoslavl, Zaporoshie, Krementshug, Podolsk (first quarter of 1922)	− 8772
Tzaritzino (first half of 1922, out of every 1000 inhabitants)	− 67
Ekaterinoslavl Province (April, May, 1922)	− 6625
Odessa (first half July, 1922, out of every 1000 inhabitants)	− 85.5
Elisavetgrad, out of every 1000 in 1922	− 91[20]

The state of depopulation in the famine districts during 1921–22 can be judged of by the following figures:

The population of the Tartar Republic during the years from 1920 to 1922 had a decrease of 470,000, that is, of 20 per cent.; the population of Bashkiria, of 33 per cent.; the Ural District, of 25 per cent.; the Kertsch Ujezd, of 33 per cent.; the Pougatscheff District in the Province of Samara, of 50 per cent.; the population of Cherson, of 60 per cent.; etc.[21]

Let us now take up the statistics of the capitals. We see that since the beginning of the war the death, birth and marriage rate underwent a change from year to year. Nineteen hundred and twenty to nineteen hundred and twenty-one brought a certain amelioration, but unfortunately it was not typical for the whole of Russia. From 1920–21 the conditions of life in capitals began to improve at the expense of the provinces of Russia. In most of the districts of the Soviet Russia this amelioration was not forthcoming, in many places the conditions grew even worse.

For every 1000 inhabitants there were in the years:

	Marriages		Births		Deaths	
	Petro-grad	Moscow	Petro-grad	Moscow	Petro-grad	Moscow
1912	6.5		27.6		22.6	
1913	6.3	5.8 for the	26.4	28.9 for the	21.4	23.1 for the
1914	6.0	5.5 years 1910-14	25.0	31.0 years 1911-13	21.5	22.1 years 1910-14
1915	5.0	4.1	22.5	27.	22.8	20.2
1916	4.7	3.9	19.1	22.9	23.2	21.2
1917	8.5	5.3	17.8	19.6	25.2	28.0
1918	9.2	7.5	15.5	14.8	43.7	45.1
1919	20.7	17.4	13.8	17.5	72.6	46.2
1920	27.7	19.6	21.8	21.9	50.6	? [22]
1921	26.7	?	36.0	?	27.8	

These figures show clearly that revolution has a much greater influence over the death rate than war has, and it also causes a greater reduction in the birth rate. On the other hand (and therein it does not resemble war) it greatly increases the number of marriages. However, till 1920 marriages were relatively childless. Only since 1920–21, when the conditions of life in the capitals were ameliorated (at the expense of the rest of Russia), can we mark a decrease of the death rate and an increase of the birth rate which, having been kept down during a whole series of years, now gave a record figure. In 1923–24 the birth rate began to go down, approaching to nor-

---

[22] " Statistical Material for St. Petersburg," book V, 1922, 19. *Red Moscow,* 1917-20, pp. 64, 66, 69.

màl level. The number of marriages again began to show a slight decrease which grew more evident during 1923.[23]

Such are a few concise figures concerning the influence of the Russian Revolution on the growth and decrease of the population. Only when the revolutionary movement began to ebb did death's spoil begin to diminish and life to increase.

Similar facts had to take place, and did take place, during other revolutions. The mightier the scale of the revolution the more manifest its effects. We are going to quote some historical and statistical witnesses.

THE REVOLUTION OF 1870–71

The increase of the population for every 1000 inhabitants :

```
1868 ............................... +  1.6
1869 ............................... +  2.2
1870 ............................... −  2.8
1871 ............................... − 12.2
1872 ............................... +  4.9
1873 ............................... +  2.8
1874 ............................... +  4.8 [24]
```

I know perfectly well that these figures were greatly influenced by the Franco-Prussian war. But they also were influenced by the revolution, which influence tended in the same direction. This is particularly manifest in the growth and decrease of the death and the birth rate in the Department of the Seine.

THE REVOLUTION OF 1848–49

Its influence was somewhat mitigated by the colossal dearth of 1847 and on the contrary the excellent harvest of 1848–49. And still the revolution has not remained

---

[23] I have not the data for 1922 and 1924 before me, but I know such was the movement of the birth rate and marriages.

[24] Levasseur: *La Population Française*, Vol. II, 6-11.

without visible influence on the decrease of the population.
For every 1000 inhabitants we have an increase of:

1846	4.1
1847	1.5
1848	2.9
1849	0.3
1850	5.3
1851	4.8
1852	4.3 [25]

THE REVOLUTION OF 1789 AND THE FOLLOWING YEARS

We have no exact figures as to the increase and
decrease of the population during the great revolution.
But we possess figures of the pre-revolution times and
those of the last days of the revolution. Towards the
end of the reign of Louis XVI there were 38–39 births;
in 1800 only 33.1 for every 1000 inhabitants. Also there
were more marriages in Louis' time, whereas in 1800 we
find only 7.3. In Louis' time the death rate was 30 per
1000. In 1800, 27.8; in 1801, 28.0; in 1802, 31.9; in
1803, 32.4.[26]

We see that the number of deaths and marriages has
remained more or less stationary in the years preceding
the revolution and at its close, but the birth rate is lower.
Historical witnesses quoted by Taine speak of the colossal
increase of the death rate during the revolutionary years
and of the decrease of the birth rate, especially in the
cities which were the battlefields of revolution.

THE GERMAN REVOLUTION, 1848–49

Oettingen writes: " These years were characterized by
the sudden decrease in the growth of the population."
The coefficient for Prussia is as follows:

---

[25] Levasseur: *Ibid.*, 6-11.
[26] Levasseur: *La Population Française,* Vol. III, 509.

Years
1814–28 .... 1.71
1828–40 .... 1.35
1840–46 .... 1.27
1846–49 .... 0.45 1850 again sees an increase.[27]

THE RUSSIAN REVOLUTION, 1905–06

The increase of the population for every 1000 inhabitants:

1903 .... 18.1
1904 .... 19.6
1905 .... 13.1
1906 .... 17.1
1907 .... 18.7

The influence of the Russian-Japanese war can be traced in these figures. However, not only that of the war, but that of the revolution of 1905 as well.

We do not possess sufficient statistical knowledge concerning the revolutions of antiquity. But about the more important ones which were accompanied by civil wars we have the testimony of contemporaries, who clearly depicted the state of affairs. We have already mentioned the testimony of Ipouver as to the colossal death rate during the Egyptian Revolution. We have seen that the same took place during the Chinese revolutions, and have also quoted testimonies as to the immense death rate of Rome during the lengthy chronic revolutions and seditions towards the close of the Republic. Historians and contemporaries speak of the decrease of the birth rate. The contemporary Varro writes: " Formerly women prided themselves on having many children. Now, when a husband desires children, she answers: ' Do you not know what Aenii said? Better three times to be in danger during battle than to give birth to a child once.' " [28]

This tremendous falling off of the birth rate explains

---

[27] Oettingen: *Die Moralstatistik*, 273-4.
[28] Mommsen: III, 537-8.

the numerous attempts of contemporary statesmen to stimulate the increase of confinements. Already the Gracchi fixed a remuneration for all who had begotten legal children. Cæsar set apart certain lands for such as had three children, and deprived childless women under forty-five years old of certain rights, at the same time giving privileges and preference to those who had posterity. The famous *leges Juliæ* (*lex Julia de maritandis ordinibus, lex Julia et Papia Poppea,* a whole series of laws proclaimed by Augustus) are directed towards the increase of the diminishing population. War and endless revolutions " have made the population barren." [29]

A similar state of things existed in Greece. The growth of the population was at a standstill from the end of the third and the beginning of the second centuries B.C. The birth rate fell abruptly. The depopulation so vividly depicted by Polybius commenced. This epoch, as is well known, is that of the acutest, most bloodthirsty revolution which, with short intervals of peace, occupied the whole period (the revolutions of Agis IV, Cleomenes III, Nabis). [30]

Outward wars and civil revolutions called forth the same identical results. We do not know whether the number of marriages had increased or decreased during these epochs, but we do know that marriage grew to be much less durable: divorce and sexual license more frequent. To sum up: we hear of the same process we now witness in Russia. It is probable during all lengthy and important revolutions, in which great masses of the population take

[29] See details in the cited works of Ferrero, Mommsen, Otto Seek, Rostovtzev, Duruy and others.

[30] See Fahlbeck: Cited works. E. Meyer: *The Population of Antiquity.* Review: " Population," Moscow, 1897, pp. 50-53 (Russ.). Niese: *Geschichte der Griechen und Macedonischen Staaten,* Gotha, 1903, Part III, 9-11, the above-cited work of Pöhlmann.

part, that the increase and decrease of the population follows the same natural lines.

The tremendous growth of the death rate and falling off of the birth rate during the epoch of the Jacqueries and civil wars in France during the second half of the fourteenth and the beginning of the fifteenth centuries we have already quoted. The same must be said of the seditions and civil wars awakened by the religious revolutions in France during the second half of the sixteenth century. The result was a new depopulation: *Les guerres de religion ont été une période de décadence. Les campagnes se dépeuplerent.* "The population of France which had gradually recovered from the losses of the 100 years' war decreased again." "Out of 1500 families living in Provence in 1575 only 500 remained fifty years later." [31] The same could be seen in other towns.

During the Jacqueries and revolutions of the sixteenth century in Germany and at the time of the Hussite Revolution, which was accompanied by bloodthirsty civil war and wars with outward foes, we see the same picture.[32] The same can be said of the Russian Revolution of the seventeenth century. "Graves are to be seen on all sides like hillocks," writes the contemporary author Palitzin.[33]

The facts above cited make us believe that the same must have taken place during all deep-rooted and bloodthirsty revolutions. Their final result is the same: a plentiful sacrifice of human life to the goddess Death.

---

[31] Levasseur: *Histoire des Classes Ouvrieres*, Paris, 1900, Vol. II, 55 and foll.

[32] "The population decreased dreadfully and the revolutionary war weakened the nation terribly." "The towns were depopulated, the villages likewise." "The death rate was terrible because of famine and want." Denis: *Op. cit.*, 255, 263, 328, 477-8.

[33] Karamzine: *History of the Russian State*, Vol. XII; 79-80 (Russ.).

3. Revolution as an Instrument of Negative Selection and an Aggravation of Hereditary Race Qualities.—
Revolutions not only call forth a numerical change of the population, but, what is much more important, change the quality as well. Contemporary warfare, unlike that of antiquity, exterminates the "best" and favors the survival and propagation of the "worst;" the least healthy, the least capable, least talented, those that have least will power.[34]

The same, and more, can be said of every revolution accompanied with civil war and bloody conflicts. It is an instrument of death, exterminating from both sides, specially all that is best, healthiest, most capable; all that is above the average; the gifted, strong-willed, intellectually qualified elements of the nation. Here the efforts of both belligerent sides are directed toward the extermination of the leaders and the best of the enemy's camps. First one side exterminates the best elements among its adversaries —then the other. As a result the country loses " the best " of both parties. As in every other ordinary war, both the fighting armies are composed of the healthiest, most capable (the weak and sick do not enlist), of the bravest, most energetic, strong-willed—those whose convictions and moral reflexes are most steadfast, who are intellectually more developed. The gray mass, without will or initiative, indifferent to all but its own welfare; the sick, the undeveloped generally try to stand aloof from the struggle; do not push themselves to the front, do not protest, remain in the shade, and, consequently, perish in

[34] See my article: *The Influence of War;* also Vaccaro: *Les Bases Sociologiques du Droit et de l'Etat;* Novikoff: *Les Luttes entre Societés Humaines;* Lapouge: *Les Selections Sociales;* Nikolai: *Die Biologie des Krieges;* P. Jordan: *La moisson humaine, Revue intern. de Sociologie,* 1911, pp. 673-712. About the influence of the last war see Döring: *The Great War and the General Development of the Population* (Statistical, Review, 1920, Nos. 5-8, Russ.).

much smaller numbers. The percentage of the loss of the
best for every 1000 men is much greater than that of the
second rate.

The same result is also achieved by the revolution in an
indirect way. Destitution, famine, want, which come in
their wake, fall more heavily on the " Intellegentzia," the
cultured class, on those who are earning a livelihood by
mental labor. Being badly adapted to hard physical labor
and physical privations this category is helpless under such
conditions. There is but little demand for their labor ; its
remuneration decreases. Apart from this the nervous system of the cultured responds much more intensely to all
the horrors of the revolutionary struggle, than, for
instance, the nervous system of the unskilled workmen.
These circumstances tend to exterminate the cultured class
and explain the high death rate within it, as compared with
the death rate of the intellectually undeveloped mass, especially representatives of muscular labor.

The political emigration of revolutionary epochs also
contributes to these results; for it often draws away from
the country the most precious and superior elements.
Ostracism in antiquity, political emigration among the
mediæval Italian states, the exile of heretics from Spain,
the Huguenots from France, the political emigration of
the last centuries, and the revolutions of the eighteenth
and twentieth centuries have carried away much first-
class human material out of the forsaken countries.   If
we sometimes see obsolete types among the emigration we
must not forget that amongst its ranks we find men like
Themistocles, Aristides, Plato, and the best blood of Spain.
Dante, Michelangelo, Chateaubriand, de Maistre, Lafayette, Louis Blanc, Mazzini, Herzen, etc.   We can be of
different opinion as to the value of their work, but we
cannot deny their superiority.   The same can be said of

the whole mass of the political emigration of the " white " and " red " camps. As a whole, the general level of it is higher than that of the mass which has remained. The reason why it has had to emigrate, or is exiled out of the country, is because it will not comply, because it has a will of its own, and appears dangerous to the conqueror. Under such conditions it is comprehensible why revolutions murder as well as exile " the brain, the will and the conscience of the country," why they are instruments of a " negative selection."

" Give of your best," was the Roman demand to the soldier during conscription. " Give the best to Death and Exile," is the slogan of revolution. *Parcere subjectes et debellare superbos*—is particularly adapted to revolutionary struggles. But this is not all. The death of " the best seed," the destruction of the bearer of the best hereditary qualities of the people means these will not be transmitted to posterity at all, or will be transmitted in a much smaller degree. The biological hereditary fund of the nation is impoverished, degraded and deteriorated. For " such as the seed is, will the harvest be." This is all the more important, as the chief actors during revolutionary epochs are generally, comparatively, young men who have not yet exhausted their parental productiveness. Gowin has proved that revolutionary and reform leaders are seldom above the age of 40.[35]

Franklin said: " It will be chiefly in the future that we will have to pay for the bill drawn up by the war." This is still more true of revolution. It not only drains the best living blood of its country, but the common biological hereditary race fund of the nation—its coming generation. It degrades its quality and causes its decadence, in propor-

[35] B. Gowin: *Correlation Between Reformative Epochs and the Leadership of Young Men*, 1909.

tion to the bloodthirstiness of the revolutionary strife, to
its cruelty and the number of its victims.

Another way by which revolution deteriorates the biological qualities of a nation is in weakening the health
and nervous system of the survivors. These latter, being
mostly but second-rate material, are degraded all the faster
by famine, cold, poverty, diseases and epidemics, the terrible abnormal conditions of life—these inseparable comrades of bloody revolutions. Under such conditions the
survivors grow still weaker. This is specially the case of
all those conceived and born during revolutionary epochs,
and of the young generation. They have to pay by loss of
health and by their own degradation, for the sins of their
fathers, for " Revolution's Conquests," for all its crimes
and exploits. Let us prove it by figures.

THE RUSSIAN REVOLUTION

1. Whereas the general loss of life for these years
equals 13.6 per cent., the loss of men averaging from fifteen to sixty years of age, that is, of the healthiest, most
capable part of mankind, is estimated at 28 per cent.[36]

2. The loss has been mostly that of men, not women.
Instead of there being 99.6 women to every 100 men, as
has been the case before the war, we now have 125 women
to every 100 men.[37]

3. The more cultured, gifted population of European
Russia which had created the Russian State lost one-
seventh, that of Asiatic Russia only one-thirtieth of
their population.[38]

[36] *Economist,* Nos. 4-5, Petrograd, 1922, article of Raphalovitch
(Russ.).
[37] See *Statistical Yearbooks of Russia, for 1913,* p. 60, and for
the years 1918-20 (Russ.).
[38] *Material of the Central Statistical Administration,* book III,
p. 4 (Russ.).

4. On both sides it was mostly the morally upright who perished; those that possessed steadfast moral reflexes and a strong feeling of duty. They did not conceal their convictions, did not change them, as the unprincipled did; they protested and struggled; they were to be found on posts of danger, and . . . they perished. Struggling against brutally hard odds, surrounded by lies, pilfering, cynicism, they neither stole, nor swindled, nor violated, and, as a result, they starved and perished. Quite other was the position of the morally defective and cynical. Among the turbid waters of the revolution they felt themselves in their element. They changed opinions as fast as circumstances demanded it of them, swindled, were brutal, profiteered, occupied lucrative posts and lived in luxury. The conduct of the first tended towards its extinction, that of the second towards its thriving.

5. The intellectually qualified were the chief sufferers. During warfare the percentage of loss among officers is generally higher than that of soldiers. In civil war this is still more evident. Nearly all the corps of officers gave up their lives on the battlefields of the civil war. Officers were killed, burnt, drowned, torn to pieces, their heads hammered in.[39] Yet the corps of officers, beginning with the under-officers and sergeant major, are the " brains " of the army, its soul and cultured aristocracy. This is specially the case of the Russian officer corps of revolutionary times; they were nearly all of the people, not of the aristocratic class.

Let us now turn to the university-educated men. In England, according to Galton, 2000 men out of every million have received a university education. In Russia no more than 500 out of a million. But their loss was not

---

[39] See details, Denikin's: *Outline of Russia's Seditions,* Vol. I, book I, p. 104 (Russ.).

(500x16) 8000 out of the sixteen millions of the victims of the revolution, but many times more. Twenty or thirty thousand would be the minimum at which it could be estimated; in other words their loss was three to four times greater than that of the mentally less qualified.

The same happened to the village teachers. The percentage of those who perished was much greater than the percentage among the rest of the population.

The death rate among the Petrograd professors during 1918–22 was six times higher than the death rate of peace times, and twice higher than the rate among the rest of the population of Petrograd in 1918–21.

Still greater was the loss among the noted men of science; among authors, artists, those great national *élites*. During the years 1917–23 we lost a great number of these rare men. The following is the list of those who died or were killed: Academicians: Anutschin, Shachmatov, Turaeff, Lappo-Danilevski, Markov, Ovsianniko-Kulikovski, Famintzin, Sobolevski, Arseniev, Shimkevitsh and Inostrantseff. Noted men of science: Palladin, Belleliubski, Tugan-Baranovski, Lopatin, Tagantzeff, Dogel, Pokrovski, Hvostov, E. Trubetskoi, Vvedenski, Kistiakovski, Rosin, Lasarevski, Andreev, Block, etc. Their death rate was terrific. And Russia, who had always been poor in cultured men, is now, after the years of revolution, positively beggared. " The brain and the conscience " of the country is half dead and still dying out. (See the detailed description of university life in my book—*Leaves from a Russian Diary*. E. P. Dutton Co.)

Similar is the fate of men of energy and will-power such as: Korniloff, Duchonine, Alekseef, Metropolitan Benjamin; Bolsheviks like Sverdloff, Lenin and Volodarski; many social-revolutionists and others. Nearly all who were strong and had will-power, who dared to struggle against the Bolsheviks have been exterminated by them. Similar will be the fate of the Bolshevik leaders after the fall of the latter. The " élite " of both sides are exterminated *ad majorem gloriam* of the revolution and counter-revolution. And even these few élite, who in consequence of special circumstances are still alive, very soon burn out, wear themselves out, amidst their feverishly tense work, or are indirectly murdered in prison, exile, amid the wasting atmosphere of terror, violence and famine.

Take all this into consideration, add to it the emigration, and you will understand that the nation's best blood, her brain and conscience have perished, or are exiled out of Russia.

But all this is not sufficient. The revolution has in a great measure degraded the survivors, especially the younger generation. This degradation is now already visible and manifests itself in a whole series of symptoms. First of all: the weight of new-born babies is considerably below what it used to be. Secondly, the percentage of still-born children is much greater.[40]   Thirdly, their vitality is lowered; the percentage of death during the first days is much greater than in peace times. Such facts have been brought out by the investigations of Professor Litchkous, Valitzki and others.

Fourthly, the growth of the younger generation is stunted due in part to absence of vitamines of growth. Two thousand medical examinations of children in the Lesshaft Institute of Petrograd give us the following figures. They also very opportunely demonstrate the horrors of so-called " Children's Homes " organized by the communists. The results obtained among the boarders or the

---

[40] See *Medical Work*, February 1, 1921, article by Litchkous and Valitzki (Russ.).

internes of such homes, colonies and asylums are worse than those among the " externes," that is, children living with their parents.

Age	The Stature of the Children of 1921-22		Petrograd's Children in peace times	
	Boarders	Externes	Asylum of Prince Oldenburg	Children of the Poorest Classes of Petrograd
7	105.9	112.0	—	118.0
8	112.8	115.8	—	118.5
9	117.4	122.5	—	122.9
10	121.8	126.6	132.0	126.8
11	126.0	129.5	133.4	130.4
12	131.8	134.5	138.2 [41]	132.01

A similar picture can be seen all over Russia. This reduction is very clearly seen in the Red Army. The average stature of the soldier is less than that of the pre-war soldier. The examination of the same two thousand children has demonstrated a whole series of defects in the organism and the formation of the skeleton, the dimension of the chest, in the lymph-apparatus, and so on. The horrors of the revolution, the famine, cold and privations have set a tragic seal on the organism of the younger generation, on those who were conceived and born during the revolution.

Fifthly, sexual license and civil war have immensely heightened the prevalence of venereal diseases, including syphilis among the population. According to the most moderate calculation their percentage has gone up six or seven times in comparison with peace times.

During the congress of syphilologists in May, 1923, it was established that syphilis and gonorrhœa were making great strides among children under fifteen years of age,

[41] Viazemski: *The Changes of the Organism During the Period of Its Development,* Vol. I, 66 (Russ.).

and that its development among the Red Army has surpassed even that of 1920 (the reports of Doctors Tapelson
and Fedorovski).[42]

The same must be said of tuberculosis. The percentage
of tuberculosis has advanced tremendously. At the present moment it carries away more victims than cholera or
typhus.[43] A great percentage of the population has, at
some time or other, been ill with typhus or typhoid.
According to Tarassievitch, in 1919 twenty per cent. of
the inhabitants had had typhus.[44] Add to this different
forms of typhus. All of these are still wildly raging in
Russia. To this must be added cholera, influenza, scurvy,
the dysentery, malaria, all kinds of catarrhal illnesses, and
dozens of others which ravage the whole country. Small-
pox, diphtheria, measles, anthrax, plague and especially
malaria are still increasing. During ten months of 1923
only 4,888,000 were ill with malaria. All these illnesses
now give much higher per cent. of mortality than before.[45]
Not only the seven, but the seventy-seven plagues of Egypt
are devastating the population of Russia.

A great increase of psychical illnesses among the population has been called forth by the nightmares of the
revolution, by famine and other accomplices of the former.
Psychical illnesses have taken colossal proportions, spe-

---

[4] *Dni,* No. 193, *Rul,* No. 777 (Russ.).

[4] See *Dni,* No. 103. Among the Smolensk metal workers the
prevalence of tuberculosis has attained 41 per cent.; among the
printers 43 per cent.; among the workers in chemical productions 50
per cent., etc. Such figures were formerly unknown in Russia.
Quoted from the Moscow Newspaper *Troud* (Labor), citing the paper
Dni, No. 185 and *Rul,* No. 768. During 1920-22 more than two million
died from tuberculosis. *Isvestia,* No. 265, 1922.

[44] Tarassievitch: *The Epidemics of the Last Years in Russia,*
Social Physician, No. 1, p. 48 (Russ.).

[45] See article of Prof. Danilevsky in *Physicians' Work,* 1922
(Russ.). See the official *Report of the Commissariat of Public Health,*
Moscow, 1924 (Russ.).

cially in the famine districts.[46] These illnesses are still
increasing. In Moscow their total number was 2700 in
1923 and 3250 in 1924. Neuroses, psychoses, progressive
paralyses, traumatic and paranoiac illnesses, early feeble-
mindedness, epilepsy and so on are still progressing. (See
Isvestia, May 30, 1924, the interview with Professors
Udin and Gannushkin.)

I presume that all we have said is sufficient to consider it as proved that all our previous statements are fully
applicable to the Russian Revolution. It has produced a
terrific devastation among the Russian population both
qualitatively and quantitatively. It has sown the germs
of degeneration. In the light of such facts, much in past
history grows clearer. The influence of other revolutions
being called forth by the same reasons is similar to what
we have described. The difference is one of degree, not
of kind. The ancient On-Chou and Ipouver, contemporaries of the Egyptian Revolution, wrote: " Men have
grown small " . . . " Nowhere, nowhere are Egyp-
tians to be found." " All perishes." " The people are
wounded and corrupted at the very core." " The nation is
like a broken reed." " There is no pilot. Where is he
today? Or does he sleep? " " His strength is not seen." [47]
In such exclamations of the contemporaries we again
see the revolutionary negative " survival of the unfittest."
We also note the degradation of the survivors. " Thanks
to the famine and other calamities people have deterio-

[46] See Gorovoy-Shaltan: The Question of Psychical Illnesses
Among the Population Under Existing Conditions, *The Journal of
Psychology, Neurology and Experimental Psychology,* St. Petersburg,
1922, p. 34 and foll. (Russ.). Ossipoff: *Psychical Illnesses in
Petrograd* (Russ.). *Isvestia of the Health Commissariat,* 1919, Nos.
7-12. See also *Isvestia,* February 15, 1922. *Petrogradskaia Pravda,*
March 10, 1920. *The Red Paper,* January 31, 1920, and others.
[47] Vikentieff: The article quoted above, pp. 283, 290, 294 (Russ.).
Turaeff: *Ancient Egypt,* 60-61 (Russ.).

rated to such a degree that the living cannot be separated from the dead. Men walk on earth like dead fish." " The great and the humble say: I want to die. The people is likened to new-mown flax." [48]

The influence which the Roman Revolution had at the close of the Republic is sufficiently known. Perhaps it devastated Rome qualitatively no less than the Punic wars. " The rebellions of the peasant Italics, as to the number of victims, can only be compared to the Punic wars, and they did not draw to a close before all the more energetic, reasonable and cultured among the Italics had perished wholesale." The seditions during the civil wars of Sulla and Marius, those of the First and Second Triumvirates destroyed the remainder of the " best " offspring of Rome's founders. During these struggles perished first of all the "élite": the Gracchi, Spartacus, L. Drusus, Catiline, Pompeius, Marc Antonius, Cæsar, Flaccus, Memmius, Cicero, Sertorius, etc. " Sulla and the soldiers took Rome and exterminated their adversaries' leaders." The victory of Marius " called forth innumerable persecutions and executions of the opponents and brought forth a very ocean of filth and treachery." The contemporary Appian writes : " Immediately, from all sides, detectives rushed in to find out and destroy senators and knights; they were destroyed, without number." The new victory of Sulla produced hecatombs. In Rome alone: " Tens of thousands of Italy's noblest sons perished." The following episode characterizes the cold-bloodedness of the destructors. During a sitting of the Senate on November 3, 82 B.C., the cries of the butcheries reached the ears of the senators. They were somewhat disturbed, but Sulla, without interrupting his speech, quietly said: *Hoc agamus, patres conscripti, seditiosi pauculi meo iussu occidentur.* " Sen-

---

[48] *Ibid.*, p. 295.

ators, let us continue; they are only executing, according to
my order, a small number of rebels." And this small number was only   . . .   8000. The same repeated itself
during the struggle of the First and Second Triumvirates.
At the time of Cæsar there existed only fifteen to sixteen
patrician families. After the patricians had disappeared,
the families of the nobles, the equestrians and the Roman
ruling classes also faded away. Rome was no more. In
its stead came the freedmen, the slaves, the barbarian races
and the " depraved " of all nationalities. As a result " all
that possessed initiative, all that was proud of its glorious
past was partly exterminated, partly degraded, partly emi-
grated." The best biological fund of the people was
annihilated and because of that " the richly creative Italy
began to fade and grow dim. The new people (mostly
composed of slaves and barbarians) were incapable of
renewing the country's life." The downfall of Rome's
glory had been made inevitable. Two centuries longer it
still stood, but, beginning from the third century, Rome's
state began to fade toward its doom.[49]

The same could be seen during the Greek revolutions.
During the revolution of the fourth and fifth centuries
before Christ: " Everywhere the tyrants had the same
policy of violence: their principle was to destroy all that
was superior;" with the fall of a tyrant perished the
noblest and best of his adherents.[50]

The same repeated itself during the revolutions of
370, 412 and 427, and later during the second and third
centuries B.C. " All who were above the average were

---

[49] Rostovtzev: *The Birth of the Roman Empire,* 28, 17, 19, 41-2.
Mommsen: Vol. III, 422-3, 463-4, 75-76. Fahlbeck: *La Decadence des
Peuples,* 370. See Ferrero: *The Rise and Fall of Rome,* Moscow, 1916,
Vol. I-III (Russ.). Otto Seek: *Der Untergang der Antiken Welt.*
[50] F. de Coulanges: *La Cité Antique,* 1905, p. 324.

murdered," [51] " masses of distinguished citizens were executed and exiled." [52]

But the sum total is the same: the impoverishment
and the degradation of the " biological fund " of Greece,
and the beginning of the end.   Here also the " élite " perished in the struggle: Polycrates, Hippius, Hipparchus,
Ephialtes, Cleon, Alcibiades, Socrates, and many others of
the killed and still others were exiled.   Similar effects
repeated themselves during the later revolutions both in
Europe and on other continents.

One of the reasons of the rapid downfall of the young
Arabian people and Caliphates, who had begun their
historical existence so brilliantly under the banner of
Islam, were the constant wars and civil revolutions in the
course of two to three centuries, till the best part of the
nation's blood was drained. [53]

The same results were also called forth by the Jacqueries and revolutions of France in the fourteenth and
fifteenth centuries.   As a result we see a colossal deterioration, impoverishment and wildness of France during the
fifteenth century. [54]   Afterwards the *Guerres de religion
ont été une periode de decadence* (religious wars were
a period of deterioration). [55]

Another revolution, which is very instructive from this
point of view, is the Hussite, as well as the war following it.   During a few years of civil war and slaughter
the most remarkable leaders of the Catholics, Taborites,

---

[51] Pöhlmann: *History of Antique Communism and Socialism,* 479
and foll. pages.
[52] Niese: *Geschichte der Griechischen und Macedonischen Staaten,*
Gotha, 1899, 2 Teil, 563 and the foll. pages.
[53] See details, Müller: *History of Islam,* Vol. I-IV.
[54] See the concise characteristic of Levasseur: *Histoire des Classes
Ouvrieres,* Vol. I, 535 and the foll.   *Les gens de métier épuisés et
appauvris par la lutte, etaient rentres dans le silence.* The same
happened to the peasants.
[55] *Ibid.,* 55.

and Utraquists—Zeliv, Sadlo, Huss, Zizka, Procopius
the Great, Procopius the Lesser, etc.—the unconquerable
terrible "Warriors of God" perished. All of the best
were exterminated—only the riffraff remained. The
destruction of the Czech state was being prepared and was
unavoidable after the Battle of "The White Hill." [56]

The same negative selection, although not on a very
extensive scale, can be seen during the English Revolution of the seventeenth century. Not only in Ireland
whose population was ruined and ravaged both quantitatively and qualitatively, but also among the English and
Scotch, the loss of the best men, both among royalists
and their opponents, was very considerable. Whatever
our opinions may be of men like: Strafford, Laud,
Montrose, Campbell, Hamilton, Lockyer, Derby and others
on the one side; and of men like: Hampden, Blake, and
Cromwell on the other, and many others whose lives were
offered up during the revolution; however much we praise
or blame the royalists or republicans, we cannot deny that
they were no ordinary men.

We need not speak of the French Revolution of 1789.
During ten or fifteen years nearly all the leading royalists,
Girondists, and Jacobins perished: Mirabeau, Condorcet,
Brisso, Guadet, Danton, Marat, Robespierre, Desmou-
lins, Lavoisier, Babeuf, Chénier, Hebert and others. They

[56] See Denis: *Huss et la Guerre des Hussites.* Already during the
Battle of Wyshegrade nearly all the offsprings of the powerful and
famous houses were killed. In the later civil wars "the aristocracy of
birth, fortune and talent were exterminated or exiled." During the
last Battle of Lipanach the remaining 16,000 of "God's Warriors"
were killed. "The Czechs conquered the Czechs." The price paid was
the complete annihilation of the Czechs. Its final destruction took
place somewhat later, after the Battle of the "White Hill," but "that
final destruction had been prepared and can be explained by the losses
sustained during the revolutionary period," pp. 255, 263, 328, 347-8,
431-4, 437, 478.

all mutually exterminated each other.   Only the second-
rate royalists, Jacobins and moderates were preserved.
During the terror of the revolutionary years the best
blood of the nation was spilt.   The revolution made havoc
chiefly among men.[57]   The revolution and its wars swept
away men between twenty and twenty-eight, those most
capable for work, and such elements as were above the
average and were gifted with a strong will.   During the
course of ten or fifteen years the nation was completely
spent.   Instead of the terrible revolutionary soldiers who
were now drawn away to the front, a secondary kind of
material floated to the top.   Waterloo demonstrated the
results of such a process.   Even a genius could not conquer with offspring of such secondary material; born during the horrors and starvation of the revolution.   Here
also we see the development of syphilis, venereal diseases
and epidemics, called forth by starvation, degradation and
other revolutionary conditions.   It is known that the stature of the French recruits born during the revolution and
Napoleonic wars and a little later was considerably below
the average.   On the other hand the percentage of recruits
whose health and physical defects (infirmities of all
kinds) made them unfit for military service was much
higher.   For instance, in 1831–35 out of 10,000 young
men 875 were acknowledged unfit for military service,
being too low of stature.   In 1856–60, 613.   Out of
10,000 men only 6357 were fit for service in 1831–35.   In
1856–60, 6707.   These recruits were born during the last
years of the Empire.   The same fact has been previously
noticed among recruits born during the second period of

---

[57] See the memoirs of Lord Malmesbury and other contemporaries
whom Taine quotes in Vol. VIII.   See Levasseur: *La Population
Française,* Vol. III, 519, 532, *Hist. des Classes Ouvrieres,* 1903, Vol.
I, 276-7.

the revolution.[58] It is just from these years of revolution
that the deterioration of the French population commenced.
The same *mutatis mutandis* can be said of the revolutions
of 1830, 1848 and 1870. The ravages were not as profound, but the tendency was similar. Among the murdered and exiled of both camps many stood high above
the average, and the whole of the population was up to a
certain point weakened and deteriorated by the revolution.
The posterity born in Paris in 1871–72 was so defective
that it received the nickname of " children of the siege and
revolution "—*les enfants de siège et de la révolution*. The
percentage of still-born children was also heightened.
For every 10,000 new-born babies in the Department of
the Seine there were in:

> 1867–68 .... 698 still born children
> 1869–70 .... 750 still born children
> 1871–72 .... 765 still born children
> 1873–74 .... 694 still born children [59]

The development of syphilis and sexual disease was
also prominent. The year 1848–49 gives the highest figures for syphilis in France from 1845 to 1854. Among
the prostitutes (*filles insoumises*) in 1847 one out of every
6.5, and in 1848 one out of every 5.6 was infected with
syphilis. In Banlieu it was one out of every 57 girls in
1847, and one out of every 37 in 1848. In Paris it was
one out of every 154 girls in 1847, and one out of every
125 in 1848. Among the *filles isolées* one out of every
351 in 1847, and one out of every 131 in 1848 was
infected with syphilis.[60]

---

[58] Boudin: *De l'accroissement de la taille et des conditions d'aptitude militaire en France, Mémoires de la Societe d'Antropologie,* 1 serie,
Vol. II, 7 Mai, 1863. Villermé: *Memoires sur la taille de l'homme en
France, Annal d'Hygiene, publ.,* I. Anouchin: *The Geographical
Distribution of the Masculine Population of Russia,* St. Petersburg,
1884, p. 25 and foll. (Russ.).
[59] Oettingen: *Op. cit.,* 703.
[60] Oettingen: 698, *Parent Duchatelet, De la Prostitution dans la
ville de Paris,* Vol. I, 691.

A Russian author, Shulgin, compared war and revolution to lice. All we have said demonstrates that revolutions bring in their wake: alcoholism, sexual license, typhus, cholera and death. To this number we must still add syphilis. The development of psychical illnesses has also been proved. In this respect the years 1830–31, 1848–49, 1872–73 give a sharp increase in the number suffering from paralysis. " In no other year do we see such an increase of them as in 1830–31, an increase of from 9 to 14 per cent.; in 1848–49, an increase of from 27 to 34 per cent.; and in 1872–76—as a result of the events of 1870–71—an increase of 37 per cent." [61]

All that has been stated here proves that the influence of the Russian Revolution is typical.

The practical deduction of all that has been said above is, that he who desires the extermination of his people, the decrease of the birth rate, the deterioration of the racial fund of the nation, the destruction of its noblest elements, the degradation of the survivors, plague, cholera, typhus, syphilis, psychical illnesses, should prepare a violent revolution and render it deep-rooted and widespread. It is one of the best ways to achieve the abovementioned effects. Those who do not desire them can uphold reforms, not bloodthirsty revolutions.

---

[61] Oettingen: 68.

PART III

CHANGES IN THE STRUCTURE OF THE
SOCIAL AGGREGATE IN PERIODS OF
REVOLUTION.

CHAPTER XII

CHANGES IN THE STRUCTURE OF THE SOCIAL AGGREGATE IN PERIODS OF REVOLUTION

1. **General Remarks Concerning the Structure of the Social Aggregate.**—Every social aggregate is composed not directly of individuals, but of a whole series of groups —religious, family, professional, proprietary, legal, political, etc.—which serve, as it were, as intermediaries between the social aggregate and the individual.[1] They represent those tissues and organs which in their totality form the social aggregate.

Along with this dispersion of the social aggregate into groups or strata, there is the fact that the individuals belong not to one, but to many groups at once, which do not coincide in general membership with each other. The total of those groups to which the individual belongs, and the place which he occupies in each of them, may be called the "system of social coördinates," which determine his position in "social space," his social weight, his social aspect and the character of his behavior.

The composition of each of those groups of the social aggregate is not always the same, it changes in the course of time. Some individuals leave a given group and go into another (from one party, family, religion, proprietary class, profession, into another party, family, religion, etc.).

---

[1] For the sake of brevity the problem of the composition of the social aggregate is outlined here in a most general and not very accurate way. For the same reasons I was compelled to use occasionally figurative terms, like "organism," "organ," "tissue," etc. A detailed analysis of the composition of the social aggregate, and of all the problems connected with it, will be found in the second volume of my *System of Sociology* (Russ.) and will be given in my book: *Social Mobility* (now in the process of preparation).

New members come to make up for those who have left. This means that in every aggregate there exists a circulation of individuals from one group into another, their transposition in the system of social coördinates. The composition of every "tissue," or "organ" of the social "organism" undergoes a constant change. Each of those groups resembles a pond with a stream that flows in and a stream that flows out, a stream of coming new members from other ponds, and another stream flowing out, and carrying old members to other groups, whereas all those groups taken together go to make up what may be called the general structure of the social aggregate.

The number of outflowing members is not always equal to that of incoming members, so that we observe fluctuations in the volume of those groups. Some of them grow larger and swell, others grow smaller and shrink. Occasionally it happens that all the members of a given group (let us say, a party) leave it and the group disappears entirely. Sometimes individuals, on leaving their old groups, do not go over to any of the existing ones but form a new one.

It must be said, however, that under normal conditions all those processes go on in an organized way, according to a definite system, without jumps and cataclysms. Both the circulation of individuals and the changes in the volumes of groups proceed gradually and, relatively speaking, slowly (although at a different rate in various aggregates). This is due to the existence in every aggregate of a complicated mechanism which regulates the transposition of individuals in "social space," their distribution between various groups, or various strata of the same group, their "selection" for this or that group, regulating also thereby the fluctuations in the volumes of groups.

Owing to the existence and operation of such a "mechanism of distribution" the above-outlined processes of transposition of individuals and of fluctuations in the volumes of groups go on gradually and smoothly, without breaks. As a rule, they do not destroy the elasticity, the constancy, the stability and the definiteness of the structure of the social aggregate. Just as the processes of circulation of blood and of interfusion in a normal organism do not impede the constancy and the definiteness of its structure and its form, so the processes of normal circulation of individuals and normal fluctuations in the volumes of groups that compose the social aggregate, do not prevent the latter from preserving the same "morphological type," the same structure, the same, so to speak, social-architectural style.

These introductory remarks were necessary in order to understand the character of the changes which the social aggregate undergoes in periods of revolution.

Let us analyze those changes.

2. Deformation of the Structure of the Aggregate in the Periods of Revolution.—A revolution means not only a perversion of the behavior of individuals, and a change in the composition of population, but also a radical transformation of the structure of the social aggregate as it has been defined above.

We may ask ourselves: What are the characteristic features of the revolutionary deformation of the structure of the social aggregate? What is the difference between the processes of fluctuation in the volumes of groups and of change in their composition, as well as of circulation of individuals, in revolutionary and in normal times?

I have emphasized above that under normal conditions the structure of the aggregate is, notwithstanding those processes, constant and stable. Likewise, the mechanism which regulates the selection of individuals, their distribution between various groups and their circulation, functions with a certain regularity.

A quite different picture is presented to us in the first period of revolution. Like a debilitated or putrefying organism, the structure of the social aggregate suddenly becomes weak, formless and crumbles to pieces. Social border-lines suddenly disappear. The mechanism which used to regulate the circulation becomes paralyzed. And the circulation consequently becomes " anarchical." No brakes exist any longer, and the individuals are carried off by the flood of revolution and move about without any plan or system, outside the usual " blood and lymph " vessels. We are present at the sight of a destroyed ant-hill: no style, no form, no order whatever. Just a putrefying corpse with disorderly moving cells, wandering from one organ into another, breaking the tissues and thereby destroying the normal structure of the organism.

The second period of revolution is that of the rebuilding of a new structure of the aggregate. The " turbidness " disappears little by little; the outlines of social groups become again visible. The mechanism of selection and circulation which brings them into a system and serves as a regulator is restored. At the end of this period the restoration may be said to be more or less complete. We see again an aggregate having its own type, its own form, regaining its elasticity. Contrary to the generally prevalent opinion, the new structure is not radically distinct from the " old régime." Indeed, it resembles very much the old one; only the inhabitants of the various rooms of this essentially old building are new. The building itself is the same, apart from the signboards and some slight alterations.

Following are the differences in this respect between revolutionary and normal times:

1. The processes of change in the composition of social groups and of circulation of individuals in the first period of revolution go on much quicker and affect a larger number of people;

2. The amplitude of fluctuations in the volumes of social groups is much wider;

3. Old groups are extinguished and new ones formed;

4. The mechanism regulating the selection, distribution and circulation of individuals is different, and its operation leads to different results as far as the distribution of individuals in the " system of social coördinates " is concerned;

5. In the second period of revolution we notice a " return to the old order " which finds its expression: (a) in the reverse circulation and the tendency of the transposed individuals to return into their pre-revolutionary state; (b) in the contraction of the amplitude of fluctuations; (c) in the restoration of the old mechanism of selection and distribution; (d) in the fact that the structure of the aggregate approaches the pre-revolutionary type, although does not quite coincide with it;

6. If it is true that the position of the individual in the system of social coördinates determines his social aspect, his " soul " and his behavior, then the intensified transposition of individuals within the social space must be accompanied by an intensified " rearrangement of souls." The members of the aggregate, changing their places in the system of social " coördinates," ought to change also their " souls," their behavior.

Let us comment upon these propositions.

3. **Changes in the Composition of Groups. Velocity and Generality in Circulation.**—The rate at which pro-

ceed the changes in the composition of groups is determined by the velocity of the social transposition of individuals and by the number of the transposed individuals. The velocity of the transposition or circulation may be measured by the distance covered by the individual in the social space, within a given period of time. In those groups where there exist consecutive degrees in the upward movement, *e.g.,* from the lowest to the highest rank, from a clerk to a minister, from a beggar to a millionaire, the social distance covered by the individual or the velocity of circulation may be measured by the number of degrees which he climbed or descended during a given period. In other groups where there is no such continuity of ranks or gradation the velocity of circulation may be measured by the number of transitions of the individual from one group into another (from one party, one family, one religion, etc., into others).

The generality of circulation, or the number of the transposed individuals, may be measured by the number of persons who have changed their position into the system of social coördinates.

Thus measured, both the velocity and the generality of " circulation " prove to be much greater in the revolutionary periods than in ordinary times. The changes in the composition of groups within the social aggregate occur much quicker and with greater intensity.

Let us begin with the changes in the composition and with the circulation within the occupational, legal and proprietary groups.

In all those groups the processes of change in the composition and of circulation of individuals not only from one occupation into another, but also from one stratum of the legal and proprietary pyramid into another, become in the first period of revolution much quicker and acquire a mass character.[2]

The individuals, as it were, are elevated all of a sudden from the lower parts of the proprietary or legal pyramid to the very top of it, or on the contrary they precipitate downward with the same catastrophic rapidity and suddenness. The same may be observed with regard to the change of occupation: in one or two years the individual changes his occupation several times, often to very dissimilar or even diametrically opposite. In normal times in all those changes, whether elevations or falls, there is a certain gradualness: the individual gradually changes from a beggar to a rich man, from a small clerk to a higher official. He does not change his profession so quickly and suddenly. Apart from countries with an intense circulation like the United States of America, any considerable changes in this respect occur in most aggregates only in the course of generations.[3]

During a revolution the picture changes. That which

---

[2] It is always necessary to compare the same aggregate in the normal and the revolutionary period, and not different aggregates.

[3] Cp. Sorokin: *System of Sociology*, Vol. II, ch. V. Ammon has demonstrated that in Karlsruhe only 14 per cent. of the village newcomers go over to the middle class in the first generation, and only 4 per cent. become officials; in the second generation 49 per cent. enter the ranks of the middle class, and 10 per cent. become officials; in the third generation the last figure is increased to 25 per cent. Ammon: *Die Gesellschaftsordnung*, 1895, p. 143 and foll.

On the other hand, P. Mombert having examined 1653 persons who were admitted to the Legal Test in Baden, as candidates for high public offices, and 6373 *Lehrerseminaristen* has pointed out the same gradualness of upward movement. P. Mombert: *Zur Frage der Klassenbildung, Kölner Vierteljahrshefte für Sozialwissenschaften.* Heft. 3. "Theoretically speaking," says Mayr, "the man is quite free in the choice of his profession, nevertheless, the son of a laborer usually becomes a laborer himself; the son of an industry-worker, an industry-worker." Mayr: *Regularity in Social Life* (Russ. ed.), p. 132. F. Chessa arrives at a similar conclusion in his monograph: *La Transmissione Ereditaria delle Professioni.* Torino, 1912. Cp. figures and data in Vol. II of my *System of Sociology*.

was impossible under normal conditions becomes possible now.

Let us begin with the Russian Revolution. With the assistance of my pupils I carried out in 1921–22 an investigation of the social circulation in Petrograd, during the years of the revolution. Eleven hundred and thirteen persons were subjected to investigation. The main results are as follows: Of those 1113 persons every one had at least once changed his original occupation in the period from 1917 to 1921. Having summed up the total number of changes of professions, I divided that figure by 1113, and thus obtained the average number of changes of profession which amounted to five. Even for America, not speaking of Petrograd, such a rate of professional circulation would be abnormal.

A similar process went on as regards the legal and proprietary displacement of these persons. All of them were removed from the old places. The majority became impoverished; a comparatively small section became rich. Their " social position " also changed sharply.

Two examples will prove the rapidity and sharpness of those changes. A former Senator and Deputy-Minister, during three and a half years of the revolution, has passed consecutively through the following stages: A starving gardener, a prisoner in concentration camp, a dealer in powder against cockroaches, a clerk in a coöperative shop, a typist in the Academy of Sciences, a teacher in the Agronomic School, a member of the Board of an Agricultural Association, a photographer. A former village lad, eighteen years old, had been consecutively in those years: A Red Army soldier, a factory worker, a party propagandist, arrested and condemned to death by the Whites, a member of a factory committee, an administrator of finances in a provincial town, a Red Army officer, a student, a member of the Provincial Committee of the Russian Communist Party, chairman of the Provincial Extraordinary Commission, a member of the All-Russian Central Executive Committee and a prosecuting counsel.

Although not all those people had so many changes as these two, yet at any rate all of them passed through more vicissitudes than they did in normal times. It is precisely during revolutions that, as the song goes, " Fate is playing with men; now it elevates them, now it throws them into an abyss."

Such is the picture of revolutionary circulation seen with the aid of a miscroscopic analysis. It is but a miniature copy of what is going on on a large scale among the Russian population.

From the beginning of the revolution, but especially after the Bolshevik *coup d'état* in October, there occurred an occupational, proprietary and legal cataclysm. On February 27th and in the first days of March, 1917, all former rulers, down to the policemen, as well as the dominant class, *i.e.*, the gentry, were removed from their position in the legal pyramid. Instead of rulers they became helots, deprived or semi-deprived of rights. Their places were taken partly by the representatives of the middle class of industry and trade, partly by those who occupied the lower parts of that legal pyramid, by the representatives of workers and peasants, and partly at last by the persecuted nationalities of Russia (the Provisional Government and the First Council of Workers', Peasants' and Soldiers' Deputies). The composition of the commanding class became—both socially and ethnographically —quite different. At the end of October there came a new explosion which finally buried the gentry and brought to the surface a new layer consisting of workers, soldiers,

Lumpen-proletarians and village paupers on the one hand, of international adventurers of all countries (Radek, Rakowsky, Sadoul, Varga, Rothstein) and the worst elements of Jewish people which filled all the commanding posts—on the other. " Those who were nothing had become everything," and *vice versa*. Communists, together with the paupers and the dregs of society who supported them, became a new " gentry."

The same thing happened as regards proprietary groups. As a consequence of " nationalization " and " communization " nearly all the rich people have become poor, while some of the poor have become rich. Along with this process there was going on the process of general impoverishment and levelling of proprietary standards.

A similar revolution occurred with respect to occupational diffusions. Many representatives of manual labor —workers and peasants—took to brain work as commissaries, propagandists, factory managers, etc.; on the contrary, many intellectuals, like teachers, professors, students, writers, employers and factory managers, were compelled to earn their living by manual work and become factory workers, guards, agricultural laborers, woodcutters, dockers, station porters, etc. Both of the former and the latter, according to Zinoviev, " changed their profession nearly every month." [4]

To be brief, it was a real earthquake which turned over all the social layers and radically changed the composition of groups, the relation between the rulers and the ruled, the privileged and the disinherited, the rich and the poor, and affected also the composition of various professional groups. Such is the essence of the social change in the first period of revolution.

In 1921 began the process of reverse circulation. The

---

[4] " Eleventh conference of the Russian Communist Party," p. 23.

mass transposition of individuals did not prove successful. Side by side with the people who were thrown off the top of the legal and proprietary pyramid on account of their unsuitableness and who were elevated there on account of their abilities, the revolution swept down a number of people who were quite able to occupy the upper places, at the same time elevating such as had no suitable abilities or experience. When the destructive period came to its end in 1920–21, and it was necessary to begin the work of creation, this became manifest at once. " Born rulers," " organizers " and " rich men " who had been unjustly thrown aside, began again to climb upwards, whereas the " born slaves," " paupers " and people good only for manual labor began to slide downwards. In the army the posts of generals, commanding and staff officers were allotted again to former generals and officers, who had been till then either imprisoned or serving in the White armies (Generals Brussilov, Klembovsky, Dostovalov, Noskov, Borissov, Verkhovsky, Lebedev, Slastchev and others). On the other hand many a revolutionary commander with the exception of the " born strategists " was dismissed or lowered in his rank.

The same happened in other branches of governmental administration. By 1922–23 in the majority of them all the leading posts were already occupied by specialists, *i.e.*, former ministers (*e.g.*, Nekrassov, Kutler, Pokrovski, etc.), officials, professors, etc. In the State Trusts, in the Councils of National Economy, while the supreme organs were composed up till 1921 almost exclusively of workers, during 1921–22 a change took place so that there were on the board of State Trusts only two workers and one " bourgeois specialist." Throughout 1922 and in 1923 the percentage of workers continued to diminish still further. According to the data furnished by an investigation of 1306 factory managers only 39 per cent. were former workers. Of the remaining 61 per cent. the majority belonged to the category of former employers and managers.[5] Three years before the picture was quite different. This rising of the " former people " and the sliding down of the upstarts is not yet complete, but it is still going on.

A similar process is going on within the proprietary and professional groups. The " new bourgeoisie " is to a considerable extent composed of the old one. The village " koolak," [6] the town trader, the employer and the profiteer having disguised themselves under the cloak of " nepmen " [7] and " red merchants " are again climbing to the surface. The same kind of reshuffling is taking place also within the professions.

On the whole, the reverse circulation, the tendency to return into pre-revolutionary state is obvious. In many cases this return is already an accomplished fact. The social groups begin to be filled with their old, pre-revolutionary members. It is true a certain part of those who have been placed in a new position in the first period of the revolution (especially the Jews) will remain there and thus " dilute " the old elements; but only a small part. Such is the circle of the revolution, such are its *corsi* and *ricorsi*. Now (in 1924) this circle is being completed.

The same phenomena, in a different form, may be observed in other groups.

From the data about the movement of divorces (see above ·" on the perversion of sex reflexes ") it follows that the inter-family circulation of individuals is also proceeding at a mass rate.

---

[5] *Les Dernières Nouvelles,* No. 972.
[6] A rich peasant.
[7] From " NEP " which means " New Economic Policy."

The same may be said of the political groups. A large number of people have passed during these six years—in a country with an undeveloped party-life—through many parties from monarchism to communism and have returned into their original non-party state. In this respect the velocity and the generality of circulation were also quite extraordinary.

As to the inter-state circulation (not in the sense of crossing the frontier territorially, but in the sense of belonging to this or that state), we are faced with a similar picture. For years and years—leaving aside a small number of emigrants—the Russian nationals remained such. After the revolution hundreds of thousands and even millions of people became—sometimes against their will—nationals of other states: Finland, Esthonia, Latvia, Lithuania, Georgia, Poland, the Ukrainia, Roumania, whereas many others—million *émigrés*—became subjects of no state whatever, people "without a country." A great part of all those people changed their nationality more than once; originally Russian subjects, they became citizens of Georgia, and then again subjects of Soviet Russia.

A similar picture is presented by the inter-religious circulation. A great mass of believers became atheists at the beginning of the revolution, some went over to the Evangelical Christians or to other sects; some became Roman Catholic converts. In 1922 various groups, like the "Living Church," the group of "Church Renewal," the old "Apostolic Church" separated themselves from the Orthodox Church headed by Patriarch Tikhon. Thus began an additional circulation within those religious groups. In 1921–22 began also the opposite process. A greater part of all these people returned into the Orthodox Church. The influence of the latter increased; the persecutions of religion and its servants instead of weakening the Church, strengthened it and augmented the number of its active adherents, leading to a renewal of Orthodoxy.

Here then also a large number of people have passed in the course of six years through a series of religious and atheistic groups which was not the case in normal times.

The territorial circulation is no exception from this general rule. In spite of the destruction of transport, it may be asserted that during these years the population of Russia has been much more nomadic than before. The revolution has turned over and set moving huge layers of population which never thought before of abandoning their residence. It flung them, and continues to do so, from one place to another over the whole borderless Russian plain. In 1917–18 hundreds of thousands of people from the starving towns went to the country; [8] then with the beginning of the civil war huge armies began to ramble about over the whole territory of Russia, covering distances from Vladivostok to Poland and from Archangel to the Crimea or Persia. In 1921–22 millions of starving people fled from the famine-stricken areas. Besides, thousands of Jews were driven to the capitals by the danger of pogroms, by the eager desire to make fortunes and by the opportunities for speculation and plundering that existed there. Millions of people lost their " homes " and became mere tramps, whom the revolution drove from place to place, even as far as Warsaw, Constantinople and Tunis. Instead of a sedate Russia

---

[8] *E.g.*, the population of Moscow amounted on February 1, 1917 to 2,017,000; on August 26, 1920 it was only 1,028,000. In Petrograd there were before the revolution 2,420,000 people; in 1918—1,469,000; in 1919—900,000; in 1920—740,000. V. the *Red Moscow* and the *Statistical Materials for Petrograd*, Vol. V, p. 19. Altogether about eight millions left the towns in the period from 1918 to 1920 (See the miscellany *During 5 Years*, 1922, p. 295).

there was a disturbed ant-hill with ants wandering in all directions.

However, beginning with 1921–22, *i.e.,* when the civil war was over, a tendency towards " settling down " could be observed also here. Demobilized soldiers came home. People who fled from the towns were gradually returning and the town population began to grow again. According to the census of 1923, the total town population increased to 16,330,274 (15,730,490 in 1920). The population of Moscow which amounted in 1920 to 1,028,000 increased to 1,542,874; the population of Petrograd increased from 740,000 to 1,067,328.[9]

Instead of Russia wandering " on foot, on horseback and in carts," as she was in the first period of revolution, we have a Russia " sitting quietly in one place like Ilya Murometz."

The same may be said of the circulation between various other groups and associations: scientific, artistic, literary, etc. In all of them the position of their members and the composition of the groups themselves changed repeatedly during this period.

In other revolutions similar things happened. To the increased rapidity and generality of circulation—proprietary, legal, professional and political—in the Egyptian Revolution the following observations of Ipouver testify: " He who had no property of his own, has become now a well-to-do man. Poor people have become rich, while the owners of property have become indigent. The former owner of clothes is going about in rags, whereas he who never wove for himself possesses linen; he who never built a boat for himself is the owner of a ship now; he who never had any bread, possesses corn-bins, and his stores are full of other people's property." And " the

---

[9] *Economic Messenger* (Russ.), No. 2, pp. 207-09.

rich and the princes are starving . . . A man who used to be well-off is now tortured by thirst in the night; noble ladies starve and say: if we only had something to eat," etc. It is clear from this what a great proprietary upheaval there was.

" The former slaves," he goes on, describing the legal circulation, " have become the masters of slaves." " The children of the princes are thrown into the streets and crushed against the walls . . . Not a single former official has retained his place," etc.

The revolution affected also the occupational circulation. " The builders of pyramids have become agricultural laborers," the princes have to do hard manual work, whereas some pitiful nedjes have become aristocrats and are living an idle life; the slaves of yesterday—who are the rulers of today—are resting on sumptuous couches, etc.

From the remarks of this writer about the invasion of foreigners it is clear that many have changed their nationality. There was also an intense interreligious circulation.

" The earth has been turned up like the disk of a potter," is his summary of the general picture.[10] We see from all this that during a short period of time great changes in the composition of groups and an enormous circulation altered the whole aspect of Egyptian society, and turned it topsy-turvy. The like happened in Rome in the last days of the Republic towards the end of the first revolutionary period. The Roman aggregate in this period may be compared to a boiling pot with madly circulating particles inside it. The victory of every dictator beginning with Gracchus (followed by Marius, Sulla, Anthony, Pompeius, Cæsar, Augustus, etc.), means the substitution of one upheaval for another and a radical

[10] See Vikentieff: Passim.

change in the composition of the majority of social groups. With every change of dictator "he who was nothing becomes everything" and *vice versa.*

The rapidity and the generality of circulation may be judged by the fact that the composition of the governing class repeatedly underwent radical changes during this period. The patrician aristocracy speedily disappeared in the process of revolution. By the time of Cæsar only fifteen patrician families were left. Their place was taken by the equestrians. But that did not last long. Owing to constant revolutions the rich quickly lost their fortunes, and on the contrary, the poor, if they had some cunning, easily made such. The proprietary circulation went forward at a greatly accelerated pace. Besides, there appeared on the stage liberated slaves, proletarians, criminals and international adventurers. Every struggling party tried to attract them to its side, and had to pay for their support by giving away offices and estates, by liberating the slaves, etc. Consequently, more and more newcomers penetrated into the governing class, and by the time of Cæsar and Augustus this class consisted chiefly of such *parvenus.* "In Augustus' time the emancipated slaves had an almost exclusive privilege of occupying the posts of higher and lower officials. . . ." The men nearest to Augustus . . . were again his personal slaves and emancipated slaves." [11]

Similar processes characterize other revolutions, too —such as the French Jacqueries, the Paris Revolution, the Jacqueries in Germany and England, the Russian

[11] Rostovtzev: *The Birth of the Roman Empire*, pp. 134-35. See also the works of Mommsen, Duruy, O. Seeck, Fahlbeck. Also Bouglé: *La Démocratie Devant la Science*, pp. 81-82; Woltmann: *Political Anthropology* (Russ. transl.), p. 279; Sensini: *Teoria dell' equilibrio. Rivista Italiana di Sociologia*, 1913, and above all Pareto: *Trattato di Sociologia Generale*, Vol. II, where he gives a detailed analysis of this circulation.

"trouble" of the seventeenth century, the Hussite Revolution.[12] The first period of revolution is always characterized by a social "avalanche": the aristocracy is immediately brought down, the rich plundered, new rulers and leaders from the lower classes come speedily forward, the composition of the governing classes undergoes a radical change (Watt Tylor, John Ball, the leaders of the French and German Jacqueries, E. Marcel, *les Maillotins,* the butchers, Caboche, Zizka, H. Huss, Zeliv, Procopius, the "Taborites," the "Orphans," etc.). As soon as the revolution has been suppressed, or naturally completed, there begins the "reverse circulation;" after the suppression of the rebellion of W. Tylor, of the French and German Jacqueries and revolutions, of the "Prague compactants" and of the Russian trouble, old commanding classes—to a certain extent pervaded with the new element—appear again on the surface.[13]

The same phenomenon we observe in the English Revolution. Its first stage consisted in the general overthrow of the higher aristocracy (of the cavaliers and of the upper layer of the Anglican Church hierarchy) with the King at its head, and in the general elevation of the next layers which formerly exercised but a slight influence in the commanding class. The next stage signifies a further sliding down of this class and the rising of the "middle," and to some extent of the lower classes, with Cromwell at its head. "The main landowners, the rich

[12] "Now," says a contemporary of the Hussite Revolution, "it is not the old group of men that rules in Prague. Now the most noble by birth, by estate or by talents have been either executed or banished. Tailors, carpenters, workers of all trades have filled the Council; there are in it even foreigners and peasants who came no one knows where from," Denis, p. 330.

[13] For details see the above-mentioned works. For France see a special monograph: Kolabinska, *La Circulation des Élites en France Depuis la fin du XI-e Siècle Jusqu à la Grande Révolution,* 1912.

citizens, the nobles, abstained from public affairs and did not participate in administrative committees or local courts; the power passed into the hands of the men of humbler classes who greedily stuck to it and proved able to act energetically, but not to retain it in their hands. They enjoyed, with great avidity, the pleasure of ordering, of ruling, of believing and calling themselves 'the chosen sons of God.' " [14]

The Protectorate of Cromwell, the dissolution of the Long Parliament, the abolition of the House of Lords, etc.—such are the main sign posts that characterize this second "avalanche." It was followed by the third, by the numerous attempts of the still lower orders (the levellers, the millenarians, the mystics, the diggers), to overthrow the Government of Cromwell, and the middle class, upon whose support it rested. This outburst was, however, suppressed by Cromwell who in 1653–55 came resolutely forward against all such attempts. At the end of his protectorate began the reverse circulation which found its expression in the sharp breach between Cromwell and the extreme groups which represented the lower classes (cp. his speech in the Parliament on January 22, 1655, his reply to Fick, etc.), in the dissolution of the Barebones Parliament, in the attempt to play with the upper orders and to incorporate them into the governing class.[15]

This process of reverse circulation ended in the Restoration. "It was not only the monarchy that was restored: together with the King, the big landowners, the rural gentry, all the nobility whom the Republic and Cromwell had eliminated from public affairs, took their

---

[14] Guizot: Vol. I, 133, XVI.
[15] " Cromwell had united himself with them and thereby radically changed his position: from a democrat, he became an aristocrat; from a revolutionary, he became a conservative." Guizot: Vol. III, 65, Gardiner: Vol. III-IV.

old places in the Government. The Episcopal Church was also restored." [16]

A similar circulation took place within other groups: religious, political, professional, territorial, etc.

In the French Revolution these processes were still more strikingly manifested. The first general transposition was accomplished in four or five months. August 4, 1789, saw the overthrow of the aristocracy and the higher clergy and the substitution for it of the *tiers état* which " was nothing and has become everything." At the same time the peasants, who were freed from the feudal dependency and exempted from feudal rates, moved to a somewhat higher station. The Legislative Assembly and the National Convention symbolize the further stages of this progress. The men of 1789 and the Girondists are driven aside by the lower class, by the intellectual proletarians, the workers, the peasants, the criminals and the dregs of society who occupy now the chief posts in the administration, who form the first Jacobin Committees, the main bulk of the clubs and sections which play the decisive rôle in politics. Some of their members in two or three years cover an enormous distance in " social space ": from ordinary lawyers, veterinaries, actors, tailors, carpenters, unknown officers, workers, peasants, journalists, etc., they become persons of weight and influence occupying high posts and having the power to dispose of the lives of their countrymen.

The same is true of the proprietary pyramid. The abolition of privileges, the confiscation and seizure of property, the plundering and the emigration ruined many a rich and privileged man and reduced him to a beggarly state. On the other hand, that and the purchase of

---

[16] Guizot: Vol. I, pp. li-lii.

national estates helped to create the *nouveaux riches* of
the " fat revolutionaries."

The general circulation within religious groups—
from faith to atheism, from the " unsworn " Church to
the " sworn " one, from one sect to another, from the
" worship of superstition " to the " worship of reason,"
etc.—went on with no less rapidity.

The growth of inter-family circulation has been
already noted above (see chapter on sexual reflexes).

It is hardly necessary to mention that the cases of a
free or obligatory change of nationality due to the emigration, to the conquest of new provinces, etc., became
very frequent in that period. The extent of territorial
circulation was also great. In the period of the Directory
and in the first years of Napoleon's Consulate began the
process of reverse circulation in all those groups. It was
completed during the Restoration when the large mass of
people returned into their original state, with a slight addition of the most " tenacious " newcomers.

Exactly the same happened in the revolutions of 1848
in France, Germany and Austria; in the revolution of
1870–71 in France; in the revolution of 1905 in Russia;
in the revolutions of 1918 in Germany and Hungary
(where the process of reverse circulation is not yet completed), the only difference being that all those revolutions, with the exception of the French of 1871 and the
Hungarian, were not of a thoroughgoing character and
the general circulation provoked by them was rather
superficial and confined chiefly to the legal transposition
of individuals.

After all those illustrations the main thesis about the
rapidity and generality of circulation and the quick
changes in the composition of groups will appear quite
clear and beyond dispute. Such is then the main differ-

ence between the revolutionary circulation and that of the normal times.

4. Changes in the Volume of Social Groups.—The inevitable result of the extraordinarily rapid, general and disorderly circulation in the first period of revolution is a quick and sharp fluctuation in the volume (the number of members) of the social groups which compose the aggregate.

We observe during the periods of revolutions not only a change in the composition of groups, but also a change in their volume, their number, their mutual relations and consequently a change in the entire morphological structure of the population as a collective unity. I shall illustrate this with a number of facts, and in doing so I shall accompany the descriptions of changes in the volume of groups with reference to certain related changes.

The Russian Revolution: Let us take the occupational and productive groups. The years 1917–21 are characterized in this respect (1) by an almost complete extinction of the following occupational groups: (a) the employers; (b) the tradesmen; (2) by a considerable decrease in the volume of the group of industrial workers (their number fell to 46 per cent.); the dictatorship of the proletariat nearly led to the complete extinction of the latter; [17] (3) by an excessive swelling of the group of officials (nearly 30 per cent. of the whole population became government officials and agents); [18] within the group we perceive also

---

[17] Prokopovitch: p. 27.

[18] *E.g.*, according to the census of 1920, the Soviet officials constituted over 50 per cent. of the whole population of Moscow, while the remaining 50 per cent. stood at their service: the Russian capital became a town of officials. The same happened in other towns. The percentage of officials in the villages also increased. See the *Red Moscow* and the article of Larin, entitled " The amusing arithmetics " in the *Red Gazette*.

Before the war, there were 1.5 officials and gentry for every 100 people (*The Statistical Yearbook of Russia for 1908*, p. 75). Now

an abnormal increase of the controlling personnel, as
against the executive one: according to the same census
of Moscow for every two members of the executive
personnel, there were one, two or even in some Commis-
sariats three controllers; (4) by a certain increase in the
volume of the agricultural groups; (5) by a nearly complete extinction of the liberal professions (barristers,
etc.); and, finally, (6) by a generally reduced professional differentiation, due to the fact that many people,
and especially the brain workers were compelled to
become "encyclopædic," as far as their functions went,
and to satisfy by their own efforts all their wants, *i.e.,* to
sow, to cook, to wash, to split the wood, to dig in the
kitchen garden, in short, to do everything for themselves.
It is clear from this how great were the changes in the
professional map of Russia, how displaced the border-
lines became between the existing professions, leading to
the swelling of some of them and to the contraction of the
others, to the intermixture of various professions and to
their reduced differentiation.

At the end of 1921–22 began the reverse process: the
group of employers and tradesmen reappeared again and
began to grow; the number of officials sharply diminished
("the reduction in staffs"), liberal professions sprang

the number of Soviet officials alone has enormously increased. If we
take the number of people who are subsidized by the State, we obtain
the following figures:

> 1918–19 there were 12 million officials
> 1919–20 there were 23 million officials
> 1921–22 there were 35 million officials

35 million officials in a country with 130 millions of population make
27 per cent. (instead of 1.5 per cent. before the war). These figures
speak clearly of the extent to which this group has swollen during those
years; they also show that instead of abolishing bureaucracy and
State apparatus in general, the Communists have created a new,
unheard of bureaucratic machinery and an all-pervading State mechanism. Truly: *ducunt volentem fata, nolentem trahunt.*

again into existence, the tendency toward "functional encyclopædism" began to disappear and functional differentiation became again prevalent.[19]   A similar process was going on in the field of proprietary differentiation. Not only the composition of the various layers of the proprietary pyramid, as shown in the foregoing section, but also the form of the latter and especially the number and the magnitude of layers, changed in the course of the revolution.   From 1917–20 are the years of general impoverishment, of the diminishing proprietary differentiation, of the lowering of the proprietary pyramid.[20] Private property was confiscated and the whole upper section of the pyramid was thereby cut off.   In the lower parts the process of the levelling went on.   This may be gathered from the decrease of economic differentiation

---

[19] According to the data of the Statistical Department of the Moscow Council in 1922–23, the number of employers in Moscow increased by 600 per cent. in the period 1921–23; that of accountants and clerks by 400 per cent.; that of engineers, architects and technicians not in the State service by 350 per cent.; and that of people engaged in private trade by 318 per cent.   The number of "nepmen" increased fifteen times as compared with the rest of the population; that of their clerks and assistants—seven times (*Dni,* 1923, No. 245).

On the other hand, there continued the "reduction in staffs." Thus, towards July 1, 1923 the staff of the Commissariat of Transport was reduced by 25 per cent.; a further reduction of 20 per cent. was contemplated for January 1, 1924.   Yet with all those reductions the relation between the number of officials in the Central administration of the Commissariat of Transport and the total number of workers in the same institution, three times exceeded that of 1915 (in 1915 1 : 90, in May, 1923, 3 : 90).   See *Dni,* No. 248.

[20] The annual national income per capita was:

1913 .... 101.35 roubles
1921 .... 38.60 roubles

The monthly wages of a worker were:

before the war 22   roubles
1918 .... 8.99 roubles
1919 .... 6.77 roubles
1920 .... 7.12 roubles
1921 .... 6.95 roubles
1922 (first half) .... 8.22 roubles

Prokopovitch: *Op. cit.,* pp. 119, 135.

among the peasants and workers. In 1918 the ratio
between the highest wages of a skilled worker and the
lowest wages of an ordinary laborer was 175 : 100. This
relation was not to be exceeded under fear of penalty.
Of the peasants' households there were in twenty-four
provinces of Soviet Russia :

	with no sowing area	with sowing area up to 4 dess.	with sowing area from 4 to 8 dess.	with sowing area over 8 dess.
1917	11.4 per cent.	59.1 per cent.	21.6 per cent.	7.9 per cent.
1919	6.5 per cent.	74 per cent.	16.4 per cent.	3.1 per cent.

The percentage of households with many or with no
horses diminished, and that of households with one
horse increased.[21]

From those data we may judge of the general impoverishment and of the contraction of the proprietary
pyramid.[22] The revolution produced an economic equalization, not by enriching the poor, but by making the
rich poor and by contributing to a general impoverishment. That, of course, did not prevent the small clique
of rulers and their satellites from becoming rich, but this
is only a partial result which does not counter-balance the
general ruin. The result is that instead of a pyramid we
have a kind of trapezium with a small steeple on the top
of it.

In 1921 began the reverse process of growing proprietary differentiation with a tendency, as yet feebly
developed towards an increase of the national income.
Both in towns and in villages the economically strong ele-

[21] See A. Khriastchev and B. Knipovitch in the miscellany *About
the Land*, Vol. I, 25, 34; Procopovicz: pp. 29-30.
[22] During the periods of economic impoverishment the proprietary
equalization is quite a common phenomenon. The periods of economic
prosperity are on the contrary characterized by an increasing proprietary differentiation: the pyramid grows higher and steeper. P. Sorokin:
System of Sociology, Vol. II, 406 and foll.; Schmoller: *Die
Einkommensverteilung in alter und neuer Zeit. Bullet. de l'Inst. de
Stat.*, Vol. IX, part I.

ments again occupy the predominant positions, attaining to it by labor, by speculation, by frauds, by legal seizures. Again we see an enormous contrast between poverty and wealth. In 1922–24, with the whole country brought to the utmost limit of ruin, this contrast acquires very acute forms, especially in towns. Here the luxury of European capitals is to be seen side by side with people dying from starvation. In villages the "koolaks" and the "paupers" predominate; comparatively large households and households with no sowing area at all increase in numbers at the expense of the medium ones. For example, in Pensa province the percentage of the peasants without horses was in:

1917 .... 36.8
1920 26
1922 37

" The tendency of the increase of the percentage of the poorest and of the richest elements at the cost of the middle peasants is quite clear," says *Pravda*.[23] To sum up, the destroyed pyramid of proprietary relations has begun to reform.

Such are the processes that have been accomplished within the proprietary pyramid in the course of six years by the revolution and that would have required decades under normal conditions.

The rearrangements within the legal pyramid were just as violent. Here also not only the composition of the "privileged" and the "disinherited," of the "ruling" and of the "ruled" classes was affected, but the form of the pyramid, that is to say, the number and the magnitude of the layers that composed it as well. The gentry, the big landowners, the high officials and the merchants dis-

---

[23] *Pravda*, Nov. 21, 1923. See also: Iakovleff: *Village as it is,* 1923 (Russ.).

appeared from the upper section of it. Their places were taken by the new officials and the new aristocracy, but in a modified proportion.

Before the revolution the hereditary nobility counted about 300,000 people. The number of communists who took its place as a privileged class was in 1920-21— 600,000; in 1922—420,000; in 1923—372,000. Before the revolution the number of officials, together with the nobility, did not exceed three millions, whereas in the years 1918-20 that number fluctuated between twelve and thirty-five millions. Those examples show how great were the changes in the magnitude of the various layers of the legal pyramid. If we did imitate the communists and regard all the officials and the privileged class as parasites, we should be forced to admit that the revolution not only did not exterminate the parasites, but that it led to the increase of their number.

The structure of the medium parts of the pyramid has also changed. Formerly there were no civilly disinherited people, and the will of the government, beginning with the Czar, was limited. The life of every citizen was secure, and the rights of man and citizen were fairly large, as far as personal and proprietary immunity and freedom of press, meetings and associations were concerned. After the October revolution the picture radically changed. The contrast between the privileged class and the remaining population became much more sharp: the rights and privileges enjoyed by the former were practically unlimited, those of the latter reduced to nothing. The citizen of Soviet Russia resembled a snake whom every commissary could, and did, crush under his foot.

Instead of a pyramid of rights and privileges there was an even plane of the lawless equality of some and of the unlimited whim of the others.

In 1922 the tendency towards the reconstruction of the pyramid begins to be felt. Both theoretically and practically the volume of rights enjoyed by the population starts to grow, at the same time the whim of the new governing class is gradually circumscribed. The number of officials and the number of the members of the communist party considerably diminish. Not many years are needed in order that the pyramid should be completely reconstructed quite apart from the question whether the monarchy will be restored or not: in either case the difference will be that of labels and personal composition, and not of the essence.

We have seen above that considerable changes occurred also as regards the State territory and the population. The former was contracted by 710,000 square wersts, the number of people who became the nationals of other states amounting to 28,571,000.[24]

Still more striking are the changes in the party relations. At the beginning of the revolution there existed in Russia the following big parties: (1) the monarchists; (2) the Octobrists; (3) the industrial party; (4) the cadets (constitutional-democrats); (5) the labor party; (6) the social democrats, and (7) the social-revolutionaries. After the first weeks of the revolution the first three of those parties practically ceased to exist. On the other hand, the socialistic parties began to swell like bubbles; especially that of the social-revolutionaries. Out of a small illegal group it became in the course of a month a big party with a membership of over one million. In the elections to the bodies of self-government (municipal, etc.) in the summer of 1917 it received more than one-half of the total votes. The communist party hardly existed as a party in March, 1917; but in July it was

[24] *Statistical Yearbook of Russia for 1918-20*, pp. 1-7.

already strong enough to attempt a *coup d'état*. From August its popularity went on increasing, whereas the influence of the socialistic parties was already on the wane. In October the communists succeeded in carrying out their *coup*, almost without resistance. All non-socialistic parties now disappear, the socialistic ones lose their members and only the communists go on growing. In 1918–20 the extinction of all parties but the communist is completed, their remnants continue an illegal existence, but the entire political stage belongs to the communists. In 1921–22 begins the decline of the latter, and at the same time the place of the old parties is being taken by some new groups; we witness the birth of a new monarchist, a new republican and a new "non-party" party. From this it may be seen with what cinematographic rapidity did all those party changes proceed.

The extraordinary fluctuations in the volume, in the number and in the position of social groups, which are so clearly perceived in the Russian Revolution, happened also in other revolutions.

Let us take the great French Revolution. In the course of one or two years the whole morphological structure of the population of France was changed. The upper layer of the legal and proprietary pyramid, represented by 270,000 members of the privileged class, 130 bishops and 120,000 to 140,000 clerics, was removed. Their places were taken by the upstarts from other classes, but it is unlikely that their number was equal to the number of the "privileged" class under the old régime. Still more unlikely it is that the form of the legal and proprietary pyramid, the number and the position of layers in it remained the same. Though we are unable to prove it exactly with figures in hand, we know that great changes took place in this respect. The wealth amounting to

2,992,538,140 livres—which had been owned by 120,000 to 140,000 clerics—was disbursed among new owners. General proprietary differentiation diminished. The position of the peasants improved both legally and economically; the position of other classes, of the workers especially, became worse. On the whole there was a "contraction" of the legal and proprietary pyramids, notwithstanding the fact that over the impoverished and disinherited mass of the population there appeared a tiny layer consisting of a few upstarts. The same happened to the other groups. The volume of the French State— its population and its territory—at first contracted and then expanded again. In two or three years the volume of political groups—the royalists, the Feuillants, the Girondists, the Jacobins and the anarcho-communists underwent radical changes. Similar changes took place within religious and professional groups, as well as in the administrative division of the State.

In other words, the old structure of the French social aggregate changed so radically and so quickly that the period 1789–95 may be called the period of "deformation" and "turbidity," in which the social border-lines are hardly visible. Only in the beginning of the nineteenth century did the outlines of a new France become clear and distinct; the reconstructed pyramids of legal and proprietary groups reappear again; the border-lines between religious, political and professional groups are again sharply outlined.

Similar phenomena characterize the English Revolution of the seventeenth century, the Russian Revolution of the same century, as well as mediæval and ancient revolutions. Although we have no precise data about the extent of the changes that took place in them, the fact of those changes is sufficiently proved by various historical testimonies.

5. " Dissociation " of " Abnormal " Cumulative Groups and Formation of the New Ones.—The social groups of which the population is composed may be divided into simple and complex (cumulative) ones. By the former I understand such groups as are united together by one cardinal similarity or by one social bond (*e.g.,* by similarity of religion, of profession, of party, of wealth). By the latter I understand such groups as are united together by two or more of such simple social bonds. As examples of such complex social groups may serve a social class, as a totality of people united together by the volume of rights, by the similarity of occupation and by the social position; or a territorially-linguistic group as a totality of people who live in the same territory and speak the same language. There are a number of such cumulative groups.[25]

In examining the structure of those complex groups we discover among them " normal " and " abnormal " cumulative groups. The point is that not all kinds of simple bonds are easily combined with each other, and not all those combinations are enduring. Thus, *e.g.,* the criterion of " wealth " easily attaches itself to the criterion of " privilegedness," and it is difficult to combine it with that of privation of civil rights (disfranchisement). Therefore, cumulative groups such as " the rich and the privileged " or the " poor and the disinherited " occur frequently enough, they are normal and stable, not easily dissoluble; whereas cumulative groups such as " the poor and the privileged " and " the rich and the civilly disinherited "

---

[25] See the theory of cumulative groups in my *System of Sociology,* Vol. II.

are very rare (abnormal), and when they do exist they are not stable and easily dissolve. The same is true of the cumulative groups consisting of "people who perform professional functions essential for the life of the aggregate and the privileged " and of "people leading parasitic life and the civilly disinherited." Those groups are normal. The opposite combinations occur more rarely and usually they dissolve easily. The former combinations are "normal cumulations," the latter "abnormal cumulations," bound to dissolve. The appearance in some aggregate of such "abnormal cumulative groups " is one of the signs of the coming "reaction of transposition," *i.e.*, of the coming dissociation of such an abnormal cumulation and of the formation in its place of a new normal cumulative group.

In the chapter on the causes of revolutions we shall see that an excessive development of such abnormal cumulative groups is characteristic of the pre-revolutionary periods. Those groups grow up gradually, like abscesses in a physical body, and they last for some time through the sheer force of "inertia." Revolutionary epochs are characterized by a speedy disappearance of such abnormal cumulative groups, *i.e.*, by a quick "reaction of transposition." To this is largely due the so-called "purifying" work of the revolution. I will illustrate the above with a few facts.

What is the picture we see in Rome on the eve of the revolutionary period (the movement of the Gracchi) ?

1. An aristocracy that is poorer than the newly-born bourgeoisie (the equestrians), but enjoys greater privileges and prevents the "new people" from entering the ranks of the governing class.

2. An aristocracy that has ceased to perform socially-

important functions, has degenerated and become to a considerable extent parasitic, but is still privileged.[26]

3. A bourgeoisie that is richer than the ruined aristocracy, but does not enjoy all the rights and privileges.

For those "abnormal" cumulations to exist was enough to ensure that a struggle would begin between them.[27]

It did begin. The "reaction of transposition" became manifest already at the time of G. Gracchus, who granted several new privileges to the bourgeoisie (the equestrians) who were thus made almost equal in importance to the senators.[28]

Had the class of equestrians itself proved adequate to the situation—perhaps things would not have gone further than a "bourgeois revolution," which would have led to the dissolution of the old aristocratic group ("the privileged, the parasitic, the poorer") and of the new bourgeois group ("the richer, the civilly disinherited") and to the formation of new groups ("the rich and socially useful, the privileged" and "the poor, the civilly disinherited") in their place. But the equestrians proved just as incapable as the old nobility.[29]

Besides, several other classes, like the proletariat, the peasants and the slaves, became implicated in the struggle started by the nobility and the equestrians, thus contributing to the deepening of the revolution. A whole century

---

[26] From 151 B.C. on the "new people" begin to be excluded from the high offices. "The aristocracy itself begins its political career not in a military camp, but in the antechambers of influential persons." It has degenerated, become parasitic and shows neither its former virtues, nor the self-denial, nor the sense of duty, nor the ability to rule. Cp. Mommsen: Vol. II, 69-75, 132-34, 158, etc. It has become unworthy of itself "both politically and morally."

[27] "Between the noble and the wealthy there existed a feeling of hostility." Mommsen: Vol. II, 112-13.

[28] Mommsen: Vol. II, 112-13.

[29] Mommsen: Vol. II, 73, 211.

of struggle, leading to the nearly complete extinction of both parties and causing an enormous social upheaval, was necessary in order that new normal cumulative groups might emerge by the time of Cæsar and Augustus when the wealthy became also the privileged and *vice versa.* Notwithstanding all the vicissitudes of the revolution its result was the usual one: the formation of "normal" groups in the place of "abnormal."

A similar picture is presented by the English Revolution of the seventeenth century.

Here, "some great changes in the relative power of the various classes of society took place before the revolution which were not followed by the corresponding changes in the government." The privileges of the lords and of the court aristocracy were enormous although "the House of Commons was now three times as rich as the House of Lords. The inhabitants of the towns, the provincial gentry, the farmers and the small landowners had no such influence upon state affairs as would correspond to their social importance. They had grown in numbers, but not risen in rank. Hence—their proud and powerful spirit of ambition. The democracy was looking forward to elevation and trying to make its way through the ranks of the weakened aristocracy." [30]

This means that apart from other "abnormal" cumulative groups there were here two main groups: (1) "the privileged aristocracy, the poorer" and (2) "the civilly disinherited, the wealthier" (the bourgeoisie and the other classes represented in the Parliament). Those groups began to fight one another; consequently they dissolved in the process of revolution and their place was taken towards 1688 by "normal cumulations." In this

---

[30] Guizot: Vol. I, p. IX.

"reaction of transposition" consisted the work performed by the revolution.

The same may be said of the French Revolution. Before the revolution we have in France: (1) the enriched *tiers état,* "energetic, intelligent, ambitious and persistent" and yet "nothing" as far as the volume of rights is concerned; and (2) the aristocracy which had been systematically ruined and brought to a lower economic level, as compared with the bourgeoisie—degenerated, leading a parasitic existence, yet enjoying enormous rights and privileges.[31] The same is true of the upper clergy.

Such a situation could not be lasting. Either the "sword of the aristocracy" had to obtain gold and again become socially useful in the protection of the public, or the gold of the bourgeoisie had to buy privileges and turn the *tiers état* from "nothing" into "everything." It was this latter that happened. The bourgeoisie "was carried to the high pitch of madness by the inequality." It hated the aristocrats and aspired to freedom in the hope of obtaining power.[32] "The vanity (of the bourgeoisie) has created the revolution, freedom was but a pretext," as Napoleon picturesquely, and yet precisely, put it.

Thus began the struggle between those groups. As usual the other classes became involved in it and the struggle developed into a real revolution. In the complex body of revolutionary dramas, tragedies and comedies the above-mentioned "reaction of transposition" played the main part. Its result was the dissolution of the "abnormal" cumulative groups and the formation of normal ones, *viz.,* "the rich, the privileged" and "the poor, the

[31] For the characteristic of those groups see Taine: *Les Origines de la France Contemporaine,* Vol. I, ch. I and foll.; also de Tocqueville and Madelin: Vol. I, ch. III.
[32] Madelin: I, 37-43.

civilly disinherited " (no matter by what means the privileges and the wealth were obtained).

The same state of things we see in the Russian Revolutions of 1905 and 1917.

The cumulative group of nobility which monopolized the privileges and the power was—from the second half of the nineteenth century—gradually becoming impoverished. The land—the main wealth of the nobility—was passing out of their hands. At the beginning of the twentieth century the nobility was quite poor as compared with the new commercial and industrial bourgeoisie. But looked upon from the point of view of rights and privileges it was still in the same extraordinarily favorable position. Both those groups: the nobility and the bourgeoisie —not speaking of the others—became " abnormal." The Russo-Japanese war gave a stimulus to the " reaction of transposition " which found its outcome in the revolution of 1905. The result was: a diminution of the privileges of the nobility and the growth of the influence of the industrial and commercial group (the Duma, the Gutchkovs, the Konovalovs, the Riabushinskys, etc.). Yet, the " reaction of transposition " was not quite complete. But for the war, it would have probably developed along the lines of " evolution." In the period from 1905 to 1914 the influence of the nobility annually decreased, while that of the bourgeoisie grew accordingly. The war made the competition between them still more acute. The bourgeoisie placed itself at the head of the opposition to the government of the nobility which proved incapable to rule, yet did not wish to surrender its position. Thus began the revolution in the first stage which accomplished the above-indicated " reaction of transposition." The nobility was put aside, the authority passed into the hands of the Provisional Government which was to a great extent composed of the representatives of the big bourgeoisie (Tereschenko, Lvov, Konovalov, Buryskkin, etc.). But the unusual conditions created by the war drove into the struggle the other social groups, too, with quite different interests and aims, which they set out to achieve. Consequently, the revolution transcended the limits of the struggle between the nobility and the bourgeoisie. However, notwithstanding that deepening of the revolution, the accomplished "reaction of transposition" remains its most important and enduring result. The nobility has ceased to exist as an abnormal group. If some members of it do elevate themselves to the ranks of the "privileged," it is not in their capacity of parasitic aristocrats that they do so, but as active and energetic men who make their fortune by hook or crook. Together with the members of the old and of the new ("communistic") bourgeoisie, they form a new normal group: "the rich, the privileged" which is destined to occupy the commanding social positions. On the other hand, the "impoverished nobles" are brought low and have to join the group of "the poor, the disinherited."

Such is the main result of the Russian communistic revolution. Its balance has been, as usual, right. It does not matter whether the gold attracts the privileges, or the violence of the privileged and the non-privileged obtains the gold; it is only essential that the place of an "abnormal" group should be taken by a "normal" one. This object has been achieved, no matter by what means.

Those examples show what I mean by the "reaction of transposition." Of course the dissolution of the abnormal cumulative groups accomplished in the process of revolution is not confined to those two main groups. Many other groups undergo the same change. It is not my task here to enumerate them: that is merely a *questio facti* in

every given case. Every social aggregate has such blisters
or abscesses which are cut and destroyed by revolutions.
It is true that frequently while some splinter is being
extracted, the whole organism becomes infected, that the
surgical knife of the revolution cuts without sense, and
causes serious wounds, inexcusable in the case of an intelligent surgeon, but only political romanticists may demand
knowledge and experience from a revolution. It would
be strange to demand from a blind elemental force that it
should know the art of surgery. Being a revolution is a
sufficient excuse for being a "bungler" in this case.

**6. Changes in the Mechanism of Selection and Distri-
bution.**—The fact that the interrelation of groups and
the circulation of individuals proceed in a different way in
the ages of revolutions means that that mechanism of the
social aggregate which regulates the selection and distribution of individuals within social space, *i.e.*, within the system of groups and in the various strata of the same
group, is also different.[33]

Granted all the multitudinous varieties of this mechanism in various aggregates, its main task may be summed
up as the distribution of individuals more or less according to the law: "to everyone according to his abilities,
especially the innate ones." A violent and lasting transgression of this law cannot be safely allowed in any
aggregate. Otherwise, as the proverb goes, "the baker
will start making shoes," the ordinary draught horse will

---

[33] By this mechanism I mean, using the words of O. Ammon: *Die
Einrichtungen, welche dazu dienen sollen, die Individuen "auszulesen"
und jedes auf den Platz zu bringen, den es vermöge seiner Veranlagung
am besten ausfüllen kann*. This mechanism consists of two kinds of
devices: the first are meant to hinder the elevation of incapable individuals, the second—to further the rise of the talented and capable
ones.

See O. Ammon: *Die Gesellschaftsordnung*, 1895, p. 52 and foll.
For details see my *System of Sociology*. See also below the chapter
on "the causes of revolutions."

play at a racing horse, the born slave will assume the functions of a ruler—in a word, all social functions will be badly performed, the aggregate will succumb to a disease which will lead to a social crisis.

Apart from periods of decadence and such as precede a revolution when such a perversion of social status is what we really see (cp. below, chapter on the " causes of revolutions ") in any sound social aggregate, this mechanism as a rule works fairly well. Consisting on one hand of a series of preventive devices (such as the demand for experience, examinations, etc.), and on the other of a series of favorable conditions which presume abilities and are not so absurd as they may seem at first (such as the descent from a talented family, pecuniary welfare, good references, etc.) it performs in normal times fairly well the function of " sifting " the individuals, and distributes them, if not ideally, at least not too badly.

This picture changes strikingly in the periods preceding a revolution and in the revolutionary periods.

The normal mechanism becoming distorted in the pre-revolutionary periods ceases to operate during the revolution and is superseded by a quite different one. With a few exceptions, this new mechanism of selection and distribution usually proves a failure, i.e., it works contrary to the law : " to everyone according to his abilities."

In the first place, when the old mechanism breaks up hundreds and thousands of people arbitrarily seize upon the important functions without any test of their abilities or examination. Some speech which pleased the mob, or the energetic participation in the murder of the " enemies of the people," or some such thing makes up for a serious test of abilities which would be necessary in normal times. This is enough in order to understand why so many adventurers and " bakers disguised as shoe-makers " emerge in the first period of the revolution.

Let us observe the professional selection during the revolutions. Under normal conditions, in order to be admitted into any profession—and especially into the highly skilled professions—it is necessary for an individual to prove his professional ability and experience. The individual prepares for his future occupation and is subjected to various tests, such as learning, practical test, examinations, carrying out of several tasks, etc. Without such preparation and test he cannot be admitted into, and excel in, such a profession. We do not entrust the construction of a locomotive, the teaching of children, or judging to the first comers.

During revolutions this condition is in most cases brushed aside. Instead of professional ability, especially as far as skilled professions are concerned, there is the " revolutionary certificate, faithfulness to the cause of revolution and revolutionary merits; " " unrevolutionariness " is, on the contrary, a criterion of general inability. I do not exaggerate. From the beginning of the Russian Revolution we see this happening. The whole ruling class, down to the last policeman, was at once dismissed, although there were in it many able professional men. And, conversely, " revolutionaries " and the " sympathizers " were chosen for the rôles for which they were not in the least prepared. The maximum of revolutionary fervor was regarded as a sufficient guarantee of universal abilities.

This became still more striking after the October revolution. The distribution effected by it, not only in the administration, but also in the field of economics, was simply absurd. Engineers, experienced managers and organizers of undertakings were purposely driven out from the factories and workshops, on the plea of cleansing the industry from parasites and class enemies. "The presence of a skilled engineer in a factory was regarded as a sign of conciliatory policy towards the bourgeoisie, incompatible with the principle of the dictatorship of the proletariat." [34]

"We must ruthlessly sweep away our class enemies from all the decisive economic organs, not leaving them there under any pretext or upon any considerations whatever"—such was the leading opinion of the communists.[35]

It is not surprising, then, that at the head of the undertakings were placed workers who could not sign their names, journalists who had no idea whatever of economics. In 1921 began the work of cleansing and of elimination of all incapable elements. It is not yet completed. The state of things in 1922 may be gathered from the results of an *enquête*. Of 159 responsible managers of industrial undertakings:

13 per cent. had higher education
24 per cent. had secondary education
63 per cent. had preliminary education

About 70 per cent. were formerly simple peasants, workers and office clerks without any special experience. Among those 159 people were only six skilled engineers.[36] The results of the *enquête* held in 1923 show that a further purification has taken place. There were among 1306 managers of undertakings:

22.6 per cent. with higher education
24.9 per cent. with secondary education
52.5 per cent. with preliminary education [37]

---

[34] Prokopovitch: *Op. cit.*, p. 38.
[35] In the magazine *The National Economy*, 1918, I, p. 19.
[36] *Economic Life*, 1922, No. 268, Prokopovitch: pp. 40-41.
[37] *Isvestia*: Quoted after *Les Dernières Nouvelles*, No. 972, June 23, 1923.

Only 61 per cent. of them were designated by the communists themselves as quite capable to occupy their posts, 30.3 per cent. were marked as " feeble " and 8.7 per cent. as incapable.

If such was the position in 1922–23, after the purification, it is easy to imagine what a staff of managers there was in 1918–21. At the head of the industrial undertakings were placed revolutionary Mayflies transformed out of former *émigrés,* old party workers, journalists and such-like people who knew nothing about the work they were to do, and merely helped to create a " multitudinous vacuum." [38] One of the communists, Gastev, thus characterized the situation: " A tailor was placed at the head of a big metallurgical concern, a painter at the head of a textile works. . . With such an apparatus only people of the *bohême* and not people who deal with state affairs, could imagine that something was to be done. It is high time that we stopped that *bohême,* that incessant prattle." [39]   The same we see everywhere. For example, as late as the summer of 1923, the Commissary of Justice, Kursky, pointed out that " 80 per cent. of the justices of the peace have no idea of law." [40]   And such a state we have also in 1922–23, 1446 " red justices " were dismissed in the process of " cleansing." [41]

Those facts show the extent of the distortion of the mechanism of selection and distribution which works now

---

[38] Procopovicz: p. 38.

[39] " Acts of the 1st All-Russian Conference of the Councils of National Economy," pp. 71-73.

[40] *Dni,* No. 243.

[41] See official *The Weekly Magazine of the Soviet Justice* for 1922-24 and *The Magazine of the Soviet Law,* 1922, No. III.   See also N. Timasheff: " About the Soviet Justice " in *The Peasants' Russia,* No. VII, pp. 155-61 (Russ.).   See also my article about the Soviet Court and Justice in *Michigan Law Review,* Vol. XXIII.

quite contrary to the principle " to everyone according to
his abilities." Fords and Carnegies may exist among
peasants and workers, but they cannot be created by the
order of the government. They succeed by manifesting
their organizing abilities, and not by showing their revolutionary fervor. They prepare for their future rôle, they
possess some experience, they overcome obstacles, and do
not, mechanically and all of a sudden, from tailors become
managers of metallurgical works.

It will be easily understood that such an absurd distribution became one of the causes of the economic and
industrial disorganization. When that disorganization
reached its limit, the communists themselves began to
complain. In 1922 began the cleansing of the second
period of the revolution, *i.e.,* the restoration of a more
normal mechanism of selection and distribution, coupled
with the recognition of the principle of " professional pre-
paredness " and suitability. The incapable elements began
to be excluded, and instead of them " bourgeois specialists " were invited. One of the chief blunders was realized. The inability of the majority of the communists to
perform their new functions was such that in March,
1922, Lenin himself welcomed the coming financial crisis
as a means to throw out the mass of communists. This
crisis, he said, " might be even useful: it will expel the
communists from various state trusts. Only we must not
forget to do it. . . . We might draw some profit out
of this crisis and do the cleansing thoroughly, not
as it is done by the Central Committee of the Communist Party." [42]

The same took place in other professions. Good pedagogues, students, eminent professors were thrown out if

[42] See *The Eleventh Conference of the Russian Communist Party,*
Kiev, 1922, p. 26.

they happened not to be communists, and instead of them were put " red teachers," " red students " and " red professors " who had no knowledge, no experience. The distribution was based not on the principle of professional suitability, but on the principle of faithfulness to the Soviet Government and Communism. The drawbacks of the pre-revolutionary period were carried to absurd lengths. Just as formerly noble descent was preferred to abilities, so now proletarian descent meant more than anything else. Just as formerly people who belonged to the opposition were shunned, although they were excellent specialists, so now—even in a greater degree—opposition to communism led to exclusion, to arrest, sometimes to execution. Just as formerly " protection " played an important part, so—and even more now—good relations with, and proximity to, the Government, opened the way to the most incapable people. If formerly bribes and presents, flattery and servility helped individuals to rise, now they played the chief part.

It would be useless to go on enumerating facts. The picture of the bad functioning of the mechanism of selection and distribution in the first period of the revolution is sufficiently clear.

Of course, I do not mean to say that under such general redistribution there were no capable people among those who " slipped through " or that among those who were swept aside there were none who deserved it. It would be simply incredible, had there been no such exceptions; but there were exceptions—and in the Russian Revolution very rare. If this was not evident in the first —destructive—period of the revolution, it became so in the second—constructive—period. With it began at once the above-described " reverse circulation," the elevation of the unjustly displaced and the "sliding down" of the upstarts.[43]

The same happened in other revolutions. Let us take the Paris Commune of 1870-71. Both the "Central Committee of twenty sections" and the Commune were composed "of people entirely unknown to the population." "Who are they?" exclaimed many people after reading the signatures.[44] The commanding positions were occupied by people who were totally unprepared and belonged to all sorts of professions (painters, mechanicians, druggists, laborers, etc.).[45]

Can we wonder that such a government was unable to cope with the tasks that stood before it. "After the first week the Commune proved weak and light-minded, possessing no military plan, incapable of finding its way amidst the difficult problems of the moment," say its own members.[46] Even if the Commune were not suppressed, there is no doubt that with the restoration of the

---

[43] This reverse circulation is still going on. In a telegram of June 16, 1923 we read: "The Council of Labor and Defense has proposed to the Council of National Economy to carry out a radical reorganization of the industrial councils and to appoint as members of the latter solely the persons who used to occupy corresponding posts in large industrial concerns." *Dni,* No. 192.

[44] Gregoire: Vol. IV, 311, 322-30.

[45] "Over 56 members (out of nominal 90) had been formerly imprisoned or banished. They brought with them all the rage, the irritation, the passion of the men who are exasperated. Behind them was the excited crowd of the political, scientific and literary bohême, of the café-gossip, who postponed till tomorrow the carrying out of their grandiose plans." Vallès thus describes them: "out of a café-table they have made a chair for themselves and there, under a gas-lamp, they talk out their books: days and evenings pass, they have already talked out 30 chapters, and not written even 15 pages." Gregoire: *Ibid.,* 342. Lissagarés: *Op. cit.,* 178-79.

[46] Lissagarés: p. 214; "The Executive Commission was unable to command. The Central Committee did not wish to obey." At the head of it stood "incapable people, upstarts." "The unsatisfactory composition and the lack of knowledge were becoming every day more and more evident." *Ibid.,* 230. See the whole of ch. XVII which describes the loose organization of public institutions.

normal mechanism of selection the majority of those upstarts would have been thrown overboard.

In the Revolution of 1848, the Provisional Government was proclaimed in a haphazard way and composed of casual people.[47]   The mechanism of social selection ceased to exist and all sorts of casual people slipped through the hole and seized the functions of government for which they had no special aptitude.   This happened also in the lower administrative degrees.   The posts of the prefects and sub-prefects were occupied by revolutionary commissaries and assistant commissaries, among whom there were many not only incapable people, but downright scoundrels. The amount of revolutionary ardor served as the criterion of suitability.[48]   Is it to be wondered, then, that this government " greatly contributed to the disorganization of France." [49]

The results of such a bad selection and distribution manifested themselves as early as 1848–49 when many of the " upstarts " were not reëlected; in 1850–51 the work of cleansing proceeded further; it ended in 1851 in a *coup d'état,* after which we notice again the growing importance of " specialists," of business-like people, the distribution according to abilities and other features already familiar to us.

Thanks to similar defects of the mechanism of selection, many incapable elements penetrated into the commanding class in the German Revolution of 1848.   " A

---

[47] " By what right? rejoined Lamartine when questioned about the right by which the government ruled.—By the right of blood, the right of fire swallowing our buildings, of nation without leaders. By the right of most faithful and courageous citizens." What is that if not a poetical interpretation of the Roman: *res nullius primo occupandi cedit!* Gregoire: Vol. III, 5.

[48] *Ibid.,* 35.   " The republicans of 1848 demanded the dismissal of those who did not prove their attachment to the Republic by taking part in conspiracies or secret societies."

[49] *Ibid.,* 10.

great number of madcaps appeared on the stage who
wanted to make use of the movement for their own hob-
bies. There were gentlemen, for instance, for whom the
abolition of the custom of taking off the hat when greeting
somebody meant infinitely more than the awaited Constitution." [50] In the Frankfort Parliament we see nothing but an incessant prattle and inability to act.[51] Journalists appear in the rôle of military leaders, poets in the
rôle of economists, in a word " shoemakers " acting as
" pastry cooks." No wonder, then, that in the course of
one or two years the " reverse selection " threw overboard
many an " upstart " and elevated again those who were
undeservedly cast off.

As to the French Revolution: Before Termidor there
was a general banishment of people who formerly occupied
the commanding positions. After Termidor began the
opposite wave. Seventy-three exiled deputies immediately
returned to the Convention; they were followed by sixteen
Girondins. Then the process went on still faster: the
Constitution of the year III meant a return to the proprietary restrictions in the electoral law. Nearly all the
Jacobins were cast out from the important offices. In the
by-elections held in accordance with the " two thirds
law " it was " the moderate former deputies of the Constituent Assembly; the former Feuillants or the men hostile to the declining régime " who came off as victors.[52]
That showed itself still more strikingly in the elections in
Germinal of the year V, when royalists, including the former ministers of Louis XVI (Fleury), the agents of Louis
XVIII, the white terrorists and moderate bourgeois and

---

[50] Bloss: p. 110.
[51] Thus, *e.g.*, it was originally proposed to devote 292 sittings to
the first reading of the " Fundamental Rights " alone. This figure
was then diminished, but not sufficiently. Bloss: pp. 258-9.
[52] Madelin: II, 198.

conservatives were elected. That process continued under Napoleon and ended in the Restoration. The same happened to the professional, religious and other groups. The mechanism of selection which in the first period of the revolution, side by side with capable and tenacious individuals, allowed incapable ones to pass through, began to work better in the second period, performing the same work of cleansing which we saw it doing in the Russian Revolution. In the second period of the revolution, the demand for "special preparation," for "professional aptitude," for "business-like methods" already played an important rôle. Under Napoleon it became predominant. His own collaborators were chosen by such tests. The general map of social distribution radically changed.

The same process went on in the English Revolution, although here the distortion of the mechanism of social selection was not so great as in the Russian Revolution. As the revolution deepened, not only the outspoken royalists, but many professional specialists were cast off. Of 506 members of the Long Parliament there remained in 1649 only 100, chiefly people with highly-developed servile instincts.

After the execution of the King even such republicans as Fairfax, Sidney, Vane, etc., were removed. Of forty-one members of the State Council twenty-two refused to take the oath and were dismissed. Many excellent judges, hundreds of officials and aldermen were also removed. The culminating point in this respect was reached in the Parliament (1653) which was composed of people hardly capable of performing their functions.[53] After this the mechanism of social selection began to work normally, as may be seen in the composition of the Protector's Council

[53] Guizot: Vol. III, 56 and foll.; Gardiner: *History of the Commonwealth*, 1903, Vol. I, 5-9, Vol. II, chs. XXVI-XXVII.

constituted in accordance with " the Instrument of Government." " The members of the new Council were of the type of men who usually rise to ascendancy after a revolution has run its course—men of practical efficiency opposed to further changes in the State and, above all, to anything savoring of fanaticism. Such men are usually content to devote themselves to the task of carrying on government without taking into account the theories on which any special government is founded. Such were the instruments of Napoleon, and such, too, were the councilors of Oliver," as Gardiner rightly observes.[54] This improvement of the mechanism of selection and distribution went on further.

Is it not the same in all other revolutions? Did not the prolonged Hussite Revolution lead in the second period to the reverse circulation of the moderate elements—the courtiers and the Calixtines who were cast off in the first period? Were not many of the ill-starred Taborites and Orphans brought down after the " Compacts of Prague " of 1433 (see Denis, pp. 330, 348, 469-73)? Did not the principle of " business-like people " clearly triumph at this moment? And in what did the numerous Jacqueries and revolutions of the fourteenth and fifteenth centuries end in France? In the strengthening of the monarchy which surrounded itself with excellent specialists and business people who helped to create a great France. What was the result of the Russian trouble of the seventeenth century? The increase of the Czar's power, the rise to ascendancy of the old commanding classes, the overthrow of the new rulers, the growing importance of " business principle " in social selection, the triumph of specialists in the persons of professional bureaucrats.[55] What was the

---

[54] *Ibid.*, Vol. III, 3.

[55] Kliutchevsky: *Russian History*, Vol. III, 198-271, Platonov: *Lectures on the History of Russia*, 1917, pp. 355-6, 361.

result of the Roman revolutions? Cæsar and Augustus surrounded by " business people " chosen from various classes of society, down, it is true, to slaves and liberated slaves.

From this summary survey we see that our conclusions regarding the changes in the mechanism of social selection and distribution were right. The Russian Revolution is typical in this respect. But that general similarity which we perceive in all revolutions does not exclude the possibility of variations as to the details: the extent of the distortion of the mechanism of selection, the percentage of people unsatisfactorily distributed in the first and in the second period, the rate at which the disorganization and the restoration of the mechanism of selection proceed, the percentage of " upstarts " who fit in with their new functions, etc. All those are but partial differences which do not invalidate the above-stated essential resemblance.

7. **What Psychological Types are Climbing up in Revolution?**—The changes in the mechanism of selection and distribution of individuals which were described above may be traced also in another way, *viz.*, by analyzing the " psychological types " which are on the one side carried to the top of the legal and proprietary pyramid, and on the other left at, or brought to, the bottom of it.

In this respect, too, the revolutionary selection is quite distinct from the normal one.

The main differences may be thus summed up. Since in the first period of revolution the main task is that of destruction and the activities are confined to struggle and intrigues connected with it, the leading rôle in this period inevitably falls to energetic people, with dominating destructive impulses, to narrow-minded people who do not

want, and cannot foresee, all the calamities that are bound
to be brought about by unlimited destruction, to people of
a " single idea," some of whom are unbalanced maniacs
and fanatics, full of unsatisfied ambitions, hatred and exas-
perations, indifferent to other people's sufferings, in a
word, people with feebly-developed (restraining) habits,
and with all their liking for nice phrases, little sociable. On
the contrary, peaceful, compassionate people who are
accustomed to create, not to destroy, who are sane and
broad-minded enough to understand the dangers of an
unlimited destruction, who usually weigh their actions and
act carefully, people with strong restraining instincts,
well balanced and not extreme—have no chance of succeeding in the first period of revolution. They are left
in the shadow, brought to the bottom, and are bound to
remain passive.

It is not surprising, therefore, that the first period of
a revolution carries to the top all sorts of adventurers,
some among them are maniacs, victims of mental disorders, together with criminals, murderers, prostitutes and
dregs of society who belong to the same psychological
type. Madelin is right when he says : " In the period of
crises all that there is dark in the nation rises to the surface—' white scum, red scum.' " [56] General opinion that
such persons are sociable is absolutely wrong. Sonorous
phrases of such leaders are nothing but a " beautification "
and " veiling " their exceedingly inferior egotistic and—
very often—insane nature. This fact now became clear
for psychologists and psychiatrists. With few exceptions
we can say the more radical, extreme and " pompous " in
his " speech-reactions " the man is (" Welfare of Mankind," Liberty, " Annihilation of Exploitation," etc.) the

---

[56] Madelin : Vol. I, 8.

more careless is he in reality about everything excepting himself and his rather rude impulses.[57]

Since, on the other hand, revolution always means war, it cannot help thrusting to the foreground professional soldiers. If questions of justice are to be decided by physical force, and the " weapons of arbitration " are to be replaced by the " arbitrament of weapons," the growth of the influence of the soldiers—be it Cæsar or Augustus, Cromwell or Dumouriez, Napoleon, Monk or Wrangel, Zizka or Procopius, MacMahon or Ludendorff—is inevitable. The revolution, which looks so contemptuously upon militarism and *soldatesca,* is itself militaristic in its essence, and inevitably leads to the rule of militarism. Thrusting forward of the military leaders is an indispensable function of every revolution. When all questions begin to be solved by violence, " the interference of people belonging to the military class, and possessing a military force, in the political revolution " becomes inevitable.[58] Thus it was in Rome, thus it has been ever since. Those men usually end by killing their mother—the revolution— and on her tomb they erect a throne of dictator or emperor for themselves.

To the third psychological type whose ascent we witness during revolutions belong " cynical schemers," people skilful in political manœuvring, scoundrels on a large scale who know whither the wind blows and are ready to change their conditions when necessary, for whom there is nothing sacred except their own welfare. Among them we often come across excellent specialists of their trade.

[57] See S. Paton: *Human Behavior,* 451-52 pp. F. H. Allport: *Social Psychology,* 111-19, 368-74 pp. Le Bon: *La Revolution Française,* 87, 223-25 pp. E. Burke: *Reflections on the Revolution in France,* in the Writings and Speeches (Little, Brown Co.), Vol. III, 284, 311-12, 321-22, 347-48 pp.
[58] Mommsen: II, 160.

Usually men of this type pass safely through all the periods of revolution and restoration. Once risen to a position of ascendancy they remain there. By adroit manœuvres and changes of opinions they manage to please all governments and run less risk than the first two types. Usually men of this type, together with the professional soldiers, act as immediate successors and grave-diggers of the revolutionary heroes of the first type.

As examples of the first type may serve: Lenin, Trotzki, Zinovieff, Latzis, Radek, Kedrov, Dzerdzinsky and many thousands of Russian communists who ascended from various classes: criminals and bandits, workers and peasants, ruined aristocrats and bourgeois, ill-starred journalists and writers, etc. The majority of them have passed through years of imprisonment and hard labor which could not but tell upon their nerves, which in its turn explains the fact that instead of an earthly paradise they have introduced the régime of hard labor.

Bela-Khun and his colleagues in the Hungarian Revolution; K. Liebknecht, R. Luxemburg and several other communists in the German Revolution; the majority of the members of the Paris Commune; Struve, Hecker, Bakunin, Blum, Blanqui and the Blanquists in the Revolution of 1848; Marat, Robespierre, St. Just, Danton, Carrière, Babeuf and many other Jacobins in the French Revolution; leaders of the fifth monarchy and of the extreme sects in the English Revolution; Adamites, Piccards and many Taborites in the Hussite movement; W. Tylor, Caboche, many demagogues in the Roman revolutions—all those are men of the first type.

Marius, Cinna, Sulla, Sertorius, Anthony, Pompeius, Cæsar, Augustus, Zizka, Procopius the Great, Cromwell, Fairfax, Monk, Dumouriez, Napoleon, Wrangel, Cavaignac, MacMahon, Brussilov, Slastchev, Budenny, Tukhatchevsky, Frunse, Kamenev, etc.—are the examples of this second type.

Krassin, Steklow, Nekrassow, Kutler, leaders of the " smienoviekhovtsy," of the " Living Church;" all those Gredesculs, Sviatlovskys, Elistratovs, Kirdetzovs, Jordanskys and many others in the Russian Revolution; Cenek de Wartenberk, Talleyrand, Tallien, Merlin, Barras, Carnot, Fouché, Sieyès, Cambacerès and others in the French Revolution; dozens of " changelings " such as H. Mildmay and Whitaker in the English Revolution—personify the third type.

From adventurers, the insane and fanatics to military dictators and cynical schemers—such are the phases of the revolutionary development.

As soon as the revolutionary current is dammed up, the men of different psychological types begin to fill the commanding classes.

However unpleasant are the men of the third and the second type they must be preferred to those of the first—cynical schemers at least know how to live and permit the others to do so, whereas the irreconcilable revolutionary sectarians neither live themselves nor let the others. Revolutionary (and counter-revolutionary) fanaticism is more terrible than any cynicism—such is the bitter truth which history teaches us.

8. Changes in the Behavior and Psychology of the Transposed Individuals.—The place occupied by the individual in the system of social coördinates is not quite indifferent from the point of view of his behavior and psychology. The character of the social groups to which the individual belongs and the place occupied by him in every such group have a decisive influence upon his psychology and behavior. *Ceteris paribus,* our behavior is determined by the character of the groups to which we

belong and by the place which we occupy in them. If those groups are mutually antagonistic and impose on their members contradictory rules of behavior, then our " ego " will be also full of contradictions and will subjectively reflect the objective fact of antagonism of various social groups to which we happen to belong. Our behavior in this case will be self-contradictory, inconsistent, hesitating. There will take place in our psychology a collision of incompatible obligations and aspirations. In our behavior we shall resemble a ball which is being pushed in opposite directions. If on the contrary all the groups to which we belong show a mutual solidarity, our " ego " will remain wholesome and united, our conscience will be quiet, our sense of duty will undergo no fluctuations. Our behavior in this case will be consistent and resolute. We shall resemble a ball which is being pushed by various impacts in the same direction. It is not difficult to understand why there is such connection between the position of the individual in the system of social groups and his behavior. The fact that one belongs—voluntarily or involuntarily— to this or that group (religious, party, family, state, economic, etc.) involves the pressure of that group upon the behavior of its members and the necessity for these latter to fulfill various actions and duties (towards family, state, profession, religion, etc.). Being a member of a definite family, one cannot help carrying out a series of actions which are involved in that fact. Likewise, being a citizen of a definite state, or a member of some definite profession, or religion, one cannot help performing certain functions and thereby fulfilling one's rights and duties as a citizen of the state, as a member of the Orthodox Church or as a member of some profession. Between the individual and the groups to which he belongs there is a kind of electric wire which transmits to the individual the cur-

rents that emanate from those groups, and make him
respond to those currents.

Our behavior seen from this point is to a great extent
a mere combination of reactions to the "stimuli" and
"orders" emanating from those groups. The same must
be said about our ego. This big ego consists, as it were, of
a multitude of little egos ("ego" of the member of the
family, "ego" of the member of the profession, "ego"
of the member of the party, etc.), which represent various
social groups to which we belong and every one of which
has its own "sphere of influence" in our soul. It is easy
to understand therefore that, granted the equality of other
conditions, the behavior of the individuals must be
regarded as the outcome product of the pressure of those
groups to which he, voluntarily or involuntarily, belongs.[59]

In accordance with the above-stated propositions " a
man who belonged to the group of poor and disinherited,
and earned his living by manual work, let us say, of a carrier, on passing into the group of rich and privileged and
on changing his profession from that of a carrier to that
of a minister, will inevitably change himself. Otherwise
he will be unable to retain his new position. If formerly
he had the interests, the psychology, the behavior and the
manner of life of a proletarian, now he will have the
psychology, the behavior, the interests and the manner
of life of a master. With this transformation the little
"egos" of a poor and disinherited man and of a carrier
will be, so to speak, taken from him and replaced by the
little egos of a rich and privileged man and of a minister.
Unless such a transformation takes place, this man will

<hr>

[59] For the proofs of this proposition see my *System of Sociology*,
Vol. II, ch. VI and Passim. From the psychological point of view the
phenomenon of the multitude of psychical affiliations in one individual,
their solidarity and their collisions, has been fairly rightly explained by
the school of Freud. See, *e.g.*, Freud: On *Psycho-analysis*, Passim.

not retain his newly-gained position: either he will relinquish it, or he will be swept away. It is easy to understand, therefore, why every government, no matter to what class its representatives belong, will inevitably have its own interests, psychology and behavior, different from the interests, the psychology and the behavior of the people ruled by it." [60]

Since revolutions lead to the general transposition of the individuals in the system of social coördinates they also lead to the general transformation of the behavior and of the " souls " of the transposed individuals. Figuratively speaking, a revolution always means not only a general transposition of the individuals, but also a general transposition of the " forms of behavior " and of the " souls." During the first period of revolution, when, as we saw, the old system of coördinates becomes distorted, a corresponding change and " turbidness " takes place in the souls of men. Old views and opinions, old rules of behavior are swept away while the new ones have had as yet no time to crystallize themselves. The transposed individuals who have lost their old egos, but not yet obtained their new " souls " resemble people whose behavior has lost its former stability and who are at a loss where to turn. From *socii* they change into mere biological individuals. Their psychology becomes disorganized and primitive. The preventive habits disappear. The gulf between that which is permitted and that which is not, exists no longer. The sense of rights and duties becomes slack. No longer directed by the groups to which they used to belong, for those groups are disorganized, the individuals now commit much of that they would—with their " old soul " —regard as inadmissible and disgusting.

[60] Sorokin: *System of Sociology*, Vol. II, 452-53.

Then the first period ends. The disturbed social sea begins to settle down, the " turbidness " disappears, the system of the social aggregate undergoes the process of crystallization. Parallel with it goes the process of crystallization in the " souls " of the individuals. Those who have returned to their social positions restore their old " ego " and their old behavior. Those who have been transposed little by little adapt themselves to their new position and gradually obtain the " souls " and the forms of behavior which correspond to their new position in the system of social coördinates. We need not be surprised, therefore, when we see a former monarchist in the rôle of an ardent communist or *vice versa,* a former proletarian who used to protest against the persecutions of workers, now—in the rôle of a commissary shooting them or prohibiting their strikes, *i.e.,* doing exactly that which the governors and the policemen did, a former advocate of the freedom of press and meetings, now—as a chairman of some Soviet, proclaiming all liberties as counter-revolutionary prejudices; a former enemy of death penalty and militarism, now—in the rôle of a military commissary or a member of the Extraordinary Commission—engaged in the wholesale destruction of men and advocating a " ruthless war." The manner of life of those people (their housing, nutrition, clothing, general standard of life) changes accordingly, as well as their attitude, their gestures, their reflexes of speech, their tastes and opinions. The same is applicable to those who have been brought down by the revolution.

Such a general transformation of the behavior and of the psychology is quite inevitable and is due not so much to the versatility of those people, but to the fact of their transposition in the system of the social aggregate. Let us look at some facts which illustrate this.

Who stood at the head of the punitive expeditions which destroyed whole villages and executed peasants for non-payment of rates, for disobedience and criticism? In most cases—former workers and former peasants who used to protest against infinitely milder measures of the old government in dealing with the same peasants. Now they were ruthlessly punishing the mutineers. Is that not a striking change? The point is that those workers were put in the position of rulers and policemen, and this caused a transformation of their behavior and their psychology. They have obtained the same " soul " which their predecessors used to have and therefore they do exactly the same that the leaders of the punitive expeditions and the chiefs of the police used to do, only much more coarsely and ruthlessly.

Who abolished freedom of strikes in 1918–24, declaring them to be the result of counter-revolutionary propaganda, engineered at the expense of the enemies? [61] Former workers and revolutionaries who—before they came to power—ardently advocated freedom of strikes and laughed when the government tried to explain them as a result of foreign bribery or malicious agitation. Now, having occupied the position of the old government they have " put on " its " garment of behavior," and acquired its soul, its opinions and its psychology.

What did Lenin, Trotzki, Zinovieff and other leaders

---

[61] Several Bolshevik proclamations upon this subject (*e.g.*, to the striking workers of the drain factory in Petrograd in 1921) were an exact reproduction of the similar proclamations of the Czar's government, the only difference being that the Bolsheviks threatened the strikers with more severe punishments, and instead of " Jewish and Japanese money " they put, adapting themselves to the circumstances— " the money of the Entente," while instead of " revolutionary rioters : social-revolutionaries, social-democrats and other Jewish freemasons " they said : " counter-revolutionary rioters : social-revolutionaries, social-democrats." Koltshakists, White Guards and other rabble supported by the Entente. This is the whole difference.

of Bolshevism preach in their speeches, their books, leaf-
lets and articles before they took power into their hands?
They preached freedom of speech, of press, of meetings,
of the manifestation of popular will, the necessity to
abolish the death penalty and to stop the war. What did
they preach and do when instead of ordinary journalists
and propagandists they became ministers and supreme
rulers? Exactly the opposite to what they preached
before, and at the same time precisely that which had been
done by the Czar's government, if not worse. Their old
" souls " were taken out of them and replaced by the souls
of unlimited despots and policemen. It will be said that
the Bolshevik government had its own reasons for such
propaganda and actions, that they were dictated by
necessity. But then every government has its own reasons and does such things not for sheer pleasure, but only
of necessity.

The general transposition of individuals led to the
general transformation: those who obtained new positions in the system of social coördinates acquired also
the "soul" and the "garment of behavior" of their
predecessors.[62]

One of the main demands of the revolutionaries of the
nineteenth century was the demand for all kinds of liberties. They usually accused the old régime of tyranny.
But what happened when the authority passed into the
hands of revolutionaries? In the first days unlimited free-

[62] Very often this change of behavior and psychology is nothing
short of the imitation of the overthrown predecessors. Thus, e.g., the
red cadets of the R.S.F.S.R. are copying precisely the habits of the
old officers. "We notice among them a tendency towards petty-
bourgeois ideology and the acquisition of the habits of the Czarist
officers' caste," is the judgment of the communists themselves. See the
address of Shubin at the Military Schools' Conference, printed in the
Military Messenger, 1923. Quoted after Dni, No. 243. The same is
everywhere including the State Political Department which resembles
exactly the old Police Department.

dom was as a rule proclaimed; then, as we saw above, all
the liberties were abolished.

Members of the Central Committee and of the Paris
Commune of 1871 were, before they came to power, all
of them advocates of liberties and enemies of the death
penalty.[63] In a month or two their behavior radically
changed. All the newspapers which they regarded as
undesirable were suppressed, the guarantees of personal
freedom were abolished, freedom of speech and press also,
courts-martial were introduced and a number of innocent
hostages were shot.[64] To sum up, we see here a complete negation of all previous declarations and demands
and an exact reproduction of those features of the Versailles Government which they themselves criticized. It
might be said again: those measures were dictated by
necessity. Yes, of course, but every government that
introduces such measures sees a necessity for them, and
the real reason is that every new occupant of authority
must needs inherit the main features of the psychology
and the behavior of his predecessor. Otherwise he will
be overthrown.[65]

The same was repeated in the case of Jordan, Giskra,

---

[63] As late as March 20, 1871 they indignantly rejected the accusation to the contrary and proudly declared in the *Journal Officiel*:
"We have not signed a single death verdict; the National Guards
have not taken part in a single execution." *Paris Commune, Acts and
Documents*, 1920, p. 17 (Russ.).

[64] See *e.g.*, the resolution of May 17, 1871 (*Acts and Documents*),
pp. 124-29. "Away with pity, we say; away with mercy; away with
forbearance," thus runs the resolution of April 6, 1871 which introduces courts-martial. "In view of the urgent necessity the Commune
decrees: 10 hostages are to be shot as a punishment for the murders
committed by the Versailles lot.," etc. *Ibid.*, p. 126.

[65] We see this also in our days. In many European countries it
has become almost a rule to begin one's political career as an
extreme socialist and then in climbing higher to grow more and more
moderate and on entering the government to become a domesticated
socialist-bourgeois (Clémenceau, Viviani, Briand, Ebert, German
social-democratic-ministers, MacDonald, etc.).

Rüder, Kapp, Geld, Fröbel, Brass, Bauer and others in the German Revolution of 1848, who began as revolutionaries and ended by becoming the mainstays of order.[66]

Let us turn now to the great French Revolution. Against what did the Jacobins protest prior to their rise to power? Against tyranny, despotism, *lettres de cachet,* political persecutions, and other restrictions of freedom. What did they wish for? Freedom, manifestations of popular will, republic, carrying out of the principles of the "Declaration of Rights," etc. What did they do and proclaim after their rise? The exact opposite of all that. Did they respect the will of the people and let it manifest itself? No. This was shown clearly in the debates of December 27, 1792, concerning the fate of the King. When Salles proposed in the Assembly that the will of the people should be appealed to and made known, Robespierre spoke passionately against this proposal. "Virtue," he admitted, "is always carried out by the minority." St. Just made a still more important admission: "Appeal to the people. . . . Does it not mean the restoration of monarchy?"[67]

The point is that when the will of the people coincides with their own, they are ready to appeal to it, when not . . . hundreds of "ideologies" are invented, such as, in this case, that of a chosen minority, and the will of the people is trampled upon. Did not the old régime do the same, although in a milder form? Were not the activities of the Jacobins after their rise to power a blatant negation of all their previous declarations? In dispersing the meetings with armed force, in excluding the undesirable members of the Legislative Assembly, in depriving them of rights, in using sheer force, in abolishing all guarantees

[66] Bloss: pp. 224, 247, 262, 277, 279, 320-1, 341, etc.
[67] Madelin: II, 31.

of freedom and carrying the terror to the utmost pitch—
did they not rise against themselves and copy most cruel
and wilful of all despots?   Is it not a complete change of
" soul " and behavior?   A closer study of that transformation leads to the discovery of some curious details.   The
old régime used to fake the elections in its favor—they do
it twice as much.   The old régime tried to assure the
necessary majority by violence and various machinations.
They did the same, e.g., when they decreed that two-thirds
of the Convention were to be elected from among them.
Did they not protest against the King's veto?   And having
become members of the Directory, they, in the person of
La Réveillière, claimed that veto for themselves.

We need not point to the members of the Directory, to
the " fat " revolutionaries who inasmuch as they got
" fat " and rich and climbed to the top of the social ladder,
changed their opinions and behavior: those who used to
preach equality now stuck avidly to the titles of mar-
quesses and dukes; those who took part in the overthrow
of monarchy now became its ministers.

Those are but sundry facts.   But is not the history of
the revolution full of them?   Did not the same happen to
thousands of people who were transposed in social space?

Likewise it was in the English Revolution, beginning
with Cromwell.   In reading his speeches and analyzing his
actions we see through the veil of frequent appeals to God,
how, with the change of his social position, his behavior
and " soul " also changed.   Did he not bring the King to
the scaffold for not wishing to take into consideration the
will of the people, for not respecting the Parliament, for
interfering with liberties and for religious persecutions?
Yet, what does he do when he takes the King's place?   He
dissolves the undesirable parliaments, interferes with lib-

erties, does not pay any heed to the will of the people, creates the " Protector's Council " instead of the " Star Chamber; " instead of establishing the Commonwealth he favors the proclamation of himself as a Lord Protector and virtual King; arbitrarily fixes the taxes; arbitrarily arrests and punishes his enemies; in a word, Cromwell, the revolutionary, and Cromwell, the Protector, are two different people, with different " souls." [68]

The same may be said of a great number of other people who rose to the top. They imitated the behavior and the souls of their predecessors. " Step by step, the government of the Commonwealth was to accommodate itself to its true position, and to rule by means which every one of its members would have condemned if they had been employed by Charles or Strafford," rightly observes the historian.[69]

The same happened to the religious groups. Prior to their becoming the privileged Church the independents

---

[68] In a conversation with E. Calamy, when the latter objected to the principle of monarchical power as unlawful and inapplicable, Cromwell replied: " Unlawful?—No. But why is it inapplicable?" Calamy said: " For the majority of the nation is opposed to it and nine-tenths will be against you." " What if I disarm the nine and will hand the sword to the tenth, will it not do?" Guizot, Vol. III, 29. Was it not Cromwell who used to defend the right of the Parliament to overthrow and to execute the monarch? Yet in 1654 he, while dissolving the Parliament that did not suit him, said: " On your part not to recognize this (Cromwell's) seal, to sit here and not to recognize the authority (Cromwell) on the strength of which you do it . . . is the gravest crime which a man can commit against the God's Providence." Ibid., 116. Reading those words of Cromwell one involuntarily thinks that they might have been uttered by Charles I who actually did on many occasions say almost exactly the same.

[69] Gardiner: Hist. of Commonwealth, Vol. I, 55. For facts see ibidem. The authors of The Hunting of the Foxes were quite right in remarking that " the old King's person and the old lords are but removed, and a new King (Cromwell) and new lords with the Commons are in one House and so we are under a more absolute arbitrary monarchy than before." Gardiner: Ibid., Vol. I, 33.

fought for religious toleration, whereas Laud and the Episcopal Church did not want to acknowledge it. Later their rôles changed. The former adherents of religious toleration became its oppressors, while the former oppressors became its advocates.

Was not the struggle for complete freedom of interpretation and preaching of the Word of God the main claim of the Hussites before they acquired power? On how many occasions did they sign special covenants in order to secure that claim! Yet as soon as the Taborites and the Utraquists came to power the picture changed. Zizka embarked upon a wholesale destruction of the Adamites and other sects for their interpretation of the Gospels, and declared and carried on a ruthless war against all the dissenters. The same occurred in Prague where the Utraquists organized a mass inquisition, arrested and killed all those who did not believe according to their wish. Before their rise, the Bohemian revolutionaries denounced the rich and denied private property. Then having seized other people's wealth they keep it to themselves and become ardent advocates of private property. Did they not protest against the oppression and the robbing of the people? Having come to power they began to oppress and to rob more ruthlessly than the old rulers ever did.[70]

This general transformation of the behavior of the transposed individuals is not confined to the examples that have been adduced above. We observe it in all successive revolutions. It is universal and manifold. Every individual on coming into a new position changes more or less his behavior, his soul, i.e., his convictions, his beliefs, his tastes in conformity with this new position.

---

[70] Denis: *Op. cit.*, 278-83, 294 and foll., 348-49.

Only a long social education, a frequent change of occupation under normal conditions (as in the United States of America), a rich and many-sided experience and a genuine and deep-seated sense of morality may somewhat mitigate that transformation. Outside those conditions, it is inevitably sharp and conspicuous in all countries during the periods of revolution.

PART IV

THE MODIFICATION OF SOCIAL FUNC-
TIONS DURING REVOLUTIONARY
PERIODS.

CHAPTER XIII

THE MODIFICATION OF SOCIAL FUNCTIONS DURING REVOLUTIONARY PERIODS

I. GOVERNMENTAL FUNCTIONS

LET us now speak of the chief modifications which take place in the social processes of a Revolutionary Society.

We shall commence by studying them in their relation to government and politics. Treating the subjects from the standpoint of a mechanism whose business it is to regulate the conduct and interrelationship of different members of an aggregate we must have in view two mutually opposed kinds of societies. 1. A society in the midst of which the conduct and mutual relations of its members are regulated from outside, in a compulsory manner, by a controlling power; their own free will and agreement not being taken into consideration. Here the domain belonging to such controlling functions of the government is very considerable, its authority is immense and its intervention —limitless. It issues orders with authority; decides on the activities which the individual should embrace, the work which should be performed by him; whether he should marry or not, what he should believe, think, wear or eat, etc. The members of such a society resemble puppets, which the governing authorities pull by a string. Whereas the governing authorities can be likened to a single central dynamo-machine bringing into action and controlling the movements of these puppets.

The amount of liberty, independence and self-government granted to the citizens is very restricted; this is the case in all domains: economical, professional, religious, that of the family, that of culture, etc. There are no limits to the intervention of the government. This type of society possessing such a central compulsory governmental mechanism for controlling the conduct of its citizens can be called a centralized despotic one. 2. Quite opposed to this type is a society in which conduct and mutual relations are controlled by the members themselves; where their own free will and agreement play an important part; where independence and liberty reign supreme; and the authority, intervention and controlling functions of the government are comparatively restricted. In such a type of society nothing is needlessly forced upon the members in a compulsory manner by the government. Here the government only prescribes: methods of coöperation, the other choices remain with the individual. He himself chooses his own religion, his point of view, his own ideology and occupation. The individual, not authority, decides whether he will marry or not; what economical agreement he will enter upon; what he is going to produce, and how much of it; what he will wear, and eat, and drink; where he is going to live, etc. In this case it is, as if, besides the small dynamo-machine of the government, each individual possessed a special dynamo-machine of his own which set him in motion and controlled his behavior. Such a type of society can be named a democratic or independent self-government. Each of these two types are but rarely found in a pure unmixed stage. But different societies of the past and present assume a character which is nearer either to the first or the second type.

We must now try to find out in which direction the transformation of social organization progresses during revolutionary periods. Does it deviate toward compulsory state intervention or toward autonomy. The answer to this problem is the following: 1. During the first revolutionary stages we witness a sharp deviation of social organization in the direction of uncontrolled anarchical autonomy. 2. It is speedily supplanted by a deviation of an opposite character; which brings on a stage of despotic state intervention surpassing pre-revolutionary despotism. 3. Only after the termination of the revolution does this state intervention, as well as the despotism born of it, decrease. The deeper, the more violent, the revolution— the sharper will such deviations be.

Up to the present time a great majority think that revolution and freedom are synonymous. It seems needless to say that such a belief is unfounded, unless we call a society of despotic state intervention a free type; unless we understand freedom of action to be the freedom of the puppet put into motion by authority.

For, apart from the first half-anarchic period, revolution is: 1. The decrease of the independence, the rights and the liberty of citizens. 2. It is the increase of intervention, tutelage and other controlling functions of the government, or in other words, it is the growth of a despotic state intervention at the expense of free autonomy. Such is the result to which everyone has to come who wants to acquire an objective viewpoint of the controlling organization of society and the conduct of citizens and authorities during revolutionary periods; every one who does not judge events by revolutionary " vocal reflexes," loudly proclaiming the merits of liberty.

In private life we already have learned to judge of people according to their deeds, not their words. Unfortunately this principle has not quite reached the realm of social science and our judgment of historical events is not always colored by it. Revolution is rich in slogans and anthems in honor of liberty. But how poor is it in corresponding deeds.   It resembles an adroit sharper enveloping his doubtful actions in sonorous words.   There are many who admit that the liberty and independence of citizens decrease during revolutions, but console themselves with the thought that after the termination of the revolution they will again increase : this they attribute as merit to the revolution.   There is no doubt that after the end of the latter the ascending line of despotism and state intervention will actually fall, in comparison to the level it had attained during the revolutionary period.   But this fact only corroborates the statement that revolution and independent self-government are incompatible; that they mutually exclude each other; that the development of independence after a revolution is attained in spite, not because of, the latter.   Consequently, it seems somewhat difficult to ascribe the merit of it to the revolution.   It is also a mistake to suppose that post-revolutionary independence is much more widespread than that of the pre-revolutionary period.   The autonomy and freedom of Roman society during the times of Cæsar, Augustus and his successors diminished, rather than increased, as compared with pre-revolutionary times,[1] with the period preceding the changes in Roman society which were brought on by the Gracchi.   The régime of tyrants which followed the Greek Revolution can scarcely be considered less despotic than that which had existed before the revolutionary period.   France emerged from the revolutions of the fourteenth and fifteenth centuries much more centralized and less independent than she had been formerly.   It is from this period that the unlimited power of the king dates. The Czech Government grew to be infinitely more des-

---

[1] "As result of the revolutions : national liberty has come to an end, and Rome witnesses not the reign of democratism, but of monarchism." Mommsen: Vol. II, 96. Alas! that is nearly always the case.

potic after the revolutions; its population—more devoid of rights and more subjugated. We witness the same after the troubled times in Russia, during the seventeenth century: they produced the consolidation of imperial power, the abrogation of existing forms of self-government, the development of centralization, bureaucracy and despotism. It is difficult to consider the period of restoration in England as a time of freedom (Charles II, James III,) or that of Napoleon I, who transformed the whole of France into one immense "barrack-room;" or of Napoleon III, who was the offspring of the Revolution of 1848; or the régime of Admiral Horti and the Bavarian monarchists after the Revolutions of Hungary and Bavaria in 1918–19.

Even if in some cases—and that only when the revolutions had not been very deep-rooted—the post-revolutionary régime was not less independent than that of pre-revolutionary times, neither was it essentially superior to it in this respect. Often, as we have just mentioned, the independence of the former régime has been less widespread than that of the latter—consequently, I cannot admit popular opinion to be correct, that revolutions give a rich fruition of liberty at a later period. First of all, this is not the case; secondly, if it were, the merit of it would belong not to the revolution, but to the peaceable activity of the population, that had had enough of revolution; and thirdly, countries like England, which have known nothing of revolutions during many centuries (seventeenth to twentieth) have not only not lost liberty, but have spread it far and wide to a degree unknown to societies shaken by the storms of revolution. This once more indicates the fallacy of the popular opinion.

Let us now turn to our theme: the deviation of social organizations in the direction of interventional state despotism during periods of revolution. It is unavoidable because the principal factors causing the development of despotic state intervention are: 1. war; 2. the increase of hunger, pauperism among the masses, and the existence of material inequality. From this standpoint the state intervention brought on by the war can be called " Military Socialism " (following the terminology of Russian communists) ; and the state intervention, brought on by poverty " Hungry Socialism." The above-named part played by war has been brilliantly demonstrated by Spencer.[2] The part played by hunger as a factor of state intervention has been investigated by me.[3]

A deep-rooted revolution is synonymous with the worst kind of war, and at the same time, synonymous with want, famine and pauperism among the masses; consequently, the reason why the structure of revolutionary society is transformed into a state despotism grows very evident. It is unavoidable that the functions of authority should grow much more extensive, because revolutions always mean an exceptionally energetic destruction of the old régime; people are transferred from place to place, property changes hands, the whole social structure and all social processes are transformed. It is evident that without an extremely serious extension of the functions and activities of force and authority such immense transformations could not be accomplished. The one is called forth by the others, and every revolutionary government is forced to be energetic, and violent, and must intervene in all spheres of social life. Even in the realm of economics, in the conduct and relations (where such an inter-

---

[2] Spencer: *Principles of Sociology.* Chapters about a military and industrial type of society; see also my article " Influence of War on Social Organization," *Economist*, No. 1, 1922; an article "War and Militarization of Society." *Collective Work*, Nos. 3-4, 1922 (Russ.).

[3] See my article: " The Influence of Famine on the Social Organization," *Economist*, 1922, Nos. 2, 4-5.

vention must be out of place), we can witness it during periods of revolutions. These are periods "par excellence" of compulsory state intervention in economical life (Zwangswirtschaft).

During the Roman and Greek Revolutions in reality contracts and obligations were annulled. The ways and means of production, distribution and exchange of worldly goods were controlled by the government. A whole series of governmental monopolies was introduced; the alimentation of the population was concentrated in the hands of the government. The personal independence of citizens in all questions regarding their mutual relations was restricted to a minimum. We see such a state of things both when a revolutionary dictatorship was in the hands of the rich and when in those of the poor (the tyrants of the fifth and sixth centuries; in the revolutions of the fourth century; during the reign of Agis, Cleomenes, Nabis, and during the activity of the Gracchi, Marius, Sulla, Drusus, Crassus, Pompeius, Cæsar, Marc Anthony and Augustus). The only difference between these two kinds of dictatorship was that the social groups spoliated by them were different in each case; but each revolutionary government requisitioned property in a most unceremonious manner, and in this respect its functions grew without measure.

A similar picture is to be seen in serious revolutions of later days. The same arbitrariness and intervention in the economic relations of the members of society; though the forms it assumes are not always similar.

The organization of active communistic aggregates in Münzer and Mühlhausen, when all the implements of production were communized and private property was annulled, is a clear proof of the above. We know that the same took place during the Revolution of Huss. The

decree of July 26, 1420, proclaimed the property of the
emigrants, Germans, clergy, and the opponents of the
Hussites to be confiscated; later on that of the rest of the
rich as well.   In Tabor, among the Taborites, private
property was annulled.   The peasants were mercilessly
stripped of all they possessed.   Shortly, individual independence was completely destroyed.[4]

The English Revolution shows us the same picture.
This is proved (1) by the very numerous arbitrary confiscations which were practiced by revolutionary governments and which in Ireland took colossal proportions; (2)
by the energetic struggle with the merchants which was
called forth by famine; by the establishment of fixed
prices; a fixed rate of profits, by governmental control
over the distribution and exchange of goods; (3) by arbitrary taxation and fines; (4) by compulsory loans
demanded from the rich and the city and (5) by a whole
series of monopolies introduced by the government.[5]

Colossal confiscations of land and property took place
among the emigrants and all such as were not acceptable
to the Jacobins.   Church property was nationalized.   We
witness requisitions " of bread, cattle, linen, boots," etc.,
on an immense scale.   In Marseilles Barras forced 20,000
people to give away two shirts each.   In Lyons Fouché
confiscated the boots and shoes of private individuals;
edicts were proclaimed, such as the one of November
10th, which requisitioned one-eighth of the pigs belonging
to private individuals; " others fixed the rate of wages,

<hr/>

[4] See Denis: 228, 261-2, 281-7, 330 and others.
[5] " The sequestration and confiscation of property was performed
in the most exasperating and revolting manner . . . it was so arbitrary
that no one knew where he stood or what his future would be like."
" A great many people were taxed heavily and the taxes collected with
violence."   " The people were taxed exorbitantly," etc.   Guizot: Vol.
I, XXIII, 194, Vol. II, 221-2.   Gardiner: Vol. I, 24, 49, 251-2, 311-12,
Vol. II, 22, 187, 200; Vol. III, 322, 328-30, 254 and others.

the price of products, the method of ration cards; compulsory labor taxes, compulsory enlistment of laborers; the " Maximum " law issued May 4 and September 30, 1793; the decrees of August 19 and 23, 1793; that of September 29, October 2, November 24, January 28, 1794; arbitrary and insupportable taxes and levies—all these and many others loudly proclaim the growth of state intervention in the economic realm. During the French Revolution the inviolability of private property was proclaimed, but never carried out.[6]

The same, in other forms, took place during the Revolution of 1848. This is eloquently demonstrated by the inauguration of national workshops and the attempt made to exercise control over many peaceable economic relations.

The extension of the controlling functions of the government in the economical realm during the Paris Commune, during the German, Hungarian and especially the Russian Revolutions of the years 1917–22 do not require any corroboration.[7]

The juridical annulment of private property, the extensive scale on which nationalization of land, plants, and household goods was performed, the limitless requisitions and confiscations, the complete centralization and monopoly over produce; the concentration of distribution and consumption in the hands of the government and government officials; the abolition of private commerce; the destruction of free labor and a free choice of occupation;

---

[6] See F. v. Haeke: *Zusammenbruch und Aufstieg des Französischen Wirtschaftslebens,* 1789-99. München, 1923, 96 and foll., 109-11. *Uberhaupt gibt es während dieser Schrekenzeit niemand der auch nur etwas besitzt, der eine Stunde seines Lebens und seines Besitzes sicher wäre,* 120.

[7] It is characteristic that the beginning of the development of riots in Germany (August, September, 1923) corresponds to the development of state intervention. The government of Stresemann—with its compulsory loan, with the discount of exchange, with its colossal attempts of control are but single examples of a general fact.

the abolition of inheritance; the introduction of labor taxes; the transformation of all the population into state slaves, working under the control of governmental authorities—all these facts of the Russian Revolution (the Bavarian and Hungarian as well) are but a complete expression of the usual revolutionary tendencies, which, however, have seldom in other revolutions attained such extreme expression.

The " Russian experience " in constructing a communistic society, which seems so unique, is in realty only the extreme manifestation of state despotism (or Zwangswirtschaft). The fundamental factors—war and famine—which call forth the development of state intervention were dealt out to Russia in an unusual measure (seven years of the World and Civil Wars, plus a tremendous development of pauperism), consequently it is not astonishing that state intervention, under the name of " Communism " which was later on christened by Lenin himself as " Military Communism " attains an unusual development. Taking all this into consideration we can only be struck to witness the naïve belief held by many who see in the extreme manifestations of despotic state intervention the symbol of a new and more perfect society. He must be truly naïve and ignorant who can conceive such an appreciation.

If we see a certain growth of state intervention even in economic life, it is not surprising to see it intruding into the moral domain and trying to regulate mutual relations. In this respect there can be no doubt as to the growth of despotic state intervention: it is flagrantly evident in every revolution. Dictatorship is an institution indissolubly bound up with every deep-rooted revolution. The question of the dictatorship being " white " or " red," individual or collective, is of secondary importance—it always denotes the presence of an authority which is unrestricted by any bonds, has the right to act after its own free will, and also the power to infringe the rights of others. Such is the actual state of the case. This revolutionary tyrannical power can be either in the hands of Greek tyrants, or in those of the dictators and triumvirates of Rome, or in the hands of E. Marcel and Caboche, of J. Zizka and Procopius, John of Leyden or F. Münzer, Cromwell or the Jacobins, Blanqui, L. Blanc, Caussidière, the Paris Commune or the Russian communists—it is all one in this respect: they all oppress the population with a heavy hand, not taking into account existing laws and rights. Normal laws and guarantees of individual inviolability and freedom are abolished. A " war footing " and extraordinary tribunals are introduced instead (the che-ka, revolutionary tribunals and courts-martial), which exterminate hundreds of people, throw thousands into prison, and annihilate all previous guarantees. Freedom of speech, press, association, assemblies (as we already have shown in this book) are annulled. Freedom of creed grows to be a fiction even in so-called religious revolutions (England, Bohemia). Freedom of teaching, education, and learning as well as freedom of movement is greatly restricted. In general, whatever the line of conduct of mutual relationship we speak of; everywhere we see that intervention, tutelage and compulsion take colossal proportions and that the independence of all citizens—except those of the clients and hangers-on of the governing authorities—is greatly restricted. The citizen is bound hand and foot. He is no more an independent individual—he is transformed into an object for the demonstration of the dictator's power. The centralization of all power in the hands of a dictator, a *Comité de Salut Public,* the Council of the State, or the Central Committee of the Russian Communistic Party has the same effect. All the functions of authority: legislative, executive and juridical, are concentrated in the hands of a small group. It is useless to expect "moderation or justice" under such conditions.

The militarization of social life during those revolutionary periods which are accompanied with civil war also demonstrates the immense growth of state intervention. Society is transformed into one great barrack-room; the nation—into an army; the government—into a dictator who uses his power over society at his own free will.

All these important symptoms render our proposition irrefutable. As we found abundance of facts to substantiate it in its application to economic life, so also in its application to other social relations corroborating facts are so numerous that it is not difficult to cite them; but two or three taken from the most deep-rooted revolutions will suffice for our purpose. Let us turn to the English Revolution: 1. Instead of normal authority belonging to the House of Commons, the House of Lords and the King, all power is concentrated first of all in the hands of a small group; later on in those of Cromwell alone. "Cromwell, Ireton and Harrison ruled the council of officers and the council of officers ruled the State," is the short summary of the existing situation by the author of *The Hunting of the Foxes.* Later on the centralization of autocracy and power in the hands of Cromwell reaches its zenith. 2. "To uphold the severe political tyranny it was necessary to introduce a juridical tyranny as well. The republican parliament did not scruple to make use of it." For the soldier it introduced court-martial; for the opposition—extraordinary tribunals. For all arrest, exile and incarceration—without any judgment whatsoever. "Parliament struck terror into the hearts of men and cut off the heads of all who were superior." "When incorruptible judges refused to condemn, Cromwell insulted, deprived of office, threw into prison advocates and judges with an insolence unparalleled even during the darkest times." The system of indefinite, arbitrary condemnations, so typical of revolutionary periods, grows to be very widespread. Judgment is according to the dictates of a revolutionary conscience, not according to the law. 3. "Nearly from its first stages the revolutionary government attained the extreme limits of political tyranny. Every one who was not on its side was deprived of office. The opponents of the republic were deprived of all political rights and their positions grew to be similar to those of the helots." 4. Liberty of press was annulled, and a severe censure and other measures of restriction were introduced far outstripping those of Charles I. 5. It would seem that religious liberty at least ought to have existed. But . . . "the same party, the same individuals who during half a century had so steadfastly struggled to acquire religious liberty . . . having attained power, categorically refused all liberty to three numerous classes: to the Catholics, to the adherents of the Episcopal Church and to Free Thinkers." [8] They were persecuted, thrown into prison, deprived of office, their property confiscated; they were condemned to death. 6. As to self-government and respect towards the will of the nation a similar condition is all too well proved: by numerous dissolutions of parliament and expulsion of

[8] See Guizot: Vol. I, XXII, XXVII, XI-XII, 125-6, 134, 270; Vol. II, 135, 51-2, 123; Vol. III, 19, 31, 35, 150-1, 147-60 and others. Gardiner: *History of the Commonwealth*, Vol. I-IV, Passim.

such members as were displeasing to the reigning authorities; by the cassation of the London City elections; by the exile of the elected Lord Mayor and Aldermen; by the exclusion of all officials that were displeasing to the reigning authorities; by the introduction of the institution of the Militia and the General Mayors, whose function it was to control, denounce and crush all opposition, and who treated the monarchic part of England as a conquered nation. 7. The infringement upon liberty of assemblies, association and locomotion is proved by numerous arrests; by the dispersion and prohibition of meetings, the closing of theatres and other resorts of pleasure; by exiles and prohibition of residing in London and other cities; by orders requiring parents to keep their children and servants at home, with the exception of a few permitted hours; by the permission to seize and throw into prison every suspected individual, etc. 8. The situation with regard to liberty of education and thought is demonstrated not only by legislation concerning the press, but by the "cleansing of the universities," the expulsion of undesirable rectors and professors and nomination of government candidates.

All these facts are eloquent enough and demonstrate the growth of despotism and state intervention during the English Revolution—which is the most virtuous of all revolutions.[9]

These features of "military and famine socialism" or state intervention are clearly to be seen in the Bohemian

[9] "They (the revolutionary government) promised liberty, but in reality they were tyrants," is the summary of Guizot, Vol. I, 19. "It is never possible for men of the sword to rear the temple of recovered freedom. Honestly as both military and political leaders desired to establish popular government, they found themselves in a vicious circle from which there was no escape." Such are the closing words of Gardiner: Above-cited work, Vol. I, 1.

Revolution. 1. The whole country was transformed into one immense barrack-room, governed by the most merciless discipline. 2. Religion soon grew to be compulsory and had to comply with given rules: Catholics, Free Thinkers and Taborites were persecuted and executed by the Utraquists; the Utraquists by the Taborites and all belonging to other creeds by Zizka and his adherents. They began by proclaiming religious liberty and "ended by refusing to live in peace with all such as belonged to another creed." Similar was the attitude of the Utraquists. "A veritable inquisition was established: Fifty individuals known for the orthodoxy of their belief were intrusted with the office of tracing and spying upon all those who were of different faith and did not subscribe to the dogma of the Utraquists. They had the right to incarcerate them and give them over into the hands of civil authority. 3. Education was also regulated by compulsion. 4. Liberty of thought, word and press were annulled. 5. Instead of justice—arbitrariness. 6. In Tabor even clothing, games, food, occupation were subjected to compulsory regulation. 7. We also witness a complete contempt towards the electors: brute force taking the place of the nation's will.[10]

This development of despotism is still more clearly defined during the French Revolution. Here we witness: 1. The concentration of power in the hands of a small group and Robespierre. 2. A tremendous centralization which was only following and still further developing the centralization of the *Ancien Régime*.[11] 3. A complete

[10] See Denis: *Op. cit.*, 222, 239, 261, 265 and foll., 281-3, 330, 278-9, 282-3 and foll.

[11] See Tocqueville: *L'Ancien Régime et la Revolution*, 1877, pp. 234-43 and foll. The whole of the second book and the 3d chapter of the 3d book. Taine: *La Revolution*, Vol. III, 1885, *Le Programme Jacobin*, 69-159.

abrogation of liberty: of speech, press, association, assemblies for all but the adherents of the governing party. 4. The militarization of the whole country. 5. The annulment of personal inviolability. 6. The substitution of " extraordinary tribunals " for the usual courts of justice. 7. Persecution replacing religious liberty.[12] 8. Persecution of all belonging to another political faith. 9. The abolition of self-government; an evident contempt for the will of the people and that of the electors, for instance, the expulsion and execution of the members of the National Assembly, of the organs of self-government, etc. 10. The crushing of liberty of thought. 11. The restriction of liberty of locomotion, etc.—all this is well-known and irrefutable.

Hérault de Séchelles was right when he proposed " to throw a veil over the Statue of Liberty," and it was actually thrown over it. " The intervention of revolutionary authority in all realms of private life; the oppression of labor, traffic, property, family, education, religion, morals, and feelings—such is the program and practice of the Jacobins." [13]

Even during the darkest days of the *Ancien Régime* tyranny had scarcely if ever attained to such a level as it did during the revolution: never, probably, did the population possess so few rights in regard to the government, and never was the government more autocratic than it was during the revolutionary dictatorship.

During the Russian Revolution these same features were still more evident. We witness a total abrogation of

---

[12] " We, the Convention, are authorized to change religion," such was the opinion of the ruling authorities.

[13] Taine: *Ibid.*, Vol. III, 120-1. See the whole of chapters I and II of the second book of this volume.

all the rights of the population and unlimited despotism exercised by a small group of Bolsheviks and their clients —such is the concise and exact description of the state of things in 1918–22. 1. All power is centralized in the hands of some five or six individuals—members of the Political Bureau of the Russian Communist Party. 2. Absolute abolition of liberty of speech, press, assemblies and association. 3. The abolition of tribunals and laws. They are replaced by the arbitrary judgment of the Che-ka and the revolutionary tribunals.[14] 4. A complete loss of all rights, even the right to live. 5. The annulment of religious freedom. 6. Annulment of liberty of thought, whenever it refuses to conform to the dogma of Communism. 7. The abolition of all real elections and all organs of self-government. 8. Arrests, executions and exile of all dissenting from the opinions and dogma of those in power. 9. The abrogation of all proprietorial rights. 10. The restriction of the right of locomotion. 11. Compulsory—direct and indirect—regulation: of food, clothing, lodging, activity, education, teaching, profession, even of hours allotted to sleep and working, etc. In short, we see a complete despotism by the government, a full centralization, a many-sided tutelage and thorough regulation on one side, and, on the other, a complete loss of rights; citizens are looked upon as objects for the demonstration of authority; individuals are transformed into puppets; human beings regarded like inanimate objects.

Such is the picture of the " liberty " given by the Russian Revolution.

I shall not turn for more corroboration to other fully-developed revolutions. But I dare positively affirm that

---

[14] See Sorokin: *The Soviet Court and Justice in Michigan Law Review*, Vol. XXIII.

these features—in a smaller or greater measure can be found in each of them.[15]

What we have already said proves that the state of the Egyptian slave, building pyramids, or the state of the population in the Eastern Despotism: the freedom of an arbitrary despot granted to a population unprotected by law, is the only liberty that there is any reason to expect to be given by revolutionary epochs. That is why the words: "A violent revolution" and "liberty" appear to me not as something synonymous but, on the contrary, as something incompatible. From this standpoint Flaubert was right in saying, in his *Education of the Senses,* that "behind every implacable revolutionary is hidden an inborn policeman." This sounds paradoxical, but is nevertheless true.

---

[15] The legislation expressed in the decrees of March 12, 1848 by the commissaries of the revolutionary government are typical for the activity of the revolutionary authorities. We cite the following words:

"What is your plenipotence. It is limitless. As agents of revolutionary authority you are also revolutionary. You are answerable only to your own conscience. The obligation of directing everybody is laid upon you. There must be no compromises, no concessions."

The same thought is still more clearly expressed by Louis Blanc. See Gregoire: Vol. III, 37-38.

"The Paris Commune of 1871 could get the upper hand only by oppressing its enemy. Its government grew to be a veritable tyranny. The members of the Commune did not admit of the least criticism and stifled every independent voice. They tried to inspire terror, filling the prisons with suspect individuals and hostages. Then, when the decisive hour had come, they tried with all their might to wreak vengeance on their opponents. Their papers did not cease demanding the most bloodthirsty revenge." Gregoire: Vol. IV, 411.

CHAPTER XIV

THE MODIFICATION OF SOCIAL FUNCTIONS DURING REVOLUTIONARY PERIODS

II. ECONOMIC FUNCTIONS

1. THE first feature we witness in the modification of economic life during revolutionary times is the growth of the state intervention and corresponding decrease of independence of the citizen. We have just spoken of this feature. 2. Secondly, revolution unavoidably leads to the decrease of productiveness in the country, to general pauperism, thereby calling forth the destruction and disorganization of the whole economical life of society. Such is the chief result of its influence. Parallel to it we find other secondary features. 3. In its first stages revolution often minimizes the inequality of material wealth, levelling everybody to a state of equality in poverty. During the second period economic inequality augments and often surpasses that of pre-revolutionary periods. 4. We have already shown how briskly the exchange of position between the rich and the poor takes place. 5. These effects manifest themselves in proportion to the length and deep-rootedness of the revolution. When the revolution is short-lived and not over-sanguinary these effects may be of little consequence.

An objective observer cannot avoid admitting that these are the results of revolution and not the promised "land of milk and honey." This is particularly evident in the Russian Revolution of 1917–24.

The following figures are eloquent enough. The gross receipts of Russian industry in contemporary Soviet Russia, excluding Siberia and Turkestan, according to the Bolshevist statistics, calculated in millions of gold rubles, are as follows:

1912	6059.2
1920	835.8
1921	870.0
1922	963.5 [1]

The national revenue in gold rubles calculated per capita of the population was:

		Per cent.
1913	101 rubl. 35 kopeks	100
1916–17	85 rubl. 60 kopeks	84.5
1921	38 rubl. 60 kopeks	38.1 [2]

The productiveness of different branches of industry can be seen from the following table. Taking the productiveness of 1913 to be equal to 100 per cent. we find:

Different branches of industry	1913	1918	1919	1920	1921	1922	Oct., 1923 March 1924
Coal	100	42	29	27	31	34	60
Metallurgical	100	12.3	2.6	2.4	3.0	3.9	—
Naphtha	100	44	49	41	42	49	65
Iron	100	0.2	—	1.6	1.6	2.2	14
Textile							
linen	100	75	45	38	25	46	49
wool	100	—	19	23	17	27	58
cotton	100	—	6.2	5	7.4	17	—
Sugar	100	24	6	6	7	—[3]	—[4]

Agriculture was in a similar " flourishing " state. This is evident from the area of arable land and the amounts of grain and other products harvested in P. S. F. S. P. calculated in millions of dessiatins.

[1] *On the New Ways,* book III, 1923, pp. 178-88 (Russ.).
[2] Prokopovitch: Above-cited work, p. 119.
[3] *Economic Upbuilding,* No. 2, Moscow, 1923, p. 34 (Russ.).
[4] *Isvestia,* May 28, 1924.

1909–13	1914	1915	1916	1917	1918	1919	1920	1921	1922	1923	1924
83.5[a]	88.5	85.1	78.2	78.2	..	..	62.3	54.9	42.2	59.3	69

a As a Medium.

1909–13	1914	1915	1916	1917	1918	1919	1920	1921	1922	1923
53.9	53.1	72.3	60.1	49.7	44.1	38.3	38.7[a]			
62.3	65.4	87.1	71.7	57.7	47.6	34.3	32.7[b]	31.1	50.8	42.2[b]
50.7	39	64.4	45.7	44.4	36.0	35.5	28.5[c]		(average)	

a The harvest of rye per dessiati calculated in pouds.
b The product of winter wheat per dessiatin (in pouds).
c The product of summer wheat per dessiatin (in pouds).

In consequence of this breakdown of agriculture Russia—which had exported up to 650,000,000 pouds in pre-
war times—was brought during the years 1921–22 to a
state of famine and cannibalism. In 1924–25 at least seven
million of the Russians again have to starve, according to
the announcement of the Soviet Government. The revolution nourished the Russian nation not with the *poule au
pot* (chicken broth), but with beefsteaks made out of the
flesh of . . . its own children.

Similar was the condition of other agricultural
products:

	1914	1916	1920	1921	1922
Flax					
Area calculated in thousands of dessiatins.	1.311	945.5	321.1	292.3	347.1
Harvest					
in thousands of pouds.	24083	14722	4500	5500	....

[5] N. Kondratieff: *The Control Over the Bread Markets During
the Years of War and Revolution,* Moscow, 1922 (Russ.). I quote the
figures concerning the arable area during the years 1921-22 from
the report of the People's Commissary of Agriculture, 1922. *Economic
Life,* No. 163 and September 2, 1923.

	1915	1916	1921	1922	
Cotton wool					
Area calculated in thousands of dessiatins.	520	578	130	52	
Harvest		15 mill.	— 600–700 thousands.		

	1916	1918	1920	1921	1922
Tobacco					
Area calculated in thousands of dessiatins.	6750	2967	537	221	?
Harvest calculated in thousands of pouds.	69.00	28.28	7.66	2.76	5.9

	1914	1922
Sugar beet-roots		
Area in thousands of dessiatins.	683.4	159.2
Harvest in berkovetzs	75660	9130[6]

Cattle breeding decreased by 40 to 50 per cent. in comparison to pre-revolutionary years.

Transportation was also destroyed. In pre-revolutionary times Russia possessed 19,000 railway engines and 437,000 railway cars. At the present moment she has only 7000 railway engines and 195,000 railway cars, and even these not in good repair. In 1913—31,000 cars were daily freighted; in 1923—only 11,500 cars.[7]

During the revolutionary years 3650 railway bridges and about 20 per cent. of the station buildings have been demolished.

[6] *Economic Life,* No. 172, August 2, 1923.
[7] *Isvestia,* No. 186, August 21, 1923.

The finances of the state are in a condition that it is not easy to fathom. The figures of the amount of paper money issued are as follows:

	Calculated in billions of rubles
1st of January 1917	9.2
1918	27.3
1919	61.3
1920	225.0
1921	1,168.6
1922	17,539.5
1923	2,138,704.5
May 1923	6,076,000.0
September 1923	171,000,000.0

The depreciation of paper money ran as follows. Taking the prices of 1913 as being equal to 1, the index of prices for the revolutionary years are as follows:

1st of January 1917	3.8
1918	23.3
1919	230.0
1920	3,136.0
1921	26,500.0
1922	182,753.0
1923	19,775,000.0 [8]

Transferring all this heap of paper into so-called " rubles of goods " we see that it was worth:

		(in millions of rubles)	
In the years	1921	1922	1923
January	44	96	101
February	44	67	106
March	37	54	116
April	40	42	104
May	49	35	114
June	42	51	—
July	37	69	—
August	43	94	—
September	56	128	30
October	71	144	—
November	80	117	—
December	96	106	—

[8] Cited from the book of Prokopovicz: 209. *Economic Review*, No. 2, pp. 235, 174. See also Rostovsky: *Crisis of New Economic Policy*, 1923 (Russ.).

The wages of the workmen (according to Bolshe-
vistic statistics) were during the dictatorship of the
proletariat as follows (inclusive of rations, lodging, etc.) :

1913–17 22	rubles monthly
1918 .... 8.99	rubles monthly
1919 .... 6.77	rubles monthly
1920 .... 7.12	rubles monthly
1921 .... 6.95	rubles monthly
1922 .... 8.22	rubles monthly [*]
1923 .... 17.32	rubles monthly

(The workmen of Moscow getting higher wages.)

In reality they were even lower. These figures clearly
demonstrate the " beneficent " influence of the revolution.
Its effect on the peasants has been still more terrible,
impoverishing them three or four times in comparison with
the pre-revolutionary period. Four years of the World
War were infinitely less destructive than four years of
revolution. As a result Russia has experienced general pauperism . . . famine . . . cannibalism . . . the extinction of
millions of the Russian population. Yet, perhaps, this
was the price paid for the acquisition of material equality?
For the annulment of private property? For the communization of the means and implements of production?
For the abolition of exploitation and the disappearance of
the army of men out of work? But alas! no. In 1918–21
there was an equality of pauperism. In 1922–24 we have
pauperism of the masses, and luxury of a small group,
unemployment—more than 1.5 million men—all negative
sides of capitalism, exploitation, inequality, destroyed
nationalized industry which gave about 400,000,000 gold
rubles of deficit for 1923, empty state fund, spent wealth of
the private people and churches, in a word, neither communism, nor healthy capitalism, but only: famine, poverty,
exploitation and recrudescence of the proprietorial in-

─────────

[*] Economic Life, 1922, No. 264. Prokopovitch: p. 135. Isvestia,
May 28, 1924.

stincts. The result is evident. Let the knights of the
revolution sing its praises. Personally I see no reason
whatsoever to do so.

What is the picture presented in this respect by other
revolutions? Perhaps it is less dreadful, but anyhow its
character is similar. Not one of them can boast that it has
ameliorated and raised the level of the working classes;
that it has equalized material wealth in a durable fashion;
that it has diminished sweating; that it has solved the problem of " labor slumps " and private property.

Observe the Hungarian and German Revolutions of
1918. One of the leaders of the former, Professor Varga,
former president of the Hungarian High Soviet of
National Welfare, eloquently depicts its influence.[10] We
witness a picture similar to the Russian Revolution, only
in somewhat milder forms, because the experiment of a
communistic revolution was not one of long duration.
The German Revolution was " Klein burgerlich " and not
deep-rooted, consequently its destructive influence did not
strike deep, and was, in a great measure, the result of the
Versailles Peace.

The part played by the Paris Revolution of 1870–71 is
well known. It aggravated the economic crisis suffered
by the people of Paris and of France whose position
already had been precarious enough. Famine, sickness,
the high death rate, the standstill of all industry and trade,
absence of work, such were its results.[11]

Similar was the part played by the Revolution of 1848.
It began by attempting to help those out of work—organizing national workshops—but it was not able to solve
the problem. Other measures undertaken by it only con-

---

[10] See Varga: *Die Wirtschaftspolitischen Probleme der Prole-
tarischen Diktature*, Wien, 1921.

[11] See Gregoire: Vol. IV, 307-8, 317, 409-10 and others.

tributed to disorganize national economic life, to increase poverty and the number of those out of work and to develop sweating.[12]

The influence of the revolutionary year of 1848 on the productiveness of the country can be seen from the following figures:

	1847	1848	1849	1850
The harvest of grain (in millions of hecto-litres)	97.6	88	91	88
Naphtha industry (in mill. of tons)	5153	4000	4049	4434
The production of cast iron	592	472	414	406
Of iron and steel	390	283	252	257
Of sugar (in mill. of quintales)	523.7	481	500.7	597.6
Cotton and flax (in thousands of kilo-grams)	47191	44759	63903	59272
Foreign trade (in mil-lions of francs)	2339	1644	2291	2555

" Since the beginning of the nineteenth century France had never passed through a series of years so troubled, so unpropitious to the development of industry and commerce as the years 1848–51." [13]

The state of Germany during the Revolution of 1848 was similar. In Berlin, " The streets are overgrown with

---

[12] " The revolution destroyed all credit. Expenses increased suddenly. The revenues had to diminish." Pagès writes: " Money flows out of the exchequer as water through an open sluice. In a week we shall be threatened by bankruptcy." " On the exchange 5 per cent. obligations were sold for 116 fr. 10 centimes on February 23rd. On March 7th, they had fallen to 89 fr. and soon after that to 55 fr." An obligatory rate of exchange is introduced and new taxes and levies. " The people felt the want of bread; neither credit, nor trade, nor industry existed. The number of men out of work increased." Gregoire: Vol. III, 25-29, 42, 135.

[13] Levasseur: *Hist. des Classes Ouvr.*, Vol. II, 454-64; see book V, Passim.

grass; the houses remain without inhabitants; the stores are full of wares, but there are no customers to purchase them; the industrious citizens can find no work, can earn nothing; the artisan grows to be a pauper."

As a total result the peasant alone had not lost, but rather gained. " The workmen had been disappointed in their expectations. The pittance doled out to them in the guise of state and public works could not, of course, better the material conditions of the working masses," etc.[14] A revolution—be it proletarian or bourgeois—reacts first of all and strongest of all on the revolutionary working class.

" The Revolution of 1830 aggravated the crisis of trade. All enterprises were at a standstill. The workmen were out of work." [15]

It is needless to speak of the influence of the Revolution of 1789. It is well known and very similar to that of the Russian Revolution. The universal poverty (the peasants suffered under it less than the other classes), the crisis of industry and finance, and trade, the depreciation of money, the labor slump, famine, the high death rate, the growth of material inequality (since 1793), famine again. All this is only too well known. Here also " the workmen and artisans were the chief victims of the revolution; the artisan lost his work, all his rights were taken away from him; the right of association, of going on strike and of voting."

" Everything was uprooted and destroyed," writes La Réveillère himself, " everything, beginning with ruined roads and ending with demolished homesteads; everything lies in ruins: friendly wayside inns and the unsettled

[14] Bloss: Op. cit., 326, 403-04, 280-81 and others.
[15] Levasseur: Op. cit., Vol. II, 5.

brains of individuals; the empty exchequer and the depraved hearts." [16]

Ein trostloses Chaos in den Finanzen, dazu einen kostspieligen Krieg, traurige Agrarverhältnisse, Handelkrisen, Lebensmittelnot Teuerung, und das Land noch rauchend vom Blute der Erschlagenen, such is the picture.[17] One hundred paper livres have fallen (from 1789–96) to 3 sh. 7d. Later on mandates were issued, but their depreciation was just as rapid.[18] Here also "the revolutionary legislation strove to attain a social levelling by confiscating the property of the clergy and aristocracy. But this was in nowise achieved. The only result was a new regrouping (*Umschichtung*). New colossal wealth was speedily heaped up." [19] If later on France succeeded in regaining economical well-being, it was chiefly due to the military pillage of Europe and other countries.

England during the period of revolution presents a similar picture. Civil war and the growth of the army engulfed the revenues of the country; ruined industry, trade, finances; increased poverty and famine. The finances of the Republican Government fell into a pitiful state. The expenses for the year 1651 had attained the figure of 2,750,000 pounds, *i.e.,* three times more than the budget of Charles I in 1635. The revenue had decreased. As a result we witness a constant deficit and therefore the augmentation of taxes, the confiscation of property and wealth, excesses, even the sale of pictures and churches in

[16] Madelin: Vol. II, 164-5, 219. See Levasseur: *Histoire,* Vol. I, book I, Passim and 288-90. Tarlé: *The Labor Class in France During the Revolution,* Vol. I, and II (Russ.). The works of Taine, Michelet, Tocqueville and others.
[17] F. v. Haeke: *Zusammenbruch und Aufstieg des Französischen Wirtschaftsleben 1789-99,* München, 1923, 87.
[18] *Ibid.,* 248 and foll. See also diagrams.
[19] *Ibid.,* 246.

favor of the empty exchequer.[20]   At the same time we witness the ruin of national economic life, general penury,
famine (1649 and other years) and want.[21]

As a result of the revolution: " The interests of the
Demos were not taken into consideration by the English
Revolution; the religious and political revolution helped
only to consolidate the interests of landed proprietors." [22]
" The condition of the poorest classes was pitiful till the
end of the seventeenth century."   " In 1696 a fourth of
the population consisted of paupers and poor." [23]

The same picture is given by the French Revolution
towards the end of the fourteenth and beginning of the
fifteenth century, a picture of general ruin, . . .
famine and death. . . .   Besides: *Les metiers de Paris
perdirent d'un seul coup leurs privilèges les plus chers,
leurs droits les plus anciens et leurs chefs les plus écoutés.*[24]

As a result of the Hussite Revolution " the Czech conquerors acquired no serious privileges for their national
and social life." [25] Already in 1425–26 " pauperism had
taken terrible proportions.   Former welfare had disappeared.   Foreign merchants did not risk to enter a country
where wild passions were having full sway.   Many towns
were lying in ruins.   The mines were forsaken.   Prague
ruled over poverty-stricken and depopulated towns.   In
the villages poverty was still more acute.   Every semblance

---

[20] See Gardiner: *History of the Commonwealth,* Vol. I, 39-41, 86;
Vol. II, 21-22, 187, 200, 211, 312-13; Vol. III, 56, 238, 257; Vol.
IV, 254.

[21] Guizot: Vol. I, p. XIII and others.

[22] M. Kovalevsky: (Russ.) *From a Direct Government by the
People to a Representative One,* Vol. II, 393. Rogers: *Op. cit.,*
432-34.

[23] Bernstein: *The Communistic and Social-Democratic Tendencies
in the English Revolution of the Seventeenth Century.   The Predecessors of Modern Socialism,* Vol. II, 239-41.

[24] Levasseur: *Hist. des Classes Ouvrières,* 1900, Vol. I, 518 gives
many details.

[25] Weber: Vol. VIII, 273.

of safety had disappeared. Friends and foes, Germans and
Czechs, Utraquists and Taborists burnt down villages,
trampled the harvest, demanded taxes. When the peasant
had given away his last ' sous ' new bands of soldiers
appeared and accused him of concluding peace with the
enemy; the peasant was again obliged to have recourse to
bribes, to buy them off with money or death awaited him.
The poor were the chief sufferers." In consequence of
this the peasants fled from the ruins of their villages; they
fled to the forests and into the cities, but here also they
perished alike, for they could find neither work, nor food.

At the commencement of the revolution equality of
wealth was proclaimed; private property was abolished.
" As a result of this communization we witness: indifferentism, idleness and soon pauperism and poverty."
Consequently, the return to private ownership soon recom-
menced: the first step towards it consisted " in the decision
only to restrict, not abolish, the rights of property." (The
" Huss Nep.," New Economic Policy). The second and
third step taken in the same direction soon followed, and the
whole process " ended in a simple migration of confiscated
wealth from the pockets of its first owners into those of
the new ones." Thereby " only the rich and nobles
profited. Out of the immense amount of wealth which
had been thrown on the market only an insignificant part
came into the hands of the peasants and workmen." And
even that part soon slipped away from them. The whole
ended in a complete restoration of private property, in a
colossal increase of material and other kinds of inequality, in the pauperization and enslavement of the peasants
by feudal lords and by new-made nobles.[26]

In Rome " the state of finances was greatly aggravated
when the revolution broke out." " The terrible revolution-

[26] Denis: 346-47, 263, 240, 284-85, 288 and others.

ary conflagration undermined finances." Poverty grew to
be widespread and intense. In 105: " The Roman citizens could scarcely boast of 2000 well-to-do families."
" The condition of free-born proletarians was scarcely better than that of slaves." The peasantry was ruined. Small
free agricultural homesteads fell into ruin. The number
of slaves increased immensely, it being constantly added to
by " masses of free-born provincial inhabitants." [27]

All this took place notwithstanding the limitless spoliation of conquered countries and all the oppression of the
provinces.[28] At the same time it did not prevent the
tremendous development of material differentiation, which
towards the period of Cæsar transformed Rome into " a
Republic of millionaires and paupers." [29]

I have already quoted the words of Ipouver and
Onchu describing the catastrophic pauperization, famine,
gradual extinction and ruin of economic life during the
revolutionary epoch in Egypt.

Here also " history repeats itself." The fundamental
results of the revolutions during the different epochs and
among different nations are identical. The factors which
produce them are as follows: 1. The diversion of human
energy from productive labor and a productive strife
against nature towards mutual strife. 2. The colossal
destructive process which is indissolubly bound up with
revolutionary strife. For cities and villages, fields and
factories, buildings and homesteads, the means and implements of production, all the fundamental forms of the
capital of society are mercilessly destroyed in the heat of
civil war. 3. The immense expenditure on the army,
bureaucracy, and war. 4. The absence of any guarantees

[27] Mommsen: Vol. II, 399, 134-37, 223 and others.
[28] Ibid., 387, 388-93.
[29] Ibid., Vol. III, 453-59, 461; Vol. II, 404-9 and others.

in the possession of property and the products of labor which takes away the stimulus to productive and intense labor.   5. The extinction of the reflexes of labor, the development of idleness called forth by the revolution.   6. Pillage, illimitable confiscations, requisitions, nationalizations, and the levelling policy of revolutions also unavoidably lead to the destruction of the stimulus to intensified labor and thrift.   7. When revolutions bring in their wake the actual abolition of private ownership, the universal communization of means of production and of the necessaries of life; when the principle of material equality is widespread—as was the case during the last Russian and Hungarian Revolutions, and also during the Revolutions of Huss and Mazdak—then the decrease in the capacity of labor and productiveness acquires truly catastrophic proportions.   In the long run such a socialization and levelling grants a premium to idleness, to mediocrity and, on the other hand, levies a whole series of fines on every form of energetic work, and punishes initiative.   If everybody receives the same amount of benefits, the lazy, being sure of receiving their share, grow to be still more lazy; the energetic and industrious, being deprived of all possibility to profit by their labor and initiative, will of course cease to spend unnecessary energy in working for the profit of the lazy.   The levelling of working capacity all over the country conforms itself to the level of the last of sluggards.   Productiveness decreases; pauperism makes itself felt.   The revolution in its attempts to abolish the faults of the private individualistic régime often resembles the farmer who kills the hen to get the eggs which it lays.

We have witnessed this during the Russian and Hungarian Revolutions.   As soon as everything but the " minimum necessary to existence " began to be taken away from the peasants, the latter reduced the area of tillage to that minimum.   As soon as the wages of all workmen were equalized (the difference between the highest and lowest rate of wages was in 1918 that of 175 to 100), the industrious and energetic ceased working and spent their time in idleness. " What is the sense of working uselessly? " On the contrary, as soon as in 1921 this principle of equality was abolished—a premium for productive labor established, and payment for piece-work introduced, the productiveness of the still existing enterprises immediately increased.

Of course if human beings were angels and worked as enthusiastically in the name of a " categorical imperative," as they do in their own interests, such need not have been the results.   But we have seen that human beings are very far from being in an angelic state; when a personal stimulus is taken away they cease working. This has happened in all revolutions which attempted a radical economic levelling and socialization.   In a smaller degree the same took place during all revolutions, for this tendency to " state intervention " and " levelling " is inherent in all of them in a greater or smaller measure.   8. The growth of " state intervention " during revolutionary periods calls forth universal poverty also in another way. First of all, because the principle of a state monopoly is substituted for the principle of competition; secondly, because the owner, the man of initiative, spurred on by the hope of profit and fear of risk, is replaced by a state employee, by a bureaucrat, quite devoid of all such stimulus (his wages being fixed), often most incompetent and having no capacity for the work he undertakes.   We witness the " official " relation of an employee instead of the energetic activity of the owner; a death-like monopoly instead of a stimulating competition; bureaucracy instead of talent; casual nominations to certain posts instead of inborn capacity for the kind of work it requires; formalism with its endless burden of " red tape " reports, correspondence, councils, commissions, sub-commissions, sections, etc., instead of the quick decisive will of the individual. It is needless to prove that such a substitution almost invariably, indeed with very few exceptions, leads to a decrease of productiveness, to routine, to stagnation, to Chinese ceremonies; it acts injuriously on the quality of work produced, renders it more expensive and leads to the impoverishment of the country.[30]   9. During revolution-

---

[30] " Each regulation calls forth new regulations; new functions of distributive agents are established; the number of state employees and this class of functionaries is greatly increased. Initiative is crushed. Regulation is carried into the most trivial details. Bureaucracy reaches its extreme limits," such are the perfectly correct remarks of Le Bon and his *Psychology of Socialism* (St. Petersburg, 1908—222, Russ. transl.).

As a result we sometimes witness that the paper used up for the correspondence accompanying a petition often surpasses the value of the object petitioned for.

" One administrator governs; three administrators investigate better methods of governing; five administrators dispute over contradictory programs, seven gossip. ' The Council of Administration ' is a meeting together of individuals, of whom some arrive an hour after the others, and others again are obliged to leave an hour before the former. They generally meet only on the stairs. It is true that some can be found among them who arrive and leave exactly, but it is generally those that would have done better not to appear at all." De Leener: *La Primauté de l'Individu, Revue de l'Inst. de Sociologie,* 1922, 427.

All these negative sides of state intervention are illuminatingly corroborated by the facts of the Russian Revolution. Which were the enterprises that gave least profits? Those which where nationalized. Where was the productiveness of work at its lowest? Also in them. Where does a limitless bureaucracy reign? Again in the same ones. To get the permission to procure a pound of nails a man was obliged to spend endless hours going from institution to institution, handing in petitions, and receiving the demanded permissions. The amount of paper used for this endless correspondence and the shoe leather worn out during this process would amount to a much greater sum than the price of the nails themselves. Anybody who has not personally experienced this can scarcely picture to himself the terrible state of bureaucracy, inefficiency, and procrastination which we have witnessed in Russia. Consequently it is not astonishing that even the communists have decided to put an end to this most idiotic of all idiotic systems. See a whole series of facts in the book of P. Masloff: *The World's Social Problem,* 1921 (Russ.).

ary processes all the negative sides of state intervention grow ten times stronger, thanks to the unsuccessful choice and inefficiency of the " new-fangled leaders " (see above) who often have not the least idea of what their office demands of them.   10. And lastly, this result is made worse by the mere numbers of the immense army of officials which state intervention requires.   In Russia it had reached (as has already been mentioned) almost 30 per cent. of the whole population.   In Austria during the years 1918–19 one-sixth of the population.   And let it be noticed that for each administrator we find two or more controlling and spying on his actions.   Such a crowd of employees represent an immense ballast of useless drones, feeding on the labor of the rest of the population.

All these reasons are more than sufficient to explain why revolutions, especially social revolutions, lead to pauperism and famine.   They also prove, particularly after the Russian and Hungarian experience, that conditions of a hypertrophied state intervention and violent, radical levelling are very profitable on paper, and very nefarious indeed in real life, at least so long as humanity has not attained an angelic state.

Socialists and communists and other adherents of a hypertrophied state intervention would do well to think of this.   This prescription for curing social ailments is quite different from what they would make us believe it to be.   Such at least is the experience of Russia and many countries in former times.   However, I have not the least desire to convert " unbelievers " swayed by their own passions.   Let him who believes not, experience himself a universal state intervention: then he shall believe, there can be no doubt of that.   But perhaps it may be too late!

CHAPTER XV

THE MODIFICATION OF SOCIAL FUNCTIONS DURING REVOLUTIONARY PERIODS

III. THE SPIRITUAL LIFE OF SOCIETY

THE general modifications in the psychology of revolutionary society have already been set forth. Let us now describe the transformations that are undergone in the functions of what may be called " the educational, civilizing system of society," or " the system of educating and adapting conditioned reflexes."

Schools, books, lectures, laboratories, newspapers, journals, etc., these are the social institutions whose function it is to harvest in, distribute and deepen human experience. By means of them the experience of one generation is passed on to those following and the knowledge of one individual is transferred to others. This system produces the circulation of knowledge, ideas and beliefs in the whole aggregate. What is the influence of a revolution on such a system? What is its influence on the spiritual life of society?

In this respect revolution acts as a kind of re-agent which helps us to discriminate between " pseudo-knowledge," " pseudo-experience " and actual knowledge and experience.

The mental " luggage," both of the individual and society, consists not alone in a certain amount of " learning " or knowledge of actual facts proved by logic and experience. The terms " knowledge " and " learning " include: theories, judgments, opinions and beliefs—often erroneous, not corroborated by actual facts, not founded on experience, but accepted as " truth " both by the individual and the masses. They can exist and be accepted as irrefutable verities till the moment of their first severe testing. To such an order belong, for instance, very numerous political and social ideologies, depicting a new perfect state of society and pointing to the " sure " means of achieving it. As soon as they are forced to face real life, their incompetence to meet the test grows evident. Revolutions, attempting to bring them into real life and attaining results opposed to the expected ones, show by experience how fallacious, utopian, metaphysical, and impractical they are. Their fallacy grows evident; their apparent scientific basis is taken away from them; their " knowledge " is seen to be a " pseudo-knowledge." At the same time many ideas which were looked upon as " superstitious " are, by this very same *experimentum crucis* of revolution, unexpectedly proved to be correct and justified.

It were needless to say that this process of selecting and examining—produced by revolutions can be wholly approved of. Thanks to it, revolutionary periods are periods of an intense " re-evaluation of all values," we witness changes in the ideology and frame of mind of society; a catastrophic breakdown of popular ideas, and a regeneration of others which had been looked upon as superstitious. Secondly, revolution itself is an immense (direct, not indirect) " school of life " insistently teaching us and in many ways leading to richer, more profound experience. This explains why a whole series of inventions and discoveries often take place during the periods, or under the influence, of revolution. Unfortunately, however, these two beneficent influences of revolution are more than compensated by many injurious ones, so that the experience gained by society is both quantitatively and qualitatively inferior to that of peaceful times.

We have shown that revolution brings disorganization of the nervous system and mental apparatus and a liberation of primitive instincts of the members of society. Under these conditions the process of "selecting" and "innovating" performed by revolution does not give the results it might have given had the nervous system and spiritual life been in a state of health. This explains the reason why revolutions are swayed from one ideological extreme to another; one "pseudo-experience" is replaced by another, standing in opposition to the former; one "superstition" is superseded by others. The exclusive dogmatism, intolerance and subjection of liberty of thought during revolutionary periods also contribute to the same effect. Revolutionary dictators, such as Robespierre, Lenin, Cromwell, Zizka and others are the most intolerant dogmatists, the most fanatic "revolutionary priests," direct descendants of the Spanish inquisitors.

However, the chief harm produced by it consists in the fact that it destroys quantitatively and impairs qualitatively the educational civilizing apparatus of society, bringing disorganization into its work and productiveness.

It is often looked upon as an accepted fact that revolution increases the number of schools (both low and high grades), the number of colleges, laboratories, books; that it perfects the system of teaching and conduces to the progress of science, etc. Insofar as it concerns revolutionary periods and deep-rooted revolutions this statement is fundamentally false. The following facts will prove this.

Let us briefly depict the facts which bear out the two propositions just set forth. We shall commence by taking in review the revolution's "faculty of selection."

Up to the time of the Russian Revolution the ideology and theories of Marx, of socialism, communism, of equality and revolution were very popular among Russian society. " The abolition of Private Property; " " Communization of Means and Implements of Production; " " the Dictatorship of the Proletariate; " " Complete Equality of Property; " " Class Struggle; " " the Downfall of Czarism and the Establishment of a Republican Order; " " the Annulment of Religion; " " the Banefulness of Nationalism and the Beneficence of Internationalism," etc. All this was accepted as irrefutable truth, defining well-proved means of achieving an ideal social order, universal welfare and happiness, fraternity, equality, liberty and a terrestrial paradise.[1]

But what did we witness when the revolution broke out and this ideology was carried out in real life and these " patent " prescriptions began to be applied? Something quite unexpected. The population has been obliged to test the correctness of its ideology and pseudo-scientific constructions not indirectly and theoretically, but directly by personal experience, to feel its inefficiency, so to say, in its own bone and marrow. It has verified them and . . . paid a tragic price for the conviction of their fallacy. As a result of it, at the present moment we find a universal disgust towards an ideology of this kind; its complete loss of credit in the eyes of the Russian population and, on the other hand, increased respect for the enterprising owner, for private property, nationalism, religion; even a more favorable appreciation of the *Ancien Régime,* wherein one is now prone to see not only the negative side, but also the positive.[2]

---

[1] See S. Frank: *The Downfall of the Idols,* 1924, ch. I (Russ.).
[2] See details, Sorokin: *Contemporary Russia,* 1923.

This example shows the "selecting" part played by revolution in the realm of knowledge and experience. Revolutionary experience has turned much topsy-turvy.

Have we not seen the same state of things in France after the practical realization of communism in 1871? Did not the downfall of the Commune betoken the downfall of ideology of communism for the contemporaries of the revolution? Were not similar social and political changes of opinion to be noticed after the Revolution of 1848 both in Germany and France; so that even the belief in a republican order grew to be less positive? Are not the 5,434,226 votes out of 7,327,345, electing Napoleon III president,[3] and the 7,839,000 "yeas" approving of the *coup d'état* to the 456,000 "nays" opposed to it—the expression of a great disappointment—with the ideology which but a short time previously was looked upon as sacred.

The great French Revolution destroyed in the course of six or seven years the fascination of the "Enlightening" philosophy of the eighteenth century. The Catholic Church, Chateaubriand, J. de Maistre and others—diametrically opposed to the philosophers of the eighteenth century—grew to be the leaders of thought.

There was a similar contrast in the later period of the English Revolution and the first years after it. Other revolutions show the same symptoms. Revolution not only performs this process of selection, but also forces humanity to learn in the tragic school of life and so contributes to a new and rich spiritual experience of society. The exceptional character of events wakens even

---

[3] "It has been noticed that the more socialistic departments gave a greater number of voices in favor of Prince Napoleon." Gregoire: Vol. II, 168. See Levasseur: *Histoire,* Vol. II, 468. It appears that the same is taking place in Italy at the present moment: the more communistic districts of Italy are those which gave birth to Fascism.

the most torpid minds, forcing them to look about, show some interest, and acquire a clearer understanding of the numerous new phenomena; it helps to widen the mental horizon and brings forth new discoveries. During these last years the Russian people have gained, through hard and painful travail, a clearer insight into many facts appertaining to government (different forms of government, the systems of elections, constitution, etc.), economical life (production, property, control, currency, exchange, concessions, etc.) and other sides of existence. Numerous new ideas have been assimilated. The necessity of education has grown manifest, certain practical habits have been acquired. The connection between the life of the individual and the life of society has been understood. The events of the last years have produced immense changes in science, especially in social science. Many ideas and statements which till now had been accepted without discussion (such, for instance, as the idea of progress, the rational nature of man, the laws of development; numerous " laws " of political economy, etc.), are now disputed. At the same time new conceptions have sprung up. Lavosier, Lagrange, Laplace, Volney, Lamarck—these names all stand in close connection to the French Revolution. " Everywhere there was life and eagerness, lectures were improvised and a general interest in them was taken." [4] Robert Boyle, John Wallis, Hobbes, Christopher Wren, Seth Ward and others—these are the names which the English Revolution has brought forth. The intensified life of Oxford and Cambridge; new social and religious conceptions, discoveries in the realm of natural science— all originated during, or under the influence of revolutionary events, though sometimes they were realized only at

⁴ Michelet : *Op. cit.,* 125.

a later date, yet they all belong to the " new " thoughts of the English Revolution.[5]

However, we have already mentioned that all these beneficent effects are neutralized for a time at least, and with the possible exception of some individual discoveries by the destructive influence of the revolution. The nervous system of society is in too disorganized a state to be able to profit by the correct results of the " selective process." It throws itself from one extreme into another, and as a result produces only distorted creative spiritual values. If before the revolution it happened to idolize certain theories, even with all their defects, it is now ready to deny even all that was and remains good in them. Formerly society bowed down before an inflated kind of " Materialism," " Socialism," " Communism," " Republicanism; " now it goes over into an opposite extreme and adopts a blind, one-sided belief in " Mysticism, " Capitalism," " Monarchism," " Primitive Conservatism," etc. In the Russian Revolution we see, on the one hand, the unbridled, ignorant and violent utopian ideology of the communists, who were ready to override the laws of science, the experience acquired in the course of many generations; many denying even chemistry, physiology, arithmetic, etc., as bourgeois branches of study, and attempting to create " proletarian " chemistry, physiology, arithmetic; on the other hand we witness the regeneration and success of the ideology of an autocratic monarchy; of a social order belonging to the sixteenth and seventeenth centuries (the extreme right group of monarchists) ; we witness an inflated mysticism (Lossky, Berdyaeff, Karsavin, Frank, Iljin, Novgorodt-zeff, the Eurasians) ; [6] the denial of the West and western culture; an extreme right point of view; the homage paid to private property, and a dogmatic repetition of stenciled,

---

[5] See Gardiner: *Op. cit.,* Vol. IV, ch. XLI.
[6] Eurasian—from the words Europe-Asia.

liberal formulas (*Dni,* " Poslednya Novosty ")—all this
lacks a feeling of measure; it lacks a careful sifting of
what is true from what is erroneous in each conception. A
" reactionary utopianism " springs up to succeed a communistic one. This spiritual weariness and this extreme Red
and White utopian standpoint grows to be clearly visible
during the last years in the spiritual life and creative
energy of the Russian population.

The dogmatic tendency which during revolutionary
periods is manifested by both sides is also unpropitious to
spiritual development. " Freedom of scientific thought is
a bourgeois prejudice, consequently all the professors and
teachers of social science must conform their lectures to
the teachings of Communism and Marxism. Those that
are of a different opinion are forbidden to teach and
deprived of their offices," such are the words of the decree
issued in 1921 and signed by the commissary Rotstein.
This decree was accepted and carried through. The same
was required of all schools, public lectures and meetings;
similar results were achieved by the prohibition of all
newspapers except the official government ones; by the
prohibition to publish all books not complying with the dogmas of communism and not approved of by state censure.
It is needless to speak of the havoc such forms of dogmatism have played in the realm of investigation and science.
A critical attitude—a condition *sine qua non* of progress
—does not exist. The population is forced to nourish
itself spiritually with the ignorant trash, that the authorities in power vouchsafe to lay before it. Under such
conditions it is unavoidable that thought and knowledge
should deteriorate. We witness the same kind of dogmatism in other circles, for instance, those of the emigrants;
but here it assumes an opposite character. Here everything that does not conform itself to the emigrant psychology and ideology is denied, not because it is actually false,

but because it is not in accordance with the accepted point of view popular in their midst. The " dogmatism " of the left is answered by the " dogmatism " of the right side.

In giving these sketches of the Russian Revolution I simultaneously describe the characteristic features of all revolutions. In all important and deep-rooted revolutions we find the same extreme viewpoints; an absence of moderation, an inability and absence of desire to differentiate between truth and falsehood; absence of mental rectitude; a shifting from one extreme to another; dogmatism ɛ ·d absence of liberty of thought and absence of criticism. These are the conditions which affect and annul the positive results of revolutions.

When the revolution is deep-rooted they are more than effected by the decomposition of the civilizing educational organization of the whole aggregate. Thanks to the daily struggle for existence, thanks to poverty, famine, want, dogmatism and intolerance different categories of schools are closed; others deteriorate. The publication of all books and papers decreases except those books that are dedicated to revolutionary propaganda, but which contribute little to knowledge, distort existing facts, and play upon the emotional side of their readers. The pedagogical staff is artificially replaced by other individuals; in most cases the change is for the worse: the capable are looked upon unfavorably by authorities and replaced by most inefficient individuals whose merit consists in their toadying before authority. The same process of selection is carried through among the pupils themselves.

The remuneration of the teachers is pitifully insufficient so that most of them either die or have themselves transferred to more lucrative posts. To these difficulties must be added that of the absence of books and other educational implements.

As a result of all these conditions national education and civilization deteriorate in proportion to the strength and deep-rootedness of the revolution. These are the results which the Russian Revolution has achieved. Naïve, ignorant, or unconscientious individuals have written much about the tremendous merit of the Soviet Power in the realm of national education. All this is nonsense. The following figures are the best refutation of such an opinion:

Years	The expenditure of the Ministry of Education	General State Budget	Increase of State Budget. The Budget of 1903 being taken as 100.	Increase of the Expenditure of the Ministry of Education. The expenditure of 1903 being taken as 100.
1903	39,353,000 g. r.[7]	1,883,000,000 g. r.	100	100
1904	42,433,000	1,906,000,000	101	107
1905	42,836,000	1,925,000,000	102	108
1906	43,989,000	2,061,000,000	109	112
1907	45,653,000	2,196,000,000	111	116
1908	53,043,000	2,387,800,000	127	139
1909	64,262,000	2,451,400,000	130	163
1910	79,840,000	2,473,100,000	131	203
1911	97,883,000	2,536,000,000	135	249
1912	118,147,000	2,721,800,000	145	300
1913	142,736,000	3,012,000,000	160	363
		without war expenses		
1914	161,630,000	3,302,000,000	175	410
1916	195,623,000	?	?	499
1917	214,221,000	?	?	544
1918	50,000,000 *	?	?	126
1919	40,000,000 *	?	?	100
1920	38,000,000 *	?	?	100
1922	36,000,000	1,700,000,000	99	91

*Not more than

---

[7] Gold rubles.

[8] *Statistical Yearbook for Russia*, St. Petersburg—1914, and 1918-20. For data of 1916-20 see S. Massloff, above-cited book. The figures for 1922 I take from the report of Lounatcharsky. *Isvestia*, December 26, 1922. In 1918-20 the expenditures in the Soviet rubles were as follows:

1918	....	3,074,343,000 sov. rubles
1919	....	17,249,374,000 sov. rubles
1920	....	114,366,070,000 sov. rubles

Taking into consideration that up to the time of the revolution a certain part of the expenditure of other ministries was in reality used for national education in 1914, the general outlay of all the ministries was approximately 200–250 mil. g. r.,[9] plus the immense expenditure for education of all the zemsky (county) and city organizations, which amounted in 1914 to 200–250 mil. r., giving the total expenditure for 1914 amounting to 450,000,000 g. rubles, we arrive at still more striking results, and it grows clearer what a tremendous backsliding has taken place since 1918 in the expenditure for national education, both absolutely and relatively to the total state budget. The percentage of children of school age that actually received education was as follows:

> In 1905 about 43 per cent.
> In 1914 about 70 per cent.
> In 1922 about 38 per cent.[10]

The number of primary schools was	Number of pupils
In 1912 .... 101,547 with	6,697,385
In 1922 .... 55,000 with	4,750,000 [11]

These figures, notwithstanding their inflation for 1922, give to the reader a clear conception of the civilizing influ-

Taking into calculation the depreciation of the ruble to be to:

January 1, 1919	230.0 times
January 1, 1920	3,136.0 times
January 1, 1921	26,500.0 times
January 1, 1922	182,753.0 times

and accepting the half of each coefficient as being the true figure for the middle of the year we shall arrive at a series of figures lower than those cited in the above given tables. See list of indices in the book of communist Preobragensky: *The Reasons of the Depreciation of Our Ruble*, 1922, 34-48 (Russ.).

[9] See Russian State Budget for 1914.
[10] See Belokonsky: *The Peasantry and Public Education*, in "Velikaia Reforma," Vol. IV, 296 p. Reports of Lounatcharsky. *Isvestia*, Dec. 26, 1922.
[11] *Statistical Yearbook for 1913*, 112-13, *Isvestia*, No. 293.

ence of revolution. Fifty per cent. of the primary and high schools have been demolished during the years of the revolution. Instead of the " Abolition of Ignorance " it seems that an "abolition of learning" has taken place. The whole " boom " raised by the Bolsheviks was nothing but an unscrupulous advertisement. School buildings are demolished, text-books, paper and pens not to be had. The teachers remaining without salaries have partly succumbed, partly hired themselves as day laborers; a certain percentage of the lady teachers have gone over into the ranks of prostitutes; only a part of the more fortunate have found other offices.[12] The best professors and stu-

---

[12] See above-mentioned report of Lounatcharsky depicting the terrible condition of teachers and schools. Here are a few official statements. "The situation of the village schools is most dreadful. There is no kerosene, no light, no newspapers, no books. The schools are empty. No teachers. Cultural activity has died." *Isvestia,* November 17, 1922. "I could torture you with terrible descriptions," said Lounatcharsky himself: "among the teachers there are dreadful conditions, beggarliness and pauperism, awful mortality and disease, suicide and prostitution. The teachers have only twelve per cent. of the minimum income necessary to live" (about one dollar a month). *Isvestia,* No. 293, 1922. "Economic situation of the students is very bad," said Bukharin in his report to the last Conference of the Russian Communistic Party in May of 1924: "The picture is terrible, the students are starving and could be called as the beggar-students, who do not have any shelter or room or income and how they are living nobody knows." *Isvestia,* May 31, 1924. "According to the appearance of the present students you can not say who are before you: whether a student or hobo or beggar. Their clothes are nothing but rags. Their faces are emaciated and pale. Such poverty and starvation influence the health of the students very much. You can scarcely find a student without catarrh of the stomach. Such life favours to the terrible increase of tuberculosis and typhus. Greater part of the students have had them. Anemia, malaria and eye-sight illnesses are quite usual phenomena among them. After three years of such a life the state will receive only the invalids good for nothing who are the burden for the country and for themselves." Such is the characteristic of the students given by Latzis—one of the cruellest red terrorists in *Pravda,* June 4, 1924. See also *Isvestia,* No. 260, 1922. Iakovleff: *The Village As It Is,* 1923, and other Bolshevist publications in which they state their complete failure and complete disorganization of the instruction and education in Russia. The description of the University-life see in my *Leaves from a Russian Diary* (Published by Dutton).

dents of the universities and.colleges have been executed, exiled or died. They have been replaced: the professors by ignorant communists; the students by communistic youth.[13]

Similar were the conditions under which newspapers and books were edited. In 1922–23 the issue of all the newspapers of Soviet Russia did not surpass the issue of only one paper, *The Russian Word—Russkoje Slovo*, in pre-revolutionary times. The number of books published, and still more that of the books bought, greatly decreased during the years of the revolution; their quality need not even be mentioned.[14] In 1923: " 89 per cent. of literate peasants do not take a single newspaper." [15]

To sum up: from whatever angle we approach the subject the result is always identical: destruction, destruction, destruction. In this respect, as in so many others, the revolution has thrown back Russia for fifty or sixty years.

Let us now ask ourselves in how far this destructive feature of the Russian Revolution is inherent in all other revolutions. I think that other deep-rooted revolutions vary in dimension—not in quality of destruction.

Like the Russian, the French Revolution was rich in promises and high-flown aspirations in the realm of national education. But " discussions and decrees are not yet actual facts. During the First Republic the number of schools closed for want of funds was greater than the

---

[13] See details Sorokin: *Contemporary Russia*. A certain mental level and capacities of the pupils are no more required for the acceptance into any given school, the only demand is a communistic trustworthiness. In 1922-23 all schools were officially closed for non-communists. It is difficult to consider such a selection reasonable.

[14] See article of Rosenberg: *In Foreign Countries*, 1922.

[15] Quoted from *Dni*, No. 250. See official book of Iakovleff: *The Village As It Is*, 1923.

See " Notes and Addenda," p. 418.

number of newly-opened ones. During the beginning of the Consulate the greater number of General Councils and prefects stated that the national education had greatly suffered and was in a pitiable state." The official report for 1792 says: " *Le mal est à son comble. Les colleges sont déserts. La jeunesse languit depuis quatre ans dans l'oisivité.*" In an official report Gregoire states: " Everything is demolished. Only twenty colleges still exist, and even they are in an agonizing condition. Out of 600 districts only sixty-seven have primary schools." [16]

These details clearly demonstrate the destructive influence the great French Revolution had on national education. In reckoning up the number of schools, the number of students, the number of literate recruits, the number of individuals having received the title of *baccalauréat ès lettres, baccal ès science, license et doctorat en droit et en medicine,* we find that during the years 1848–50 and again, 1869–71, the number either decreases or remains stationary.[17] These statistics prove that the influence of the revolutions of 1848–50 and 1869–71 was similar.

I should not like to be over-positive in stating that the effect of the English Revolution was identical, for I do not possess sufficient data pro and con to be able to do so; but I am inclined to believe that, in claiming its disorganizing influence on the education of the masses, I shall not be far from the truth.

The tremendous disorganizing influence of revolutionary periods, such as the blood-thirsty troubled times of Russia in the seventeenth century; in France in the fourteenth and fifteenth centuries and others, need scarcely be proved.

---

[16] Levasseur: *La Popul. Française,* Vol. II, 480. *Hist. des Classes Ouvr.,* Vol. I, 76, 93, 100.

[17] See the figures and diagrams of Levasseur: *La Popul. Française,* Vol. II, 487, 503, 508 and others.

During the revolutionary Roman period and under its influence: " Creative Italy began to deteriorate without having attained the highest stages of its original creative power." " The creative impulse grew barren in the realm of positive science." " Everywhere we witness the domain of routine." A wave of mysticism spreads over the country, superstition increases, eastern ideologies and cults grow more popular (Jehovah, Mithras, Isis, etc.), priest-craft gains influence. Even the system of national education is modified. Instead of positive knowledge we see the tendency to acquire form: the art of oratory, the memorizing of quotations, poetry, etc., and all outward attributes of culture.[18]

The example of the Russian Revolution makes us think that it could not have been otherwise in all blood-thirsty revolutions, if we consider the mental condition not of individuals only, but of the masses.

Of course during revolutionary epochs the masses can accept new catchwords (for instance, Filioque, the dogmas of Protestantism, of the Independents, of revolutionary times, etc.), but all these can scarcely be considered as true knowledge; and it is not likely that the masses could comprehend all their intricacies, and, lastly, that these abstract catchwords should really form an important part of human mental experience. At the same time we must not forget that in former times when society did not possess such a complex of educational and civilizing system of schools, institutes, laboratories, books, journals, lectures, etc., as are now the heritage of contemporary societies, the destructive effect of revolution should be much more insignificant. The simpler an institution, the

---

[18] Rostovtzev: *The Birth of the Roman Empire*, 101 and foll., 109 and others. Same author: *The Downfall of Ancient Civilization. Russian Thought*, 1922, book VI-VII, VIII-XII (Russ.). Mommsen: Vol. I, 860-65; Vol. II, ch. of the Spiritual and Religious Conditions.

easier is it for it to retain its integrity during social convulsions. Revolution has nothing to destroy there. But in our times the picture is different. The complex educational civilizing system of contemporary society requires careful handling; a coördination of its different parts is required, and all modifications must be introduced according to a given plan and not on the impulse of the moment; otherwise the confusion of one part reacts in the disarray of the whole, as in all high-grade complex machinery. Revolution knows nothing of this gradual and careful handling. It sets to demolishing suddenly and energetically, consequently, it is not astonishing that in the outcome not only the defects, but the system itself is destroyed. In Russia, where prior to the war and revolution, education and a spiritual creative activity had begun to make great strides forward: where during the years 1907–16 universal knowledge of reading and writing had been three-quarters achieved, and according to the law of 1909 had to be realized in 1919, we shall now be obliged to wait for many years before a return to the pre-war and pre-revolutionary level.

Let us now take in review the characteristic modifications in the ideology and frame of mind of society during revolutionary periods.

If the statement " The wish is father to the thought " be true, or, in other words, if the human impulses produce the character of man's ideology and conditions (vocal and subvocal reflexes), then it is easy to foresee in which direction his ideology will change during the first and second periods of revolution.

During the first period of revolution society is seized by an ideology and frame of mind which denounces and is ready to wreak vengeance against conditions which had oppressed the instincts of society (individual, or institutions and organizations) and which approves and stimulates in all possible ways everything that can help to liberate it from them and from all the effects which they call forth. If the impulses of property and nutrition have been oppressed by poverty and famine, success is assured to such ideologies as denounce private property and wealth; to such as encourage expropriation, redistribution and enrichment of the poor. If it be the impulses of liberty (by despotism) or personal safety (by executions, war, etc.) that have been oppressed, then those ideologies which flagellate and encourage the abolition of oppressing conditions will be popular. During such times not only the oppressing conditions will be condemned, but also those that stood in any indirect connection with them. If, for instance, some instincts have been oppressed by war and the government then all individuals and institutions which stood in connection with them, which had friendly relations towards them will also provoke the hatred of the masses; every ideology condemning them grows popular. We witness here on a large scale the same process that happens daily on a small one: " The friend of my friend is my friend," " the enemies of our enemies are our friends."

Such are only the general characteristic features of these modifications. The concrete form into which this ideology will shape itself will depend on many concrete conditions of time and place. In one case the " ideology of freedom " will proclaim the " purity of God's Word " and thunder against oppressing conditions in the name of the Gospel; in other cases the Koran is taken as a basis; or again it will refer to " Capital " and " The Communistic Manifesto " of Marx, or to Voltaire, Rousseau and Tolstoy. All these

are but details, only the " dressing " under which different
theories are being thundered against oppression, demanding the downfall of all oppressors and oppressing conditions and institutions. They are feverishly propagated not
because of their logical contents, their reasonableness and
truth, but because of the thirst to punish " oppression "
and the stimulus to perform corresponding acts. However idiotic, from a scientific standpoint, the theory may
be, it requires only that it should satisfy the above-named
condition for it to be accepted as supreme truth. And,
on the contrary, the most scientific and reasonable opinion
will remain unpopular, if it goes counter to the instincts
of the masses.

Such an absence of human logic is to be found daily;
we have seen this on an extensive scale in all countries during the war and the post-war years. But during revolutionary periods it takes particularly acute forms.

All we have said explains the popularity and widespread influence of the teachings of Tanhelm, Peter Brüs-
sen, Henry of Lausanne, Arnold Bresciano, the Paupers
of Lyons, the Catharites, Patarenes, Wycliffe and the Lollards, John Ball, Huss, Münzer, the Millenariens and other
reformers, who blamed the Catholic Church, which was
oppressing the instincts of the masses. They all blamed
the wealth, the license of the church; they encouraged the
population not to pay church dimes; they preached the
expropriation of the church's wealth, a return to " Evangelical poverty"; abolition of the feudal's and noble's
privileges; the annulment of hard taxes and duties (for
instance, the *Vision of Piers the Plowman*), etc.

All of the above explains the immense popularity
which the pamphlets of Prynne, Lilburne, the ideology of
the Levellers, the Independents had before the English
Revolution; they all thundered against the " oppressing "

conditions of the given moment (The Episcopal Church, The Star Chamber, The King, etc.). It also proves why in the middle of the eighteenth century the "enlightened philosophy" of the Encyclopædists Rousseau, Voltaire and others with its free-thinking tendency was caught up by French society; why the blood-thirsty articles of Marat, the coarse writings of Duchesne and others grew to be so extraordinarily popular during the first revolutionary periods; why the socialistic-communistic ideology of Owen, Saint-Simon, Cabet, Leroux, Proudhon, Lassalle, Marx and others spread wide and broad prior to and during the first period of the revolutions of the nineteenth century. In different ways, under the guise of "different dressings," they all "thundered" against conditions which were oppressing the revolutionary masses; they incited the latter to commit acts toward which they were already driven by their own oppressed instincts. The "dressings" vary, but the essence is always the same.

Such was the state of things before and at the beginning of revolution.

During the second period we witness a considerable modification, and the character of this modification depends on the question whether the revolution has been cut short or, whether it has taken more profound root and has had time to reach its own natural depth, thereby completely annihilating itself.

We have already seen that all deep-rooted revolutions when they begin to act upon the "prescriptions of salvation" proclaimed by all such "liberatory" ideologies lead not to a decrease, but an aggravation of oppression. The masses find themselves driven "from bad to worse." Where an amelioration of life was sought for they find only an aggravation of its evils; where plenty was expected they find famine; instead of freedom—unlimited despot-

ism.   Hence follows the natural and unavoidable turning
point in the ideology of the masses, brought on by the
same principle: "The wish (instinct) is father to
the thought."

As the oppressive conditions of the ancient régimes
led to an unheard of popularity of a revolutionary ideology, thundering against them, so now conditions of a still
more oppressive character lead to the extraordinary success of a counter-revolutionary ideology and frame of
mind; the soul of society makes a circuit of 180 degrees
and it begins to " bow down before what it had burnt, and
burns that before what it had bowed down."

That is why in revolutions which have run their full
course we witness the unpopularity of the ideology of the
first period (" *C'est la faute de Rousseau, c'est la faute de
Voltaire*") and, at the same time, a tremendous success
of ideologies thundering against the oppressive conditions
brought on by revolution and demanding their abolition.
Such is the " human comedy " in two acts which is played
before us in every fully-developed revolution.   Such is
the " logic " of human behavior and the stability of
" sacred convictions."

If a revolution has not run its full course, if it has
been stemmed; if the realization of revolutionary slogans
has not had time to call forth colossal oppression and to
show up its own bankruptcy—then such a turning point
may not be reached, or it may take place in a milder form,
be less widespread and less noticeable.   During this second
period a negative appreciation spreads (radiates) not only
over all odious revolutionary facts and events, but also
over those which are harmless in themselves, but have had
the misfortune of being connected with revolutionary
ideas.   The same happens to all positive appreciations.

Such is the fundamental rule of the modifications of

ideology and frame of mind. It explains and contains all the features of such modifications. It is like a formula of algebra in which the modifications of religious views, political sympathies and antipathies, social and juridical convictions, moral and other appreciations, esthetic tastes, the shape taken by vocal and subvocal reflexes of a given period and space are but simple arithmetic units.

The revolution itself during the period preceding it and the first revolutionary stages was looked upon by the masses as a beneficent factor. During the second period it is looked upon as an evil, or in the best of cases, ceases to call forth any enthusiasm amid the population, with the exception of a small number of " revolutionary specialists." Among contemporaries who have personally felt the " charm " of revolution the latter loses all attraction. Taine was perfectly right in saying that the idealization of the French Revolution commenced only when the generation contemporary with it was no more. The same can be said of other revolutions.

If during the first period a revolutionary ideology proclaims ideas of a primitive, mathematical equality, during the second period such ideas lose all credit. If revolution has proclaimed the abolition of private property, when the second stage is reached every communistic ideology is sure to lose all popularity. If the extreme parties (Taborites, Millenariens, Men of the Fifth Monarchy, Jacobins in 1789, Communists and Socialists during the nineteenth century) have been adored during the first period, during the second they lose the sympathies of the masses and grow to be hated. If at the high-water mark of revolution it proclaimed and supported certain tendencies of philosophical and religious thought, such as materialism, geometrism, the Cult of Reason, or certain Schools of Art, or artistic productions, the same are sure when the reaction sets in to have no more attraction : just because of their connection with revolution they lose credit and are supplanted by others often diametrically opposed to them. Chateaubriand and de Maistre take the place of Rousseau and Voltaire; mysticism, the place of materialism; a conservative ideology, that of a radical one; the " Leviathan " of Hobbes takes the place of an ideology denying the necessity of a state; a non-political professionalism, the place of the ideology of revolutionary politics.

On the other hand if during the pre-revolutionary periods, and during the first stages of revolution, the *Ancien Régime,* Religion, the Church, the old aristocrats, the old social order and traditions, are abused, we can be sure to find a great liking for the pre-revolutionary régime, a religious revival, growing sympathy towards all that had been mercilessly persecuted and insulted during the first period. As a result we witness: the restoration of the *Ancien Régime;* a quickening and revival in the Episcopal Church in England, the Catholic Church in France, and other examples of a revival of that which had seemed hopelessly buried by revolution. The " corpses " rising from these tombs are more alive than they had been before the revolution.

Such is a short outline of these transformations. Details are not always so clearly defined; we find different shades and degrees, but in their essence they all correspond to this outline. This reaction manifests itself, not by a compulsory infliction of the ideas of a group of reactionaries, but by a change in the whole frame of mind of society. " Reaction " triumphs not because a handful of reactionaries are now at the helm, but because the population has grown reactionary. The essence of this " reaction " is not something absolutely negative, distin-

guishing it from an absolutely positive revolutionary ideology, as is often supposed to be the case, but it is the
inevitable, and often perfectly rightful, corrective of the
mistakes committed by the revolution. Experience has
been the teacher and here we witness a salutary impulse
of society to protect itself from the disaster towards which
the first period of the revolution has hurried it. It is the
" drunken headache" after a period of debauch. However hard this state may be, it is still much less harmful
than a continuation of drunkenness with its satellites of
murder, brawls and scandals. The reaction after a
drunken fit leads to a sober life; a continuation of drunkenness leads to penal servitude, the madhouse, and death
under a fence, and from there to the "morgue" of
history; such is the fate of individuals, such also is the
fate of nations.

What has been said above explains the concrete picture
of the change of the ideology and frame of mind of
Russian society during the last years. Let us describe it
somewhat more in detail. This example helps to clear up
certain general statements that have been made.

Up to the time of the revolution and during its first
period, the socialistic and communistic ideologies, and
especially Marxism, were exceedingly popular in Russian
society. In 1921 the picture changes completely. Communism, and socialism as connected with it, lost every
vestige of popularity. Words like "commune" and
"socialism" were hated, they were looked upon as invectives. The names of Marx and other leaders of socialism
grew to be odious. Numerous monuments erected in their
honor were demolished by stealth or subjected to insults.[19]

---

[19] For instance in Odessa the mouth and beard of Marx were
smeared over with millet-porridge (upon which the population had
been fed for so long a time); an inscription proclaimed: "Eat
it yourself."

Communistic books and newspapers were no more read. To sum up, a cardinal and abrupt change in the ideology of the masses has taken place—Russia of the present day is the most anti-socialistic and anti-communistic country in the whole world.

The other side of this phenomenon is seen in the modification of the viewpoint towards private property and towards the personality of enterprising capitalists. Before the revolution private property was looked upon in Russia as the source of all evil. The capitalist and enterpriser were dubbed: " Parasite," " Exploiter," " Bourgeois." Now the picture changes. Private property is looked upon as something positive. It is the alpha and omega of salvation. The " bourgeois " is no more a " parasite," he is the " Organizer of National Economic Life." Now the people say: " We cannot live without the bourgeois."

Before the revolution nationalism and national feeling were but very slightly developed in Russia. Russia was perhaps the country in which national feeling was least of all evident. Nationalism was looked upon as something bad, even shameful. On the other hand, the ideology of " Internationalism " and the " Internationale " were very popular. During the first period of revolution their popularity increased still more. But 1920 was the turning point. Now all ideologies of " Internationalism " and the " Internationale " are absolutely discredited. Even the words themselves have grown to be invectives. All the classes of society are caught up in a great national feeling. " Nationalism," " National Principles and Traditions," such nowadays are the most popular catchwords in Russia.

The " Internationalists " who have turned Russia into a thoroughfare, where everything that was Russian was trampled under the feet of international adventurers;

who daily trespassed against national wealth, ruined
Russia, trafficking and selling it piecemeal and in retail
to friend and foe, dragging it to the brink of destruction,
these Internationalists naturally called forth, as a salutary
reaction, an unheard of development of national feeling
in Russian society. The same took place, as we have
shown, in the realm of religion. Former atheism and
indifferentism towards the Church have, since 1921, given
place to a religious revival. The same can be said of the
appreciation of many sides of the *Ancien Régime,* even in
regards to the Czar. Formerly public opinion was quite
negative to all its sides, now it is supplanted by an opposite
tendency to overrate its good points. There are not many
people to be found now who do not consider the *Ancien
Régime* infinitely better than the contemporary one introduced by the Bolsheviks. There are not many people who
continue to see in it only the negative sides, as they used
to do in pre-revolutionary times. There are even many
people who are inclined to consider it nearly the most perfect régime possible.

The same can be said of a whole series of other ideological facts. Very many national features which used
not to be appreciated are now treasured like something
sacred. Individualism was formerly looked upon askance,
as something opposed to socialism and collectivism; now,
on the contrary, it grows to be the most popular slogan. Materialism, which had formerly had a great vogue
of success and was energetically propagated by the Bolsheviks, is now supplanted by idealistic and mystical
tendencies.

"Cubism," "Futurism," "Super-Futurism," and
other extreme schools of art which joined hands with the
Bolsheviks from the beginning of the revolution have
also lost popularity and been replaced by other diametri-

cally opposed tendencies. The appreciation of Russian political and social teachers and leaders has also completely changed. Formerly all radical, socialistic and revolutionary authors were accounted " National Saviours " and considered to be positive types; all conservative authors and leaders were looked upon as " black sheep." Now an opposite tendency is getting the upper hand (for instance, the appreciation of Stolypin, Leontieff and others). The same tendency is visible everywhere.[20]

These facts clearly illustrate in the example of the Russian Revolution the correctness of our proposition. The concrete character of these changes of opinion may vary in different revolutions, but their fundamental essence is always similar to the one shown in the preceding statements. Here also: " History repeats itself." When we take into consideration the reasons of such changes it is easy to understand that it could not have been otherwise.

[20] See details in my book: *Contemporary Russia* and my *Leaves from a Russian Diary*. As the typical and popular examples of the ideology of the present Russian intellegentzia see the books, S. Frank: *The Downfall of the Idols*, Berdyaeff: *The Philosophy of Inequality*, Novgorodtzeff: *The Social Ideal*, P. Struve: *The Reflections on the Revolution*, Karsavin: *The Philosophy of History*, and others.

CHAPTER XVI

THE ILLUSIONS OF REVOLUTION

THE rôle played by " Tartuffe " has always had, and still has, great attraction in private and social life. Thousands of Tartuffes envelop their rather disgusting actions in the garb of sonorous words and high-flown ideas. And they succeed in achieving their aim. Often they are judged not according to their actions, but according to their words. As a result we find that the " Social parasite " attains the reputation of a " National hero "; the empty prattler and demagogue receives the halo of " Champion of Liberty "; he who despises all physical labor and all true laborers acquires the reputation of " Protector of the Laboring Classes " and builds his own career on this reputation. The man morally lax who disguises his own license under the title of " Taking up arms against old-fashioned prejudices " attains the popularity of a " liberal." The influence exercised by such Tartuffes is immense and has not been taken enough into consideration as a social factor. So was it in the past, is now, and will be in future times.

Never, perhaps, is this so sharply accentuated as during revolutionary epochs. Up to a certain degree revolution can be nicknamed the " Great Tartuffe."

Why so? Because no other Tartuffe claims the merit of so many virtues and no other possesses so few. No one is so ready to create false values: crime and brutality are dubbed heroic deeds; pygmies grow into giants; babblers into heroes; persons of lax morality are canonized; parasites looked upon as saviours. *Vanitas—vanitatum!*

Perhaps all this sounds somewhat severe, but, alas, it is only too true. All we have said till now proves this truth. A balance sheet of promises and bills run up by the revolution, on the one hand, and its actions and payments thereof, on the other, depicted in the foregoing chapters, confirms it clearly. Revolution has always been a voluntary or involuntary " bankrupt," an " insolvent debtor." Comparing the list of promises of revolution with that of its objective results we may appreciate the correctness of my statement concerning the falsehoods, cynicism, and Tartuffe-like hypocrisy of revolution. Of course, revolution gives some positive results also. . . . But even in suicide, even in the worst event in the world there are also some positive sides. The point is how great they are in comparison with the negative results? My answer is in revolution the former are a drop in the ocean of disastrous effects. These results are all the more important, because the Russian Revolution as well as many others have not been stemmed in their course. Power in Russia is still in the hands of extreme-revolutionists. All the changes have been carried through by them; they can throw the blame on no one. It is true that the leaders of the revolution can say: " This has happened against our will; we have wanted something quite different." But a statesman is answerable not only for his desires and promises, but also for the objective results of his activity. An engineer is responsible not only for the project proposed by him, but for the results ensuing from its execution. Lenin says: " We have been mistaken." But it is not sufficient to own yourself in the wrong after millions of victims have been sacrificed on the altar of your errors and other millions continue to suffer from the continuation of your experiments.

Our worst judgments of their moral standards seem to be corroborated by the ethical teaching of the revolutionaries themselves. Trotzki on the fifth anniversary of the Communistic Swerdloff University—June 18, 1923—proclaimed to the youthful generation the following moral thesis: " A revolutionary is he who is not afraid to ' uproot ' and put into practice the most merciless oppression. In these actions the revolutionary must be limited only by outward obstacles, not by moral ones. . . . Comrades! Existing conditions already present too many handicaps for a true revolutionary to allow himself the luxury of multiplying objective obstacles by subjective ones. Consequently the education of a revolutionary is first of all an abolition of all subjective obstacles (religion, morals, legal rights, etc.) which prevent this merciless oppression. That is why: We consider atheism which is an inherent element of materialism an indispensable ingredient of a terroristic revolutionary education."

This propaganda of ethical cynicism requires no commentaries. It only puts into words what has been done, and is still being done by the Russian communists. An important fact is that these negative results of all deep-rooted revolutions are attained quite irrespective of whether revolutionary authority is supplanted by a counter-revolutionary authority or not. The Russian, the French, the English Revolutions, and the Revolution of Huss were not stemmed. They ran their full course. Authority remained in the hands of the groups and individuals, who had been elevated by revolution, not in those of their opponents. And yet we find that this condition, of authority remaining in the same hands, does not prevent but rather accelerates results diametrically opposed to the promises and watchwords of revolution. The revolution proclaims one thing, but its hands accomplish something very different. Today it announces something, and the same, or the next day, it tramples upon its own promises and declarations. So it was, so it remains. And no revolutionary dare, without denying facts, justify himself by saying that " they were prevented from establishing an Eden on Earth, because their dominion was overthrown." For the greatest of revolutions such a justification is not possible. No one prevented the Taborites, nor the Jacobins, nor the Long Parliament, nor Cromwell, nor the Russian communists from establishing the promised Eden, no one but . . . "the inexorable course of events." If in giving their promises they did not calculate the odds against them, then they were utopians and hare-brained individuals, setting fire to the house and not expecting a conflagration. If they " calculated the course of events," hoping to conquer them and did not conquer, it again does not speak in their favor. If on the other hand, setting fire to the house, they knew that the course of events would be too much for them; that only ruins and victims could result from their actions, then all we can say is that such " incendiaries " are put into prison even for setting fire to a barn, let alone a whole country with thousands of victims.

I am no judge and am writing this not to find an indictment against these incendiaries, but only to demonstrate the aberration of the arguments of infatuated revolutionaries. Like all stupid individuals who are overlenient toward themselves, they are always seeking for the source of their failures not in themselves and other revolutionaries, but in other people and accessory circumstances.

If mankind can learn the lessons of history and has sensible nature indeed, he ought not to look for the outlet from the social misfortunes in revolution. If, what is more probable, his reasonableness is still insufficient, revolutions may be in the future; but for every such attempt the revolutionary society shall receive pitiless retaliation and merciless experimental lessons, all instructive enough for the contemporaries of revolution.

Is it not time to understand this very simple truth to avoid useless sufferings, destructions and victims?

PART V
THE CAUSES OF REVOLUTION

CHAPTER XVII

THE CAUSES OF REVOLUTION

1. **The Main Causes of Revolution.**—In analyzing the causes of revolutions it is best to begin with those causes which produce the revolutionary perversion of the behavior of individuals. If the behavior of the members of society manifest the changes described above, the whole social life is bound to change also, since in it are summarized the behavior and the interaction of individual members.

What are then the causes which lead to the above-described extraordinary quick and general perversions?

The question of causes put in a general form is always vague, and savors of metaphysics. I shall therefore qualify my statement. By causes I understand in this case the complex of conditions which form the nearest link preceding the revolution, in the causal chain whose beginning is lost in the eternity of the past and whose end is not discernible in the eternity of the future. Let us then at once answer the above question. The immediate cause of revolution is always the growth of " repression " of the main instincts of the majority of society, and the impossibility of obtaining for those instincts the necessary minimum of satisfaction. The remoter are whatever occasions such a growth of repression.

Such is that summary statement of the cause of revolutions, which may appear in a multitude of different particulars at different places and times. If the desire for food (or the alimentary reflex) of a considerable part of the population is " repressed " by famine, we have one cause of riots and revolutions. If the reflexes of individual self-preservation are " repressed " by arbitrary executions, mass murders or a bloody war, we have another cause of revolutions and troubles. If the reflexes of collective self-preservation of a group, for example a family, a religious sect, of a party are " repressed " by the desecration of the holy things of that given group, by the mockery at its members, their arrest and execution, etc., we have a third cause of revolutions. If the want of housing, clothing, necessary temperature, etc., is not satisfied even to the minimum extent—we have a further additional cause of revolutions. If the sex reflex, together with their variations, like jealousy or the wish to possess for oneself the beloved object, of a large group of individuals are " repressed " by the impossibility to satisfy them, by the rape and violations of wives and daughters, by compulsory marriages and divorces, etc.—we have a fifth cause of revolutions. If the instincts of ownership of the mass of people are " repressed " by their poverty and destitution in the face of other people's wealth—we have a sixth cause of revolutions. If the instinct of self-expression (according to Ross) or individuality (according to Mikhailovsky) of the mass of people is " repressed " by insults, under-estimation, constant and unjust ignoring of their merits and achievements, on one hand, and over-estimation of the less worthy people on the other—we have a further cause of revolutions.

If with the great number of individuals their impulses of fighting and rivalry, of creative work, of variety of experience and adventure and their habits of freedom (in the sense of freedom of speech and actions, or unchecked manifestation of innate inclinations, see below) are repressed by too peaceful a life and too monotonous surroundings, by work which satisfies neither brain nor heart, by continual restrictions upon freedom of communication, speech and action—we have further conditions contributing to the outburst of revolutions.

This is not a complete list of causes; we have merely tried to point out the most important impulses whose " repression " leads to the revolutionary catastrophes, and also the main groups of " repressed " individuals by whose hands the old order is to be overthrown and the banner of revolution to be hoisted up.

Either an exceedingly strong " repression " of the most important instincts, or a repression of a great number of them, is indispensable to produce a revolutionary outburst. In most historical revolutions it is the second case. Further, it is necessary that the " repression " should spread, if not over the large majority, at least over a considerable part of society. The " repression " of a small part of society exists everywhere; it leads to individual breaches of order which are called crimes. But when the " repression " becomes general, it leads to a general breach and subversion of order. This act is identical with those acts which being individual are termed " crimes "; becoming general, they are called " revolutions."

The growth of repression is, as everything else in the world, a relative conception. The poverty or the wealth of a man is measured not by what he has at present, but by what he used to have before, or what the others have. A semi-millionaire today, who was a multi-millionaire yesterday, feels poor compared with what he was yesterday and with other millionaires. A worker who earns $100 a month is a poor man in America and a rich one in Russia. The same must be said of the increase or decrease of " repression." It increases not only when the difficulties in the way of satisfying the instincts grow, but also when they decrease at a different pace with various persons and groups. On seeing a magnificently served dinner-table, a man who is quite satisfied from the biological point of view feels hungry and " repressed." A man who sees a fashionable elegant dress, or a luxurious apartment, feels badly dressed and badly housed, although he has for all purposes a decent suit and a satisfactory house. This is again a case of repression of the corresponding instincts.[1] A man whose volume of rights is sufficiently large feels " repressed " when he is faced with still greater privileges of other people.

Those examples serve to illustrate my idea and to explain why in so many cases the " repression " of instincts of certain groups in pre-revolutionary periods grew not absolutely but relatively and was due to the growth of legal proprietary and other differentiation and inequality. We must always bear in mind this relativity of " repression."

Such is then the primary and universal cause of revo-lutions. But it does not suffice. It is also necessary that those social groups which defend the existing order should lack the means for the suppression of subversive attempts. When to the growing revolutionary force of the " repressed " instincts those groups can oppose the force of restraint, and thus counter-balance the pressure, revolu-tion is not unavoidable. There will be only a series of spontaneous suppressed riots. But when the groups which stand for order are unable to exercise that restraining influence, a revolution is inevitable.

Thus we have found occasion to note (1) the growing

---

[1] " We are developing new types of destitutes—the automobileless, the yachtless, the Newport-cottageless. The subtlest luxuries become necessities and their loss is bitterly resented," pointedly remarks Patrick about the new types of American " destitute and repressed." Patrick : *Op. cit.,* 133, see also W. Weyl : *The New Democracy,* p. 246.

repression of the main instincts; (2) its general character
and (3) the impotence of the groups which stand for
order—such are the three necessary elements in an
adequate description of the conditions for the outbreak
of revolutions.

2. Why Does the Repression of Impulses Lead to
Revolutions?—Why does the growth of the repression of
the main instincts of the mass of population lead to a
general revolutionary perversion of behavior? Because
the repression of the main impulses will inevitably force
people to look for some way out, just as does the organism
which is put into unfit surroundings. Old forms of
behavior will prove unfit. It will be necessary to look
for new ones. The repressed reflex (instincts) will in the
first place exercise a pressure upon several conditioned
reflexes which prevent it from being satisfied; e.g., the
repressed alimentary reflex (instinct) will start by pressing
upon the conditioned checks which deter the individual
from acts of theft, of mendicity, of eating the food that is
forbidden at fast times and so on. Many such checks,
or habits, will cease to operate under the pressure of the
repressed instinct. He who has never been a thief,
becomes a thief and a robber; he who was ashamed of
stretching his hand for alms, becomes a beggar; a believer
ceases to observe fasts; he who always obeyed the law,
now breaks it; a former aristocrat, overcoming the feeling
of shame, takes a pair of trousers and goes to the market
in order to sell it; a man who used to be ashamed of
eating in the street, now does it quite freely; a man who
felt contempt for such and such people is now ready to
flatter them for the sake of a piece of bread, etc. (see my
book *Famine as a Factor,* where I have demonstrated in
detail the enormous perversion of behavior under the pressure of hunger and the disappearance of all conditioned

reflexes hindering the satisfaction of hunger). Disappearance of the majority of the latter which used to prevent the
satisfaction of the repressed hereditary instinct means the
liberation of the latter from a multitude of fetters and
letting it loose. At the same time it means the relaxation
of conditioned checks which heretofore deterred the individual from committing certain acts of violence, such as
theft, violation, sacrilege, etc. Human behavior begins
to develop on biological lines. The repressed instinct having cast off the conventional trammels begins to exercise
a pressure upon other instincts. Their mutual balance
disappears, and the latter also are displaced. This leads to
the rupture of a new series of conditioned reflexes and
signifies a further "biologization" of behavior and a
relaxation of the checks which deterred the individual
from committing anti-social acts. If the government and
the groups which stand for order are unable to screw up
the brakes accordingly, a revolution of behavior must
come: the conventional garment of civilized behavior is
speedily cast off and instead of a *socius* we are left face
to face with a beast let loose. Once the behavior of the
mass of population has changed the whole social order is
bound to break up.

It would be interesting to take up one by one the
major instincts of repression which have been followed
by revolution.

1. A historical study shows that a tremendous rôle
has been played in human history by hunger or the repression of alimentary reflexes. The periods of revolutions
and riots in the history of Athens and Sparta; that of
Rome (second and first centuries B.C. and third and
fourth centuries A.D.) and of Byzantium; in the history
of England: 1257–58, the beginning of the fourteenth
century, years before the Rebellion of 1381, before and

at the beginning of the Revolution of 1648–49, at the end of the eighteenth and at the beginning of the nineteenth centuries, before the Chartist movement, and at last in 1919–21, were the periods of impoverishment and repression of alimentary reflexes. The same may be said about the time preceding the French Jacquerie of 1358, and the revolutions at the end of the fourteenth and at the beginning of the fifteenth centuries; about the years preceding the great French Revolution, particularly of 1788–89, of 1830–31, 1847–48, at last about 1866–70 and 1919–21. The great impoverishment before and at the beginning of the German Jacqueries is well known. The study of causal relation between revolutions and riots in the history of Russia, on the one hand, (the riots and revolutions of 1024, 1070, 1230–31, 1279, 1291, 1600–03, 1648–50, 1662, the riot of Pougatzcheff, the greater part of the revolts of the nineteenth century, at last the revolutions of 1905–06 and of 1917) and the impoverishment and growth of famine, on the other, show that all these riots and revolutions took place in the years of the repression of alimentary reflexes.[2] However, this repression of the latter in order to produce revolution has not to go to the point of too exhaustive starvation. In this case it may bring the masses of population so low as to render them incapable of revolution. On the other hand, economic progress itself when accompanied by a too inequal distribution of the fruits of progress may produce a population powerful enough to be dangerous in the highest degree and at the same time so repressed in its most urgent instincts as to break over all restraints and resort to revolution.

That which is true of the connection between the

---

[2] The study of this causal relation in detail was given in my *Famine as a Factor*.

repression of the alimentary reflexes and the revolutionary outbursts of the past may be also applied, with corresponding modifications, to other main reflexes. The connection between their repression and the growth of revolutionary outbreaks may be also traced out. Let us take a few examples.

2. The repression of the impulse of property caused by the growth of economic differentiation always contributes to the outbreak of revolutions. It is confirmed by many facts. Why is the proletariat—both manual and brain workers—the most revolutionary of all classes of society? Because its impulses of property are more repressed than those of any other class, it owns nothing or very little; the houses in which it lives do not belong to it, the instruments of its work are not its property, its present is not secure, its future is still more uncertain, in short—it is poor as a rat. And on all sides it is surrounded by huge riches. At the sight of that contrast, its instincts of property become still more irritated just as would be the instinct of motherhood with a woman who has no children. Hence its revolutionariness, its incessant grumbling on the " bed of nails " upon which history had put it. Its ideals of socialism, of dictatorship, of the expropriation of the rich, of economic equality, of communization are the direct outcome of that repression. As soon as those instincts have been satisfied, the ideals of socialism and communism vanish, and all those proletarians become ardent advocates of the sacred rights of property.

Of whom does the army of the revolution as a rule consist? Of the paupers, of the men " who have nothing to lose, and can acquire much," of people with repressed reflexes of property. " The hungering and the slaves "— those are people to whom the revolution turns in the first instance and among whom it meets with the heartiest response. So it was in the Greek and Roman, in the Egyptian and Persian, in the mediæval and modern revolutions. Their legions were always composed of the poor. The latter were the instrument with which all the revolutions accomplished their tasks. Does it not speak clearly enough of the above-stated connection?

Was not that connection proved during the last years in nearly all the European countries? Did not the ground tremble everywhere as a result of impoverishment, hunger and unemployment? Did not the success of the communistic ideology grow parallel with the disturbances and strikes? Did it not lead to a series of revolutions? Do we not perceive the effects of that connection at the present moment in Germany, this most unrevolutionary of all nations, which stood a year ago on the very brink of the revolutionary abyss? It is enough to point out these facts in order to make the connection quite obvious.

3. Let us take further the repression of the instinct of individual self-preservation which serves to keep up the life of the individual, and the repression of the instinct of collective self-preservation which serves to keep up the life of a social group: a family, a nation, a tribe, a state, a church, generally speaking of a collective unit kept together by community of interests. The kernels of both of those sets of instincts are hereditary and both are powerful. Their repression, especially when it occurs simultaneously, often leads to revolution. As a good example of such repression may serve an unfortunate war. War is an instrument of death. It represses very strongly the instinct of individual self-preservation by causing a man to act against his will and to overcome this ineradicable protesting instinct of life. At the same time it represses the instinct of collective self-preservation by humiliating, insulting and exposing to privations the life of the whole group.

Can we wonder then that disastrous war is often followed by social explosion? The repressed instincts break the conditional reflexes, do away with obedience, discipline, order and civilized forms of behavior and turn human beings into wild hordes of mad people, like the Russian soldiers in 1917, or, to some extent, the German soldiers in 1918; men become slaves of their instincts of self-preservation, leave everything, and wildly attack the government, overthrow the existing order and hoist up the banner of revolution.

This explains why so many revolutions have broken out as a result of, or during, unsuccessful wars. All the revolutions of our time—the Russian, the Hungarian, the German, the Turkish, the Greek, the Bulgarian—did under such conditions. So did the Russian Revolution of 1905. And the Turkish Revolution which overthrew Abdul-Hamid after an unlucky war. And the French Revolution of 1870–71. Was it not due to the unlucky war, too? The French Jacquerie and the revolutions of the end of the fourteenth century came as the result of ignominious war and of the capture of John II after the Battle of Poitiers. The same is true of the English Rebellion of 1381; the revolutionary troubles with which the English Revolution began were due to the unfortunate war about La Rochelle, and developed after the unlucky war against the Covenanters. Do we not see the same in Germany, Italy and other countries at the end of the eighteenth and in the beginning of the nineteenth centuries after their defeat at the hands of Napoleon's armies? Or in Athens after the Peloponnesian war?

This incomplete list of the revolutions which have broken out in connection with miscarried wars is quite sufficient to prove our statement.

Of course, wars lead to revolutions not only because of the "repression" of the instincts mentioned, but also because of the repression of some others—thanks to the growth of poverty, hunger, cold, to the disorganizing influence of the war in general, etc. Yet the main revolutionary effect of the war is due precisely to the repression of the said instincts. Therefore people who want wars and who organize them ought not to complain against revolutions: the latter are to a certain extent generated by the former. He who sows wind ought not to complain of storm.

The above may be also applied to the régime of arbitrary authority and of unlimited executions, arrests and banishments. It also represents a complex of stimuli which repress in the highest degree the instincts of self-preservation and of self-expression of the individual. The insecurity and the lack of all guarantees created by it leads to the usual results of "repression": the growth of anxiety, discontent, indignation, as well as to the attempts to overthrow the "repressing régime."

Indirectly such a régime represses also the instincts of group self-preservation since every arrested or murdered individual had his family, friends, adherents and others who stand near to him. Sometimes, that régime represses those instincts directly by persecuting some symbol of a group, its members or its values (persecutions of religious, political, national and other groups); this raises the chances of a revolution by increasing the number of "repressed" individuals. Hence it will be understood why such a society is always "pregnant" with revolution, why its ground is laid with mines which explode upon the slightest relaxation of control. This makes clear the "revolutionizing" rôle played by the war and by the régime of arbitrary authority.

4. It is also easy to understand that the same rôle is played by the repression of other instincts, in particular of the sex instinct. The legend which says that the Roman Revolution was caused by the violation of a Roman woman by the last Roman King is not so naïve and remote from reality. *Si non è vero e ben trovato,* we can say with regard to it!

The repression of the sex instinct may be caused by various means and conditions: with some it is caused by the impossibility to satisfy it, with others by the growing depravity of the privileged classes, by the repression of the instinct of " jealousy " through the seduction and demoralization of their wives and daughters, etc. The part played by the repression of those instincts is often not paid sufficient attention. At the first glance it is not very conspicuous, yet its seriousness cannot be denied. That this is so may be seen from a multitude of revolutionary speeches and proclamations, which try to excite the indignation of the masses by pointing to the " repression " of that group of instincts. Those speeches reflect, perhaps unconsciously, the revolutionary character of that factor.

" Workers, if you do not wish to see your daughters used as instruments of pleasure by the plutocracy . . . go and rise! " [3] This appeal of the Paris Commune may serve as a good instance of such proclamations. And who can assert that the motives of rising indicated here were not often among the causes of revolutions. Does not everyone acquainted with history know that one of the main accusations preferred against the rulers by the revolutionaries of all times and nations was the accusation of immorality and depravity, of seducing the wives and daughters of people belonging to the lower classes? Study of the conditions under which many a government has been

---

[3] Gregoire: Vol. IV, 356.

overthrown will show that the sexual behavior of the rulers, by repressing the sex-instincts of the masses, greatly contributed to the outbreak of revolutions. The immoral behavior of the Papal Curia and of the Roman Catholic Clergy was one of the chief reasons why the Roman Church began to be called " The Harlot of Babylon " and lost its prestige and its hold upon the masses. Was not the hatred which the Roman Catholic Clergy inspired in the majority of the Czechs before the Hussite Revolution, and in the population of several other countries before the Reformation, due to their immoral behavior, because they " demoralized their parishioners "? [4] Were not nearly all of them accused of immorality, of having concubines and even whole harems, of living in sexual relation with their mothers and sisters, of having turned the monasteries into brothels, etc.? [5] All this could not but contribute to the " repression " of jealousy and other reflexes of sex on the part of the masses and to the loss of prestige of the clergy. And once the prestige of an authority has been lost, its existence becomes precarious.

Let us turn to Russia of 1916–17. What was it that " finished up " the Czarist régime?—" Rasputinism," the accusation of the Czarina and her Court of sexual looseness,[6] whether false or not. " Rasputinism " was one of the factors of the Russian Revolution. The same we see on the eve of the French Revolution, in the similar accusation of Marie Antoinette and her Court. Do we not also see in everyday life prestiges and reputations shaken because of immoral behavior and the scandal which it

---

[4] Denis: 13-14.

[5] Veber: Vol. VIII, 190-1. Cf. Lea: *History of Inquisition,* Passim.

[6] About this rôle of "Rasputinism" in the debasement of the prestige of the monarchy among the people and the army, see V. Shulgin: *Dni (Russkaja Mysl)* and Denikin: *Op. cit.,* Vol. I.

brings about? Finally, let us suppose for a moment that the government of some civilized modern country should claim its right for the possession of every woman and should attempt to carry that claim into practice. Need we say that the most likely result of that would be a revolution. The bare mention of such an *experimentum crucis* speaks enough as to the part played by this group of instincts.

5. The case is similar with reference to the " repression " of the impulse of freedom.[7]

Any strong restriction of communication, movement and action of the individual represses that impulse. Only when the repression surpasses the limit (just as in the case of hunger) and annihilates that instinct, be it only temporarily (see the experiments of Pavlov who killed this instinct in a dog by exposing it to prolonged starvation), that is, only when men become mere " biological slaves," that repression may not provoke a revolutionary reaction. Up to that point its growth must increase the will to resistance and the stimuli to the overthrow of the repressing régime.   That is why the régime of " oppression "

---

[7] In agreement with I. P. Pavlov, I understand by this the innate impulse which forces men to overcome the obstacles which limit their freedom of communication, of movements, of action. " In this sense the reflex of freedom is the common feature, the common reaction of all the animals, being one of the most important innate instincts. But for it, every small obstacle which the animal meets on its way would completely break its course of life. We all know well how the animals being deprived of freedom try to free themselves, especially the wild beasts which have been for the first time captured by a man. But that common fact had till now no name of its own and was not included in the system of innate reflexes." A man who has been fettered, put into prison or even shut in the " golden cage " of Paradise, has been deprived of freedom of communication, speech, etc., also tries instinctively to liberate himself, even if he runs the risk of death. All that is the manifestation and the complication of the same reflex whose existence has been pointed out by the famous Russian scholar. See Pavlov: *Op. cit.*, 208 and foll., see also there the description of his experiments.

and " despotism " inevitably leads to a social explosion, unless the forces of restraint which can temporarily postpone that explosion, or break the reflexes of freedom, are sufficiently strong. That connection between the growth of repression of the reflexes of freedom and the outbreak of disorders manifests itself so clearly in the history of all countries that we need not adduce any instances.

The same may be said of the repression of other innate and acquired tendencies. Perhaps no one of them, taken by itself, plays as essential a part as each of those enumerated above which are indispensable for the individual's existence (for, as the saying goes, " *primum vivere deinde philosophare* "), yet their rôle is not quite unimportant.

6. Let us take, for instance, the group of the reflexes of self-expression of inherited abilities. The difference of hereditary abilities with various individuals has been firmly established as a fact and already begins to be used in the selection of profession. Let us suppose then that the " mechanism of social selection and distribution " (see above) has been put out of work, and individuals are placed in positions which do not in the least fit in with their hereditary abilities: a " born ruler " is put in the position of an ordinary worker; a " born Cicero " in that of a simple carrier; a " poet by vocation " in that of a bookkeeper; a " born organizer "—in that of a tailor and *vice versa*. What will happen then?

The repression of the instinct of " self-expression " of all those people will grow very acute. None of them will be satisfied with his position and will curse the chains that bind him to the place he loathes, dreaming of nothing but their breaking. At the same time everyone of them will be likely to do badly in unsatisfying trade. Thus a group of people with repressed instincts, longing for revolution to emancipate them, will spring up. The " born

ruler " who became a worker will turn into a powerful
leader of a conspiracy; " Cicero " will become a propagandist, the " born organizer " will organize an illegal
party; the " poet " will sing the revolution; all other
" misplaced " individuals will form its army—and the
revolutionary force will be ready.

We have merely supposed such a bad and " depres-
sing " distribution of individuals in society, but our
hypothesis is not very remote from reality. We see such
a distribution of individuals in pre-revolutionary times.
The law which says : " To everyone according to his abilities," and especially the innate ones, is not embodied in
reality in those periods (see above). That is why we have
in them so many people with the repressed instinct of
" self-expression " which is still further repressed by
protection, by artificially created fame and privileges falling to the lot of the most incapable ones, of the " born
slaves " who have been raised to the top of the social
ladder. Hence the revolutionary feelings of the majority
of the " repressed " individuals, such as writers and
thinkers, journalists and poets, public men and scholars,
of the employers and the bourgeoisie, and of the mass of
people at the bottom of the social ladder who hate their
position and long to climb up and are therefore ready to
welcome any one who would deliver them from the repressing régime.

7. The same may be said of the repression of other
instincts which leads more or less to the same result. But,
as may be gathered from the present book, the revolutionizing influence of the repression of instincts usually
remains hidden. The visible pretexts of revolution are
quite different: now it is the passing of the Navigation
Act, now the introduction of the Prayer Book, now the
reunion of the *l'États Généraux,* now the struggle for a

responsible ministry or for this or that way of ballot, now the quarrel about some religious dogma, or something of that sort. To think that those concrete causes may of themselves provoke a revolution, if there had been no repression of the main instincts, would be rather naïve. They are only the spark which is thrown into the powder-magazine. They serve merely as a pretext, as a sort of safety-valve through which the discontent comes out.[8] Their own revolutionary force is not very great and does not suffice to call forth a revolutionary storm.[9] But when the repression of instincts is there, every slightest event provided it affects directly or indirectly some repressed instinct may lead to an explosion.

In other words, the performance of the grandiose tragedies, dramas and comedies of revolutions on the historical stage is determined chiefly by the repressed inborn reflexes. It depends upon them whether the play called "revolution" will be performed or not. If they say "yes," the play will be given and actors will not be lacking. The importance of unconditioned impulses is much greater than that of the totality of conditioned reflexes. The latter determine not so much that there shall be a revolution as the *mise-en-scène,* the dresses, the make-up and the character of the incidents. It is just those conventional "ideological factors" that determine the concrete forms, the soliloquies, dialogues and watchwords of a revolution: on them depends what it will inscribe upon its banner, whether it will be " Holy Land," " Utraquism," " True Belief," " Constitution," " Legal State," " Democracy,"

---

[8] The historian of the Bohemian Revolution is quite right when he says: "*Les passions humaines ont un rôle dans toutes les transformations religieuses, mais elles se cachent, se présentent sous une forme dogmatique et théologique.*" Denis: *Op. cit.,* 32. The same may be said of the other speech reactions. See Pareto: *Op. cit.,* Passim.

[9] See in the first chapter (essay) the index of the relative determinating force of various reflexes.

" Republic," " Socialism " or something else.   They also determine who will be chosen as popular heroes of that movement, whether Christ, Huss, Rousseau, Luther, Marx, Tolstoy or Liebknecht; whether the actors will discourse upon the Bible and the right interpretation of the Gospels, or upon nationalism, surplus-value and exploitation of capital; whether they will choose for their emblems and draw upon their banners a " chalice," a " Phrygian cap," a " green cheese," a " black shirt," a " five-cornered star " or something else; whether they will assemble in catacombs, in churches, in mediæval town-halls, or in modern parliaments; whether they will disseminate their views by means of parchments and manuscripts, or by means of a printing press; whether the murders will be accomplished with a club, an axe, an arch, a sword or with howitzers, dynamite, tanks and dreadnoughts.

They also determine how far the loosening of the brakes will go.   On the whole, their rôle is confined chiefly to the determination of the concrete forms of revolutions. It would be, however, injudicious to assert that once they appear on the stage, they cannot also become a *cause efficiens* of revolutions.

Oral and printed propaganda certainly is of some importance and helps to crystallize the formless feelings of discontent.   But it can be successful only when the ground has been previously prepared by the repression of the instincts of the masses.   Without this it is helpless to create any considerable social explosion.   In spite of the large expenditure of money upon the monarchist propaganda under the old régime in Russia it was of no avail, because it was contradictory to the repressed instincts.   On the contrary, the propaganda of socialism, communism and other revolutionary teachings was very contagious.   The watchwords of communism met with a great success, especially after July, 1917.

Three years have passed. The communists have monopolized the entire press, have excellently organized their propaganda, and yet their teaching which used to be so popular finds no new adherents now. Conversely, the counter-revolutionary ideas, including monarchism, are widely spread now. This example of the Russian Revolution which is not unique clearly confirms the view that the "speech reflexes" taken by themselves are not sufficiently strong. The same may be applied *mutatis mutandis* to other "ideological factors." Their rôle is confined to giving some form to the revolutionary movement; the latter is caused by the repression of inborn instincts.

3. What Social Groups Have to be Revolutionary, in Which Degree, and Why?—Supposing that our theorem is correct, it then follows: 1. That during a pre-revolutionary period we ought to find an exceptionally strong repression of a series of fundamental impulses among the masses. 2. That in any given society those individuals or groups will be disposed to revolution whose fundamental instincts of any kind are repressed. 3. As the repressed instincts of different people and groups are different as to character and quantity, then, according to the theorem, their character and quantity should determine and explain: how far the revolutionary disposition of each group will go, and, which of them will first desert the revolution and in what succession the other ones will follow. A pre-revolutionary order may have repressed in one group a series of instincts, say:

a,	b,	c,	d,	e,	f.
In another one a,	b,	c,	d,	n.	
In a third one a,	b,	m,	d.		
In a fourth one a,	f,	c.			
In a fifth one a,	h.				
In a sixth one a.					

Let the more powerful instincts and those more completely repressed be represented by the earlier letters of the alphabet. It is easy to see that the first group will become the most extremist and will be the last to fall back from the revolution, because its impulses are harder to satisfy and it is more difficult to remove the restraint put upon all its instincts. Each following group will be more moderate in its revolutionary demands and will be quicker in dropping the revolutionary movement. The repression of instinct *a* of the last group may be removed in the easiest way and that group will be the first to drop the movement This scheme follows from the theorem and explains the actual relation of different groups during revolutionary periods.[10] 4. Further, provided that the theorem is correct, those social aggregates whose prevailing conditions are more strongly repressive of the instincts of the masses than those of other aggregates, ought to be more revolutionary than the latter.

Such are the conclusions to be drawn from our fundamental theorem. Are they correct? I think that they are. Let us comment upon our propositions 1, 2 and 3. A study of pre-revolutionary conditions in any society will clearly indicate the presence of a tremendous repression of fundamental instincts in very numerous groups of that society.

What did we see before the Russian Revolution of 1917?:

---

[10] It also explains the "counter-revolutionary" restorative radicalism of the groups that had been restrained by the revolution. The more numerous the instincts and the more they were repressed by the revolution, the more extremist will these groups become in their restorative endeavors. The group of courtiers and aristocratic circles is subjected to the strongest restriction, therefore its desire of restoration is usually most radical and ardent. On the other side, groups that have been but slightly repressed by the revolution are, and will always be, very moderate in their restorative tendencies; they endeavor to retain the maximum of "Revolutionary winnings."

1. A strong repression of the instinct of individual self-preservation among fifteen or sixteen million of mobilized soldiers, that was brought about by a terrible war and its deadliness, by cold, hunger, parasites, trench-life, privations, etc.

2. A strong repression of group self-preservation instinct in 90 per cent. of the population, brought about by defeats, the incapacity of the authorities and even treason on the part of some of their agents.[11]

3. A strong repression of food instincts, subsequent to the disorganization of the country's economic life and the scarcity of food supplies in cities, acutely felt at the end of the year 1916.[12]

4. A strong repression of "instincts of freedom" induced by the martial law that was introduced all over Russia since 1914; also military censure, courts-martial, arbitrary measures of government agents, etc.

5. A repression of property instincts caused first by the impoverishment of a great part of the population owing to the war, as workmen, government officials, intellectuals, part of the bourgeoisie and peasants; secondly, by the enrichment of a minority of war-profiteers; and thirdly, by governmental interference in economic relations, as in its control of industry, the fixed prices of corn that were as always lower than market price, etc.

6. A repression of sexual instincts of the population by the dissolute behavior of governmental circles and "Rasputinism."

We will not mention here the repression of other instincts, nor the incapacity of the authorities to control

---

[11] Let us take for instance Miliukoff's speech in the Duma, concerning "stupidity and treason," that caused a commotion in the country. Miliukoff: *History of the Russian Revolution*, Vol. I.

[12] See Kondratieff: *The Regulation of Market in the Years of the War and the Revolution*, 1922 (Russ.).

and furnish outlets for such instincts; we will come back later to this subject.

Such conditions were quite sufficient to call forward a deafening revolutionary explosion. Nobody specially prepared it [13] but everybody expected it to come like a thunderstorm, ignoring only the time of its coming. It actually started like a thunderstorm. What were the groups disposed in its favor? Well—nearly 95 per cent. of the population, because some or all of the instincts in all of them had been repressed. Then began a very interesting evolution of the revolutionary demands of various groups, of the character of these groups and their successive exodus out of the revolutionary movement.

The scheme given above was constructed upon just such facts, as they were observed during this revolution. A unanimous effort of nearly all the population brought down " this restraining old régime." But in a week or two the unanimity disappeared and there set in a differentiation and division of the formerly united mass of discontented people, exactly in accordance with the number and character of their restricted instincts. In the course of the two or three days following March 12th there appeared the first split in the shape of a dualism of " Soviets " and " Provisional Government." The fall of the monarchy, meaning also the fall of the nobility, removed the restrictions imposed upon the commercial and industrial classes by the privileges belonging to the nobility and the bureaucracy; it also removed the restrictions set against the social and municipal workers, who had been refused admission to higher posts; it further removed the restrictions experienced by officers who had risen from the ranks and were crowded out by the aristocratic and guards

[13] See Mstislavsky: *Five Days* (Russ.) and Suchanoff: *Memoirs of the Revolution,* Vol. I (Russ.).

element; it also freed from restrictions vast numbers of intellectuals and officials, who saw in the old government the source and reason of the experienced military defeat. All of these groups were now satisfied; they had constituted the element who brought forward the Provisional Government and they now wanted to stop the course of the revolution. Famine, cold, privations and war, the monotony of hard work, did not concern them much, therefore their repressed instincts were more or less satisfied.

Things stood differently with the soldiers, workmen, peasants, the outcasts, criminals and unfit. The formerly enumerated classes and the Provisional Government did not intend to stop the war; therefore the fundamental restriction of self-preservation instincts of the soldiers was not removed and the soldiers could not stop at the February revolution.

What did this revolution bring to the working masses? Scarcely anything but freedom upon paper. Their economic situation had not been improved; on the contrary, starvation increased, the monotonous work at the factory remained the same. The " bourgeois luxury " that filled them with envy was still to be seen everywhere, whereas the part they were allowed to play, as a mass, in the Provisional Government was a very modest one. Practically no restrictions had been removed, neither from their food instincts, nor property, nor toil. Therefore . . . the workmen were bound to proceed with the revolution and try to further remove such restraining conditions as still existed for them, but that existed no more for the more moderate groups.

The same applies to the peasants. The February revolution had promised, but had not yet given them, the landowners' estates that were " restricting " them; it had not reduced their obligation to furnish corn and foodstuffs, but had augmented it; the labor hands that had been taken away in the form of recruits had not been yet returned and the manufactured goods had not become cheaper. Besides, their instincts of self-expression were repressed by their civil disinheritance in comparison to other classes.[14] Consequently . . . the peasantry saw no reason to oppose any further " deepening " of the revolution. Still more does the same apply to the element of criminals, outcasts and adventurers, and to the intellectual and muscular proletariat. The " muddy water " of the deepening revolution was indispensable for them. Thus appeared the first fissure. While the first-named groups were trying to check the revolution, the latter carried it on further. Since the latter party included the workmen, the enormous mass of soldiers clamoring for " peace at any price, even be it a shameful one," and the peasants, that is the three fundamental forces—the October revolution was becoming inevitable.

During the first months, the October upheaval relieved the restraint felt by all these groups : the peasants obtained a sanction and an approval of their seizure of the landowners' estates; the soldiers obtained the cessation of war and the right to go home. The workmen were given the right not to work, access to the more important administrative posts, and the right to " restrain " the " bourgeois "; also the factories and plants were given over to them. As to the scum of the population, the criminals and adventurers, they received posts in the government and acquired full freedom for their natural propensities in the form of a legalization of murder and robbery if perpetrated against " bourgeois and counter-revolutionists."

---

[14] See about this in the article of V. Maklakoff: *The Slavonic Review,* for 1923.

Hence came the strength of the October revolution and of the Bolsheviks.

But a few months passed and the picture began to change. The peasantry received nothing more, while more and more was extorted from them through unending requisitions, graft and robbery. The result was a series of peasant revolts and the beginning of their withdrawal from the revolutionary ranks, still somewhat checked, however, by the fear of a return of the estate-owners, of the old régime and of the old restriction. The Red Army found itself in a similar situation with the exception of three to four hundred thousand specially privileged pretorians of Bolshevism. The working class also experienced in 1919–20 some restriction from hunger, forced labor, bureaucratization and tyranny of the new power. A series of revolts commenced among workmen, red soldiers and peasants with the result that in March, 1921, the government was nearly overthrown; they remained in power by applying strong measures of repression, but they were compelled to remove many restrictions and to give up communism. Altogether, in order to remain in power, they were forced to augment the number of their life-guards, to induce part of the intellectuals, mostly specialists, to take service by giving them rich salaries and to call in businessmen tempting them by tolerating speculation. But in order to pay these people they had to rob the peasants more and more thoroughly and to exploit further the workmen. Such a restriction of the latter's instincts brought them in 1922–24 definitely back into the enemy camp. At present the only support of the Soviet Government consists of their pretorian guard, of the " spetz " (specialists) and partly of the " nepmen " (speculators). This would not represent a very strong support, were it not that the country is weakened by war, revolution, exces-

sive starvation, epidemics and were not the enormous territory and scattered population a hindrance to concerted
action. It may be seen, from this schematic sketch, that
our propositions 1, 2 and 3 are fully supported by the
events that took place during the revolution.

A tremendous restriction of the instincts among the
peasants, workmen, bourgeois, lower clergy and intellectuals undoubtedly also existed before the Revolution of
1789 in France.

The peasantry was restricted by unending feudal taxes
and duties as well as by the famine of 1788; the workmen
by hunger and poverty; the bourgeoisie was "driven
mad " by the privileges of the nobility; the lower clergy—
by the privileges of the higher one.   Everybody, "even
the privileged people, felt themselves oppressed."   " The
society, constrained by a despotic anarchy in the clutch
of which it struggled, hopefully concluded that a constitution would presently be granted to the kingdom." [15]

An explosion was unavoidable and soon took place.
The groups that were ripe for a revolution represented an
overwhelming majority of the population.   So far as
revolutionary extremism and the time at which different
groups abandoned the revolutionary movement is concerned, we observe here the same natural law.   As soon
as one of the groups which took part in the revolution had
obtained satisfaction for its restricted instincts, it lost all
interest in the revolution; and whenever the revolution,
as represented by its authorities, proceeded to restrain
them, that group turned against the authorities.

Here, too, the greatest extremism was represented by
the outcast intellectuals, workmen, criminals and adventurers, who formed the kernel of Jacobinism and furnished

---

[15] Madelin: Vol. I, 16-18, 35 *et seq.*   Taine: *Les Origines,* Vol. I,
de Tocqueville: *L'Ancien Régime et la Revolution,* Passim.

its principal as well as secondary workers. Allied to a series of other groups, they represented the " beaters " of the revolution. The workmen and tradesmen at first supported it, but as soon as they felt a restriction of their instincts in the form of hunger, or unemployment, of the " le Chapelier " law, of a new labor tax, or of forced labor, they immediately went over to the side of the revolution's enemies and unsuccessfully attempted to run the revolution in their own way, as in the case of Babeuf. The peasants, having freed themselves from taxes and having augmented their lands, became indifferent to the revolutionary movement; but, as soon as it restricted them with its endless extortions and requisitions, they became the enemies of the revolutionary government. The same may be said of the clergy, not to speak of the tiers-état.

Here, as elsewhere, owing to the common feeling of restraint, the revolutionary onrush was at first almost unanimous; later, owing to the difference in intensity and in number of the restricted instincts involved, it was divided into separate currents. The further the restricted extremists went, the shallower became the revolutionary stream and the farther back remained the groups who had already reached the desired freedom from restriction. At the same time the revolutionary vanguard restricted ever more these satisfied groups and pushed them back into the camp of the enemies of a further deepening and extremization. Towards the end, the restrictions inflicted by the runaway revolution were becoming as numerous as the restrictions experienced from the old régime. As a result the revolutionary authorities lost all support and finally collapsed, making room for a new government that provided a certain relief from the former's deadly tyranny.

We see a similar extensive restriction of the people's reflexes before the English Revolution. " The reign of

King Charles was a tyranny without any possible excuse."
The laws and the nation's rights were systematically violated. The King's promises were not kept. A number
of new taxes, monopolies and duties were introduced upon
such items as salt, soap, coal, iron, wine, hides, starch,
tobacco, beer, etc. The population was being ruined. The
King's forests were being enlarged by the arbitrary annex-
ation of privately-owned ones. Indubitable claims upon
property were claimed by the King. Judges and administration were corrupt. The population was being oppressed
by the cantoning of troops among them. " Every day,
arbitrariness was weighing more and more upon the rich,
because they were a source of profit, as well as upon the
poor, because they were not dangerous." " The nobles
were ordered to live in their estates." Besides all that
we find religious pressure inflicted upon the people and the
clergy, also censorship, etc.[16]   It takes special capacities
to carry out so efficiently the restriction of so many
reflexes of nearly all classes of the nation. But such
restriction could not continue indefinitely without becoming an explosion.

The further development of that process, in respect to
the radicalism of the various groups and to the time of
their exit from the revolution, corresponds to the theorem
2 and 3. To take another historic example. Before the
Czech Revolution, in the fourteenth century, freedom and
equality disappeared. " Feudalism was becoming ever
more oppressive, the taxes heavier, the duties more numerous." The oppression of people by the gentry was ever
growing. " Where could justice be sought, when the
offender was at the same time the judge . . . the peasant
was no more the owner of his field . . . the Czechs felt
more strongly every day that they were being more and

---

[16] Guizot: Vol. I, 1-70.

more reduced to slavery, a slavery still more objectionable, since it developed under foreign influence."

If we add to that their impoverishment along with the enrichment of the nobility, especially of the Germans and of the Catholic Church, also the depravity and corruption of the clergy, it will be clear to what extent the restriction of instincts had grown before the revolution, both in quantity and quality.[17]

We will not quote here any instances from other revolutions; the reader may himself check up these statements by analyzing the pre-revolutionary state in different countries from that point of view.

It follows from the above that the number of groups predisposed to revolution, especially in great revolutions, is large. These groups are exceedingly varied and involve people of the most different social positions; we may find here a professor still resentful for some slight in the past; a newspaperman offended by an editor; intellectuals "restricted" in some manner by the aristocracy or the existing conditions; a ruined aristocrat; a bankrupt financier; an exposed adventurer; a starving workman; the ever-rebellious criminal and the self-sacrificing unbalanced idealist.[18] Some are urged by cold and hunger, others by envy, cupidity, vindictiveness, fear or greed; others again by compassion and a desire to improve conditions in general.

All these motives are nothing but various forms of restriction of primary tendencies under the impulse of which the foundations of order were shaken and a way

---

[17] Denis: *Op. cit.,* 33-34.
[18] *Petits avocats sans causes, médecins sans clients, curés défroqués, robins ignorés, n'ayant comm auparavant qu'une pâle destinée . . . degénérés de l'alcoolisme et de la misère, voleurs, mendiants, misereax, médiocres ouvriers sans travail constituent le bloc dangereux des armées insurrectionneles,"* rightly remarks Le Bon. *Le Revolution Française,* 225, 61 pp.

for revolution was prepared by Rousseau and Voltaire, John Huss and Hieronymus of Prague, the Independents and Lilburne, Marx and Lassalle, Lavroff, Mikhailovsky, Plekhanoff and others. It is under its impulse that the preaching of radical or moderate " liberators " is picked up when it falls upon favorable soil in the shape of " restricted " masses. It is also under its impulse that the subsequent scattering of revolutionary forces takes place, followed by a collapse of the revolution itself.

Our proposition is also supported by the difference in the revolutionary propensities of the cities as compared with the villages. Professor Hayes rightly remarks that the city population is usually more revolutionary than the villagers.[19] The cities are more often shaken by revolutionary fever than the villages; the former begin it whereas the latter usually put an end to it. We find recent examples in Russia, Bavaria, Hungary and Italy; earlier ones in the Paris Revolution of 1871, . . . the great French Revolution, etc.

Why is this? Because man, his reflexes and instincts, are less adapted to the modern city life than to the rural. City environment is a comparatively new phenomena in the history of mankind, especially the environment of a modern industrial city. Man's entire conduct during many thousands of years had been adapted to country, not city environment. Transferred to the latter with all his old instincts, he finds himself upon a " bed of nails " to which his instincts are not adapted. Take, for instance, the great mass of a city's proletariat.

What is its environment? Work in enclosed spaces, a realm of soulless machinery of steel and coal. . . . Tremendous noise and rattle. The same work repeated from day to day, mechanical, monotonous, meaning noth-

---

[19] Cf. E. C. Hayes: *Introduction,* pp. 62, 63.

ing either to the heart nor to the brain. When and where did man's instincts adapt themselves to such an environment and can they find in it their satisfaction? Naturally not. Neither the instinct of creating or inventing, nor the instinct of variety and change of place, nor the love of adventures can be satisfied here nor many others.[20]

Add to that the fact that the proletariat has no property. Besides that, all these instincts are still more "restricted" by the fact that in the city the proletarian views the summits of plutocracy and abysses of poverty.[21] Is it to be wondered at that the city-proletariat, both intellectual and physical, is always discontented, is always seeking an issue and is permanently inclined toward revolution. It cannot be otherwise, since it cannot help turning round and round in the cage in which history has enclosed it.[22] This is exactly what we see.

It is another proof of our theorem as to the origin of revolution. From all of the above we may conclude that this theorem is established.

4. Disorganization of the Powers of Social Control.— Besides a universal restriction of fundamental instincts, there is another condition necessary in order to bring about a revolution; such a condition is an insufficient and incompetent resistance to the revolutionary outbreak kindled by the restricted instincts. By insufficient and incompetent resistance I mean the incapacity of the authorities and groups in power: (a) to meet the growing pressure of restricted instincts with a counter-pressure

---

[20] Cf. Sorokin: *City and Country.* In *Peasants' Russia,* No. IV.
[21] Hayes: *Ibid.,* 63.
[22] The restricting action of city life and man's lack of adaptability to it is shown by a number of other phenomena, as by the rapid biological deterioration of the human organism in cities, by a greater percentage of criminals, of still-born, suicides and greater mortality. Cf. Sorokin: *City and Country.* Also Mayer: *Moralstatistik,* 1917, pp. 108-09, 139, 274, 332-33, 504-05, 727-29.

398 THE SOCIOLOGY OF REVOLUTION

sufficiently strong to balance it; (*b*) to remove or weaken the conditions that produce the " restriction "; (*c*) to split and divide the restricted groups in sections and to set them against each other (*" divide et impera "!*), thus weakening the enemy; and (*d*) to provide an outlet for other restricted instincts in non-revolutionary forms.

As already remarked, a man may be as hungry as possible, but if a revolver be applied to his temple he will not touch food placed before him; the actions dictated by hunger will be repressed, be it at the cost of the death of the starving man. The same may be said of masses whose instincts are restricted. In any society, at any given time, there is to be found a more or less strong repression of some instincts of a great part of its members. If that restriction does not lead to disturbances and to mutiny, it is owing to resistance on the part of the authorities and of the non-restricted part of the society. Even more, we know of numerous cases in history when a very strong and extensive repression of the instincts of masses did not lead to a revolutionary outbreak, but to . . . the extinction of some members of the society and the servitude of others. The reason is to be found in exceedingly strong and efficient agencies of control. Vanquished countries occupied by the enemy may serve as examples. We find a great number of such cases in history, as Belgium and the part of France occupied by the Germans in 1914 to 1918; the Ruhr occupied by the French and the Belgians in 1923; and Russia, vanquished by a bunch of international scoundrels who since 1921–22 are no less hated than the Germans were hated in Belgium and France or than the French and Belgians are now hated in the Ruhr. In spite of this restriction the occupants were and are able to hold the country and to prevent an outbreak.[23]

[23] Upon the historical rôle of punishing and rewarding inhibition cf. Sorokin: *Crime and Punishment*, pp. 67-251.

In order to break out, a revolution not only needs the incentive of instinct-restriction, but also the absence of sufficiently strong and efficient resistance by the authorities and ruling circles. Do we see such an absence in pre-revolutionary epochs? Certainly.

Pre-revolutionary epochs literally strike the observer by the incapacity of the authorities and the degeneracy of the ruling privileged classes; they appear equally incapable of carrying out the ordinary functions of power, to say nothing of opposing revolution by force; nor are they able to divide and weaken the opposition, or to reduce the restrictions and provide controllable outlets for the repressed instincts in non-revolutionary forms. All pre-revolutionary governments bear the symptoms of something not unlike anæmia. Impotence, indecision, incompetence, embarrassment, light-headed carelessness on the one hand, depravity, corruption and fastidiousness on the other; such are the characteristic features of pre-revolutionary governing classes. No will, no brains, no cunning. " There is no steersman. Where is he? Or is he asleep? His strength is nowhere to be seen." " The King has lost his strength and is no more a support." Such are Ipouver's comments upon the weakness of Pharaoh's power before and at the time of the Egyptian Revolution.[24]

In Rome before the Gracchi and during the beginning of the revolution we see a similar degeneration of authority; instead of wise, energetic and powerful *patres con-scripti* we see a degenerate senate, flattering, obsequious and servile towards the mob and its leaders. " No one dares any more to sacrifice the wealth and the blood of citizens for the good of the country." Instead of heroes, we find dwarfs; instead of a great senate, a rotten ochloc-

[24] Cf. Vikentieff: *Op. cit.,* 288-300.

racy; the place of stern warriors and rulers is occupied by "a cowardly and immoral aristocratic crowd." [25]

In France, before the Jacquerie and the revolutions at the end of the fourteenth century, came the reign of King Jean, an incompetent ruler, a talentless soldier, surrounded by just such nullities as he was himself.

In England we find Charles I and his government equally unable to follow a fixed policy and only succeeding in irritating the people by their hesitations and hysterical outbursts of despotism. The government now arrests the opposition, now releases them. They start a war and do not know how to conduct it; having begun a struggle with the people they do not carry it out to the end; they are even incapable of protecting their favorites as Buckingham, Strafford, William Laud and others. "No stern purpose is felt and no powerful arm." [26]

In addition to that, we find an exceedingly wasteful court and squandering of money to provide sinecures for favorites. Pensions amounting to £18,000 in the time of Queen Elizabeth now went up to £120,000. The expenditures of the royal household went up from £45,000 to £80,000, etc. In addition to that the authorities systematically restricted by their actions the people's reflexes.[27]

Only a specifically incompetent authority can be so successful in exciting the people against itself and so clumsy in dealing with the resulting disturbance.

---

[25] Cf. Mommsen: Vol. II, 69-79 *et seq.*, 132.

[26] Guizot: Vol. I, 47, *et seq.*

[27] "Charles's tyranny, if not the most cruel was certainly the most unjust that England had ever experienced. No excuse can be found for it either in any social necessity nor in any brilliant result whereas it violated ancient rights in order to provide for unknown needs . . . It did not heed any laws nor even the king's word and had recourse to every kind of oppression." Guizot: Vol. I, 50, *et seq.*

The same applies to John Lackland and to James II and their courts.

The state of the French aristocracy and government before the revolution is notorious. . . . " The aristocracy is incapable of defense in close order and will not make the necessary concessions. . . . Richelieu had been weakening systematically the staunch character of the nobility; Louis XIV continued his work." " It has been disaccustomed from staunchness and its roots have been severed." " Owing to its worldliness, epicureanism and effeminacy it was completely debilitated." There was besides, its scandalous and immoral conduct, its complete insignificance, its fashionable but thoughtless liberalism; " its loss of confidence in its own rights; " a purely parasitical order of life and a complete misapprehension of the situation. As late as in 1789–90 " the nobility smiles and does not understand the revolution." [28]

At that time the aristocracy ceased to perform the useful functions that had long ago belonged to their ancestors, but still retained their privileges. Such a situation could not last long.[29]

The King may be a gentle, good and cheerful man, but quoting Napoleon's clever words, " When people say that the King is kind, it means that he is a bad ruler."

---

[28] Madelin: Vol. I, 30-35. Tocqueville: *Loc. cit.*, Passim. Taine: *L'Ancien Régime*, Vol. I.

[29] " Whatever an institution may represent," justly remarks Taine, " the contemporaries who observe it during forty generations cannot be considered bad judges; if they surrender to it their will and their property, they only do so in proportion to its merits . . . Man cannot be expected to be grateful for nothing, by mistake, and to grant many privileges without sufficient reason for doing so; he is too selfish and too envious for that " . . . In bygone days the privileged class did render such services, whereas now " they have ceased to perform their duty, their place has become a sinecure and their privileges a misappropriation." Taine: *Origines de la France Contemporaine*, Russ. ed., p. 8, 552-53.

Louis XVI " did not know how to will, he did not know his own mind." " His government, perhaps the most honest of all, was anything but a government for a crisis." [30]   In former days the Capets used to be the defenders of the people; they were that no longer.   " If the King is no longer the leader of the army, if he is no longer the judge of Vincennes nor the protector of the communities, then who is he? "

Next to him appeared Marie Antoinette and polished courtiers with a good knowledge of Voltaire and Rousseau, but lacking will, energy and an understanding of the situation.   Such an impotence of authorities became apparent at the beginning of the revolution on May 6, 1789, in the question of the way in which the estates were to vote; also at the scene of the *Jeu de Paume,* when the *tiers-état* refused to disperse, also in the church of St. Louis, and at the *Lit de Justice.*   The government tries at first to apply the brakes, but soon gives it up and only succeeds in irritating the people.   We see the same in its relation to the soldiers on June 24 and 28, 1789, and soon wavering, indecision and foolish irascibility permeate all the actions of the government, from the beginning of the revolution up to the death of Louis XVI. " The reins were dropped at the first moment." " Louis XVI (in May to June, 1789) considered that he was still the King, but he was King no longer.   He had no power and no authority." [31]

Did not the same repeat itself before the Russian Revolution?   Emperor Nicholas II was a replica of Louis XVI.   The empress was a copy of Marie Antoinette.   The courtiers?   Were not the decrepit Goremykin, the incompetent Sturmer, the demented Protopopoff and the abnor-

---

[30] Madelin: *Loc. cit.,* Vol. I, 47-54.
[31] Madelin: Vol. I, 86.

mal Mrs. Virouboff, etc., merely a bad copy of the court
of Louis XVI? Not one single minister with will-power
and brains; we see a collection of psychical and physical
impotents, of talentless rulers and of effeminate and
cynical dwarfs.[32]

A comparison of this picture with the state of things
but thirty years ago, in the reign of the great Emperor
Alexander III, is sufficient to show what catastrophic
results are brought about by a degeneration of power and
of the ruling circles.

And what of the nobility in general? There was
a time when it, like the nobility of France, fulfilled
important functions of administration, judgment, defending the country; when it was obliged to occupy itself
with the business of the state. Then it had a right to its
privileges. But towards the end of the eighteenth century
when a decree (*oukaze*) was issued proclaiming the nobility free from all obligations, but at the same time
retaining its privileges—the degeneration began. Little
by little it was transformed into a parasite; its privileges,
into a sinecure; its pretensions, into unfounded abuse.
A great majority of its members simply used up the
riches which had been accumulated in the past, and which
were from time to time wrenched away from the nation's
funds. Even when it grew active, as, for instance, in
1905-14 when it formed a society called: "The United
Nobility," it was clearly thinking not of the welfare of
the state and the whole country, but was actuated by the
primitive rapacious appetites of parasites.[33]

---

[32] Cf. *Letters of the Empress Alexandra Feodorovna, The Memoirs
of Witte, Beletsky, Mrs. Virouboff, Countess Kleinmichel,* and
others, where the courtiers themselves unwittingly show us a grandiose
picture of nullity and degeneracy.

[33] See M. Kovalevsky: *What Russia is due to the United Nobility,*
1914 (Russ.).

Consequently, it must not astonish us that history has summoned the " Nobility " to its tribunal and put an end to this excrescence on the body of Russia. We must also not be astonished to meet a total absence of energy in its own self-defense; in the defense of the old régime, and that of its head—the Czar. The death of the Russian nobility was devoid of all heroism.

We see similar features in other revolutions. All this corroborates the truth of our theory concerning the second cause of revolution: the degeneration of power. History tolerates rapacious, cruel, cynical governments, but only as long as these governments are strong, as long as they desire and know how to govern and insofar as, notwithstanding all their negative sides, they can also be useful to society.

But " kind " governments which at the same time are impotent; or cruel governments which are parasitical; or high-minded, but useless governments—history does not tolerate.

Such a degeneration of power amidst the governing classes if they are comparatively exclusive and caste-like grows sooner or later to be inevitable. It is called forth both by biological and social factors.[34]

The offspring of naturally talented rulers, such, for instance, as the ancestors of the Russian and French nobility, are very dissimilar to their forefathers and, instead of being rulers " by the mercy of God," grow to be " inborn slaves " totally devoid of talents necessary to a ruler.

Such a degeneration is always dangerous for society; and in moments of crisis it precipitates the catastrophe. The conditions are still more aggravated by the fact that the same process called forth by the same causes is taking place, only in an opposite direction, amidst the offspring

---

[34] See about these factors my *System of Sociology*, Vol. II.

of the former slaves. Their children are sometimes born with the qualities of an " inborn leader."

If the " mechanism of social distribution " worked perfectly, and immediately placed the first in subordinate posts, giving the position of leaders to the second, no great harm would result from this. The principle so necessary to the welfare of society of : " Every one according to his talents " (especially according to his " inborn talents "), would not in this case be transgressed. But alas! Till now not a single society can boast of so adaptive a circulation. Many conditions contribute to the fact that the unsuccessful descendants of the " Rightful rulers " remain at the summit, occupying the same position as their ancestors. The same principle remains true of the " tadpoles " among the lower classes. The balance of society is destroyed from both sides.

When the aristocracy is strong and talented no artificial barriers are needed to protect it against the competition of " newcomers." When it is talentless the artificial measures are as necessary as crutches are to a cripple, and is what actually does happen. In periods of decadence, in pre-revolutionary times, the degenerate ruling classes apply purely artificial measures to prohibit the entrance into their midst of all " tadpoles " from below and to prevent the attainment of all posts of honor by them. We witness this in Rome in 151 where the attainment of high posts was absolutely forbidden to all newcomers.[35]

Kolabinska, who has investigated the circulation of the élites of France from the twelfth century, states that from the seventeenth or eighteenth century the migration of the " tadpoles " from the lower to the higher posts was rendered dreadfully difficult by dozens of erected

[35] Mommsen: Vol. II, 69, 75.

barriers with which the degenerating ruling classes were attempting to protect themselves.[36]

The same fact can be witnessed before the English Revolution when the aristocrats with the King at their head attempted to render the circulation from the lower ranks of society upward more difficult; especially the migration of the middle classes which had developed so strongly; the attempt was even made to push the latter down by taking away from them the right of participating in the government, a right which had formerly been theirs (the attempt of the King to govern without parliament, the infringement of the people's rights, etc.).

The same took place before the Russian Revolution of 1905, when the degenerate Russian governing classes obstinately refused to admit the participation in the government of talented self-made men from other classes, refused to curtail their own rights and were even ready to deprive of office talented " Newcomers," such, for example, as Witte.

It is easy to understand that thanks to such measures the accumulation of " inefficient rulers " at the summit and " tadpoles " at the bottom increased still more.

The pressure which the latter brought to bear against the barriers which prevented their attaining high posts grew constantly stronger; as did also the feeling of oppression. Sooner or later the barriers had to be broken. The advent of troubled conditions and crises only accelerated this and rendered its manifestations more acute. The revolution burst out. All the barriers and impediments preventing free circulation were thrown down at a stroke. The cruel " broom " of revolution sweeps bare the cluttered flood. It pays no great heed to guilty or innocent.

---

[36] Kolabinska: *La circulation des élites en France,* 1912. The periods from 1610 to 1715, from 1715 to 1789.

Of a sudden the "privileged" are thrown from the top of the social edifice and many other individuals are raised up out of their "social cellars." The methods are primitively simple and elementary. An immense hole is visible in the "sieve" through which the selecting process is performed; and through this hole everything passes without discrimination.

Thanks to such an absence of judgment the results of such a primitive readjustment are far from satisfactory. Consequently, during its second period revolution must rectify its own mistakes by establishing a new "circulation" in an opposite retrograde direction. And that is actually what it does, as we have tried to prove in these pages.

If among the middle and lower classes of the population the number of "inborn rulers" is sufficient, the whole process ends in a comparatively satisfactory manner. The "tadpoles" having reached the summit stay there and amalgamate with the remainder of the non-degenerated former aristocracy, thereby readjusting the upset balance of the social organism. With time such an operation can effect a cure, so that the organism can continue to exist till a new accumulation of oppressions, parasitism and degeneracy calls forth a new explosion. But if the number of "tadpoles" at the bottom of society is insufficient or does not exist at all (such can also be the case), then we have no one to supplant degenerated authority; and such a case is sure to bring on a state of decadence. Such was the state of Rome. After the Patricians, the Nobles and the Equestrians had perished history made an attempt to find such "tadpoles" among the freed-men, among the plebs, the slaves, the barbarians—but in vain. After this source had run quite dry the death-knell of the Western Roman Empire had sounded. Such is the circuit run by history, the same endless story which was repeated before the days of Noah and is repeated even now.

5. **The General Causes Contributing to Call Forth the Second Stage of the Revolution or the Counter-revolution.**—From all that we already have said, it is quite evident that the second stage of revolution—the counter-revolution—is the inevitable consequence of the first.

After all that has already been said we can afford to be brief.

If the fundamental cause of the first stage of revolution consists in the repression of the instincts of the masses, we can be sure that the second stage will be called forth by identical reasons. Why so?

Because, as we have seen in all of the above, the first stage of a deep-rooted revolution does not remove such oppression, but very soon only aggravates it. The conduct of the masses swayed now only by elemental unconditioned reflexes grows to be anarchic: one unconditioned reflex is oppressed and overridden by the other; one individual oppresses and overrides the others. Famine increases, instead of decreasing, consequently, the reflexes of nutrition are still more oppressed. Personal safety grows more insecure; the death rate rises tremendously thanks to murders, famine and epidemics. Therefore, the reflexes of self-preservation are more and more oppressed. Confiscations of wealth, taken away first from the rich, later on from the whole population under the guise of ever-heavier requisitions and taxes, oppress the proprietorial instincts. The growth of sexual license oppresses sexual reflexes. The arbitrariness of the governing class oppresses the reflexes of liberty, etc. In short, with but few exceptions, whatever group of fundamental reflexes we touch upon in each one of them, the oppression has increased, not diminished; the more so, the more profound the revolution has been. In this "primitive chaos," *bellum omnium contra omnes,* a general oppression of all fundamental reflexes takes place. It is just during such periods that the theory of Hobbes (who by the way promulgated it after the experience acquired during the English Revolution) is justified. People grow less adapted to their surroundings and mutual relations. Their attitude towards them is summed up in the words: "It is impossible to continue life under such conditions, order is necessary, order at any cost."

And so men are taught by inexorable teachers; hunger, cold, illness, want and death; they stand before a double dilemma: to perish and die, continuing the revolutionary debauch; or to find a new outlet. Bitter and tragic experience forces men to see that much of what they had looked upon as "prejudice," much from which they had gladly "liberated" themselves was in reality the complex of conditions essential to comfortable social life; to the existence and development of society.

Now the demand for unbridled liberty is superseded by a desire of "order;" the longing for "deliverers" from the *Ancien Régime* is succeeded by a longing for "deliverers" from the revolution; or, in other words, for organizers of order. "Order" and "Long live the creators of order"—such is the universal clamor during the second period of revolution, alike: in Rome during the times of Cæsar and Augustus; in Bohemia towards the end of the revolutionary war; in England during the Protectorate; in France during Napoleon's elevation; in 1849–51, in 1871, and in Russia in 1922–24.

The same result is also called forth by the exhaustion of the masses. The mad expenditure of energy during the first period of revolution has, as its result, the speedy impoverishment of the reserve-fund of energy in the human organism. This reserve fund is not limitless. Man is no *"perpetuum mobile."* This exhaustion is accelerated by hunger and want which prevent the immense expenditure of energy of the first period from being replenished. This exhaustion acts in itself as a restraining force upon the manifestation of many reflexes. Apathy, indifferentism, a kind of drowsiness—set in. This state lays men open to be restrained and curbed by any energetic group of individuals. That which would have been impossible during the first period of revolution grows all too easy now. The population resembles an inert mass, ready to be molded. It presents favorable material for the activity of any "repressers." And so revolution, which had begun by encouraging limitless license, inevitably creates conditions favorable to the advent of despots, tyrants and to the coercion of the masses.

These two causes: the continued oppression of instincts and the exhaustion of the masses (and many other secondary causes as well) are quite sufficient to call forth counter-revolution. Why is it that the latter manifests itself in a regression, a more or less complete return to the former social structure, the old order, the old régime? Why does conduct, circulation, different party-grouping, religious, political, economic and social life again undergo such a regressive transformation?

It is not difficult to understand this. Social order is never casual, but is the result of centuries of the adjustment of humanity to its environment, and of its individual members to each other; it is the outcome of centuries of efforts, experience and strivings to achieve the best possible forms of social organization and life. Every stable social organization, however imperfect it may seem from the standpoint of immature radicalism, is, nevertheless, the outcome of an immense condensed real (not fictitious) national experience; the result of innumerable strivings, efforts, experiments of many generations to find the best possible forms compatible with existing concrete conditions. Only an ignoramus, or a man immersed in the fantasies of his own brain, can imagine that such an order, built up and existing for centuries, can present nothing but an immense nonsense, a misunderstanding, a complete mistake.[37]

We can make a paraphrase of the words of Renan and say: " That every day of the existence of any given social order is in reality a constant plebiscite of all the members of society and, if it continues to exist, it betokens that the greater part of society answers the question with a silent: ' Yes '." If the social order of a given society be such and no other it means that, given actually existing conditions, another more perfect order would either be difficult to realize or . . . it would be less perfect.

The period preceding revolution diminishes its perfection—its adaptability; renders it defective in many respects, but of course not in all. It were difficult to admit that circumstances had suddenly changed to such a degree, that the whole social structure should be utterly inadequate; that all the experience of past generations should be mistaken; all the social instincts, misleading. Defects call forth an outburst. But this outburst destroys not only the defects, but also a very great number of necessary reflexes, institutions and outward forms of conduct. Consequently when a return of social life to normal con-

---

[37] See true remarks of E. Burke: *Op. cit.,* 274-8, 346-7 pp.

ditions begins—it is natural that it again molds itself to the old outward forms, which have not lost their good qualities, which are well known, which happen to be the best possible under given conditions; all the searchings of society inevitably lead to a return toward these forms. That is why we witness their restoration. That is why society, after having made the attempt to separate itself completely from the past, returns to it again. Only such institutions, such forms of life as are truly obsolete; which, though once upon a time adequate, are now, thanks to changed circumstances, no more so, only such ones are doomed and will be supplanted by new ones. We witness such a substitution even at periods of restoration, for not a single revolution has ever ended by a complete restoration of the old order. Such is the process and such are the causes of counter-revolution.

But perhaps you will ask me: If revolution, called forth by the oppression of instincts, oppresses them still more, wherein does hope lie?

If famine, war and despotism lead to revolution, and revolution lead to still greater famine, war, despotism, do we then not face a tragic historical circuit from which no outlet can be found? How shall we unravel the question?

Exceedingly simply and for all deep-rooted revolutions in a very stereotyped, uniform manner. The question is not unravelled. It is solved at one stroke. Death solves it. This outlet never betrays and is always at the disposal of man. A society which has not known how to live, which has been incapable of carrying through adequate reforms, but has thrown itself into the arms of revolution —has to pay the penalty for its sins by the death of a considerable proportion of its members; it has to pay the contribution demanded by that all-powerful Sovereign.

Only, if after having paid that contribution it has not perished completely, will it acquire in a certain measure the possibility to exist and live; but not by cutting itself loose from the past, not by brutal mutual struggles; but, on the contrary, by a return to most of its former foundations, institutions, traditions (only the absolutely effete ones among them perish), by powerful labor, coöperation, mutual help and unity among the individual members and the different groups of society. If society is incapable of accepting this outlet then revolution ends in its complete degeneration and destruction.

Such is the solution of the dilemma of history.

NOTES AND ADDENDA

NOTES AND ADDENDA

To Page 85: Divorces.—Accurate statistics of divorces were absent in pre-revolutionary Russia. It is only known that in 1885 among the orthodox population of European Russia there was one divorce case out of every 470 marriages concluded in the same year. G. von Mayr in his *Moralstatistik* (Tubingen, 1917, p. 197) gives 1.3 divorce cases per 1000 marriages consecrated in the same year in 1893–97. Since that time to 1917 the divorce rate increased but scarcely more than twice. We saw that according to *Isvestia* in 1922 there was one divorce case out of 11.2 marriages. According to new *Statistical Abstract* published by the Soviet government (*Narodnoie Khosiastvo Sousa S.S.S.R., v tsyfrakh,* Moscow, 1924) in 1920–22 there was one divorce out of 11.7 marriages, in 1923 one divorce out of 12.9 marriages concluded in the same years (p. 34). The slight decrease of divorce rate given in 1923 may be the first symptom of the coming of restraint of sexual freedom caused by the revolution.

To Page 196: The Diminution of the Population of Russia During the Revolution.—The population of Russia was

January 1, 1911	167,003,400
January 1, 1912	171,059,900
January 1, 1913	174,099,600
January 1, 1914	about 178,000,000

(according to the *Statistical Yearbook of Russia for 1913*, II, 1–2 and for 1916, published in Moscow in 1918). In 1920 the population of Soviet Russia was 131,546,045, that of the parts separated from Russia (Finland, Esthonia, Latvia, Lithuania, Poland, Bessarabia, Karsky pashalyk) was 28,571,000; together totalling 160,117,045. This gives a diminution of the population of Russia from 1914 to 1920 of 17,000,000 or 18,000,000. See *Statistical Yearbook of Russia for 1918–20*, 6–7, 2–3. We come to the same results by deducting 31,398,000—the population of these separated parts of Russia in 1914, indicated in the Bolshevist *Statistical Yearbook*—from 178,000,000, the population of the Russian Empire in 1914, and then deducting from this the 1920 population of Soviet Russia.

A similar proportion of diminution of the population is given by comparison of the data of the census of 1916 with that of 1920. According to them, on the territory of Soviet Russia without Turkestan and Transcaucasus, we had:

	Rural population	Urban population	In the army	Total
In 1916	96.8 million	25.163 million	14.2 million	136.363 million
In 1920	99.0 million	17.620 million	5.3 million	121.920 million

See *Perspectivy rasvitia selskago khosiastva S.S.S.R.*, published by the Commissariat of Agriculture, Moscow, 1924, 77–78.

At last in *The Works of the Central Statist. Administration*, vol. I, book 3, 4–5, it is published that the population of only forty-seven provinces of Soviet Russia, where the census of 1920 was taken more carefully, diminished from 88,000,370 (in 1914) to 73,495,879 (in 1920). This gives a diminution of the population of only these forty-seven provinces of 11,504,473 or of 13.6 per cent. All these official Soviet figures stand in sharp contradiction to the figure 135,599,015 given in the same *Statistical Yearbook of 1918–20* for the population of Soviet Russia in 1914. Comparing it with 131,546,045, designating the population of Soviet Russia in 1920, we have the diminution of the population only by four million. This contradiction, however, is explained very easily. On page 62 of this *Yearbook* its authors say frankly that they diminished by ten per cent. the population of Russia in 1914 given by the previous Central Statistical Administration. In this easy way they got 135 million instead of 146–147 million. In this way they reduced the diminution of the population from seventeen or eighteen million to four million. Further it is necessary to note that even the figure 131,546,045 given for the population of Russia in 1920 is exaggerated. The authors of the *Yearbook* took the population of many parts of Russia where the census of 1920 could not be taken as equal to their population in 1916. In this way they calculate the figure considerably higher than the real population was in 1920. The above gives every reason to think that the diminution of the population of Russia from 1914 to 1920 was not less than seventeen or eighteen million.

Further, according to the Bolshevist computation, the famine of 1921–22 carried away about five million. Admitting that about two of these five million were compensated for by births we have an additional diminution of the Russian population by three million. In total from 1914 to 1922 we have the diminution of the Russian population by twenty or twenty-one million.

Of these twenty or twenty-one million about two and one-half million were the victims of the World War. (Of them 682,213 were killed, of 3,638,271 war prisoners no less than one-half had returned to Russia up to the time of the census of 1920; another half together with those who were killed gives the indicated two and one-half million. See *Narodnoie Khosiastvo Sousa S.S.S.R.* published for the members of the Russian Communist Party, Moscow, 1924, 55). About two million are emigrants. Deducting from twenty or twenty-one million these four or five million (the victims of the War and the emigrants) we have from fifteen to seventeen million of the Russian people as the victims of the Great Russian Revolution.

To Page 207: Births, Deaths, and Marriages.—The Statistical Abstract *Narodnoie Khosiastvo Sousa S.S.S.R.,* 32–34, gives the following figures (for 1000 inhabitants):

Year	Marriages	Births	Deaths	Increase or decrease
1911–13 [1]	8.1	44.1	27.2	16.9
1920–22 [2]	11.7	33.0	33.2	0.2
1923 [3]	12.9	42.9	22.5	20.4

Nineteen hundred and twenty-three shows a very great improvement in the situation. Unfortunately, the figures for 1923 based only on the thirteen best provinces which did not suffer either from great famine or from a serious civil war cannot be taken as typical for the whole of Russia. This supposition is confirmed by the census of the population of 145 villages in Ukrainia published in " Contemporary Medicine," *Sovremennaia Meditsina,* April–June, 1924, Odessa. For 1920–23 the average death rate in this part of Russia was 33 for 1000 inhabitants, the average birth rate was 26 giving still the surplus of mortality over births equal to 7 for 1000 of population.

To Page 346: Public Instruction and Education in Russia.—The figures concerning the expenses for public instruction, and the number of schools and pupils in pre-. revolutionary Russia given by me in the text concern all the Russian Empire. Now it is interesting to take the situation within the present Soviet Russia before and during the Revolution. Some statistics in this respect are given by the *Narodnoie Khosiastvo.* Though these figures are very inaccurate, nevertheless they are eloquent.

According to this official publication (p. 36) in 1914,

---

[1] European Russia.
[2] Twenty provinces which did not suffer from famine.
[3] Thirteen provinces.

the per cent. of expenses for public instruction and education from the total State budget was 5.7, in 1922–23 it was only 3.0, in 1923–24 3.9. In 1913 there was spent for this purpose by the Ministry of Public Instruction within the territory of the present Soviet Russia 126,818,000 g. rubles (p. 36). In 1923–24, according to the last report of Lunatcharsky given to the last Session of the All-Russian Soviet in October, 1924, there was spent only about 30,000,000 g. rubles. According to this report on the territory of the present Soviet Russia in 1913 there were 62,000 elementary schools with 4.2 million pupils, in 1923 there were 49,000 elementary schools with 3.7 million pupils. Briefly, this report, as well as the results of the investigation of the situation in universities published in *Isvestia*, August 22, 1924, is alarming and recognizes the greatest destruction in the sphere of education and instruction.

The growth of literacy in the old Russia could be judged from the per cent. of literate and illiterate recruits taken in the army. The data given by the *Narodnoie Khosiastvo* in this respect are as follows (p. 51):

Years	Per cent. of literate	Per cent. of illiterate
1874–83	21.98	78.02
1884–93	30.57	69.43
1894–1903	43.75	56.25
1904–13	62.62	37.38

THE RUSSIAN TITLES OF SOME OF THE RUSSIAN BOOKS AND PUBLICATIONS QUOTED IN "THE SOCIOLOGY OF REVOLUTION"

The official Bolshevist publications are marked by the letter "B"

Periodicals

Bulletins of the Central Statistical Administration of the Ukraine. Bulleteni Tzentralnago Statisticheskago Upravlenia Ukrainy. B.

The Economical Building Up. Economicheskoie Stroitelstvo. B.

The Economical Life. Economicheskaia Jisn. B.

The Economical Life of the People. Sborniki "Narodnoie Khosaistvo." B.

The Economical Review or The Economic Messenger. Economichesky Vestnik.

The Economist. Economist.

The National Economy for 1918. Narodnoie Khosaistvo, 1918. B.

Professional Journal. Professionalny Vestnik. B.

Past. Byloie.

Pravda. Pravda. B.

Isvestia. Isvestia Tzentralnago Ispolnitelnago Comiteta S. R. K. K. Deputatov. B.

The Red Paper. Krasnaia Gazeta. B.

The Review of Labor. Vestnik Truda. B.

Youth's Pravda. Iunosheskaia Pravda. B.

Proletarian Revolution and Right. Proletarskaia Revolutzia i Pravo. B.

Weekly Journal of the Soviet Justice. Ejenedelnik Sovetskoi Iustizii. B.

Peasants' Russia. Krestianskaia Rossia.

Medical Work. Vrachebnoie Delo.

Social Physician. Obshchestvenny Vrach.

Military Messenger. Voennyi Vestnik. B.

Collective Work. Artelnoie Delo.

Under the Standard of Marxism. Pod Znamenem Marxisma. B.

The Red Virgin Soil. Krasnaia Nov. B.

The Works of the Central Statistical Administration. Trudy Tzentralnago Statistichskago Upravlenia. B.

Statistical Review. Statistichesky Vestnik. B.

Statistical Material for St. Petersburg or Material for the Statistics of Petrograd. Materialy po Statistike Petrograda. B.

Psychiatry and Neurology. Psikhiatria, Nevrologia i Experimentalnaia Psikhologia.

The Russian Thought. Russkaia Mysl.

Sovremennyia Zapiski.

Days. Dni. Rul. Rul. Les Dernieres Nouvelles. Poslednia Novosti.

In Foreign Countries. Na Chujoi Storone.

On the New Ways. Na Novykh Putiakh. B.

Non-periodicals

About Land. O semle. B.

The Eighth All-Russian Congress of Soviets. VIII Siesd Rossiskoi Communisticheskoi Partii 18–23 Marta 1919 goda. B.

The Third All-Russian Congress of Professional Associations. Trety Vserossyssky Siesd Professionalnykh Sousov 6–13 Aprela 1920 goda. B.

During Five Years. Za Piat Let. B.

The Eleventh Conference of the Russian Communist Party. XI Siesd Rossyskoi Communisticheskoi Partii. B.

Red Moscow. Krasnaia Moskva. B.

Statistical Yearbook of Russia. Statistichesky Ejegodnik Rossii. (B. for 1918-20.)

INDEX

INDEX

423